TRANSNATIONAL
CONSTITUTIONALISM

An interdisciplinary perspective is adopted to examine international and European models of constitutionalism. In particular, the book reflects critically on a number of constitutional themes, such as the nature of European and international constitutional models and their underlying principles; the *telos* behind international and European constitutionalism; the role of the state and of central courts; and the relationships between composite orders. *Transnational Constitutionalism* brings together a group of European and international law scholars, whose contributions provide the necessary intellectual insight that will assist the reader in understanding the political and legal phenomena that take place beyond the state. This edited collection represents an original and pioneering contribution to the international and European constitutional discourse.

NICHOLAS TSAGOURIAS is a Lecturer in Law at the School of Law, University of Bristol.

TRANSNATIONAL CONSTITUTIONALISM

International and European Models

edited by
NICHOLAS TSAGOURIAS

CAMBRIDGE
UNIVERSITY PRESS

CAMBRIDGE UNIVERSITY PRESS

Cambridge, New York, Melbourne, Madrid, Cape Town, Singapore, São Paulo

Cambridge University Press
The Edinburgh Building, Cambridge CB2 8RU, UK

Published in the United States of America by Cambridge University Press, New York

www.cambridge.org
Information on this title: www.cambridge.org/9780521872041

First published 2007

Printed in the United Kingdom at the University Press, Cambridge

A catalogue record for this publication is available from the British Library

ISBN-13 978-0-521-87204-1 hardback

CONTENTS

LIST OF CONTRIBUTORS

Patrick Capps, Senior Lecturer, School of Law, University of Bristol

Pavlos Eleftheriadis, Fellow in Law, Mansfield College, University of Oxford

Bardo Fassbender, Assistant Professor, Humboldt University, Berlin

Tonia Novitz, Reader in Law, School of Law, University of Bristol

Julian Rivers, Senior Lecturer, School of Law, University of Bristol

Achilles Skordas, Reader in Law, School of Law, University of Bristol

Nicholas Tsagourias, Lecturer in Law, School of Law, University of Bristol

Wouter Werner, Professor of Law, Vrije Universiteit, Amsterdam

Ramses Wessel, Professor of the Law of the European Union and Other International Organisations, Centre for European Studies, University of Twente

Nigel White, Professor of International Law, School of Law, University of Sheffield

FOREWORD

This book is a product of the seventh EU/International Law Forum hosted by the School of Law at Bristol University. The origins of the Forum series lie in the recognition of a need to ensure that scholarship in European Law and in International Law remain in contact with each other, something that has become more difficult over time as the specialty of each has increased. The Forum offers an opportunity to reflect upon developments of common interest and to explore the contribution that those steeped in the thinking of the one corpus of law can make to the thinking of the other. These Fora also seek to bring together leading academics and policy-makers, again encouraging a sharing of perspectives enriching not only the debate at the Fora themselves but also the wider work of all participants.

The theme of the most recent Forum was inspired by the debates surrounding the moves to adopt a new European Constitution. The first volume in the Forum Series was published ten years ago and explored 'Aspects of Statehood and Institutionalism in Contemporary Europe'.[1] It was inspired by the observation that in the post-Soviet era new states were emerging which sought to express themselves as independent sovereign states through participation in international organisations and, in doing so, they created something of a tension between statehood on the one hand and the expanding role of international institutions on the other. In a sense, this volume continues with elements of that theme, exploring from the perspective of constitutionalism the locus of the state as an entity within the broader system of communities of states. Rather than reflect on the contours of that debate itself, the Forum sought to consider the broader issues which underpin the move towards constitutionalism – the impulse towards constitutionalism – and whether, and how, that is rooted in, and finds reflection

---

[1] M. D. Evans (ed.), *Aspects of Statehood and Institutionalism in Contemporary Europe* (Aldershot: Dartmouth, 1996).

through, existing and nascent legal structures and debates. Naturally, the outcome revealed disparities of approaches, not only between those approaching the subject from the perspective of European and International Law, but also between those approaching it from within these subject perspectives. It quickly became apparent that the core issues were not 'subject specific' but reflected different approaches to legal and conceptual understandings of the nature of constitutions and constitutionalism themselves and the points of contact between the seemingly divergent perspectives became apparent.

The essays in this volume provided the material for that journey and it is to be hoped that the reader will find them equally stimulating and thought-provoking.

Malcolm D. Evans

ABBREVIATIONS

AJIL	*American Journal of International Law*
BYIL	*British Yearbook of International Law*
CFI	Court of First Instance of the European Communities
CFSP	Common Foreign and Security Policy
CLJ	*Cambridge Law Journal*
CMLR	*Common Market Law Reports*
CML Rev	*Common Market Law Review*
Col. JTL	*Columbia Journal of Transnational Law*
EC	European Community
ECHR	European Convention for the Protection of Human Rights and Fundamental Freedoms
ECR	European Court Reports
ECtHR	European Court of Human Rights
EHRLR	*European Human Rights Law Review*
EHRR	*European Human Rights Reports*
EJIL	*European Journal of International Law*
ELJ	*European Law Journal*
ELRev	*European Law Review*
ESDP	*European Security and Defence Policy*
EU	European Union
GA	General Assembly
GATT	General Agreement on Tariffs and Trade
GYIL	*German Yearbook of International Law*
HRC	Human Rights Committee
HRLJ	*Human Rights Law Journal*
I.CON	*International Journal of Constitutional Law*
ICJ	International Court of Justice
ICLQ	*International and Comparatively Law Quarterly*
ICTY	International Criminal Court for the Former Yugoslavia

ILM	*International Legal Materials*
ILO	International Labour Organization
ILR	*International Law Reports*
IMF	International Monetary Fund
IOL Rev	*International Organizations Law Review*
JCMS	*Journal of Common Market Studies*
Max Planck UNYB	*Max Planck Yearbook of United Nations Law*
NGO	Non-governmental organisation
NIEO	New International Economic Order
OJ	*Official Journal of the European Union*
PCIJ	Permanent Court of International Justice
RC	*Recueil des cours de l'Académie de droit international*
RGDIP	*Revue général de droit international*
RIAA	*United Nations Reports of International Arbitral Awards*
SC	Security Council
TECE	Treaty Establishing a Constitution for Europe
TEU	Treaty on European Union
UN	United Nations
VaJIL	*Virginia Journal of International Law*
WTO	World Trade Organization
YEL	*Yearbook of European Law*
ZaöRV	*Zeitschrift für ausländisches öffendtlisches Recht und Völkerrecht*

Introduction – Constitutionalism: a theoretical roadmap

NICHOLAS TSAGOURIAS

Constitution, constitutionalism, constitutionalisation – these are some of the terms used to describe the political and legal culture, not only within states, but also beyond states. Often these terms take a descriptive and empirical twist; they describe empirically observable events relating to the structure and organisation of political spaces. At other times, they take a normative twist and become prescriptive and axiological. In their latter disguise they refer to the values and principles that an entity possesses or should possess, in addition to any organisational format that it may have. Regardless of what form they may take, we should acknowledge that the term 'constitutionalism' and its derivates are pregnant with promises that exert a strong appeal, and place constitutionalism at the apex of political and legal aesthetics or virtues.

It is important, then, to explain the meaning of constitutionalism before we discuss whether it operates in political spaces beyond states and, if it does, what its nature is. Constitutionalism is about the normative and structural premises of political orders; but whereas constitutions utter the forms of organisation of specific political spaces and the normative commitments of the members of that polity,[1] and whereas 'constitutionalisation' refers to a constitution-hardening process, constitutionalism is the ideology behind the process of constitutionalisation and the ideology behind constitutions as outcomes. To put it differently, constitutionalism provides the ideological context within which constitutions emerge and constitutionalisation functions.[2]

---

[1] 'A constitution is an ordering of a city in respect of its offices and particularly of the sovereign one.' *Aristotle's Politics*, Book III (trans R. Robinson) (Oxford: Clarendon Press, 1962), p. 19.

[2] 'When we speak of constitutionalism, we refer to the set of ideas and principles which form the common basis of the rich variety of constitutions which we find in many countries of the world ... Thus constitutionalism encompasses institutional devices and procedures which determine the formations, structure and orderly functioning of government, and it embodies the basic ideas, principles and values of a polity which aspires

Although constitutionalism lacks ontological definition,[3] it consists of a number of themes which acquire meaning in the particular context in which they apply. Such themes include the *pouvoir constituant*, normative and organisational principles, institutional settings, conditions of membership, exercise of political power or the interface between centres of power. Last, but certainly not least, constitutionalism is not a static property. It expands, recedes or changes direction; but it constantly provides a template, according to which laws are created, behaviours are regulated, or institutional functions are assessed.

Lest there be any misunderstanding, we should say at this juncture that 'constitutionalism' is not synonymous with 'constitution'. A constitutional document may represent the fruition in time or space of constitutionalism, but it is just one of its facets, because constitutionalism is not about a single 'constitutional moment'[4] but about a series of such moments, some more pronounced and explicit, others rather implicit or mundane. Having said that, can there be a constitution without constitutionalism? Weiler has admonished the European Union (EU) for developing a constitution without constitutionalism.[5] One may agree with such a verdict if a 'thick' version of constitutionalism is taken,[6] according to which constitutionalism

to give its members a share in government.' U. K. Preuss, 'The Political Meaning of Constitutionalism', in R. Bellamy (ed.), *Constitutionalism, Democracy and Sovereignty: American and European Perspectives* (Avebury: Ashgate, 1996), p. 11 at p. 12; T. C. Grey, 'Constitutionalism: An Analytical Framework', in J. R. Pennock and J. W. Chapman, *Constitutionalism* (New York: New York University Press, 1979), p. 189 at p. 190; N. Walker, 'European Constitutionalism and European Integration' (1996) *Public Law (PL)* 266 at 268–75; F. Snyder, 'General Course on Constitutional Law of the European Union', in *Collected Courses of the Academy of European Law*, vol. VI (1998), p. 41 at p. 56; P. Craig, 'Constitutions, Constitutionalism, and the European Union' (2001) 7 *European Law Journal (ELJ)* 125 at 126–28; C. Möllers, 'Pouvoir Constituant-Constitution-Constitutionalisation', in A. von Bogdandy and J. Bast, *Principles of European Constitutional Law* (Oxford: Hart Publishing, 2006), p. 183.

[3] W. Murphy, 'Constitutions, Constitutionalism and Democracy', in D. Greenberg, S. N. Katz, S. C. Wheatley and M. B. Oliviero (eds.), *Constitutionalism and Democracy: Transitions in the Contemporary World* (Oxford: Oxford University Press, 1993), p. 3; D. Castiglione, 'The Political Theory of the Constitution', in R. Bellamy and D. Castiglione, *Constitutionalism in Transformation: European and Theoretical Perspectives* (Oxford: Blackwell, 1996), p. 5.

[4] B. Ackerman, *We the People: Foundations 1* (Cambridge, Mass: Belknap Press of Harvard University Press, 1991).

[5] J. H. H. Weiler, 'European Neo-constitutionalism: In Search of the Foundations of the European Constitutional Order' (1996) *Political Studies (Pol S)* 517 at 518.

[6] For the thin and thick notion of constitutions, see J. Raz, 'On the Authority and Interpretation of Constitutions: Some Preliminaries', in L. Alexander (ed.), *Constitutionalism: Philosophical Foundations* (Cambridge: Cambridge University Press, 1998), pp. 152–53.

is not only about the normative and structural scaffolding of a polity, but also about its *telos*. On the other hand, one may say that where there is a constitution of some sort there is also constitutionalism, especially if we rise above the particulars and view constitutions in conceptual terms and as a whole. Be that as it may, what Weiler's criticism alludes to is the precariousness of constitutions that lack the gelling power of constitutionalism – that is, when the political or legal facts reflect or correspond loosely, if at all, to the attitudes and articulations of those that form the polity. One may say that this is the case at the international where some sort of constitutional sample can be traced, however the meaning of international constitution is contested, and no agreement as to its overall rationale exists. The reason for this state of affairs is that international constitutionalism, if not totally dormant, at best lacks momentum or confidence. To a lesser degree, the debates about the European Union's real, virtual or even invisible constitution and the debates about its content, reveal the uncertainty that afflicts those polities which lack a fully developed constitutional conscience. This is because constitutionalism provides the optic that frames the debate about constitutions, and attributes meaning to the debate and to its outcome. If the optic is missing or is blurred, constitutional visions become equally blurred or are contested.[7]

From all of this, it is possible to surmise certain points about the meaning and value of constitutionalism. Constitutionalism is the narrative behind processes of self-creation, self-perception, self-identification, or self-projection. Furthermore, constitutionalism employs prescriptive, axiological and empirical tools,[8] not only to construct but also to continuously read politico-legal spaces.[9] Finally, constitutionalism is not an absolute and total quantity but a matter of degree[10] and of sensibilities, and comes into being in particular contexts.

---

[7] G. Walker, 'The Constitutional Good: Constitutionalism's Equivocal Moral Imperative' (1993) 26 *Polity* 91 at 98–9.

[8] T. Cottier and M. Hertig, 'The Prospect of 21st Century Constitutionalism' (2003) 7 *Max Planck Yearbook of United Nations Law (UNYB)* 261 at 279–82.

[9] According to Weiler, constitutionalism is '. . . a prism through which one can observe a landscape in a certain way, an academic artefact with which one can organise the milestones and landmarks within the landscape, . . . an intellectual construct by which one can assign meaning to, or even constitute, that which is observed'. J. H. H. Weiler, 'Introduction: The Reformation of European Constitutionalism', in J. H. H. Weiler, *The Constitution of Europe* (Cambridge: Cambridge University Press, 1999), p. 221 at p. 223.

[10] N. Walker, 'The EU and the WTO: Constitutionalism in a New Key', in G. de Búrca and J. Scott (eds.), *The EU and the WTO: Legal and Constitutional Issues* (Oxford: Hart Publishing, 2001), p. 31 at p. 33.

The above account of constitutionalism is particularly important when we discuss transnational constitutionalism because, traditionally, constitutionalism has been a statist *objet d'art*. This is because states are the prototype political units which are self-referential and often endowed with a stable and written constitution. Moreover, states are infused with their own version of normative ethos. It is not difficult, then, to explain why constitutionalism is questioned in spaces beyond the state. For one thing, these spaces may not exhibit certain constitutional attributes found in states. For example, such spaces may lack a common or a coherent organisational or normative charter or lack common governmental structures. However, even in such spaces, questions arise about conditions of membership, about relations, or about the organisation and regulation of power. To the extent that members of such spaces do not lead a nomadic life, they need to devise ways to regulate their mutual interactions. Any such organisational charter may refer to a thin notion of constitutionalism but it does not preclude the emergence of thick constitutionalism on the basis of more intense normative and structural alliances and allegiances. In this case, aggregations of states that share common perspectives may form linkages based on common normative and organisational standards, principles and rules. They can also establish their own legislative, executive or adjudicative institutions to regulate their lives and mitigate conflicts about fundamental principles or rules. All of the above will eventually make the constitution of the polity and project it as a unitary and autonomous order internally or externally.[11] One such micro-order is the European Union, which is characterised by common normative patterns, is endowed with legislative, executive or judicial powers and enjoys a degree of autonomy.

Even if constitutionalism does operate in areas beyond the state, state constitutionalism often becomes the standard-bearer of comparisons.[12]

---

[11] For example, the EC is a member of international organisations such as the United Nations Food and Agriculture Organisation (FAO) and the World Trade Organization (WTO). The autonomy of the EU has been affirmed in a number of opinions such as *Opinion 1/91* [1991] ECRI-6104 at 6108; *Opinion 2/94* [1996] ECR I-1759; *Opinion 1/76* [1997] ECR 755 at 759. J. Sacks, 'The European Community's Membership of International Organizations' (1995) *Common Market Law Review* (*CMLRev*) 227; D. Vignes, 'La particiupation aux organisations internationales' in R.-J. Dupuy (ed.), *Handbook of International Organisations*, 2nd edn (Dordrecht: Martinus Nijhoff, 1998), p. 62.

[12] F. Mancini, 'Europe: the Case for Statehood' (1998) 4 ELJ 29; J. H. H. Weiler, 'Europe: The Case Against the Case for Statehood', *ibid.*, 43. For a general discussion see J. Shaw,

Such comparisons are, however, unwarranted, because they are often based on an abstract and ideal model of state constitutionalism which is not real[13] and, secondly, they fail to appreciate the different dynamics in post-state spaces. Indeed, constitutionalism in post-state spaces may give rise to a different type of intellectual or practical enquiries. Thus, we not only need to consider the particular features of those spaces and understand their different historical experiences but, above all, we need to attune the constitutionalist themes and debates to the idiosyncrasies of such orders.

For instance, constitutionalism advertises its function in circumscribing political power.[14] This reflects the particular experiences of states in their political journey through history. However, this theme acquires a different dimension at the international, because the international is not endowed with legislative or governmental powers, and enjoys no separation of powers. If there are restraints, these are of a different kind and degree and refer, for example, to the relations between states or between states and organisations. Then, one needs to see the rationale behind the restraining function of constitutionalism, which is to protect people against the exercise of political power by institutions. However, at the 'international', states are not only the *pouvoir constituant* but also participate directly in law-making and law-enforcement. Consequently, the international is not an independent entity and cannot rise above its constituents but the 'sovereign' and the 'subject' merge.[15] On the other hand, the EU has its own legislative, judicial and governmental institutions which interact at different levels and enjoy a degree of autonomy. Therefore, one may need to examine the relations between the EU, the member states and individuals as well as the relations between the EU institutions.

'Postnational Constitutionalism in the European Union' (1999) 6 *Journal of European Public Policy (JEPP)* 579; N. Walker, 'Postnational Constitutionalism and the Problem of Translation', in J. H. H. Weiler and M. Wind, *European Constitutionalism Beyond the State* (Cambridge: Cambridge University Press, 1999), p. 27.

[13] M. Poiares Maduro, 'Europe and the Constitution: What if This is as Good as it Gets?' in J. H. H. Weiler and M. Wind, *European Constitutionalism Beyond the State* (Cambridge: Cambridge University Press, 1999), p. 74.

[14] G. Sartoti, 'Constitutionalism: A Preliminary Discussion' (1962) 56 *American Political Science Review (Am Polit Sci Rev)* 860.

[15] H. L. A. Hart, *The Concept of Law*, 2nd edn (Oxford: Oxford University Press, 1994), pp. 50–78.

Further, whereas the existence of a 'demos' either in ethno-cultural or civic terms is presented as a precondition of state constitutionalism, the international has no 'demos' in the sense of a body-politic that can bind its members;[16] whereas the EU, whose subjects are states and people, exhibits some discerning elements of demos and democracy, and therefore constitutionalism in that context adopts a different meaning.[17] It has also been said that 'constitutions are about moral commitments and identity'.[18] However, in a polyvalent order such as the international, constitutionalism may be more about normative neutrality and accommodation of differences than about projection of a common value system.

What the preceding examples have shown is that constitutionalism gives rise to different type of questions in the different *topoi* to which it applies. But there is something more. Constitutionalism is not built on a *tabula rasa* but is moulded by the political struggles and accommodations that have marked any of the referent *topoi*. Within states, constitutions are often the product of disruptive or explosive events that formalise and perpetuate their outcomes. The history of the international is marked by the Westphalian accommodation and the rise of sovereign states, the self-determination struggles, the quest for peace after devastating wars, or the emergence of the human rights movement, to name some of its most characteristic moments. The European constitutionalism has been inspired by the need to contain the negative impulses of nation-states, the downplaying of sovereignty, the search for peace through prosperity, human rights and the rule of law.[19]

Having said that, one may trace in the origins of the EU a strong ahistorical streak, and a move to rewrite history from then on. Compared

---

[16] J. H. H. Weiler, 'The Geology of International Law – Governance, Democracy and Legitimacy' (2004) *Zeitschrift für ausländisches öffentliches Recht und Völkerrecht (ZaöRV)* 547 at 548.

[17] J. H. H. Weiler, 'Does Europe Need a Constitution? Demos, Telos and the German Maastricht Decision' (1995) 1 *ELJ* 219. For an opposing viewpoint, see Bundesverfassungsgericht, decision of 12 October 1993, *Treaty of Maastricht* (Brunner), 89 BverfGE 155; [1994] 1 *CMLR* 57, para. 44; D. Grimm, 'Does Europe Need a Constitution?' (1995) 1 *ELJ* 282.

[18] J. H. H. Weiler, 'A Constitution for Europe? Some Hard Choices' (2002) 40 *Journal of Common Market Studies (JCMS)* 563 at 569; A. Estella, 'Constitutional Legitimacy and Credible Commitments in the European Union' (2005) 11 *ELJ* 22.

[19] J. H. H. Weiler, 'Fin-de-siècle Europe: Do the New Clothes Have an Emperor?' in J. H. H. Weiler, *The Constitution of Europe* (Cambridge: Cambridge University Press, 1999), p. 238.

with states where historical myths and symbols play an important role in their constitution, the EU rejected the historical baggage that its members carried or the 'pathos' of national constitutional aesthetics and built itself on the ahistorical and apolitical foundations of technocratic functionalism.[20] Be that as it may, the question remains as to whether the EU has developed it own brand of constitutionalism, which has subsequently acquired its own meaning.

Although the above discussion provides only a crude schematisation of the contours that international and European constitutionalism take, it is important to keep these contours in mind, because they are often neglected in the political or intellectual excitement that the language of constitutionalism provokes.

Overview of the book

The discourse on international constitutionalism is gaining momentum, but it is still in its infancy and appears rather slippery.[21] On the one hand, there are those who deny the existence of constitutional culture or conscience at the international or think that it is not a workable hypothesis.[22] Often they reach this conclusion by transposing to the international benchmarks borrowed from state constitutionalism. One area that fuels such scepticism is the normative, executive and adjudicative heterarchies that exist in the international in contrast to the hierarchies found in states.[23] Conversely, there are those who use the language of constitutionalism to describe and analyse organised clusters within the international, such as the lego-political order of the United Nations or

---

[20] U. Haltern, 'Pathos and Patina: The Failure and Promise of Constitutionalism in the European Imagination' (2003) 9 *ELJ* 14.

[21] For a general discussion, see D. M. Johnston, 'World Constitutionalism in the Theory of International Law' in R.St.J. Macdonald and D.M. Johnston, *Towards World Constitutionalism: Issues in the Legal Ordering of the World Community* (Leiden: Martinus Nihjoff, 2005), p. 3; B.-O. Bryde, 'International Democratic Constitutionalism', *ibid.*, p. 103.

[22] 'International Law, in fact is a *law without a constitution*. And since it is not grounded in a constitution, it lacks the possibility of natural growth. Unconnected with a *society*, it cannot adjust itself to its needs.' (Italics in the original.) A. Zimmern, *The League of Nations and the Rule of Law 1918–1935* (London: Macmillan, 1939), p. 98; S. Sur, 'L'état entre eclatement et mondialisation' (1997) 30 *Revue Belge de Droit International (RBDI)* 5 at 11.

[23] M. Koskenniemi, 'Hierarchy in International Law: A Sketch' (1997) 8 *European Journal of International Law (EJIL)* 566; but see T. Schilling, 'On the Constitutionalization of International Law', *Jean Monnet Working Paper 06/05*.

that of other international organisations and regimes such as the World Trade Organization (WTO),[24] international criminal law, and international, regional, or subject-specific human rights regimes.[25] They trace in such orders constitutional characteristics or vague constitutional promises deriving from hierarchical relations, general principles, or divisions of competence.[26] To give one example, both the United Nations (UN) and its Charter are often viewed through constitutional lenses[27] because of the principles the Charter contains, and the hierarchical order it establishes on the basis of Article 103. One may want to add here the Weberian trait of 'subjective orientation'; that is, people or states looking to the Charter to find direction. On the other hand, it can be noted that the UN Charter does not offer a total constitution in the sense that it does not regulate all the areas of the international political economy, and it cannot impress itself on its members. Even further, some identify a nascent constitutionalism built around *jus cogens* principles. These serve to 'verticalise' the international lego-political order; but one may object that this is not all that constitutionalism is about, and in any case any such hierarchy is only ideational rather than real since the content of *jus cogens* is not stable.

The literature on European constitutionalism is thriving, due to the EU's declared constitutional tendencies; although one may comment that it is often replete with inquiries as to whether the EU has a constitution, whether it needs a constitution, and if it does, what is, or

---

[24] D. Z. Cass, *The Constitutionalization of the World Trade Organization: Legitimacy, Democracy and Community in the International Trading System* (Oxford: Oxford University Press, 2005).

[25] In relation to the ECHR, see *Loizidou v. Turkey* (Preliminary Objections) – 15318/89 [1995] ECHR 10 (23 March 1995), para. 75: 'constitutional instrument of European public order'. L. Wildhaber, 'A Constitutional Future for the European Court of Human Rights?' (2002) 23 *Human Rights Law Journal (HRLJ)* 161; S. Greer, *The European Convention on Human Rights: Achievements, Problems and Prospects* (Cambridge: Cambridge University Press, 2006), particularly ch. 7.

[26] For the constitutional interpretation of the international order see T. Cottier and M. Hertig, 'Prospects of 21st Century Constitutionalism' (2003) 7 *Max Planck UNYB* 261; C. Tomuschat, 'International Law: Ensuring the Survival of Mankind on the Eve of a New Century' (1999) 281 *Recueil des Cours (RC)* 10; A. von Bogdandy, 'Constitutionalism in International Law: Comment on a Proposal from Germany' (2006) 47 *Harvard International Law Journal (Harvard INT LJ)* 22.

[27] B. Fassbender, 'The United Nations Charter as Constitution of the International Community' (1998) 36 *Columbia Journal of Transnational Law (Columbia J Trans Law)* 529; P.-M. Dupuy, 'The Constitutional Dimension of the Charter Revisited' (1997) 1 *Max Planck UNYB* 1; R. Chemain and A. Pellet, *La Charte des Nations Unies. Constitution Modiale?* (Paris: Pedone, 2006).

should be, the content of any existing or prospective constitution. The literature also replicates state envisions of constitutional organisation by conflating constitutionalism with hierarchical relations, and sometimes fails to take cognisance of the Union's distinct culture.

This book scrutinises the unfolding models of European and international constitutionalism by contextualising their structural and normative premises and critically reflecting on their constitutional ethos. It merges analysis and evaluation, whilst recognising that both the international and the European domain have their own 'constitutional culture' and dynamics. By combining the study of European and international themes, this book provides the needed nexus of knowledge and critical reflection on the nature and terms of the constitutional debates within the European and international context. In particular, the book addresses a number of constitutional topics such as: (i) the nature of European and international models of constitutionalism and their underlying principles; (ii) the *telos* behind international and European constitutionalism; (iii) the role of the state and of central courts; and (iv) the relations between composite orders.

The contributors to this collection deal with the above issues from different perspectives, and some are more sceptical than others. This degree of intellectual plurality reflects the authors' understandings of constitutionalism. It is not our aim to devise a single or comprehensive model but to generate knowledge and offer the reader an intellectual framework for making sense of the political and legal phenomena beyond the state.

At this juncture it is important to explain some of the concepts we are going to use throughout this book, which is, first of all, about international and European models of constitutionalism. By 'international' we mean the international political space as the primary and total layer beyond states. That said, clusters can be formed within the international, having their own political culture such as the UN. By 'European' we mainly refer to the EU, which already employs constitutional language and has explicitly declared its constitutional aspirations, but also to other organised clusters, such as the Council of Europe, and its European Convention on Human Rights (ECHR), in particular. These organised clusters evolve from the international, but because they exhibit self-referential and self-contained constitutional dimensions which are particular to them and different from the international, they are treated separately. We also use the word *models* when we refer to international and European constitutional phenomena. Model is a construction that, in our case, represents the structure and properties of particular international or European spaces. Furthermore, the international and European models are put under the umbrella of transnational constitutionalism because, first, transnational describes spaces that exhibit patterns of organisation and law creation other than states; second, transnational alludes to transactional relations which can be horizontal or vertical but not necessarily and exclusively hierarchical; third, because of the interlacing and cross-cutting of constitutional configurations at state, international or European level. A final point should be made here by way of clarification. Often the word 'supranational' is used to describe the political situation beyond states; we have avoided this term because it evokes hierarchical relations.

Looking now more specifically into the contributions, the first part examines the role of the state, of courts and of constitutional principles.

Patrick Capps' chapter compares the arguments made by social contract philosophers to justify the creation and internal normative structure of the state with their arguments in respect of international relations. In the latter case, they reject the concept of what Kant might have called 'the universal state'. Specifically, they argue for the *discontinuity thesis*. Variants of this position fall into three relatively distinct categories: (i) the universal state is empirically impractical; (ii) the sovereign state, as an agent, behaves differently from human agents; and (iii) the state is not an agent. Each version of the *discontinuity thesis* is used to justify a different kind of order in international relations; an international order rooted upon the prudential interests of states; or an order generated without the need for legislation through a sovereign power or, finally, an order established transnationally through the regulation of sub-state linkages. For Capps the whole exercise is multidisciplinary and solutions to the problems of establishing international legal order require a very clear analysis of the problems faced in international relations coupled with solutions to the problems of normative legitimacy and with innovation in the design of international institutions.

Pavlos Eleftheriadis considers the standing of states in the European Union by looking into how institutions make decisions. Decision-making in the Union is a combination of formal equality of states with proportional equality on the basis of states' population. Proportional equality refers to the standing of states in the Council or their representation in the Parliament. He then examines two issues: the allocation of powers between the Union and member states and the principle of subsidiarity. For Eleftheriadis, both support the view that the formal equality of states is prioritised and protected. Another area under consideration is the standing and representation of states within the judicial architecture of the Union where Eleftheriadis finds in the composition of the Court and the division of competences, but also in the relations between the European courts and national ones, a reaffirmation of the privileged standing of states in the Union. From the above, he concludes that Union constitutionalism in the area of collective decision differs from state constitutionalism. It is a combination of domestic and international principles where states do not abandon their rights of statehood.

Nicholas Tsagourias explores the role of general principles of law in the constitutional reading of the international and the European Union. These general principles of law are constitutive in the sense that they mould political orders and are divided into normative-ideological and structural-organisational principles. At the international they support a derivative order, lacking autonomy and independent authority, and evolving around structural-organisational principles rather than normative ones. For Tsagourias, the international, being an open order, allows states to construct their own particular clusters such as the EU, which represents an encysted and self-referential order enjoying a degree of autonomy and authority vis-à-vis its member states or the international and one that has its own normative and organisational charter. He then goes on to examine the role of courts in the constitutional praxis and argues that when a polity has developed awareness of constitutional practices or its own constitutional culture, courts may contribute to or even initiate constitutional debates. However, for Tsagourias, the constitutional debate should ultimately be formulated and practiced primarily by the *pouvoir constituant* instead of being ring-fenced by courts.

Julian Rivers examines the principle of proportionality in international and European law by looking into how the European Court of Justice (ECJ), European Court of Human Rights (ECtHR) and the Human Rights Committee (HRC) interpret and employ proportionality. Proportionality implies a form of discretion and Rivers identifies three types of discretion: policy-choice discretion; cultural discretion; and evidential discretion. Policy-choice discretion is about necessary and balanced policy options; cultural discretion in international jurisprudence appears in the form of relativism versus absolutism; and evidential discretion is about the prognosis of costs-benefits. For Rivers, courts should take care to distinguish between the different types of discretion in proportionality but their intervention depends on how they view their role vis-à-vis the other branches of government.

The second part contains chapters which examine different forms of transnational constitutional interface.

Nigel White's contribution deals with the issue of hierarchies between regional organisations and the United Nations. For him, the UN and international law represent the universal constitutional template within which regional organisations function. The UN Charter establishes a hierarchical system by virtue of Article 103 and Article 53 which includes the primary and secondary obligations deriving from the Charter. The latter are moulded by the Security Council but, overall, these obligations are limited. They concern, for example, security, where regional organisations are subject to Security Council authorisations but with regard to non-forcible measures such as sanctions, regional organisations enjoy wider powers. In this case, it is general international law or *jus cogens* that set limits to such power. White then considers the legitimacy of the Security Council and, although he acknowledges its poor standing, he still believes that its legitimacy is grounded on the fact that it represents the international community.

Ramses Wessel discusses the multilevel constitution of the Union in foreign relations. Such a constitution is formed by the constitutions of member states complemented by that of the European Treaties. This is, for Wessel, a multilevel, albeit distinct constitutional setting where the delimitation of competences is inferred by four principles: the principle of information and consultation; the principle of loyalty; the principle of subsidiarity; and that of external representation. The first principle supports systematic cooperation; the next, loyalty, is vertical between the Union and member states and between Union institutions and member states; subsidiarity covers all the areas of Union decision; and external representation is supported by Article 24 of the Treaty on European Union, according to which the Council can conclude agreements on behalf of the Union, although member states can use the procedures in the Council to prevent this from happening. This multilevel constitution in foreign relations is not only about the European and national legal orders but extends to the global order as well.

Achilles Skordas examines the principle of self-determination as a principle of global governance. He claims that self-determination is not merely a right to statehood, but that it has become a principle for the allocation and organisation of territorial authority in global society. Moreover, as a concomitant feature of the fragmentation of international law, it permeates the operation of transnational regimes. This means that an organisation or a legal regime has reached the evolutionary threshold that guarantees the further reproduction of its internal operations (internal self-determination), and ensures its separation from the external environment (external self-determination). This development is visible in the representative examples of the regional integration regime of the EU and of the global sectoral World Trade Organization regime.

Tonia Novitz reflects on how constitutionalism has been used to enhance the legitimacy of forms of governance. She considers corporatism and deliberate governance within the ILO 'tripartite' system and the 'bipartite' process of social dialogue within the EU. Whereas corporatism, which is about the participation of management and labour in norm-creation, is concerned with output legitimacy, deliberate governance has challenged some of its premises. Deliberate governance is about input legitimacy but its contribution depends on the nature of the corporatist models.

The final section includes two chapters which contain visions of international constitutionalism.

Bardo Fassbender reviews the constitutional language used in the international and finds that it is based on the identification of fundamental rules relating to the structure of the international but also on rules that transcend state consent such as the *jus cogens* norms. The above are tenets of the international community school which is today prevalent in international law. He then examines the United Nations Charter and claims that it should be viewed as the constitution of the international community mainly on the premise that it is treated as a point of reference for international interaction.

The last chapter, by Wouter Werner, views the language of international constitutionalism as a symbol that merges facts and norms and as a device to instil unity at the international. As facts, Werner treats the world order treaties, the *jus cogens* and *erga omnes* obligations, the mechanisms that control power; all the above against a background of disruptive events such as the US hegemony and the violation of international norms. However, the normative aspects of international constitutionalism seek to provide healing and regeneration by emphasising the need for legal unity. But such attempts are seldom successful and may even produce further fragmentation. For Werner, international constitutionalism should be regarded as an important, but never-ending attempt at reaching normative closure at the international level.

PART I

States, courts and constitutional principles

1

The rejection of the universal state

PATRICK CAPPS

Introduction

Three concepts have central roles in describing, explaining or legitimising the legal orders which have come to regulate our social lives. These concepts, which are consent, obligation and institutional form, are mutually supportive and logically parasitic upon each other. This is as true for the social contractarian tradition in political philosophy as it is for modern international legal scholarship. For example, for social contractarians the idea of rational consent by natural agents (i.e. human beings) justifies certain political and legal institutional forms. In the same way, international lawyers argue that the consent of artificially constructed agents (i.e. states) gives rise to legal obligations and legal institutions which regulate international relations. In the former tradition, the state is the justified institutional form. But both traditions shy away from arguing for some analogue to what Kant called a 'universal cosmopolitan state'[1] or what Hobbes might have called a 'global leviathan'[2] and instead argue for some alternative. The familiar, decentralised and horizontal conception of international law is but one example of these alternatives. This chapter examines the reasons why the logic which provides the normative justification for the state does not do the same to justify some form of universal state.

By rejecting a universal state, most social contractarians and international lawyers adopt what might be called a *discontinuity thesis*. This thesis can be explained in the following way. As has been suggested, the consent of natural agents has a normativising effect. Consent transforms

---

[1] I. Kant, 'Idea for a Universal History with a Cosmopolitan Intent', in T. Humphrey (ed. and trans.), *Perpetual Peace and Other Essays* (Indianapolis: Hackett, 1992, first published 1784), p. 38.
[2] T. Hobbes, *Leviathan* (Cambridge: Cambridge University Press, 1991, first published 1651), see e.g. ch. 13.

stipulated norms into legal obligations. It might also transform someone who does the stipulating from a tyrant or gangster into an authoritative source of law. The construct employed to show how consent can transform the rules of the powerful into a legal order is called the social contract. It works by hypothesising a state of nature. This is characterised as an irrational state of disorder. Disorder is solved when each agent rationally recognises the irrationality of the position he or she is in when in the state of nature and then consents to the formation of legal order and state institutions. This argument shows us why it is better that our activities are coordinated, our lives made predictable and justice achieved through law. The irrational alternative we must face is the unilateral judgment of the strongest holding sway.

It is often said that while the state of nature hypothetically existed, it *actually does* or did exist in some form in international relations. Hobbes, for instance, said that in international relations states are 'in a posture of War'.[3] Kant says that it is a state of 'barbarity, rudeness', 'a brutish degradation of humanity' or a 'lawless' or 'senseless freedom'.[4] Given the argument just presented, it would appear rational for states to attempt to escape from this situation in international relations: states must rationally agree to subject themselves to an institutional mechanism designed to authentically express the general will of the world community, embodied in the idea of the universal state. Most accounts in both the social contractarian tradition and in international law reject this line of argument and it is this rejection which is called the *discontinuity thesis*. It is the central claim of this chapter that, through the development of a typology of reasons used to support the discontinuity thesis, it is possible to clarify how an international legal order might be rationally constituted. In order to set out this claim, however, it is necessary to say something more about the basic concepts of consent, obligation and institutional form which are all at work in justifying and characterising legal and political order.

Consent and international legal obligation

Explanations of how international legal obligations arise are often founded on a well-known assumption. This is that states are bound to various

---

[3] *Ibid.*, p. 63.
[4] I. Kant, *Perpetual Peace*, L. W. Beck (trans.) (New York: Macmillan, 1957, first published 1795), p. 16.

commands, prohibitions and permissions, as well as having certain rights, duties or immunities, because they have given their consent to be bound. Somehow, the *fact* of consent, coupled to other related factors (such as an absence of deception or duress, or substantive factors such as constraints implied via *jus cogens* or *jus naturae*), has a normativising effect. This simple assertion, however, belies serious conceptual complexities concerning the way consent generates international legal obligations.

For some, the consent of a state to undertake an obligation is indistinguishable from a simple act of promising.[5] So, a treaty is more like a promise to meet a friend at the Red Lion at 8 p.m. than a contract to buy a painting by Constable of Salisbury Cathedral for 85*l*. A distinctive *international legal* reason to act is not, therefore, generated by the act of consenting by the state. Reasons to abide by promises have more to do with dialectical judgments of iterative self-interest. To this explanation should also be added the controlling effect of domestic review procedures.[6] So, international obligations are not binding on states as a corpus of norms which are part of an autonomous international legal order. Rather, the body of norms to which states consent are useful in coordinating the relations between sovereign states, may be legally binding by virtue of domestic constitutional law, and ultimately any putative obligation is qualified by the doctrine of *rebus sic stantibus*.[7]

There is another way of conceptualising the role of consent in generating obligations between states. Rather than international legal norms being the mis-characterisation of bare promises, rules of thumb or a rationalisation of self-interest, an autonomous international legal order gives rise to specific legal reasons for a state to act in particular ways. If a state acts contrary to the obligations to which it has consented, it is in violation of international law rather than simply being, for example, imprudent. For the same reasons, responsibility to other states arises, and international law determines what reparations are required in order to make good the internationally wrongful act. This conception of obligation rests on a foundational norm which requires that the consent of artificial agents or corporate bodies like states is essential for the creation of international legal obligations. The act of consent, then, generates a genuine legal reason for

---

[5] On this point see C. Reus-Smit, 'Politics and International Legal Obligation' (2003) 9 *European Journal of International Relations (Eur J Int Relat)* 591 at 595.

[6] See the discussion of Jellinek's work, below.

[7] See M. Koskenniemi, *The Gentle Civilizer of Nations: The Rise and Fall of International Law 1870–1960* (Cambridge: Cambridge University Press, 2002), ch. 3.

compliance; but, for those philosophers who have considered the problem of regress in grounding legal obligation, a familiar difficulty arises.[8] This problem is that it is not obvious how states have consented to the foundational norm which makes consent a law-creating fact.[9] Furthermore, consent to the norm which establishes consent as the normative foundation of the international legal order must be based, in turn, on a prior norm which gives normative force to this foundational rule, which, presumably, must be consented to. This, when iterated, forms a regress.[10]

One very familiar way to avoid this regress is to argue that it would be functionally impossible to regulate international relations without this foundational norm being the case. Any state, if it is rational, will accept it.[11] Oppenheim employs this type of argument. He claims that international law '. . . is merely a means to certain ends outside itself'.[12] These ends are three-fold: (i) 'peace among the nations and the governance of their intercourse by what makes for order and is right and just'; (ii) 'the peaceable settlement of international disputes'; and (iii) 'rules for the conduct of war'.[13] It is the task of the international lawyer to analyse the tectonic movements of international relations, to tame them, and orientate the actions of states towards certain fundamental values. Oppenheim claimed that if those who

---

[8] See J. Hampton, *Hobbes and the Social Contract Tradition* (Cambridge: Cambridge University Press, 1986), ch. 4.

[9] This position is set out in the *Lotus Case* and is both widely accepted and highly controversial. J. L. Brierly said that this decision was 'based on the highly contentious metaphysical proposition of the extreme positivist school that the law emanates from the free will of sovereign independent States' (J. Brierly, 'The "*Lotus*" Case' (1928) 174 *Law Quarterly Review (LQR)* 154 at 155). Elsewhere, Brierly explains why he thinks it is contentious. He says 'consent cannot of itself create an obligation; it can do so only within a system of law which declares that consent duly given, as in a treaty or a contract, shall be binding on the party consenting' (J. Brierly, *The Law of Nations* (Oxford: Oxford University Press, 1950), p. 54). Therefore, there is a theoretical hole in this positivist concept of obligation despite its simplicity, popularity and intuitive plausibility. It cannot explain why international law is binding.

[10] See *ibid.* See also Koskenniemi, *The Gentle Civilizer*, pp. 230 and 354; H. Lauterpacht, *International Law, Being the Collected Papers of Hersch Lauterpacht*, E. Lauterpacht (ed.) (Cambridge: Cambridge University Press, 1975), vol. I, pp. 179–444; *Private Law Analogies in International Law* (London: Longman, 1964), pp. 54–9; and H. Lauterpacht, *The Function of Law in the International Community* (Oxford: Clarendon Press, 1933), pp. 416–20.

[11] This argument was most famously made by H. Grotius in *The Rights of War and Peace* (Indianapolis: Liberty Fund, 2005, first published in English 1654 by J. Barbeyrac). It is also made by H. Bull in *The Anarchical Society* 3rd edn (Basingstoke: Palgrave, 2002).

[12] L. Oppenheim, 'The Science of International Law: Its Task and Method' (1908) 2 *American Journal of International Law (AJIL)* 313 at 314.

[13] *Ibid.*

manage states are rational, and there is, empirically, a balance of power between states, they will accept that certain fundamental norms are binding upon them. These norms are: (i) sovereign equality; and (ii) consent as the source of international legal obligation.[14] At least hypothetically, then, each state must rationally consent to the formation of an autonomous legal order based upon certain fundamental norms. Even if such consent is hypothetical, this argument provides a set of reasons why international legal obligations are binding and in this way the problem of regress is solved.

Note that Oppenheim's account of consent works in three ways. It explains, first, how the international legal order is normatively binding, secondly, why it takes a particular form; and thirdly, how individuated legal obligations arise. The first account tells us that states have an interest in settling their disputes peacefully. States must rationally consent to a system which allows this end to be achieved. Selection of this end, in turn, rests upon certain fundamental prudential values, such as peace, that they must hold. This is an *a priori* (and realist)[15] judgment, which binds together a socio-psychological explanation of state behavior (how states do act) with a normative claim (how states ought to act).[16]

Given the first account of consent, a second account arises whereby consent gives rise to a particular institutional form in international law. This is that states have, and ought to have, rationally consented to the foundation of an autonomous international legal order. The form of this legal order is decentralised and rooted on sovereign equality and consent as the basis of international legal obligations, given the end that states must resolve their disputes peacefully. So not only does consent imbue the legal order with normativity, it also structures its institutional form. Given this institutional form, a third account arises whereby consent is a fact which explains why putative obligations become *legal* obligations.[17]

---

[14] This statement is based on Kingsbury's characterisation of Oppenheim's work. See B. Kingsbury, 'Legal Positivism as Normative Politics: International Society, Balance of Power and Lassa Oppenheim's Positive International Law' (2002) 13 *EJIL* 401–37. See also A. Perreau-Saussine, 'A Case Study on Jurisprudence as a Source of International Law: Oppenheim's influence', in M. Fitzmaurice and M. Craven (eds.), *Time, History and International Law* (Leiden: Martinus Nijhoff, 2006).

[15] H. J. Morgenthau, *Politics Among Nations: The Struggle for Power and Peace* (New York: McGraw-Hill, 1993, first published 1948), see below.

[16] M. Hollis, *Models of Man* (Cambridge: Cambridge University Press, 1997), ch. 3 at pp. 35–7.

[17] H. Kelsen, *Introduction to the Problems of Legal Theory*, B. Litschewski Paulson and S. L. Paulson (trans.) (Oxford: Clarendon Press, 1992, first published 1934).

This chapter opened with the claim that the concepts of consent, authority and institutional form are logically inter-connected. Given the foregoing reconstruction of Oppenheim's concept of international law, it is easy to see why. Throughout his account (at least hypothetical) consent gives rise to legal authority and determines institutional form. This account of the role of consent in the formation of legal order is similar to that offered by social contractarians, such as Hobbes.

For social contractarians, natural agents (such as human beings) covenant to give up their unilaterally held rights to judge and punish and transfer these rights to the sovereign. Once into the social contract, the power of the sovereign to enforce law provides a sufficient reason for compliance. Hobbes tells us: 'Covenants, without the Sword, are but Words, and of no strength to secure a man at all.'[18] But while this explains the reasons for compliance with laws once into a legal order, it does not tell us how the covenant to form a legal order comes to be binding in the first place. This is because in the state of nature there are only words and no sword. The most well-known explanation for this is that it is prudentially rational to do so. Harrison explains that '[k]eeping agreement promotes the peace because it stops the aggravation and resentment of people who are abused by the breach of their protected expectations'.[19] So even without the sword, it is better to keep at least one promise; the promise to enter into legal order.[20]

Hobbes explains that the state of nature is an imagined situation[21] in which there is no governing sovereign power. As sovereign states in their international relations have no political superior, they too can be considered in a state of nature. This is a situation of mutual fear, where it is rational for states to adopt a defensive posture; to be 'diffident' towards

---

[18] See Hobbes, *Leviathan*, p. 117.
[19] See R. Harrison, *Hobbes, Locke and Confusion's Masterpiece* (Cambridge: Cambridge University Press, 2003), p. 114.
[20] See *ibid.*, pp. 113–24 for a very clear summary of Hobbes's answers to the problem of free-riders. For another analysis of the arguments Hobbes employs to justify the rationality of the move from the state of nature to the sovereign state, see Hampton, *Hobbes and the Social Contract*, chs. 2 and 3.
[21] It is for this reason, in my view, that Hobbes's argument is not susceptible to a critique which may come from the view of law advanced by Pospisil or Sacco, who both claim that 'never was there a pre-legal social world'. See S. Roberts, 'After Government? On Representing Law without the State' (2005) 68 *Modern Law Review* (*MLR*) 1 at 8. See R. Sacco, 'Mute Law' (1995) 43 *American Journal of Comparative Law* (*AJCL*) 455; and L. Pospisil, *Anthropology of Law: A Comparative Theory* (New York: Harper Row, 1971).

each other.[22] This means that states are '. . . saddled with the constant
need to watch, distrust, anticipate, and get the better of others, and to
protect themselves by all possible means'.[23] Specifically, he argues:

> But though there had never been any time, wherein particular men were
> in a condition of warre against another; yet in all times, Kings, and
> Persons of Soveraigne authority, because of their Independency, are in
> continuall jealousies, and in the state and posture of Gladiators; having
> their weapons pointing, and their eyes fixed on one another; that is, their
> Forts, Garrisons, and Guns upon the Frontiers of their Kingdomes; and
> continuall Spyes upon their neighbours, which is a posture of War.[24]

If we are applying Hobbes's reasoning for the establishment of a uni-
vocal sovereign will, we might say this situation is irrational and that a
universal state which mimics the functions of the sovereign state is
rationally required to solve the problem of disorder in international
relations. But Hobbes rejects this conclusion. He argues that each state's
self-interest may cause them to generally act civilly towards each other in
the absence of a universal state. There is a kind of minimum sociability
in the state of nature; a basic system of trust with the *rebus sic stantibus*
qualification. Iterative self-interest is sufficient to bind states *in foro
interno* even though there no external power binding states *in foro
externo*.

Following this reasoning, there is only one choice open to the
Hobbesian international lawyer: he or she must choose a universal
state or the state of nature. This is because international law can only
exist if there is a body that authentically expresses the general will of
those states. There is no other *legal* alternative.[25] Oppenheim, on the
other hand, shows how there may be a middle way between the state of
nature and the universal state by arguing for a decentralised model of
international legal order. He claims that states will and ought to rationally consent to this decentralised order where each state consents to the
norms it is bound by, and, by and large, determines unilaterally whether

---

[22] See R. Tuck, *The Rights of War and Peace* (Oxford: Oxford University Press, 1999),
p. 130; Bull, *The Anarchical Society*, pp. 45–6; M. Doyle, 'Kant, Liberal Legacies and
Foreign Affairs' (1983) 3 *Philosophy and Public Affairs* 205–35 at 218–9.

[23] See Tuck, *ibid.*, p. 130.

[24] See Hobbes, *Leviathan*, p. 90. See also G. Roosevelt, *Reading Rousseau in the Nuclear Age*
(Philadelphia: Temple University Press, 1990), p. 38.

[25] See T. Nagel, 'The Problem of Global Justice' (2005) 33 *Philosophy and Public Affairs*
(*Philos Pub Aff*) 113 at 115.

a wrong has been committed against it (that is, unless the state has, in itself, consented to compulsory arbitration). Grotius and Pufendorf make similar claims. But this model is, for Hobbes, simply not law. It is merely a state of nature where international legal obligations are misnamed expressions of iterative self-interest. Oppenheim's view is that such norms are genuine legal obligations and they can arise independently of the universal state.

The logic of the social contract

The previous section shows how consent works to ground the concepts of legal obligation and institutional form in both international legal theory and the social contract tradition. This mode of reasoning seems intuitively plausible. As Harrison suggests, 'it is attractive to think that rightness flows from our own will'.[26] But it is necessary to look at the logic underpinning this mode of justification more systematically before we can consider exactly how various arguments for the discontinuity thesis work. This is because these arguments press against various aspects of the logic of the social contract, thus permitting the rejection of the universal state.

Hobbes realised that covenants with God to follow the moral law led to obligations *in foro interno*, but did not lead to political stability. Similar conclusions were reached by Grotius, Pufendorf, Locke and Kant, even though each disagreed as to the exact role of natural law in political and legal justification and the spiritual implications of not acting in compliance with its dictates. For all of these philosophers, the problem with the application of the moral law (whether revealed in the Bible, by inductive analysis of our social world or by a transcendental deduction of the moral implications of agency) amongst large groups of people is that disagreement emerges over what each of us is practically required to do. This is because the moral law may be interpreted differently by different people according to the circumstances, or at least permit of a range of options, some of which may be incommensurable with each other and which may produce conflict. Even when all agents attempt to comply with the strictures of the moral law, unpredictability will emerge alongside social conflict.

Hobbes's view is that this unpredictability leads each of us to be naturally diffident towards each other. As was seen in Hobbes's description of the

[26] Harrison, *Hobbes, Locke*, p. 138.

relations between states, being diffident means that we will naturally take a defensive and untrusting posture towards each other. This spirals out of control for Hobbes until it is ameliorated through an agreement to establish a social contract. Here, each individual agent's will is subsumed by a sovereign will which lays down and enforces mandatory legal norms. Other accounts of the social contract may reject the violent turbulence of the Hobbesian description of life without the sovereign, but essentially the same problem arises: if individuals can make judgments as to what is right or what is theirs and then attempt to enforce these judgments against others, then conflict and disorder will arise. This is the case even if, or perhaps more accurately, even *because*, each agent is attempting to comply with the moral law.

There are, then, two foundational components in the logic of the social contract. The first is a conception of the individual which has certain generic interests. These are, for example, interests each individual has in survival, having one's property protected or living in a society in which the moral law will be more perfectly realised. The second is an account of the problems which occur when social beings, like human beings, are in close proximity to each other. There are a number of reasons for these problems emerging. One is connected to facets of human psychology. For example, human beings tend to be short-sighted, self-orientated or sometimes governed by their passions. Then there are the physical limitations human beings have: each is roughly equal in physical strength and their brains sometimes reason imperfectly. Finally, there is competition over limited resources in their physical environment and population density is such that they cannot but interact with each other. Given these factors of social life, these agents will choose civil society and stable government because it rationally preferable to the state of nature.

David Lewis, in his book *Convention*, attempts to systematise the logic of the social contract. This is a useful summary of the comments which have been made so far. Avowedly Humean in approach,[27] the social contract is defined:

> ... roughly as any regularity R in the behavior of members of a population P when they are agents in a situation S, such that it is true, and common knowledge in P, that:
>
> Any member of P who is involved in S acts in conformity to R.

[27] D. Lewis, *Convention* (Oxford: Blackwell, 2002, first published 1969), pp. 3–4.

> Each member of P prefers the state of general conformity to R (by members of P in S) to a certain contextually definite state of general nonconformity to R, called the state of nature relative to social contract R.[28]

Note that, for Lewis, members of P act 'in conformity' to R, but R is also a 'regularity' in the behaviour of members of P and this perhaps reflects an equivocation between normative, descriptive and explanatory modes of analysis which is commonly found in game theory.[29] To explain, the word 'conformity' suggests that members of P are actually altering their behaviour, as an exercise of practical reason, so that it is in accordance with R. 'Regularity' does not seem to imply the same exercise of practical reason. Most animals act regularly, but do not choose to act in conformity with norms (and, as Hobbes puts it, ants and bees are not 'continually in competition for Honour and Dignity . . . Envy and Hatred . . . and Warre'[30]). But as Lewis considers human beings are capable of practical reason, the description of R is a state of affairs to which members of P conform because it is preferable for them to do so and R is an optimal outcome relative to the state of nature. Reading Lewis's description in line with the comments just made, S is an account of the situation (psychological, physical, social) in which members of P find themselves. R represents the set of social arrangements which, for the social contract tradition, are civil society and the sovereign state.

It is not surprising, given that the foundations of his work are in game theory, that a conception of generic human interests which make R rationally preferable is missing from Lewis's account. Instead, Lewis's conception of preferences is essentially subjective: each person can choose the ends they wish to pursue. Understood in this way, it might be too much to expect that from all the discordant interests members of P have that they all choose R as a relative optimal outcome.[31] The social contract argument, however, is based upon the claim that *whatever* an agent wills he must also will certain

---

[28] *Ibid.*, pp. 88–9.   [29] See Hollis, *Models of Man*, ch. 2.

[30] See Hobbes, *Leviathan*, ch. 17; p. 117. Kant argues that because we have this rational capacity there can be no 'systematic history of man . . . (as perhaps it might with bees or beavers)'. Kant, 'Idea for a Universal History' 29.

[31] Lewis's conventions (which differ in various ways from the social contract) (see Lewis, *Convention*, pp. 88–95) rely upon long-term coordination conventions arising as a result of iterative behaviour in the past, where precedent is a strong reason for compliance for practical reasoners. This will not work for the social contract. This is for at least two reasons. First, the state of nature is conceived as a situation where there is no regular practice in conformity with pre-existing norms (because people interpret the moral law differently). Alternatively, even if people do act in accordance with the moral law, this will do no good: I will simply have to say 'I predicted that', when I take what I

generic ends. So, the logic of the social contract is understood as concluding that the sovereign state is to be rationally preferred given that members of P have certain generic ends they must rationally accept when they find themselves in situation S.

This description of the logic of the social contract is obviously over-generalised and shrouds some important distinctions between the central protagonists of this tradition. One, which is of importance in the rest of this chapter, concerns the single step contract offered by Hobbes and the double step contract offered by Locke (along with Pufendorf and Grotius). For Hobbes, reasonable individuals rationally choose to enter civil society governed by a sovereign will. Once this step has been made, questions of right and wrong are determined by the sovereign. The idea that the sovereign might be wrong makes no sense.[32] This is because the sovereign is the 'Multitude of men . . . made One person'.[33] We have a single author of law.

In the accounts offered by Locke, Grotius and Pufendorf, the sovereign does not constitute the people in this way. Rather, the people constitute themselves as a civil or political society, and then entrust power to the sovereign to make laws on their behalf.[34] For Locke, the initial step is for individuals to consent to establish civil society; 'a single body that moves with a single will'.[35] The second step is for a majority of this body to consent to form a government which is entrusted to use its powers for the public good. For Locke, Grotius and Pufendorf the public good is a standard to which the sovereign can, in principle, be held to account by civil society.[36] For Hobbes, what constitutes the public good is determined by the sovereign.

On the Lockean account it appears possible to conceive of a society of states which mirrors civil society between human beings. This is characterised by 'guarded co-operation',[37] governed by laws (natural[38] or

---

think is mine and others take what they think that it is theirs. Yes, we can envisage a convention whereby people act prudentially. It is not, however, likely to do us much good. The convention I adopt to act prudentially because everyone else is likely to do so, produces a sub-optimal outcome relative to R.

[32] See Harrison, *Hobbes, Locke*, p. 153.

[33] See Hobbes, *Leviathan*, p. 82. See M. Loughlin, *The Idea of Public Law* (Oxford: Oxford University Press, 2003), pp. 55–7.

[34] See Loughlin, *ibid.*, and Harrison, *Hobbes, Locke*, pp. 144–52.

[35] Harrison, *Hobbes, Locke*, p. 211.

[36] See P. Pasquino, 'Locke on King's Prerogative' (1998) 26 *Political Theory* 198.

[37] See Tuck, *The Rights of War*, p. 84 and Bull, *The Anarchical Society*, pp. 25–7.

[38] See Reus-Smit, 'Politics and International Legal Obligation', 618–9.

positive) which extend beyond mere prudence, but which are not created or enforced by a universal state. This conceptual device then justifies a horizontal and diffused conception of international legal order. It is also more than Hobbes's cynical and diffident state of nature in international relations. Put another way, the idea of civil society without the state is one that can be employed to argue *against* a universal state to govern international relations.

Locke alludes to this idea between natural agents in §97–99 of the *Second Treatise*, but does not apply it to international relations.[39] One place where he refers to this possibility is in §14:

> That since all Princes and Rulers of Independent Governments all through the World, are in a State of Nature, 'tis plain the World never was, nor ever will be, without Numbers of Men in that State. I have named all Govenors of Independent Communities, whether they are, or are not, in League with others: For 'tis not every Compact that puts an end to the State of Nature between Men, but only this one of agreeing together mutually to enter into one Community, and make one Body Politick; other Promises and Compacts, Men may make one with another, and yet still be in the State of Nature.[40]

One ought to be careful not to read too much into this, but it does seem to allude to an international political community without a universal state which is similar to the arguments found in the work of Grotius and Pufendorf.

The discontinuity thesis

A universal state is characterised as an institution which subsumes the unilateral will of sovereign states through institutions which express their general will. These institutions centralise law-making, dispute-settlement and law-enforcement activities. For Hobbes and Oppenheim, the logic which justifies the sovereign state does not imply the universal state. This is called the *discontinuity thesis*.

There are three sets of reasons found in the literature to justify the discontinuity thesis. First is the argument that the universal state is impractical against standards of effectiveness or legitimacy. Secondly,

---

[39] See J. Locke, *Two Treatises on Government* (Cambridge: Cambridge University Press, 1997, first published 1690).

[40] See also §21; and C. Beitz, *Political Theory and International Relations* (Princeton: Princeton University Press, 1979), p. 60, n. 97.

it is sometimes argued that that the state, as an artificial agent, behaves in a different way from natural individuals. The third is that the state should not be perceived as a 'person' or 'agent' in the way that flesh and blood human beings are.

A. A universal state is empirically impractical

Whilst the universal state is a logical ideal, it is impractical. There are a number of varieties of this argument which often run together. The first argument sees the history of political thought as a history of developing techniques by which our social life can be effectively regulated. As Skinner and Loughlin, amongst others, argue, the nation state is a modern technique for regulating our lives and it represents a seismic change in the way in which politics is conducted.[41] This development rests upon a transformation in political ideas as well as the technological capacity to physically coordinate social activity via a centralised state (e.g. through improvements in communications). At present, cosmopolitanism might be considered not sufficiently developed (both intellectually and practically) to challenge the dominance of the state as a regulatory technique and it is for this reason that the universal state is impractical.[42] A more radical version of this hypothesis is that the entrenched power interests are better served by a state of nature in international relations and therefore it will be impossible to achieve a universal state. The other, normative, side of this argument is to claim even if the universal state was technically possible, it would collapse into a tyrannical form of government.

Anne-Marie Slaughter makes both the technical and normative arguments in the polemical opening to her article in *Foreign Affairs* in 1997.[43] She states that: '[m]any thought that the new world order proclaimed by George Bush was the promise of 1945 fulfilled, a world in which international institutions, led by the United Nations, guaranteed international

---

[41] Q. Skinner, *The Foundations of Modern Political Thought* (Cambridge: Cambridge University Press, 1978), vol. I; Loughlin, *The Idea of Public Law*, ch. 5.

[42] On these points, see the work of Daniele Archibugi. Perhaps the articles which deal with these issues most systematically are 'The Reform of the UN and Cosmopolitan Democracy: A Critical Review' (1993) 30 *Journal of Peace Research* (*J Peace Res*) 301–15 and 'Models of International Organisation in Perpetual Peace Projects' (1992) 18 *Review of International Studies* (*RIS*) 295–317.

[43] A.-M. Slaughter, 'The Real World Order' (1997) 76 *Foreign Affairs* (*Foreign Aff*) 183. Many of these claims are also set out in her book, A.-M. Slaughter, *A New World Order* (Princeton: Princeton University Press, 2004).

peace and security with the active support of the world's major powers.'
We could consider that when she alludes to the 'promise of 1945' she is
referring to an analogue to the universal state in that it is an attempt to
'guarantee international peace'. She then claims that '[t]hat world order
is a chimera' and then states the technical and the normative versions of
the impracticality argument: '[e]ven as a liberal internationalist idea, it
is infeasible at best and dangerous at worst.'[44] She substantiates these
conclusions by claiming that the universal state:

> ... requires a centralized rule-making authority, a hierarchy of institu-
> tions, and universal membership ... [E]fforts to create such an order
> have failed. The United Nations cannot function effectively independent
> of the major powers that compose it, nor will those nations cede their
> power and sovereignty to an international institution. Efforts to expand
> supranational authority, whether by the U.N. secretary-general's office,
> the European Commission or the World Trade Organization, have con-
> sistently produced a backlash among member states.[45]

The problem with this justification, it should be pointed out, is that it is
not possible to infer from the truism that human beings have failed to
transcend the state in the past to the general truth that they cannot do it
in the future. This is merely a replication of the riddle of induction. Her
assumption is that 'a regularity in the past is *pro tanto* good evidence that
it will hold in the next case'. The problem is that 'the number of past
cases is not necessarily the arbiter of merit of the theory' operating as a
general truth about human social life.[46] One could avoid this conclusion
if abderitism (where human life is at a 'permanent standstill', any
progress or decline is an 'empty activity of backward and forward
motion', and 'all the interplay of members of our species on earth
ought merely to be regarded as a farce'[47]) was the case. But I cannot
see how one might demonstrate this to be true.

The same point is made by Kant, and in Slaughter's earlier work she
draws directly on his writings.[48] He argues that:

> [t]he idea of international law presupposes the separate existence of many
> independent but neighbouring states. Although this is a condition of war

---

[44] See Slaughter, 'The Real World Order', 183 and *A New World Order*, p. 8.

[45] Slaughter, 'The Real World Order', 183.   [46] See Hollis, *Models of Man*, p. 48.

[47] I. Kant, 'Contest of the Faculties', in H. Reiss (ed.), *Political Writings* (Cambridge:
Cambridge University Press, 1991), pp. 179–80.

[48] See A. Burley, 'Law Among Liberal States: Liberal Internationalism and the Act of State
Doctrine' (1992) 92 *Columbia Law Review* 1907.

(unless a federative union prevents the outbreak of hostilities), this is rationally preferable to the amalgamation of states under one superior power, as this would end in one universal monarchy, and laws always lose in vigor what government gains in extent; hence a soulless despotism falls into anarchy after stifling the seeds of good.[49]

Although Kant's arguments are often equivocal on the subject of the solution to the problem of disorder,[50] this quote represents his strongest affirmation of this version discontinuity thesis. The loss of 'vigour' he refers to corresponds to the technical ineffectiveness of global institutions. The 'soulless despotism' implies the normative illegitimacy of a universal state.[51]

The more radical version of this argument is that the universal state is impractical because of entrenched power structures. Those who benefit from these power structures are set to lose too much if there is a universal state. Therefore, it cannot happen. Whilst not endorsing the despondency of this claim, Allott does clearly recognise the barrier to the development of international law produced by entrenched power structures.[52] One of the central claims of his work is that the very concept of the sovereign state alienates human beings from the possibility of achieving his vision of the universal state. Instead, we have a 'misconceived international society' which is 'formed in and for the reality of the ruling-classes of their state-societies'.[53] The lack of controls on state behaviour expressed in the Vatellian inter-state system '... was most welcome of all to the political and administrative sections of the ruling classes, who could speak to each other and compete with each of and conflict with each other across the frontiers, safe in the fastnesses of their self-contained internal-external state-systems'.[54]

---

[49] See Kant, *Perpetual Peace*, p. 37.   [50] See note 90 below.
[51] See J. Rawls, *The Law of Peoples* (Cambridge, Mass.: Harvard University Press, 1999), p. 36.
[52] P. Allott, *Eunomia* (Cambridge: Cambridge University Press, 1990). See also E. J. Hobsbawm, *Nations and Nationalism* (Cambridge: Cambridge University Press, 1990), chs. 1 to 3. Hobsbawm says, for example, '... governments had considerable domestic interest in mobilizing nationalism among their citizens' (p. 89). This was coupled with 'a rejection of new proletarian socialist movements, not because they were proletarian but also because they were, consciously and militantly *internationalist*, or at the very least non-nationalist' (p. 123).
[53] See Allott, *Eunomia*, p. 250.   [54] *Ibid.*, p. 249.

B. *The state is different from natural individuals*

The second version of the discontinuity thesis rests on the argument that there is a difference between natural agents, such as human beings, and artificial agents, such as states. It was shown in the last section that the logic of the social contract rests upon some presuppositions about the socio-psychological traits and vulnerabilities of human beings. It is argued that these presuppositions do not apply to states in their relations with other states. One argument which supports this version of the discontinuity thesis is that states act differently because they act reasonably or can auto-limit themselves in a way in which human beings cannot. The second argument is that states can co-exist within an international society where legal obligations can arise without a universal state. A third argument is that states are not vulnerable in the same way as flesh and blood human beings are.

Hobbes tells us that chaos and disorder are found in the state of nature when natural agents act prudentially. Some have argued, however, that states, in international relations, will auto-limit themselves. Auto-limit means that they will act with restraint in accordance with various obligations, and tend to comply with the promises they make. Therefore, Hobbes's maxim that 'Covenants, without the Sword, are but Words, and of no strength to secure a man at all'[55] does not *always* apply in international relations. Stability and order is possible in international relations because states can act with self-restraint in a way that human beings cannot.

One variant of the auto-limitation argument is that states *qua* states can auto-limit themselves. A second variant is that it is only democratic states which can auto-limit or otherwise act reasonably or with restraint. The first variant rests on two factors. Initially, the sociological, political or economic environment in which sovereign states act is different to that found in the state of nature between human beings. Arguments of this type – for example, realism – tend to rest on the claim that prudence or iterative self-interest is a strong constraining factor in international relations.

It might be wondered how prudential rationality provides more of a constraint in international relations than it does in a state of nature between human beings. This argument is not readily forthcoming and sometimes rests on a Hobbesian claim that states acting prudentially produces some level of predictability, and this is the best that can be achieved. Answers might be that there is more stability in international relations because there is a relatively small number of states or because they are economically or

---

[55] Hobbes, *Leviathan*, p. 117.

politically interlinked in ways which human beings cannot be.[56] So, Hobbes's 'foole' might think that he can get away with secretly breaking promises in societies inhabited by millions of subjects but states might be less likely to be able to take the free-riding approach simply because other states are likely to have a better idea of what other they are doing, and it is easier for other states to publicise breaches of obligations.[57] It might be that a state can become a pariah who should not be trusted far more easily than the seasoned fraudster within such a state.

The second factor which explains how states auto-limit themselves is the constitutional law of the state itself. International norms are not legal because they are validated by an autonomous international legal order, but because they emanate from self-legislation.[58] Natural agents and Hobbes's sovereign state bind themselves *in foro interno* and rules are not externally or publicly enforced against them. The idea of self-legislation is different because it is *enforced* against the state through *public law*. Furthermore, the capacity of states to legislate internally is no different from their capacity to legislate externally: both are an expression of the state autonomy by which the state legislates to bind itself.

This is the approach taken by Georg Jellinek in his 'two-sides' theory.[59] The juridical side leads to the conclusion that the state was not subject to a higher law such as international law, but rather had a 'will' that bound itself. The problem identified by critics of Jellinek was that such an obligation vanishes once the state changes its mind. It might, then, be questioned whether an obligation which can be disobeyed is really an obligation. But this mistakes two core elements of Jellinek's approach which map onto the considerations just outlined. The second, sociological or psychological, side to Jellinek's theory takes into account 'the structural constraints imposed on State will by the environment'.[60] His second response is that the state is capable of self-legislation. He says that public and administrative law is an exercise in self-legislation, but it is slightly odd to think of such norms as a set of contingent norms which can be violated at will. So why should it then be presumed that international law is any different to state public law when it comes to the binding effect of self-legislation?

---

[56] It is the case that if biological beings were as inter-linked as, for example, two states which had a longstanding trading relationship with each other, we would say that they were symbiotic. See Roosevelt, *Reading Rousseau*, p. 34.

[57] See Harrison, *Hobbes, Locke*, pp. 121–4.

[58] See Koskenniemi, *The Gentle Civilizer*, pp. 186, 189 and 198–206.

[59] *Ibid.*, and see G. Jellinek, *Allgemeine Staatslehre* (Berlin: Häring, 1914).

[60] See Koskenniemi, *The Gentle Civilizer*, p. 201.

The more restrictive version of the auto-limitation argument is that it is only states *qua* democratic states that behave reasonably. Kant suggested that line of reasoning might serve to regulate international relations when he claimed:

> The republican constitution ... gives a favourable prospect for the desired consequence, i.e. perpetual peace. The reason is this: if the consent of the citizens is required in order to decide that war should be declared ... nothing is more natural than that they would be very cautious in commencing such a poor game, decreeing for themselves all the calamities of war ... on the other hand, in a constitution which is not republican, and under which the subjects are not citizens, a declaration of war is the easiest thing in the world to decide upon, because war does not require of the ruler, who is the proprietor and not a member of the state, the least sacrifice of the pleasures of his table, the chase, his country houses, his court functions, and the like. He may, therefore, resolve on war as on a pleasure party for the most trivial reasons, and with perfect indifference leave the justification which decency requires to the diplomatic corps which are ever ready to provide it.[61]

Doyle tests Kant's speculation empirically. He finds that liberal states[62] exist within a 'zone or peace' of 'a pacific union', and inducts the following thesis: '*Even though liberal states have become involved in numerous wars with nonliberal states, constitutionally secure liberal states have yet to engage in war with one another.*'[63] Relations between liberal states are, therefore, peaceful and cooperative but '[l]iberal states are as aggressive and war prone as any other form of government or society in their relations with nonliberal states'.[64] His reason for peace between

---

[61] See Kant, *Perpetual Peace*, p. 12. See also, Kant, 'The Contest of the Faculties', p. 185: '... if the rules of man's own species regard him as such and treaty him accordingly, either by burdening him like a beast and using him as a mere instrument of their ends, or by setting him up to fight in their disputes and slaughter his fellows, it is not just a trifle but a reversal of the ultimate *purpose* of creation.' See Rawls, *The Law of Peoples*, p. 44–54.

[62] Liberal states are defined as having four characteristics: (i) judicial equality and civil rights; (ii) democratic institutions and freedom from internal and external despotism; (iii) protection of private property rights; and (iv) a market system of exchange.

[63] See Doyle, 'Kant, Liberal Legacies', 213.

[64] *Ibid.*, 225. Liberal states are aggressive towards non-liberal states for three reasons:

1. 'Imprudent vehemence' on the part of liberal states in the validity of their value systems coupled to the liberal impulse to provide humanitarian support to those who suffer at the hands of non-liberal states.
2. The principle of non-intervention is only restricted to liberal states in some circumstances.

liberal states is that 'their constitutional structure makes them – realistically, different'.[65] The specific reasons he gives for the occurrence of this phenomenon are as follows:

(i) In liberal states, citizens have some control over the declaration of war. Furthermore, the rotation of officials 'is a nontrivial device that helps ensure that personal animosities among heads of government provide no lasting, escalating source of tension'.[66]

(ii) '[D]omestically just republics, which rest on consent, presume foreign republics to be also consensual, just, and therefore deserving of accommodation.'[67]

(iii) The 'spirit of commerce' provides for deep connections to develop between liberal states.[68]

Doyle does not unequivocally support the normative implications of his thesis, but the corollary of his thesis is that war would cease to occur if all states were liberal. His argument, therefore, supports the discontinuity thesis because the universal state is not logically required as a mechanism to provide order in international relations. This normative argument, which is based upon promoting liberalism globally through the strengthening of trans-governmental linkages, coupled to criteria of procedural legitimacy,[69] is Slaughter's solution to the problem of institutionalising international order without a global state.[70]

A third argument is advanced by Grotians such as Hedley Bull. Their argument rests upon the claim that a legally regulated society can exist between agents independently of the emergence of a state. This is rooted on the Grotian and Lockean argument set out in the last section that principles of natural law provide tangible legal obligations between individuals and structure their basic social relations: 'if natural law is

---

3. Liberal states tend to be suspicious of non-liberal states because of the latter's closed and often secretive governmental institutions. So, when the 'Soviets refuse to negotiate, they are plotting a world takeover'. This suspicion also leads to the limited development of economic ties between liberal and non-liberal states.

[65] Ibid., 235. These reasons in some part suggest that we might be approaching the problem of conflict in international relations in a wrongheaded fashion; that it is what goes on within the state rather than the actions of the state qua artificial agent itself which are important. This consideration will be dealt with in the next section. But, at least in part, for Doyle, democracy has an important pacifying effect for the actions of states as corporate entities.

[66] Ibid., 230.   [67] Ibid.   [68] Ibid., 232.

[69] For example, 'global deliberative equality'.

[70] Slaughter, 'A New World Order', 11 and passim.

as Grotius supposes, then people have a basic right not to be harmed in their lives, bodies and possessions. They have a right to have their agreements kept.[71] Therefore, '[w]hen this does not happen, there is injustice, and where there is injustice, restitution and punishment are permitted by natural law'.[72] The state only emerges to institutionalise and enforce communal systems of property rights. But this system based upon natural law can provide a framework within which a society of states can emerge. States, 'lacking a superior (under God) and bound only to natural (and divine) law, may justly declare war and attack, destroy, and sieze the property of other states when that state has acted unjustly'.[73]

This decentralised system of law, for Grotius, regulates the activities of states. Tuck says that this is a form of society which lacks 'a genuine community of interests or resources. Its sociability extended only as far as was necessary to justify a private right of punishment'.[74] But, crucially, this international society precludes the need for a universal state but does allow international laws to arise independently of it.

Bull largely accepts the Grotian claim that a society of states is sufficient to regulate international relations.[75] However, he argues for a thicker conception of society in which states 'regard themselves bound by certain rules in their dealings with one another'.[76] This thicker conception of international society is in part analytical and in part historical. Analytically, Bull considers that there are certain norms which are accepted by states as being necessary for social life in international relations to occur. These are an 'empirical equivalent'[77] of Grotian natural law and concern the preservation of an international society of states, maintaining the independence of states and providing a limit on violence and the stabilisation of property rights.[78] This has to 'be set against the cultural and historical forces that had helped shape the consciousness of society at any particular time and moulded perceptions of common values and common purpose'.[79] Institutions – such as the

---

[71] Harrison, *Hobbes, Locke*, p. 145.
[72] *Ibid.*   [73] *Ibid.*   [74] Tuck, *The Rights of War*, p. 88.
[75] See Hurrell's preface to the second edition of Bull, *The Anarchical Society*, at ix. The word 'sufficient' is used here with reference to Bull's claims that to develop a more comprehensive conception of world order was 'premature global solidarism' (*Ibid.*, at xxii) or 'confused international law with international morality or international improvement' (p. 38).
[76] See Bull, *The Anarchical Society*, p. 13.   [77] *Ibid.*, p. 6.
[78] *Ibid.*, pp. 16–18.   [79] A. Hurrell's Introduction to *The Anarchical Society*, p. xi.

'machinery of diplomacy' – are built upon the norms derived from both of these sources in order to make international society operate smoothly. In this way, Grotians accept the discontinuity thesis by claiming that the state of nature in international relations is regulated through an international society. This precludes the logical requirement of the universal state to govern international relations.[80]

Bull's argument for the discontinuity thesis rest upon three claims. His first claim is that civil society can exist independently of government. So, he accepts a Lockean or Grotian conception of international civil society which can exist independently of the institutionalisation of sovereign power. Then he says that human beings cannot do very much without a social contract. Industry and agriculture are predicated on a stable system of property rights and personal security. But while this is true for human beings in their relations, all these activities, as a matter of fact, can occur with a society of states in international law.[81] So, one of the key reasons for the state does not, in the same way, give rise to a reason for the universal state.

Bull's final claim is justified by a different kind of argument. This is not that states will tend to behave reasonably in international relations. Rather it rests on Hobbes's argument that states do not have the same vulnerabilities as natural agents. As has been shown, Hobbes claims that diffidence will give rise to a basic level of sociability in international relations and in fact Tuck describes this as a very thin conception of society in international relations, and so it might be similar to Grotius's claim on this matter.[82] But human beings are in exactly the same position; they are unlikely to be sociable with each other unless it is in

---

[80] *Ibid.*, pp. 44–50. Something like this idea is backed up by ethnographic studies of law in non-state societies. See Roberts, 'After Government?', 9.

[81] On this, see Tuck, *The Rights of War*, p. 98. It might be said in response to Bull's point that some sorts of modern collective activity might be inhibited or precluded in a society of states.

[82] It ought to be pointed out that some have questioned whether there is indeed a qualitative difference between the Hobbesian 'thin' conception of international society, on the one hand, and the Lockean or Grotian 'thick' conceptions of international society, on the other. Tuck (*The Rights of War*, p. 102) quotes Rousseau's *Emile*: 'Hobbes relies on sophisms, and Grotius on the poets; all the rest is the same.' See also Harrison, *Hobbes, Locke*, p. 160. If we contrast Bull (which is a modern Grotian approach) with realism (which is Hobbesian in approach), this distinction is clearer. But even here it is not obvious why a realist rationale would, by necessity, provide a thinner conception of international society than that which is advanced by Bull. This much is admitted by Stanley Hoffmann in the introduction to Bull, *The Anarchical Society*, at xxvi–ii.

their occurrent interest to do so, and Hobbes thinks that this is rationally sub-optimal. This being the case, this very thin conception of sociability in international relations is clearly irrational, and the universal state might be implied.

Hobbes, as has been shown, rejects this conclusion. He thinks that there is a dis-analogy between the relations between natural individuals and international relations and it this argument which supports his view of the discontinuity thesis. Hobbes, according to Harrison and Bull, initially claims that the defensive posture adopted by states in the state of nature is 'expensive, and, it might seem, pointless' and states 'get locked into a mutually expensive posture of defence'.[83] Harrison makes the argument just stated: '[y]et, if rational self-interest is really as Hobbes describes, whereby people placed in state of nature have reason to escape to the greater security of the state, then it might seem that the separate sovereign states should also have escaped by now into the greater security of a single sovereign world government.' Harrison then sets out the discontinuity thesis when he says: 'something has to be different at the state level.' Bull says much the same thing: 'States are ... very unlike human individuals.'[84] This difference is as follows:

> ... as well as analogies there are also dis-analogies between states and individuals. It is important for Hobbes that in the state of nature everyone be effectively equal in strength ... and that they are all equally weak. As he puts it in *Leviathan*, 'the weakest has strength enough to kill the strongest' ... Even the strongest sleep. So no one (at least for Hobbes) has sufficient strength for security. They need a greater strength; hence they need the artificially constructed strength of the great Leviathan. This, however, does not apply to states, as least not obviously so. The weakest here cannot topple the strongest. States do not go to sleep. Hence, at least for some of them, there is both the possibility and the desirability of going it alone (that is, defending themselves by their own exertions) in a way that has no analogue with respect to individual people.[85]

---

[83] Harrison, *Hobbes, Locke*, p. 94.

[84] See Bull, *The Anarchical Society*, p. 47. He identifies that it is Spinoza that initially develops a Hobbesian 'states don't sleep' argument. Spinoza says: '... of course, a man is overcome by sleep every day, is often afflicted by disease of body or mind, and is finally prostrated by old age; in addition, he is subject to troubles against which a commonwealth can make itself feel secure.' See Spinoza, 'Tractatus Politicus, III, ii', in A. G. Wernham, *The Political Works of Spinoza* (Oxford: Clarendon Press, 1958), p. 293. See also Doyle, 'Kant, Liberal Legacies', 220 and Roosevelt, *Reading Rousseau*, p. 37.

[85] Harrison, *Hobbes, Locke*, p. 96.

For the Hobbesian, this argument is certainly *prima facie* plausible. For some states it might well be prudentially rational to 'go it alone', and, if so, this is a conclusive reason for accepting the discontinuity thesis. This argument has a number of implications. First, it might give a justification for a unilateralist US foreign policy since the collapse of the USSR. Furthermore, it might be rational for weak states to band together in defensive pacts, or even to pool their sovereignty and form larger cohesive state units, but it does not imply the universal state. It should be noted that this argument relies upon Hobbes's claim that states can render themselves relatively invulnerable. This is an empirical claim which we might seriously question given the proliferation of weapons of mass destruction.

C. State is not a person

The final version of the discontinuity thesis is that it is a fundamental mistake to consider the state as an artificial agent and such a claim presupposes an obscuring and misplaced ontology. This presupposition is that what is of concern is the relations between states and it is on this that a disordered state of nature in international relations is predicated.

Slaughter makes this argument in an article from 1995.[86] It starts by rejecting realism: '[f]or Realists, power is the currency of the international system. States interact with one another within that system like billiard balls: hard, opaque unitary actors colliding with each other.'[87] Specifically, this is a rejection of three assumptions. First, realists 'believe that States are the primary actors in the international system, rational unitary actors who are functionally identical'. Second, 'they assume that State preferences, ranging from survival to aggrandizment are exogenous and fixed'. Third, 'they assume that the anarchic structure of the international system creates such a degree of either actual conflict or perceived uncertainty that States must constantly assume and prepare for the possibility of war'.

Some, for example Hans Morgenthau, accept the realist diagnosis of international relations, but find it deeply troubling as a mechanism to regulate international relations. He tells us that the realist premises form a 'debilitating vice that was present at its birth [which] continues to sap its strength'.[88] He then claims that 'international peace cannot be permanent without a world state, and that a world state cannot be

---

[86] See A. Slaughter, 'International Law in a World of Liberal States' (1995) 6 *EJIL* 503.
[87] *Ibid.*, 507.   [88] Morgenthau, *Politics Among Nations*, pp. 342–3.

established under the present moral, social, and political conditions of the world . . .', and then seems to accept the impracticality version of the discontinuity thesis.[89]

Slaughter would agree that this undue pessimism is caused by the realist ontology of international relations which is presupposed by most international lawyers, but she considers the way forward is to re-orientate our ontology. For Slaughter, the 'real business' of international relations takes place at the 'sub-national' level and, therefore, it is important to look more closely at how decision-making takes place within states. This means that inter-relations between sub-state agents (such as court, banks, enforcement agencies) should be understood as a significant source of transnational relations alongside the traditional concerns of high politics with which realism seems focally concerned.

This explanatory claim is then taken further: transnational linkages are stronger and more frequent within democratic and capitalist states. This *explains* why liberal states are more reasonable than illiberal states and thus confirms Doyle's thesis. So, it is not that liberal states behave better, but rather that there are more transgovernmental inter-linkages between the individuals and institutions who live, or are situated, in liberal states. It is not the hermetically sealed, prudentially rational, sovereign state that is the subject matter of international relations. Nor is it the reasonable democratic state that does not go to war with other democratic states. Both of these arguments belie the real explanation, which is that there are systemic reasons why the individuals who live in relatively open (i.e democratic and transparent) and trade-orientated societies do not go to war with each other.

This leads to the normative conclusion, which is that if we increase transgovernmental linkages then we reduce the likelihood of war. It is possible, by short-circuiting the premises of the social contract argument, to achieve peace without global governance. Rather, order is achieved through the regulation of transgovernmental linkages, and a universal state is not necessarily required to achieve this.

Institutionalising international law

The three versions of the discontinuity thesis tell us why the universal state is not a logical conclusion of the logic of the social contract. Of these versions, the *impracticality* argument is essentially defeatist. The

[89] *Ibid.*

act differently and *not a person* arguments reject the premises upon which the social contract logic is built. I suspect that those who hold the second and third justifications, however, have as their inspiration, the first. This general despondency about international law does not necessarily follow, however, if it is employed to justify some other way of regulating international relations. By way of conclusion to this chapter, some more systematic comments will be made about these alternatives.

The *impracticality* argument reveals two positive arguments. The first is that because it is impossible to achieve the universal state, the next best alternative is to consider a 'surrogate' to it. Kant, for instance, argues for a 'free federation, the surrogate of the civil social order, which reason necessarily associates with the concept of the law of nations'.[90] What this surrogate might look like, or whether it is indeed a surrogate, is ambiguous in Kant's work. The second argument rests on the claim that the ends we want to achieve through legal regulation are better served by *not* having a universal state. So, if we want an international legal system which promotes, for example, legitimacy, transparency or diversity, then the best option is to avoid a universal state, and, perhaps, favour a diffuse or horizontal conception of international law.

Regarding the *act differently* argument, a universal state is rejected in favour of a state of affairs whereby iterative self-interest or self-legislation will normally keep international relations stable, and to some extent, predictable. On the other hand, modern Grotians, such as Bull, argue – in a different way to the Kantian – for a decentralised and horizontal conception of international law.

The *not a person* argument tends to be used to imply a much more haphazard system of international governance, which may at times be ineffective and opaque, but which generally achieves the objective of securing peaceful coordination between states. The solution to social disorder – which exists between human beings and groups of human beings at all levels – can be achieved through comity, conflicts of law, diplomacy, conferences, colloquia and assemblies rather than through formal and potentially ineffective or unjust international global institutions. Added to this might be a general requirement that this solution is governed by overarching normative concepts such as 'global deliberative equality' to ensure that every relevant person has a say in decision-making.[91]

The discontinuity thesis tells us that international relations is different in significant ways to the relations between natural agents and it is these

[90] Kant, *Perpetual Peace*, p. 19.   [91] Slaughter, *A New World Order*, 29.

differences which drive these alternatives to the universal state. How this thesis is characterised would, therefore, seem to be a key judgment which must be made when arguing for various institutional forms to govern international relations. If this judgment is unclear, then the argument for international law will also be unclear. For example, Kant argues, at various parts of his work on international law, for 'a federative alliance ... given a priori by the principle of right',[92] 'universally valid public laws', 'a league of peace', 'a common external power', 'a convention ... analogous to a universal state', a 'system for the legal settlement of ... differences'[93] and a 'universal *cosmopolitan state*'.[94] He also argues that:

> [t]he spirit of commerce, which is incompatible with war, sooner or later gains the upper hand in every state. As the power of money is perhaps the most dependable of all the powers (means) included under the state power, states see themselves forced, without any moral urge, to promote honorable peace and by mediation to prevent war whenever it threatens to break out. They do so exactly as if they stood in perpetual alliances ...[95]

While I think that Kant is best interpreted as arguing for some analogue to a universal state, the above paragraph might lead some to equivocate as to the validity of this interpretation. It would be my guess that, at least in part, this problem is caused by a lack of clarity about the problem of international relations which he faced. For example, he seems confused as to whether states can act reasonably in a way which human beings cannot. By taking the 'spirit of commerce' approach, it might be surmised that he does think that they act differently and hence he supports the discontinuity thesis. However, when he characterises the problem as one whereby states decide 'what is right by unilateral maxims through force',[96] this is the same problem which is faced by natural agents. He, then, might be understood to reject of the discontinuity thesis and accept a universal state characterised as a 'league [whereby] every nation, even the smallest, can expect to have security and rights, not by virtue of its own might or its own declarations regarding what is right,

---

[92] *Ibid.*, p. 51. See also G. Wallace-Brown, 'State Sovereignty, Federation and Kantian Cosmopolitanism' (2005) 11 *European Journal of International Relations* 495.

[93] Kant, *Perpetual Peace*, p. 44.   [94] Kant, 'Idea for a Universal History', 38.

[95] Kant, *Perpetual Peace*, p. 32. See also J. Rawls, *The Law of Peoples*, p. 46; and C. Montesquieu, *The Spirit of Laws*, A. Cohler, B. Miller and H. Stone (trans.) (Cambridge: Cambridge University Press, 1989), ch. 2.

[96] Kant, *Perpetual Peace*, p. 19.

but from this great federation of peoples alone, from a united might, and from decisions made by the united will in accord with laws'.[97]

This confusion might be taken further into an analysis of the history of international law. It is fairly obvious, for instance, that the United Nations, which has strong analogies to the universal state, has been forged from oblique conceptions of a horizontal, diffuse system of international governance.[98] If we take the history of political ideas seriously, this may reflect deep ideological differences over the ways in which international relations are different from the relations between natural beings, which results in skewed and confused approaches to institution building.[99]

Finally, the despondency which is associated with the discontinuity thesis probably comes from the power the state has as the quintessential form of political organisation we can imagine. To argue for the universal state is to ask for new forms of political and legal organisation of our social world. Alongside globalisation, Kuper has argued that there is '. . . a glaring absence of a corresponding increase in our capacities to exercise political control over this enmeshed world. This deficit is partly due to a peculiar way in which our practical imagination is constrained';[100] a deficit which breaks down into three deficiencies of international legal thought. First, there is little agreement on how the problem of disorder in international relations should be understood. Should the discontinuity thesis be accepted, and if so, in what form? Secondly, there is little agreement on the various ends that we want to achieve through international legal regulation. Finally, the possibilities of international legal regulation beyond the state are often constrained by analogies to state institutions (e.g. global accountability = global democracy). More appropriate institutional mechanisms need to be developed in order to achieve effective and procedurally just decision-making procedures on a global scale. This is an interdisciplinary project which combines international relations, moral and political philosophy and international law. Embarking on this project may go some way to revolutionising[101] thinking on international law *beyond the confines* of the sovereign state.

---

[97] Kant, 'Idea for a Universal History', 34.
[98] See A. Hurrell, 'Global Inequality and International Institutions', in T. Pogge (ed.), *Global Justice* (Oxford: Blackwell Publishing, 2003), pp. 40–1.
[99] See Skinner, *The Foundations*, Preface.
[100] A. Kuper, *Democracy Beyond Borders* (Oxford: Oxford University Press, 2004), p. 2.
[101] Here I mean, revolutionary in the sense re-described as 'evolutionary' by Kant in 'The Contest of the Faculties', and E. Fromm in 'The Revolutionary Character', in *The Dogma of Christ* (London: Routledge, 1963).

2

The standing of states in the European Union

PAVLOS ELEFTHERIADIS

Introduction

Many European Union (EU) lawyers believe that we ought to compare EU law to constitutional law, and the European Union's institutions to those of a state. Leading authors describe the core of EU law as the 'constitutional law of the EU',[1] or have argued that the Union is an 'autonomous political authority'[2] or that it can be compared to a nascent 'republic'.[3] The state analogy is supported by the suggestion that Europe has embarked on a journey towards 'ever closer union'.[4] The leading European philosopher Jürgen Habermas has written that he hopes to see the Union form strong federal-like institutions so as to accelerate the creation of a European 'public sphere'.[5] Such views have, for a long time, been presented as the most progressive and forward-looking accounts of the EU. They have also helped to develop the law. The Court of Justice of the European Communities (ECJ) has ruled that Community law is a 'new legal order' that constitutes a hierarchical legal order vis-à-vis the national legal systems and that the treaties constitute the 'constitutional charter' of the Union.[6] The doctrines of direct effect

---

[1] See, for example, K. Lenaerts and P. van Nuffel, *Constitutional Law of the EU* (London: Sweet and Maxwell, 2004).

[2] K. Lenaerts and D. Gerard, 'The Structure of the Union According to the Constitution for Europe: The Emperor is Getting Dressed' (2004) 29 *European Law Review (ELR)* 289.

[3] A. von Bogdandy, 'The Prospect of a European Republic: What European Citizens are Voting On' (2005) 42 *CMLRev* 913.

[4] This is the well-known phrase employed in the preamble of the Treaty of Rome. For an unusually forthcoming federalist argument, see G. Verhofstadt, *The United States of Europe* (London: Federal Trust, 2006).

[5] J. Habermas, 'Why Europe Needs a Constitution' (2001) 11 *New Left Review* 5. For a more extended argument along the same lines, see J. Habermas, 'The Postnational Constellation and the Future of Democracy', in J. Habermas (ed.), *The Postnational Constellation: Political Essays*, M. Pensky (trans.) (Cambridge: Polity Press, 2001), p. 58.

[6] Case 294/83, *Parti Ecologiste 'Les Verts' v. European Parliament* [1986] ECR 1339, para. 23.

and supremacy have brought EU law very close to the model of a federal public law. The theory that underlies much of the interpretation of EU law by the Court of Justice seems to be a theory of public law analogous to that of federal legal systems.

Yet, such interpretations leave much unexplained. They offer a working account of EU law in that they accommodate the supremacy of the internal market rules and the direct effect of secondary law created in Brussels. Nevertheless, they do not satisfy a more theoretical desire for completeness and generality. A closer look at the EU law in its entirety, including the treaties, the institutional balance between states and the institutions, the case law of the Court of Justice on competences and subsidiarity (and even the institutional design envisaged by the new Treaty Establishing a Constitution for Europe[7]), shows that the Union is fundamentally different from a state legal order. The fuller picture shows that the EU has features that go well beyond those of conventional constitutional structures. When seen in its entirety, the constitutional architecture of the EU exhibits a persistent respect for the allocation of roles and powers between states and the centre in a form that is unique to the Union.

The problem with all constitutional analogies is broadly this. A constitution of a state is normally built on the construction of powers around the institutions of government, and on a set of fundamental principles that define public rights and duties in a conclusive way. The key to these rights and duties is the idea that state power is exercised by means of collective decisions, i.e. decisions from which members cannot opt out. The legal materials of the EU, by contrast, do not exhibit these features. There is an ordering of institutions and some collective and representative decision-making, but the states retain distinct roles in many fields. The Union's institutions are given broad powers, but such institutions still do not enjoy the comprehensive role of their domestic counterparts. As a result, the public rights and duties of citizens (and their governments) are primarily determined by national laws and constitutions and only secondarily by European Community law. The

---

[7] See the Draft European Constitution, published as 2004 Treaty Establishing the Constitution for Europe, *OJ* C 310, 16 December 2004. For the various stages to the drafting of this text, see the earlier Draft Treaty Establishing a Constitution for Europe, CONV 850/03, 18 July 2003 (prepared by the Convention for the Future of Europe) and Draft Treaty Establishing a Constitution for Europe, CIG 86/04, 25 June 2004 (drafted by the Intergovernmental Conference). The Treaty was signed in October 2004 by the member states' governments. The process of ratification has now been suspended, after failed referenda in France and the Netherlands in May and June 2005.

constitutional architecture of the Union exhibits a complexity, for which domestic constitutional law has no use. All constitutional analogies mislead us into neglecting this complexity.

The unique feature of the EU's constitutional architecture is the division of labour between member states and the Union in legislative, executive and judicial functions. As I will show, this is a very different arrangement from the separation of powers we find in domestic constitutions, and cuts across all three functions of government. This allocation of powers between states and the Union requires the working out of new principles, uniquely appropriate to the European Union.

In this chapter I shall therefore try to describe some of the basic features of the position of states in EU law. I will look, first, at the position of states in the composition and procedures of the main Community institutions. I will then examine the particular allocation of functions between states and the Union. Finally, I will look at the judicial framework. Such analysis is necessary before we embark on a discussion of the most fitting general political and constitutional principles explaining such arrangements. As in other areas of the law, a general theory should be close to the record of the complex practices of lawyers and courts. The theoretical framework must be appealing but must also remain faithful to its materials. On the basis of such materials, my argument will be that the appropriate starting point for the political and constitutional theory of the EU is not be a comparison with constitutional law but a new and unique cosmopolitan framework for states.

Collective decision-making

A key concept in understanding the EU is that of a collective decision. States are typical examples of institutional collective action. The international community is an example of absence, in principle, of collective action. The EU stands somewhere in between. It is an international organisation but its institutions combine both international and domestic patterns of decision-making.

Political decisions are collective in the sense that, once the process begins, the members of a political society cannot opt out of such decisions. Citizens are bound by the decisions reached, even if they disagree with the result or even refuse to participate in the process. There is little collective decision-making in international politics. In international relations important decisions are usually reached by diplomatic conferences in the form of treaties, which are not collective decisions in the sense intended here. Every state is in principle free either to join or not join in the decision. It is free to join or not a particular agreement according to public international law. Any state can ignore the treaties it does not subscribe to, unless such a treaty is taken to be a codification of international custom.

In international relations, collective decisions are therefore the exception, not the rule. In the absence of a world political society or a world state, the occasions of collective enforcement of decisions is rare. Such exceptions occur in some international organisations, which occasionally reach decisions that are binding on everyone, even on those not consenting to them. In the EU, by contrast, we do have very wide-scope collective decisions within the Community's policies. The enactment of a Directive or a Regulation is binding even on those member states that voted against it in cases of majority voting, or abstained in cases of unanimity.[8]

Collective decisions create the following complexity. One may disagree with the decision but approve the procedure. Alternatively, one may agree with the decision but not with the procedure. Procedure raises the question of its legitimacy, irrespective of the particular outcomes. Collective decisions under some previously outlined procedure are not therefore the same thing as the actions of a group. A non-organised group (which could range from a revolution to a peace march) acts without procedures, perhaps by force or accident. There is no point questioning how a crowd moves or how a queue is spontaneously formed. Only the result can be evaluated, not the procedure. By contrast organised collective decisions invite questions of legitimacy in addition to questions of substantive success. To put it another way, legitimacy is a distinct virtue of institutions, quite apart from their tendency to produce correct results.

In addition to being collective, some decisions are also representative. This means that even those who did not participate in its formation may also by covered – in some relevant sense – by the decision. The idea of representation here is just a formal one. When an absolute monarch issues, say, a Royal Ordinance, his decisions are collective in their effects, in the sense that they are intended to bind everyone, even those who disagree. They are also representative in that they claim to bind also those who did not participate (and could not participate on account of the particular constitution). The decision is not properly collective or representative in the normative sense, but collective and representative

---

[8] See Article 205(3) EC, according to which abstention does not prevent adoption of an act by unanimity.

only in the formal sense employed here. We need such formal concepts to distinguish collective and representative decisions from decisions that happen to have the same influence on some other basis (because the monarch is popular or wise). We also need them in order to point out the ways in which the monarchical decisions are flawed, because they claim to bind those who under a monarchical constitution have no voice. If they seek to have collective and representative effects, they must also be collective and representative in the full normative sense.

Modern political life offers examples of collective representative bodies that claim to bind and do have the power to bind everyone, including those who disagree (those bound by the collective nature of the decision) and those who are not even present in the process (hence those 'represented'). In domestic law such bodies are ordinarily parliaments, boards of directors or cabinets of ministers. We may then draw another distinction by saying that a person or state or other entity may enjoy a certain standing in a collective body, reflected by the number of votes it controls in the process. Or we may say that the person or state or other entity is represented by a number of persons. Standing and representation are related, but different, concepts. Hence, a Foreign Office official may sit on a committee controlling a number of votes on behalf of his state (standing) or a number of persons may sit on a body representing the electorate of their state, each with their own voice and vote (representation).

In an obvious sense all state actions in international relations are representative. All governments represent their peoples. Such peoples are never present even when diplomatic conferences are held. Representation, in this sense, is always a feature of international relations. But we are interested here in a second level of representation, when a government may be represented by other governments. The Security Council of the United Nations is an example; it reaches binding decisions for everyone, even those governments who did not sit on the Council in any particular year, but only voted in the election of the non-permanent members. The Security Council's decisions are representative in this second level sense, in that they bind other governments, and in the first level, deeper, sense, in that they are taken in the name of peoples. It is clear that the idea of representation in international law is more complex than in constitutional law.

In ordinary constitutional practice, collective and representative decision-making is very common. Legal and philosophical argument claims legitimacy for such structures through complex principles of fairness or principles of justice. Constitutional law and practice normally provide a set of answers to the questions of legitimacy of procedures. Representative democracies normally settle on some form of words for rules of appropriate decision-making, combining equality, accountability and geographical and numerical criteria. It is hard to enumerate all of such practical criteria here. They have to do with the particular virtues of institutions within particular political and historical situations (a distinct field of political theory, contrasted to the virtue of individuals or the correctness of decisions). Such institutions emerge slowly, often as the unintended consequence of conflicting actions, and are justified on historical or local grounds that normally defy summary or classification. It is the task of constitutional law to manage them for each particular political society.

Unitary states, for example, mostly follow a simple criterion of electoral representation according to population within certain locations. A certain number of electors in a particular place choose one representative. In the United Kingdom, for example, all parliamentary constituencies are of roughly equal numerical size and elect one Member of the House of Commons. Gerrymandering aside, the same is true in the House of Representatives in the United States.[9] But the similarity is deceptive. Federal states generally introduce more complex variations. The US Senate, for example, does not represent populations but only constituent states: every state has two senators, irrespective of its size. The situation is more complex still in the US Presidential Electoral College. Every state elects a number of delegates but in most cases only the winning candidate within any state is consequently represented; the system is thus a mixture of the representation of states and populations. The US constitution thus follows a complex scheme of representation. It follows a principle of the representation of populations in the House of Representatives, a principle of the representation of states in the Senate and a mixed system of representation of both states and populations in the election of President. We may thus conclude that in the US the political process (including Senate, House of Representatives and the President) combines the representation of populations with the representation of states. From this preliminary discussion we may identify the three possible models of representation: a representation of states, a representation of populations, and a mixed principle combining both of these.

---

[9] This is true at least in principle. For the most recent position of the US Supreme Court on drawing congressional districts on racial (not allowed) or political (allowed) grounds see *Hunt v. Cromartie*, 526 U.S. 541 (1999).

International decision-making

In international relations, the rule is that every state is present, with its diplomats, 'around the table'. Collective decisions are the exception. Representation of governments is rare. In the formation of treaties we have neither collective decisions nor representation. A state is not bound by a treaty it does not enter (nor can it be legally compelled to participate in the drafting of such a treaty). Decisions bind only those who agree with them. Examples of such exceptions include the process of decision-making in the Security Council of the United Nations or the decisions of the International Monetary Fund (IMF). It would be instructive to examine the principles behind them, if indeed there are any. It is clear that the standing of states within these collective bodies varies.

It has been noted that in domestic decision-making we can distinguish between the standing and the representation of states or populations. But such distinctions are insufficient to explain the differences between the Security Council and the IMF. We need more sophisticated distinctions. It is clear that the sovereignty of a state is a different kind of criterion to the size of its population. We may, therefore, outline four abstract models of collective decision-making. The standing or representation of a state may be determined by 'formal equality', 'criterial equality', 'formal inequality' or 'criterial inequality'. It will be obvious that the four types are created by linking two parameters: first, the type of the arrangement and, second, the ground for the arrangement.

The 'formal equality' of states denotes their equal standing or representation (the form) on the formal basis (the ground) that they are sovereign states. The clearest example is the rule that every state shall have one representative or one vote and decisions shall be reached by the majority of votes. This rule follows the general pattern of state sovereignty, enunciated in Article 2(1) of the Charter of the United Nations (UN Charter), according to which the UN is based on 'the principle of the sovereign equality of its Members'. The equality of states in law-making is of course manifest in the negotiations for treaties, where there is no collective decision to be made. But it is also evident in collective decisions. In some international bodies equality requires that either all have a power of veto (unanimity rule) or that none does (majority rule). The first variation, the unanimity rule, is endorsed, for example by the procedures of the Council of the North Atlantic Treaty Organization (NATO), which makes decisions only with the consent of each of the representatives of the member countries. The second variation of formal equality, the majority rule, is adopted by the Committee of Ministers of the Council of Europe, where some issues require unanimity of votes cast, others a two-thirds majority, and others a simple majority.[10] The criterion of the standing of states in both cases is formal equality, because no distinction is drawn between the various states on account of their size, their economic or military power, or any other criteria. Everyone has one vote (whatever the particular significance of that vote according to the particular decision mechanism, unanimity or two-thirds or simple majority). The standing of all states is the same, even if the relative weight of their votes will depend on the voting mechanism.

The second model of collective decision-making is 'criterial equality', according to which the standing or representation of a state (form) is proportional to some distinct feature (ground) going beyond sovereignty. Even though, in this model, voting rights may vary for each state, the way in which such rights are calculated will be the same for all. In this sense any resulting inequality in the standing of states as participants in the process does not upset the principle of equality, because it follows a distinct criterion, such as size of population, or monetary contributions or some other public criterion which is applied equally to all. Hence we may draw the conclusion that such a system is not one of inequality but one of proportional or criterial equality. An example of such proportional equality is the allocation of votes in the Board of Governors of the International Monetary Fund. This is the organisation's highest decision-making body, which allocates votes to participating countries' decisions according to their contributions to the Fund in terms of IMF quotas of Special Drawing Rights (SDR).[11] Therefore, all states are equal, at least in proportion to their IMF quotas.[12] Could we employ a criterion of population as a criterion of proportional equality? Such a model could perhaps lead to a principle that states should have votes or individual representatives in proportion to the

---

[10] See, for example, Article 20 of the Statute of the Council of Europe.

[11] The quota determines a member's voting power in IMF decisions. Each IMF member has 250 basic votes plus one additional vote for each SDR 100,000 of quota. Accordingly, the US has 371,743 votes (17.1 per cent of the total) and Palau has 281 votes (0.013 per cent of the total).

[12] There are two possible variations to this scheme. The first is that the criterion pursued may be a substantive one, for example the financial contribution to the IMF. This marks 'substantive' proportional equality. The second version can follow a formal, inflexible criterion. The Council of the EU, for example, allocates votes in the procedure of qualified majority voting in a fixed way (reflective size at the time of the conclusion of that treaty), irrespective of substantive features (e.g. subsequent changes in population). This is 'formal' proportional equality.

size of their populations. If such a criterion were endorsed, the principle of sovereignty might be radically altered. This is not how international relations work today. Neither the General Assembly of the UN nor any other collective body in the UN adopts a criterion of population.

The third model is that of 'formal inequality'. Here the decision-making structures do not claim equality for participating states (form): some states are treated differently independent of circumstances, conditions or substantive criteria (grounds). They are formally unequal. This is the structure endorsed by the Security Council (SC) of the UN. Of the 15 members of the Council, five are permanent members whose 'concurring' vote must be included among the nine necessary votes.[13] The standing of the permanent members is unequal (form) on the strict basis that the UN Charter says so, irrespective of their current power, influence, population, or of any other criterion (ground).

A final possibility is 'criterial inequality', i.e. a system of collective decision-making where one member may be treated unequally, e.g. given fewer votes or no votes, according to a substantive criterion. This is a very unusual structure but not entirely unknown; in the EU, for example, there is a procedure according to which a member may lose its voting rights if it is found guilty of risking a breach of democratic principles, and of other principles such as human rights.[14] The loss is not proportional to the offence, but absolute. Yet such a model is very unusual and has never been applied by the EU. In most instances criteria are applied in proportion to their weight, not in an 'on-off' fashion, and therefore this type is not significant for any practical purposes and will not be discussed further.

What do these models teach us about collective decisions in international practice? The most interesting feature is the variety of the observed procedures. One might think that the first model, formal equality as provided for in the UN Charter, would be the model for all international decisions. It should be the most appealing to states. Yet, in many cases, states accept that collective decisions are necessary. For the sake of peace or prosperity or certainty, they give up their right to opt out and they also give up their right to formal equality based on sovereignty. When circumstances require, as in the IMF bodies, some form of proportional equality is preferred. But the criterion then is a substantive one, the level of contributions to the Fund.

---

[13] See Articles 23 and 27 of the Charter of the United Nations. An abstention by a permanent member does not defeat a resolution.

[14] Article 7 of the 2002 Treaty on European Union. Such states also lose the right to vote at the meeting where such sanctions against them may be decided.

The oddest structure of the four is that endorsed for the SC. Here we have formal inequality established explicitly by the UN Charter. It is hard to see this as an example of fairness, or indeed an expression of any principle. But the additional voting power of the five permanent states – which is to last indefinitely even if the influence of these states may be waning – could be seen as an incentive for them to participate in a collective system of peace. It is an *ad hoc* guarantee of stability in the circumstances of post-war peace. The strongest states in the world need incentives to abide by a multilateral system of peace. It is clear that they have the most to lose by abandoning the recourse to power, since they are the most likely to win wars. Their additional power in the SC is a recognition, perhaps that the institutions of peace need to coincide with these nations' self-interest. They need a guarantee that the multilateral institutions of the UN will not turn against them. Their veto power in the Security Council is that guarantee.

European Union decision-making

Is any one model of decision-making adopted as the preferred model for EU legislation? How different is the EU from the mechanisms that have been examined? We shall have to look at the composition of the relevant bodies and their procedures in detail.

The composition of the bodies is the simpler question. The EU follows here the model of formal equality in some of the institutions. There is one official for each member state in the Council, one judge appointed at the Court of Justice from each member state and, since Nice, one member appointed in the Commission (although in the last two cases, judges and Commissioners are not strictly representatives of the state that appoints them). The composition of the European Parliament is, nevertheless, different. States here are represented by Members of Parliament, elected in national elections according to their political affiliation. Here we have more accurately the representation, not the standing of states. In the composition of the European Parliament the principle of formal equality is rejected; states do not have an equal number of MEPs. We have something like criterial equality, albeit approximate. States have more or fewer MEPs according to their populations, but with a minimum number for the smallest states. After the recent accession of new members, the United Kingdom and France have 78 Members of the European Parliament (MEPs), Italy has 77 and Germany, with a much larger population, has 99. Conversely, Cyprus and Luxembourg have six and Malta five, in great disproportion to their much smaller populations. The European Parliament follows, therefore, neither formal equality based on sovereignty, nor a simple criterion of the size of populations. The composition of this body seems like a mixture of the criteria of population and statehood.[15]

The situation is more complex when we turn our attention to voting procedures. The question is complicated by the fact that there are many processes of law-making; for brevity's sake we shall concentrate on the main ones. Co-decision is now the main law-making mechanism for secondary legislation (Article 251 EC). As is well known, the process involves the Commission, the Council and the Parliament. In most cases (except when it wishes to approve an amendment to which the Commission objects) the Council decides, in this procedure, by qualified majority, i.e. on the basis of an allocation of weighted votes. Whereas the composition of the Council reflects formal equality (everyone has one minister present), the standing of each state as reflected on voting power varies (on account of their different voting rights). The amendments brought about by the Treaty of Nice and the 2004 accession did not change this principle of the allocation of weighted votes significantly.[16] Under the current arrangement, which follows the most recent Accession Treaty signed in Athens in 2003, the four largest states have the same number of votes (29), with Spain and Poland following not far behind (27), whereas the smaller states have at least four votes and Malta three, irrespective of their much smaller size. This means that the main decision-making procedure in the Council does not follow a formal equality principle either. States do not all have the same votes. Nor does it follow criterial equality, a principle reflecting a representation of populations. Instead, states are represented by a mixture of formal and criterial equality; there is a minimum of representation for all states but also a population criterion. The mixing of the two seems to follow the pattern endorsed for the composition of the European Parliament. Smaller states have higher standing than mere reference to population size might require, hence their standing is distinct from population.

---

[15] The principle is reaffirmed in the Treaty Establishing the Constitution for Europe, *OJ* C 310, 16 December 2004: Article 1–20, para. 2: 'The European Parliament shall be composed of representatives of the Union's citizens. They shall not exceed seven hundred and fifty in number. Representation of citizens shall be degressively proportional, with a minimum threshold of six members per Member State . . .'

[16] See, for example, K.StC. Bradley, 'Institutional Design in the Treaty of Nice' (2001) 38 *CMLRev* 1095.

The Treaty establishing a Constitution for Europe sought to introduce a new method of calculating a qualified majority in the Council, which required that a measure should have the support of at least 55 per cent of the member states, representing at least 65 per cent of the total population. The arithmetic of the votes has now been changed – giving more weight to the larger states – but the principles behind it have not. We still have a mixture of a formal principle, as the first majority is based on the formal equality of all member states, and a criterial principle, since the second majority is dependent on population. The Treaty explains this solution by establishing in Article I-45 a general 'principle of representative democracy', which has two parts. The first provides for a familiar constitutional principle: 'The working of the Union shall be founded on the principle of representative democracy.' The second part provides, however, for a representation of states: 'Citizens are directly represented at Union level in the European Parliament. Member States are represented in the European Council and in the Council of Ministers by their governments, themselves accountable to national parliaments, elected by their citizens.' This new article gives a more or less accurate account of the complex practices already followed by EU institutions. The standing of states is separate from that of their populations.

These various solutions for law-making would suffice, perhaps, to justify the conclusion that unlike other international organisations, the EU avoids in most cases the principle of formal equality and endorses some variations of a principle of criterial equality. Nevertheless, the most fundamental process of law-making in the EU is the making of the treaties, a process which also involves deciding who is to be a member. Here, the area of the most fundamental decisions of the EU, we find a strict adherence to formal equality. The procedure is that of public international law, allowing states to freely enter into or reject international treaties. There is no difference to standing or to representation among states and all decisions are taken by unanimity.

Nevertheless, such decisions are in some sense collective. The level of integration reached by the member states is such that it is not realistic to say that groups of members can choose whatever course of action they like. It is not realistic to think that some amendments to the treaties will apply to some and not to others. This has been followed in some cases (for example, in the single currency and the Schengen Treaty) but this concerned relatively limited areas of policy and in any event met with the agreement of everyone. Hence, a negative position by one member on a proposed treaty amendment is a veto that binds effectively everyone. Constitutional change in the EU is in effect a collective decision as much as in the domestic case, at least in the sense that the views of the collective body (when there is a failure to reach unanimity) effectively blocks change for everyone, even those that are for the proposed change.

Even after the 'Convention' models of the making of the Charter of Rights and the Constitution, the member states retain full control of treaty amendments through intergovernmental conferences, where members enjoy full and equal sovereignty as states. Unanimity is the only rule and there is no departure from the principle of formal equality, although, strictly speaking, the decision is not even one of representation, unless one considers that citizens whose rights are affected by EU treaties in a way that they are not by other international treaties are represented before such conventions by states.[17]

This analysis may, then, be concluded as follows. The institutional arrangements of the European Union combine the formal equality of states in the composition of many bodies (Court, Commission, Council, Treaty Revision), with the proportional equality of states on account of their populations in both their standing in some bodies (Council) and their representation in others (Parliament). But states generally enjoy higher standing than is reflected by their populations. In other words, statehood has a distinct higher in the allocation of decision-making power. And even though the voting processes in all institutions are described without reference to particular states (a sufficient number of votes is required, irrespective of who is behind them), the voting patterns in qualified majority voting and the mode of representation in the European Parliament are determined by reference to the constituent members of the Union.

Substantive powers and subsidiarity

The institutional arrangements just outlined offer only a partial view of EU law and institutions. There is a great deal more detail, and more legal

---

[17] The issue of representation arose only in the new 'Convention' that met to discuss and vote on the new treaty revisions. Although the 'convention method' for the creation of the new European Constitution involved a hint of representation, it adopted the same principle of formal equality in its composition as required by treaty negotiations. All states had the same number of representatives irrespective of their size. The Convention was mostly a delegation of states, not a parliament of peoples. Moreover, its decision-making procedure was one of 'consensus', not majority voting; and in any event, its decisions were not binding.

constraints, in the way these institutions function. We must now proceed to examine the powers that these institutions are called to exercise,
according to the standards of established legal principles. It is common
ground that the ultimate rules for the allocation of Union powers lie
with the treaties. There is no 'inherent jurisdiction' or customary
sources of power, such as is found in British constitutional law. The
treaties are the ultimate source of constitutional power in the EU.

In some senses this reflects well-established practice in states that have a
written constitution, subject to interpretation by a dedicated constitutional
court, such as Germany, Italy or South Africa. The European Court of Justice,
similarly, follows a very strict line on the sources of EU law. Nevertheless, in
the case of the EU, such self-imposed limitations also reflect the fact that the
foundation of the Union is an international treaty. The well-known principle
of *pacta sunt servanda* is a main principle of public international law and
implies a duty on each state to respect its agreements with the other members
and with the EU itself. Hence, a reason for the strict compliance with the letter
of the treaties might be not just a theory of constitutional legal positivism, but
also a duty of respect owed to the other parties. In other words, it is owed to
the states that their mutual agreements are strictly followed.

It is in fact one of the most secure principles of EU law that all of the
Union's powers must be explicitly based on the treaties and that all
secondary law issuing from the EU (and all national law in the relevant
areas) must conform to the treaties. There are many examples of this
restriction having real effects. In the leading *Marshall* case, for example,
in spite of elaborate arguments to the contrary offered by counsel, the
Court of Justice refused to extend the direct effect of directives to
horizontal relations because this would be incompatible with the explicit
distinction between directive and regulation established by the Treaty:

> With regard to the argument that a Directive may not be relied upon
> against an individual, it must be emphasized that according to Article 189
> (now 249) of the EEC Treaty the binding nature of a Directive, which
> constitutes the basis for the possibility of relying on the Directive before a
> national court, exists only in relation to 'each member state to which it is
> addressed'. It follows that a Directive may not of itself impose obligations
> on an individual and that a provision of a Directive may not be relied
> upon, as such, against individuals.[18]

---

[18] Case 152/84, *Marshall v. Southampton and South-West Hampshire Area Health Authority
(Teaching)* [1986] ECR 723, para. 48; see also Case C-91/92, *Paola Faccini Dori v. Recreb
Srl* [1994] ECR I-3325.

In addition, the EU treaties introduce clear legislative disabilities binding all Union institutions. In numerous ways the Treaty establishing the European Community (EC Treaty)[19] outlines a principle of enumerated powers for the Union as a whole. Article 5 EC provides the general foundation as follows: 'The Community shall act within the limits of the powers conferred upon it by this Treaty and of the objectives assigned to it therein.' A Treaty Article will provide for the necessary powers in certain policy spheres, and will specify the procedures according to which the measure is to be agreed. In all cases, there is a duty to give reasons (Article 253 EC), which includes mentioning the legal basis.

The principle of enumerated powers can often create disagreements, especially when there are two possible bases for EU action, providing for different decision procedures. There are two types of problems. The first is the question of whether the legal basis is the right one, which matters for procedural reasons. The second is whether the competence exists at all.

The first type of question is exemplified in the case of the *Working Time Directive*,[20] where the United Kingdom (UK) sought the annulment of a directive concerned with the organisation of working time in various fields of the economy.[21] The Directive had been adopted on the basis of Article 118A of the Treaty as it was then,[22] which provided for a qualified majority in the Council in areas of health and safety at work. The UK claimed that the measure should have been proposed under Article 94 EC,[23] which provides for unanimity in areas that affect the establishment of the Common Market. The Court ruled that the Directive was properly adopted on the basis of Article 118A, apart from one minor provision that had to be annulled.

The second type of problem arose in the *Tobacco Advertising Case*.[24] Here the question raised by Germany was not as to the precise basis of a measure from amongst many possible bases in the Treaty and the relevant procedures, but on whether the power existed anywhere in the Treaty at all. The measure was claimed by the Commission and the

---

[19] Treaty establishing the European Community (consolidated text), *OJ* C 325 of 24 December 2002.

[20] Council Directive 93/104/EC of 23 November 1993 Concerning Certain Aspects of the Organization of Working Time, *OJ* 1993 L 307.

[21] Case C-84/94, *United Kingdom v. Council of the European Union* [1996] ECR I-5755.

[22] The Treaty has now been substantially amended and renumbered; this Article is now Article 137 EC.

[23] Article 100 of the EC Treaty prior to amendment.

[24] Case C-376/98, *Germany v. Parliament and Council* [2000] ECR I-8419.

Council to fall under Article 95,[25] the provision that, as we saw above, provides for measures promoting the 'establishment and functioning of the internal market'. The Court held that 'a measure adopted on the basis of Article 100a of the Treaty must genuinely have as it object the improvement of the conditions for the establishment and functioning of the internal market'.[26] The task of the Court was accordingly to examine if the measure in question pursued the objectives stated. The problem with the Directive under review was that it did not make it easier to buy and sell tobacco products on the internal market, but that instead it sought to make it more difficult. By banning advertising of tobacco in Europe it made the rules the same for all, but these rules were not rules designed so as to achieve the 'internal market'. They were rather health rules, making it harder to advertise smoking in order to protect consumers from its harmful effects. The Court found that Article 95[27] was wrongly invoked and that the Directive had to be annulled in its entirety. The *Tobacco Advertising Case* shows that the Community cannot act in areas where it does not have competence.

Both types of problems can be traced to the obligation of the Community institutions to respect the rights of states. In the first case, the correct legal basis safeguards the role of states in the appropriate decision-making procedure. In the second case, states retain exclusive powers to regulate the particular field.

Even in areas of shared competence, the Union must act under the constraints of the principles of subsidiarity and proportionality, under Article 5 EC. The cases here do not offer much in the way of substantive criteria,[28] but the principle has general application. The Subsidiarity Principle was introduced in the Maastricht Treaty and rephrased in the Amsterdam Treaty. The second paragraph of Article 5 TEC now reads as follows:

> In areas which do not fall within its exclusive competence, the Community shall take action, in accordance with the principle of subsidiarity, only if and insofar as the objectives of the proposed action cannot be sufficiently achieved by the Member States and can therefore, by reason of the scale or effects of the proposed action, be better achieved by the Community.

---

[25] Previously Article 100a.   [26] Above, note 24, para. 84.   [27] Previously Article 100a.
[28] See T. Tridimas, *The General Principles of EC Law* (Oxford: Oxford University Press, 2006), pp. 175–92.

The 1997 Protocol on Subsidiarity states that:

> In exercising the powers conferred on it, each institution shall ensure that
> the principle of subsidiarity is complied with. It shall also ensure com-
> pliance with the principle of proportionality, according to which any
> action by the Community shall not go beyond what is necessary to
> achieve the objectives of the Treaty.[29]

The principle of subsidiarity was meant to check the creeping expansion
of the Community's powers, and it applies only in areas of 'shared
competence'. Yet, it has been hard to apply by the courts and the ECJ
has rarely used it. Even the *Tobacco Advertising* judgment did not
employ the principle of subsidiarity, despite the fact that the German
government raised it. One of the problems is that the principle requires
us to make a judgment as to who can achieve 'better' the objectives of the
Community, the states or the Community itself. This is a very indeter-
minate criterion and the Court rightly has refrained from invoking it.

Proportionality, on the other hand, means that a measure must be
appropriate, and necessary to achieve its objectives. The standard
expression used by the ECJ is whether the measure employs means
that correspond to the importance of the aim and whether it is necessary
for the achievement of that aim.[30] There are, therefore, two dimensions
to proportionality. First, that which we could call the criterion of 'suitability': is the measure in question suitable to achieve a legitimate aim?
The second dimension could be called the criterion of 'necessity': is the
measure necessary to achieve that aim or are there less restrictive alternatives? At the heart of the second criterion lies a consideration for the
individual freedom or other interests that may be compromised by the
aim in question. The proportionality test is therefore a balancing test
between competing aims. The principle of proportionality in legislative
action appears in Article 5(3)[31] EC: 'Any action by the Community shall
not go beyond what is necessary to achieve the objectives of the Treaty.'
It is obvious that the balance to be achieved here is between the effectiveness and uniformity of Community policies on the one hand, and
something like the rights of states to self-government on the other.

---

[29] Protocol on the Application of the Principles of Subsidiarity and Proportionality [2004]
OJ C310/207, para. 1.
[30] For further discussion see Tridimas, *The General Principles of EC Law*, pp. 177–80.
[31] Formerly Article 3b(3).

This is why proportionality is required: the EU should not compromise the independence of the states without good reason.

The ECJ had recognised that proportionality was important for the Community's competences even before the Maastricht Treaty came about (which brought into force what is now Article 5). The Court has stated the principle as follows:

> According to the Court's case-law, in order to establish whether a provision of Community law complies with the principle of proportionality, it must be ascertained whether the means which it employs are suitable for the purpose of achieving the desired objective and whether they do not go beyond what is necessary to achieve it (see, for example, the judgment in Joined Cases 279/84, 280/84, 285/84 and 286/84 *Walter Rau Lebensmittelwerke and others v Commission* [1987] ECR 1069, paragraph 34).[32]

The ECJ then ruled that Germany had not shown that the measures in question had failed the two criteria, and the Court said that for a measure to fail the second criterion it must be 'manifestly disproportionate'.[33] This view was confirmed in another significant case mentioned above, the *Working Time Directive Case*.[34] In this area, therefore, the review by the Court will be only at the margins; it will only intervene if there is 'manifest error'. Nevertheless, it is a secure principle of EU law that the legislative power of the collective institutions in the EU is checked by the allocation of competences between the EU and the member states.

Similar principles bind the main executive body of the EU, the European Commission. Its powers are extensive in some areas, for example in competition and external trade, but they do not extend to the full range of modern executive action by national governments.[35] There is no power over the main political issues of the day, such as criminal law, family law, pensions, taxation, defence or foreign affairs. The restrictions to the Commission's executive powers are the same as in legislation; the competences of the EU are arranged for the union as

---

[32] Case C-426/93, *Germany v. Council of the European Union* [1995] ECR I-3723, para. 49.
[33] *Ibid*, para. 50.   [34] See above, n. 21.
[35] See A. Moravcsik, 'In Defence of the "Democratic Deficit": Reassessing Legitimacy in the European Union' (2002) 40 *Journal of Common Market Studies (JCMS)* 603–24 and A. Moravcsik, 'The European Constitutional Compromise and the Neofunctionalist Legacy' (2005) 12 *JEPP* 349–86. Dashwood also observes that the Commission lacks the ordinary powers of coercive action normally enjoyed by national executives: see A. Dashwood, 'States in the European Union' (1998) 23 *ELR* 201 at 211.

a whole, not for particular institutions. Hence, the disabilities that apply to legislative action also apply, *mutatis mutandis*, to executive actions: powers must be expressly granted by law and they must be exercised according to the principles of subsidiarity and proportionality.

As in all other administrative systems, the Commission occasionally undertakes to introduce delegated legislation, and in such cases its decision-making mechanisms resemble those of the Council. If the Council delegates some of its powers to the Commission, usually by means of a Regulation, the Council sets up Committees of State Representatives to oversee and approve the Commission's work, a procedure which is formalised in the *Comitology Decision* of 1999.[36] According to this Decision, there are three possible Committees: (a) an Advisory Committee; (b) a Management Committee; or (c) a Regulatory Committee. The choice of procedure depends on the subject-matter, based on criteria that are now included in the Decision. The three methods are arranged in ascending power for the state representatives: hence, delegation does not always give much additional power to the Commission.

This brief examination of the powers of the Union confirms the principles that we encountered in the institutional arrangement. There is a strong recognition of the equal standing of states as authors of their own laws and masters of the treaty that unites them. Here the sense of equality is that of formal equality, based, one assumes, on the rights of sovereignty. The areas where collective decision-making is expected to apply are carefully circumscribed. The exercise of powers in the EU in terms of collective and representative decisions does not fail to respect the equal standing of its members as sovereign states.

The judicial architecture

The judicial architecture of the EU comprises both the ECJ and the Court of First Instance, and the national courts. Their relations are complex, but a closer examination shows a strikingly strong position for the member states.

The composition of the Court of Justice is in principle that of an international court, where the principle of formal equality is followed. There is one judge from each member state; unlike a federal court, judicial appointments are based entirely on national criteria. The twenty-five judges are appointed

---

[36] *Council Decision 1999/468/EC laying down the Procedures for the Exercise of Implementing Powers Conferred on the Commission* [1999] OJL 184/23.

by the governments of the member states under a principle of strict formal equality between states. The eight Advocates-General are appointed on a rotating basis that equally respects the formal equality of states.

This account of collective decisions has so far covered legislative and executive decisions. Can we say that the judicial function can, in principle, be described in terms of collective decision-making? I think we can. An ultimate appellate court, whose judgments bind not just the parties but also all other courts and all state bodies, reaches decisions that bind those that disagree with it and in that sense is engaged in collective decision-making. A judicial decision is also representative in the formal sense, since it binds those who did not (and could not because of the nature of the institution) participate in the process. Of course, the subject-matter of judicial decisions separates them from other collective and representative decisions of the political field. But, in all relevant senses, the decisions of courts – and primarily those of the supreme court in each jurisdiction – are expected to be collective and representative in the sense described here.

We reach then an interesting and perhaps surprising conclusion. Despite the doctrines of direct effect and supremacy and the theoretical construct of the 'new legal order', the judicial architecture of the EU is an area where, uniquely in the EU, we do not have collective action. We do not because the European Court of Justice is not the highest appellate court for the member states. It is the highest court of the Union, but its institutional relationship with the courts of the member states is not hierarchical in order to enable the collective effect to work directly. As is well known, according to its case law and the case law of member state courts, the judgments of the ECJ are both directly effective and superior to all national judgments. Nevertheless, this principle does not find expression in the judicial architecture established by the Treaties. The ECJ and the national courts sit parallel to each other, not in a relation of superiority or subservience. National courts are charged with making preliminary references to the Court of Justice. Yet, any ECJ judgment is conditional on its reception by the national courts and the national jurisdiction. The relationship between the court structures has been correctly identified as one of 'legal pluralism'.[37]

---

[37] This is very well described by Neil MacCormick in his *Questioning Sovereignty: Law, State and Nation in the European Commonwealth* (Oxford: Oxford University Press, 1999), pp. 97–121. See also N. W. Barber, 'Legal Pluralism and the European Union' (2006) 12 *ELJ* 306–30.

It is a well-known feature of the EU that the legal systems of the member states remain in principle independent of that of the Union. In the *Huber* judgment, for example, the Court repeated that national law is something distinct from Community law:

> None the less, Commission approval of a national aid programme does not in any way have the effect of conferring on that programme the nature of an act of Community law. In those circumstances, where an aid contract is incompatible with the programme approved by the Commission, it is for the national courts to draw the appropriate inferences from this in regard to national law, by taking account of the relevant Community law in applying national law.[38]

Although the doctrines of direct effect and supremacy have brought national law and European law very close to one another, the general rule is that they remain distinct.

The point is well illustrated by looking at the complex rules regarding the jurisdiction of the Court of Justice. There are five routes by which a case comes before the ECJ and none of these routes implies a hierarchical relation with a national court: (1) the ECJ has jurisdiction to hear a case when a state takes action against another state (Article 227 EC); (2) it enjoys jurisdiction when the Commission takes action against a state (Article 226 EC); (3) when a national court makes a preliminary reference apropos of a domestic case (Article 234 EC); (4) when the ECJ hears an appeal from the Court of First Instance (CFI); (5) when it hears a direct action by an individual or an EU institution against an act of an institution (Article 230 EC).

It is obvious that the Court of Justice is not a 'supreme court' of Europe. The missing link is that it cannot hear appeals from national courts. Since, in addition, individuals have very limited direct access to the court as a forum of first instance (under the direct action of Article 230 EC), the judicial function of the Court for the member states remains limited. This does not mean that the Court is weak. It only suggests that the Court, for all its power within the Union, does not occupy the institutional position of a high appellate court, i.e. as a court that has the power to issue collective and representative decisions binding on all other bodies, judicial, legislative or executive.

---

[38] Case C-336/00, *Republik Österreich v. Martin Huber* [2002] ECR I-7736, para. 40. See also Case 33/67, *Dietrich Kurrer v. Council* [1968] ECR 179, at 193, where the Court had declared that the Community is 'composed of States, each of which retains its own national legal order'.

In principle, member states' legal systems remain therefore largely autonomous. National courts are to implement EU law directly, but they are to do so on their own terms. They need not change the judicial or other procedural methods with which they apply the law. Their procedures and remedies remain autonomous.[39]

There are, however, two conditions for such autonomy. The first is the principle of equivalence: the procedural rules enforcing Community law must be no less favourable than those applied in domestic law actions. The second is the principle of 'effectiveness': the application of national procedural rules should not make the protection of Community rights excessively difficult. The two conditions were summarised in the *Peterbroeck* judgment:

> [T]he Court has consistently held that, under the principle of cooperation laid down in Article 5 of the Treaty, it is for the Member States to ensure the legal protection which individuals derive from the direct effect of Community law. In the absence of Community rules governing a matter, it is for the domestic legal system of each Member State to designate the courts and tribunals having jurisdiction and to lay down the detailed procedural rules governing actions for safeguarding rights which individuals derive from the direct effect of Community law. However, such rules must not be less favourable than those governing similar domestic actions nor render virtually impossible or excessively difficult the exercise of rights conferred by Community law . . .[40]

Hence, as long as the national procedural rules are not ineffective or discriminatory, procedural independence is secured.

The principle of procedural autonomy has been limited by a related development in the area of remedies; it has been affected by the *Francovich* principle and its later manifestations.[41] In that case the ECJ created an entirely new remedy, a state liability for damages for failure to

---

[39] This was first established in Case 33/76, *Rewe-Zentralfinanz eG et Rewe-Zentral AG v. Landwirtschaftskammer für das Saarland* [1976] ECR 1989.

[40] Case C-312/93, *Peterbroeck Van Campenhout SCS & Cie v. Belgian State* [1995] ECR I-4599, para. 12; see also Case 33/76, *Rewe-Zentralfinanz eG et Rewe-Zentral AG v. Landwirtschaftskammer fuer das Saarland* [1976] ECR 1989, para. 5; Case 45/76, *Comet v. Produktschap voor Siergewassen* [1976] ECR 2043, para. 12–6; Case C-96/91, *Commission v. Spain* [1992] ECR I-3789, para. 12; and Joined Cases C-6/90 and C-9/90, *Andrea Francovich and Danila Bonifaci and others v. Italian Republic* [1991] ECR I-5357, para. 43.

[41] Case C-9/90, *Andrea Francovich and Danila Bonifaci and others v. Italian Republic* [1991] ECR I-5357.

implement Community law. The reasoning of the Court in this case was that Italy's failure to implement a Directive that did not meet the conditions for direct effect (Directive 89/987) should not impair the 'full effectiveness of Community rules' and the 'protection of the rights which they grant'.[42] This doctrine is as creative as were the doctrines of direct effect and supremacy, and is equally distant from any particular Article of the Treaties; the Court said it was 'inherent in the system of the Treaty'. It is hard to reconcile with national procedural autonomy, especially since the Court has now offered substantive criteria for the application of this remedy. *Francovich* offered a tentative set of criteria, but they have now been supplemented by the later ruling in *Brasserie du Pêcheur*, where the Court stated that there were three conditions:

> [T]he rule of law infringed must be intended to confer rights on individuals; the breach must be sufficiently serious; and there must be a direct causal link between the breach of the obligation resting on the State and the damage sustained by the injured parties.[43]

This broad statement was clarified in further cases, such as *British Telecom*[44] and *Denkavit*,[45] in both of which the Court did not find a sufficiently serious breach. The problem with the three criteria is that they are simultaneously Community criteria, and national standards. They require national courts to apply Community criteria in what is fundamentally a procedural issue.

The later *Köbler* judgment has made further inroads into national procedural autonomy.[46] In this case the Court ruled that governments are to be held liable for a breach of EC law even when the breach is the result of a judgment of the highest national court, a decision which means that lower national courts can review judgments of their own higher courts. The ECJ insisted that this extension of state liability does not undermine the principle of *res judicata*, because it does not overturn the judgment of the national court. Nevertheless, it is hard to reconcile

---

[42] *Ibid.*, para. 33.

[43] Joined Cases C-46/93 and C-48/93, *Brasserie du Pêcheur SA v. Bundesrepublik Deutschland and The Queen v. Secretary of State for Transport, ex p. Factortame Ltd and others* [1996] ECR I-1029, para. 51.

[44] Case C-392/93, *R v. HM Treasury, ex p. British Telecommunications plc* [1996] ECR I-1631.

[45] Cases C-283, 291 and 292/94, *Denkavit International BV, VITIC Amsterdam BV and Voormeer BV v. Bundesamt für Finanzen* [1996] ECR I-5063.

[46] Case C-224/01, *Köbler v. Austria* [2003] ECR I-10239.

the continuing authority of a court's decision with granting compensation for its consequences. *Köbler* represents a departure from the fundamental rule that national judicial systems remain autonomous.

Nevertheless, *Köbler* is an isolated case. In all other situations the allocation of powers between national courts and the Court of Justice has been maintained. The most important such instance is the issue of access to the Court by individuals under the direct action procedures of Article 230 EC. There are two kinds of applicants in direct actions. The first kind, 'privileged applicants', are the Parliament, the Council, the Commission and the member states. They have the right, under Article 230 EC, to bring actions for annulment of any act, without showing that they have a special interest in starting proceedings before the ECJ. Private persons or companies, by contrast, have the right to bring actions under Article 230 EC only under certain conditions, namely 'against a decision addressed to that person or against a decision which, although in the form of a regulation or a decision addressed to another person, is of direct and individual concern to the former'. What is 'direct and individual concern' in the case of regulations or decisions addressed to others? The classic statement of the relevant criteria was given in the *Plaumann* case. The Court stated that it means that an applicant:

> ... may only claim to be individually concerned if that decision affects them by reason of certain attributes which are peculiar to them or by reason of circumstances in which they are differentiated from all other persons and by virtue of these factors distinguishes them individually just as in the case of the person addressed.[47]

A very considerable case law has arisen, interpreting this statement. The criteria have, for a long time, seemed too narrow. The Court of First Instance sought to reverse the *Plaumann* criteria in its *Jégo-Quéré* judgment of 2002.[48] In that judgment the CFI followed an earlier Opinion of Advocate-General Jacobs,[49] and ruled that the 'right to effective judicial protection' required that the *Plaumann* doctrine be amended to allow more individuals access to the ECJ. The basis of the extension was the fact that the Treaty established a 'complete system of legal remedies and procedures designed to permit the Community judicature to review the

---

[47] Case 25/62, *Plaumann and Co. v. Commission* [1963] ECR 95.
[48] Case T-177/01, *Jégo-Quéré & Cie SA v. Commission* [2002] ECR II-2365.
[49] Case C-50/00 P, *Unión de Pequeños Agricultores v. Council of the European Union* [2002] ECR I-6677.

legality of measures adopted by the institutions.'[50] The implicit premise of this argument is that the 'right of effective judicial protection' was to be protected by the courts of the European Union directly, not the courts of the member states.

Yet on appeal, the Court of Justice struck down the judgment of the CFI and refused to endorse the analysis of the Advocate-General.[51] In its judgment the Court ruled that it was for the member states to set up a judicial system protecting the rights of their citizens. The Treaty has 'established a complete system of legal remedies and procedures designed to ensure review of the legality of acts of the institutions'[52] but under this system the jurisdiction of the European courts is supplemented by that of the national courts, under the system of preliminary references. Under this allocation of powers, the court concluded: 'it is for the Member States to establish a system of legal remedies and procedures which ensure respect for the right to effective judicial protection.'[53]

Hence, not only the composition of the Court of Justice, but also its own recognition of the limits to its jurisdiction, provides evidence of the fact that the judicial functions of the European Union are clearly demarcated between the Union and the states. The effect of EU law in domestic jurisdictions – smooth and uncontroversial though it is today – depends on the reception of this law by national courts. Its direct effect and supremacy is conditional on that reception, which cannot be reviewed by the ECJ directly. Despite the inroads, therefore, into the national legal systems made by the principles of direct effect and supremacy and the development of special Community remedies in subsequent case law, the fundamental organisational principle of the judicial function within the EU is the clear division of powers between the Union courts and the domestic courts. The judicial sphere is an area where the EU does not proceed by collective and representative decision-making. The guiding principle here is institutional and state autonomy, rather than collective decision-making.

Conclusion

What are the conclusions, if any, to be drawn from this analysis? I have suggested a new way of approaching the nature of EU institutions and the place of states within them. The first question I asked is whether we

---

[50] Case T-177/01, *Jégo-Quéré & Cie SA v. Commission* [2002] ECR II-2365, para. 50.
[51] Case C-263/02 P, *Commission v. Jégo-Quéré & Cie SA* [2004] ECR I-3425.
[52] *Ibid.*, para. 50.   [53] *Ibid.*, para. 31.

can talk of collective decision-making in the EU and if so in what areas. It was established that many areas of EU action (e.g. judicial decisions) do not involve collective action at all or they do only in a partial and modified way (e.g. treaty amendment). The second question was what principles determine the standing and representation of states within the collective processes of the EU according to established law and practice. It was observed that just like federal states, the constitutional and institutional principles of the EU were a mixture of formal equality and proportional equality according to population. Nevertheless, the mixture was quite different to that of a federal union. That standing of states in the EU is consistently higher.

These observations give us a good sense of the uniqueness of the Union. What makes the EU unique is the fact that the areas where it enjoys the power of collective action are very carefully circumscribed and that within the areas of collective action the main principle is formal equality or at least modified criterial equality of states according to population. The position of the constituent entities, the member states, is therefore much stronger in the EU compared to any other federal or national structure.

This equal standing of states within the EU requires that we approach the EU constitution with distinct conceptual tools. In *The Theory of Justice*, John Rawls reminds us that that domestic legal systems make particularly strong claims on the people to whom they apply. Political societies have centralised political institutions and uniform legal systems. Rawls writes that 'what distinguishes a legal system [from rules of games or private associations] is its comprehensive scope and its regulative powers with respect to other associations'. This means that the 'legal order exercises final authority over a certain well-defined territory . . . These features simply reflect the fact that the law defines the basic structure within which the pursuit of all other activities takes place'.[54] This all-encompassing role of a legal order – and the parallel role of a constitution that serves as the comprehensive and authoritative foundation of such an order – is based on the basic premise that all political action is collective action and its choices are meant to bind everyone.

In the EU the structure of institutions and powers is different. There is no uniform legal order, i.e. a single hierarchy of rules and single hierarchy of institutions. Instead, power is distributed between the Union and the member states in complex ways determined by explicit constitutional

---

[54] J. Rawls, *A Theory of Justice* revised edn. (Cambridge, Mass.: Harvard University Press, 1999), p. 207.

principles laid out in the treaties and interpreted by courts. The basic rules establish relations not only between central power and the citizen, but also among the various member states, between member states and the EU and (especially in the area of the four freedoms) between member states and the citizens of other states. The domain of such new relations is neither the domain of ordinary politics nor the domain of diplomacy and international relations. It is a mixed institutional arrangement, where international decisions have legal and political effects according to the doctrines of direct effect and supremacy both internationally (pursuant to the supervision of the ECJ) and domestically (following national courts). In this new domain the various legislative, executive and judicial powers are distributed among the member states and the Union in a way that consistently respects that autonomy and distinctness of states. As we saw, these arrangements do not always follow formal equality. They do, nevertheless, grant equal standing according to some relevant criterion to the constituent members of the Union and their peoples.

This is why the tools of constitutional law alone must be insufficient to explain the institutional nature of the EU. They cannot capture the equal standing of states within the structure of the Union. The more we try to apply domestic constitutional law principles to EU law the more we miss the distinctness and indeed the uniqueness of the institutions before us. An appropriately comprehensive theory of the EU must therefore be able to accommodate the international dimension of the Union as a unique union of states. Of course, in addition to principles from international law we need new principles, which elsewhere I have called 'cosmopolitan', to accommodate the distinct weakening of sovereignty as a principle within the Union.[55]

The resulting constitutional architecture of the Union is therefore this. The members of the EU have created a voluntary cooperative organisation giving rise to substantive principles combining domestic and international ideals. They have formed a democratic union opening their borders to each other's citizens, in order to establish, fully and effectively, an area of both liberty and peace. In so doing, however, they do not abandon the rights of statehood that their citizens collectively enjoy according to their own constitutional traditions. The EU is an open and democratic union of liberal peoples but it is also a union of states.

---

[55] P. Eleftheriadis, 'The European Constitution and Cosmopolitan Ideals' (2001) 7 *Columbia Journal of European Law* 21–39; P. Eleftheriadis, 'Cosmopolitan Law' (2003) 9 *ELJ* 241–63.

3

The constitutional role of general principles of law in international and European jurisprudence

NICHOLAS TSAGOURIAS

Introduction

One can find in European and international legal literature many inventories or accounts of general principles of law.[1] This is because the phrase 'general principles of law' has polysemous meanings and is credited with multiple roles. In this chapter, I do not offer another inventory of general principles of law or discuss the content of particular principles, but examine their role in the constitutional reading of the international and European Union political order. In other words, this chapter is a study of constitutional patterns prescribed by general principles of law. For this reason, I shall first explore typologies of such principles, and then look at how the European and international constitutional culture is defined by them. My attention will then be turned to the forces that vie to organise the international and the EU political space by focusing on the role of the International Court of Justice (ICJ) and the Court of Justice of the European Communities (European Court of Justice; ECJ) in applying or interpreting general principles of law.

---

[1] T. Tridimas, *The General Principles of EC Law* 2nd edn. (Oxford: Oxford University Press, 2006); J. A. Usher, *General Principles of EC Law* (Harlow: Longman, 1998); B. Cheng, *General Principles of Law as Applied by International Courts and Tribunals* (Cambridge: Grotius, 1987); G. Herczegh, *General Principles of Law and International Legal Order* (Budapest: Akadémiai Kiadó, 1969); H. Mosler, 'General Principles of Law' in *Encyclopaedia of Public International Law*, vol. 2 (Amsterdam: North-Holland, 1995), p. 511.

Typologies of general principles of law

Traditionally, general principles of law are identified with certain principles of legal technique or logic such as the principles of estoppel,[2] res judicata,[3] proportionality,[4] prescription,[5] and so on that municipal courts or tribunals often employ in order to decide cases.[6] These principles are then transplanted into the international or European order because of their general standing as principles of law: that is, as principles of an autonomous episteme.[7] This was indeed the approach taken by the drafters of Article 38 of the ICJ Statute, which included general principles of law in the sources

---

[2] For cases, see, before the Permanent Court of International Justice (PCIJ), *Chorzów Factory (Germany v. Poland)*, Jurisdiction, Judgment of 26 July 1927, (1927) PCIJ Series A, No. 9, p. 31; *Legal Status of Eastern Greenland*, Judgment of 5 April, 1933, (1933) PCIJ Series A/B, No. 53, pp. 69–73; *Diversion of Water from the Meuse (Belgium v. Netherlands)*, Merits, Judgment of 28 June 1937, (1937) PCIJ series A/B, No. 70, p. 25; and before the ECJ, Case 148/78, *Ministero Pubblico v Ratti* [1979] ECR 1629, para. 22; see also Cheng, *General Principles*, pp. 141–9.

[3] ICJ, *Effect of Awards of Compensation Made by the United Nations Administrative Tribunal*, Advisory Opinion of 13 July 1954, (1954) ICJ Rep. 46 at 53; ECJ, Case C-224/01, *Köbler v. Austria* [2003] ECR I-10239, paras. 38–39. Cheng, *General Principles*, pp. 336–72.

[4] ECJ, Case C-331/88, *R v MAFF, ex p. Fedesa* [1990] ECR I-4023, paras. 12–13; Case 11/70, *Internationale Handelsgesellschaft mbH v. Einfuhr- und Vorratsstelle für Getreide und Futtermittel* [1970] ECR 1125, 1147; ICJ, *Military and Paramilitary Activities In and Against Nicaragua (Nicaragua v. United States of America)*, Merits, Judgment of 27 June 1986, (1986) ICJ Rep., 14 at 94, 103; *Legality of the Threat or Use of Nuclear Weapons*, Advisory Opinion of 8 July 1996, (1996) ICJ Rep. 226 at 245; Tridimas, *General Principles*, pp. 136–74; Usher, *General Principles*, pp. 37–51; J. Rivers, Chapter 4, below.

[5] Cheng, *General Principles*, pp. 373–86.

[6] H. Lauterpacht, *Private Law Sources and Analogies of International Law* (London, New York: Longmans, Green, 1927), pp. 69–71; H. Lauterpacht, *The Development of International Law by the International Court* (London: Stevens & Sons Ltd, 1958), pp. 158–65; Ripert, 'Règles du droit civil', 580–3.

[7] Cheng, *General Principles*, p. 390: '[t]he general principles of law ... are indeed the fundamental principles of every legal system. Their existence bears witness to the fundamental unity of law ...'; A. Verdross, 'Les principes généraux du droit dans la jurisprudence internationale', (1935 II) 52 *RC* 191 at 203; ICJ, *Corfu Channel Case (United Kingdom v. Albania)*, Merits, Judgment of 9 April 1949, (1949) ICJ Rep. 4 (Judge Azevedo, Dissenting Opinion, 104); Separate Opinion of Judge Ammun in *North Sea Continental Shelf Cases (Germany v. Denmark; Germany v. Netherlands)*, Merits, Judgment of 20 February 1969, (1969) ICJ Rep. 3 at 134–5. For a more critical approach see P. Weil, 'Le droit international en quête de son identité', (1992 VI) 237 *RC* 9 at 144–151 and P. Weil, 'Towards Relative Normativity in International Law' (1983) 77 *AJIL* 413 at 423–30.

of international law.[8] According to Lord Phillomore, 'the general principles ... were these which are accepted by all nations *in foro domestico* such as certain principles of procedure, the principle of good faith, and the principle of *res judicata*, etc.'[9] That said, neither the international nor the EU should borrow or apply such general principles of law 'lock, stock, and barrel', but they should first assess their suitability.[10] As the Permanent Court of International Justice (PCIJ) said with regard to the concept of responsibility, it is found 'in the very nature of law' but when it is raised in relations between states, acting as public powers, 'the law to be applied is public international law'.[11] In the same vein, according to Mr Advocate-General Lagrange, the ECJ:

> ... is not content to draw on more or less arithmetical 'common denominators' between the different national solutions, but chooses from each of the Member States those solutions which, having regard to the objects of the Treaty, appear to it to be the best or ... the most progressive.[12]

---

[8] Article 38(1)(c) of the Statute of the International Court of Justice. See also ICJ, *Right of Passage over Indian Territory (Portugal v. India)*, Merits, Judgment of 12 April 1960 (1960) ICJ Rep. 6, at 11–2; G. J. H. van Hoof, *Rethinking the Sources of International Law* (Antwerp: Kluwer, 1983), 131–68; W. Friedman, 'The Uses of "General Principles" in the Development of International Law' (1963) 57 *AJIL* 279; R. B. Schlesinger, 'Research of the General Principles of Law Recognised by Civilised Nations' (1957) 51 *AJIL* 734; H. C. Cutteridge, 'The Meaning and Scope of Article 38(1)(c) of the Statute of the International Court of Justice' (1952) 38 *Transactions of the Grotius Society (T Grotius Soc)* 125 at 128; P. Ripert, 'Règles du droit civil applicable aux rapports internationaux', (1933) 44 *RC* 569. For an alternative opinion, see L. Kopelmans, 'Quelques réflexions au sujet de l'Article 38, 3 du Statut de la Cour Permanent de Justice Internationale' (1936) *Revue General de Droit International Publique (RGDIP)* 285.

[9] Permanent Court of International Justice. Advisory Committee of Jurists. *Procès-Verbaux of the Proceedings of the Committee*, 16 June–24 July 1920 (The Hague, 1920), p. 335 (hereinafter cited as *Procès-Verbaux*).

[10] ICJ, *International Status of South West Africa*, Advisory Opinion of 11 July 1950, (1950) ICJ Rep. 128 (Sir Arnold McNair, Separate Opinion, 148); *Corfu Channel Case* (Judge Krylov, Dissenting Opinion, 71); *South West Africa (Ethiopia v. South Africa; Liberia v. South Africa)*, 2nd Phase, Judgment of 18 July 1966, (1966) ICJ Rep. 14 (Dissenting Opinion of Judge Tanaka, 300); International Criminal Tribunal for the former Yugoslavia (ICTY), *Prosecutor v. Furundzija*, Case No. IT-95-17/1-T, T Ch II, Judgment, 10 December 1998, para. 178; ECJ, Case 11/70, *Internationale Handelsgesellschaft mbH v Einfuhr- und Vorratsstelle für Getreide und Futermittel* [1970] ECR 1125 at 1134, para. 4; also see Opinion of Mr Advocate-General Roemer in Joint Cases 63–69/72, *Werhahn v. Council* [1973] ECR 1229 at 1260. See also I. Brownlie, *Principles of Public International Law* 6th edn (Oxford: Clarendon Press, 2003), p. 16.

[11] *Russian Indemnity Case* 11 *RIAA*, 431 (1912).

[12] Case 147/61, *Hoogovens v. High Authority* [1962] ECR 253 at 283–4.

According to another interpretation, general principles of law are general and often substantive norms which are distilled from other sources of
law such as from treaty or custom.[13] For instance, international jurisprudence often equates principles with customary rules, as in the *Nicaragua*
case, where the ICJ said that 'the principle of non-intervention . . . is part
and parcel of customary international law'.[14] Although this may be true
in international law, custom is not a recognised source of EU law and,
thus, general principles can only be distilled from the treaties or other
posited legislation. To some extent this is what the ECJ did when it
introduced human rights as general principles of law. It grounded them
on the constitutional traditions of member states and the international
conventions to which they are parties.[15]

Be that as it may, judicial or academic inventories often refer
to principles that have normative and ideological dimensions.[16] For
example, in the *Reservations to the Convention on the Prevention and
Punishment of the Crime of Genocide* Advisory Opinion, the ICJ said that
'the principles underlying the Convention are principles which are
recognised by civilised nations as binding on States, even without any
conventional obligation'.[17] The Court was referring in that instance to
the principle of humanity; in such cases, the scope of general principles
of law extends 'beyond the limit of legal positivism' and assumes 'an
aspect of supra-national and supra-positive character'.[18] In the same

---

[13] G. Scelle, 'Règles Générales du droit de la paix' (1933 IV) 46 *RC* 327 at 435–7;
Kopelmans, 'Quelques réflexions', 293–5; G. Schwarzenberger, 'The Fundamental
Principles of International Law' (1955 I) 87 *RC* 191 at 201; G. Tunkin, 'Co-existence
and International Law' (1958 III) 95 *RC* 1 at 26; H. Kelsen, *Principles of International
Law*, R. W. Tucker (ed.) 2nd edn (New York: Holt, Rinehart and Winston, Inc., 1967),
pp. 539–40; B. Vitanyi, 'Les positions doctrinales concernant le sens de la notion de
"principes généraux de droit reconnus par les nations civilisées" ' (1982) *RGDIP* 48 at
56–61.

[14] *Nicaragua Case*, at 106, para. 202.

[15] Case 29/69, *Stauder v. City of Ulm* [1969] ECR 419 at 425, para. 7; Case 11/70 *Internationale
Handelsgesellschaft*, paras. 3–4.

[16] For example, Tridimas includes among others the principle of fundamental rights, and
the principle of equality. See also Article 6(2) TEU.

[17] *Reservations to the Convention on the Prevention and Punishment of the Crime of
Genocide (Advisory Case)*, Advisory Opinion of 28 May 1951, (1951) ICJ Rep. 14 at
23; at 134; *Application of the Convention on the Prevention and Punishment of the Crime
of Genocide (Bosnia and Herzegovina v. Yugoslavia)*, Provisional Measures, Order of
8 April 1993, (1993) ICJ Rep. 23; *Prosecutor v. Furundzija*, para. 183.

[18] Dissenting Opinion of Judge Tanaka in *South West Africa* (1966), p. 298; Verdross, 'Les
principes généraux', 195–203; A. Verdross, 'Principes généraux dans le système des
sources', in *Recueil d'études de droit international en homage à Paul Guggenheim*

vein, the Union's Charter of Fundamental Rights links the enumerated rights to the 'indivisible [and] universal values of human dignity, freedom, equality and solidarity'.[19]

The different readings of general principles of law and the different views about their status are symptomatic of more profound enquiries about the nature of the international or EU constitutive process. In subsequent sections I shall address these issues, but suffice to say here that condensing general principles of law into judicial aids makes them relatively innocuous and, similarly, attaching general principles of law to custom or treaties tames their potential by making them subject to state consent.[20] As a matter of fact this is what Article 38 of the ICJ Statute insinuates by demanding that general principles of law should be 'recognised' by 'civilised nations'.[21] Above all, it deflects attention from the study of normative or ideological principles; which, as it will be seen, are not neutral but, instead, are full of meaning and potential and their study raises important questions about the nature of constitutional orders and the rationale behind patterns of political and legal organisation.

At this point an explanation of the meaning of 'general principles of law' will be offered. General principles are primary propositions that refer to values or goals and are 'consequentially oriented'.[22] When applied to particular formations, general principles become their points

(Impremerie de la Tribune de Genève: Genève, 1968), p. 521 at pp. 522–6; A. Favre, 'Les principes generaux du droit, fond commun du droit des gens', in *Recueil d'études*, p. 366; H. G. Schermers and D. F. Waelbroeck, *Judicial Protection in the European Communities* 5th edn. (Deventer/Boston: Kluwer, 1992), p. 27.

[19] Preamble to the Charter of Fundamental Rights of the European Union, 2000 *OJ* (C 364) 1, 7 December 2000.

[20] PCIJ, *The Lotus Case (France v. Turkey)*, Merits, Judgment of 7 September 1927, (1927) PCIJ series A, No. 10, p. 16; ICJ, *South West Africa (Ethiopia v. South Africa; Liberia v. South Africa)* (1966), 14 at 34–5. See also G. Herczegh, *General Principles of Law and the International Legal Order* (Budapest: Akadémiai Kiadó, 1969), pp. 34–9; G. M. Danilenko, *Law-making in the International Community* (The Hague: Martinus Nijhoff, 1993), pp. 1–15. An opposing viewpoint may be found in Descamps, who said during the drafting of Article 38 of the ICJ Statute that 'it would be a great mistake to imagine that nations can be bound only by engagements which they have entered into by mutual consent'; *Procès -Verbaux*, 323.

[21] C. de Visscher, *Theory and Reality in Public International Law*, P. E. Corbett (trans.) revised edn (Princeton, New Jersey: Princeton University Press, 1968), p. 400. Concerning the meaning of 'civilised nations', see *In the Matter of an Arbitration between Petroleum Development (Trucial Coast) Ltd and the Sheikh of Abu Dhabi* (1952) *ICLQ* 247 at 250–1. For criticism, see *North Sea Continental Shelf Cases* (Separate Opinion of Judge Ammoun, 132–40).

[22] G. Zagrebelsky, 'Ronald Dworkin's Principle Based Constitutionalism: An Italian Point of View' (2003) 1 *International Journal of Constitutional Law (ICON)* 621 at 628; P. van Dijk,

of reference in the sense that they act as assumptions turned into propositions about how they should be constituted. To put it differently, general principles represent, define, and explain the constitution of a polity and when they enter its constitutional conscience as legal precepts they become general principles of law in the sense that they translate in legal terms the normative and organisation principles of the polity. These general principles of law are then divided into two categories: normative-ideational and structural-organisational.[23]

Normative-ideational are the pivotal and archetypal principles of a particular order, being its *creator spiritus* and *raison d'être*.[24] In the words of Mr Advocate-General Dutheillet de Lamothe, they contribute to the 'philosophical, political, and legal substratum' of the referent order,[25] and as such they provide unity, consistency and direction thereto.[26] Moreover, their function is axiological and deontological. Such principles in the international are the principles of peace and

'Normative Force and Effectiveness of International Norms' (1987) 30 *German Yearbook of International Law* (*GYIL*) 9 at 14: '. . . the normative standard implied in [a principle] may concern a set of values and the quality of the behaviour as such.' G. Del Vecchio, *General Principles of Law*, F. Forte (trans.) (Boston: Boston University Press, 1956), p. 102: '. . . the general principles have an ideal and absolute character which virtually transcends the established juridical system to which they belong, they have no validity against the special rules which compose the system, nor can they violate them. However, they definitely have a certain validity over and within the specific rules, whose loftiest reasoning and animated spirit are represented by those general principles'; R. Pound, 'Hierarchy of Sources and Forms In Different Systems of Law', (1933) 7 *Tulane Law Review* (*Tul L Rev*), 475 at 483; R. M. Dworkin, *Taking Rights Seriously* (London: Duckworth, 1977), pp. 22–31; S. D. Krasner, 'Structural Causes and Regime Consequences: Regimes as Intervening Variables' (1982) 36 *International Organization* (*Int'l Org*) 185 at 186.

[23] Verhoeven divides such principles into '*axiomatique*', '*structurels*' and '*communs*': J. Verhoeven, *Droit International Public* (Bruxelles: Larcier, 2000), pp. 252–4; Schermers and Waelbroeck, *Judicial Protection in the European Communities*, pp. 27–9; J. Bengoetxea, *The Legal Reasoning of the European Court of Justice* (Oxford: Clarendon Press, 1993), pp. 71–9; O. Wiklund and J. Bengoetxea, 'General Constitutional Principles of Community Law' in U. Bernitz and Joakim Nergelius, *General Principles of European Community Law* (The Hague: Kluwer Law International, 2000), p. 119; F. Snyder, 'The Unfinished Constitution of the European Union: Principles, Process and Culture', in J. H. H. Weiler and M. Wind, *European Constitutionalism Beyond the State* (Cambridge: Cambridge University Press, 2003), p. 55 at pp. 60–2.

[24] A. Verdross, 'Les principes généraux du droit dans la jurisprudence internationale', (1938) 45 *RGDIP* 50 at 52.

[25] Opinion of Mr Advocate-General Dutheillet de Lamothe in Case 11/70, *Internationale Handelsgesellschaft* at 1146.

[26] As Judge Weeramantry said in a Dissenting Opinion: '[t]he general principles provide both nourishment for the development of the law and an anchorage to the mores of the community. If they are to be discarded in the manner contended for, international law would be cast adrift from its conceptual moorings.' ICJ, *Legality of the Threat or Use of*

humanity,[27] whereas in the EU, the principles are of 'ever closer union among the peoples of Europe', liberty, human rights, and democracy.[28]

Structural-operational principles represent the coordinates of a particular order that assist in organising and managing relations therein.[29] They derive from normative-ideational principles and maintain a particular order in the image of the normative principles. Structural-operational principles are, amongst others, the principles of sovereign independence and equality, self-determination, non-intervention, *pacta sunt servanda*,[30] and in the EU, the principles of primacy,[31] direct effect,[32] subsidiarity[33] and conferral of powers.[34]

Nuclear Weapons, Advisory Opinion of 8 July 1996 (1996) ICJ Rep. 226 at 493; M. Virally, 'Les roles de "principles" dans le développement du droit international', in *Recueil d'études*, 531 at 543: '... ils constitutent une idée-force ...'; M. Virally, 'Panorame du droit international comtemporain', (1983 V) 183 *RC* 9 at 174–5.

[27] Preamble and Articles 1 and 2 of the UN Charter; ICJ, *Corfu Channel Case*, 22; *Military and Paramilitary Activities In and Against Nicaragua (Nicaragua v. United States of America)*, Merits, Judgment of 27 June 1986 (1986) ICJ Rep. 14, at 112–4; UN General Assembly (GA), *Declaration on Principles of International Law Concerning Friendly Relations and Co-operation Among States in Accordance with the Charter of the United Nations*, UN Doc. A/RES/2625 (XXV).

[28] Preamble and Article 6 TEU; Article I-1 TECE, Article I-2 TECE; ECJ, Case T-135/96 *UEAPME v. Council* [1998] ECR II-2335 at 2371, para. 89.

[29] ICJ, Separate Opinion of Judge Moreno Quintana, *Case Concerning the Application of the Convention of 1902 Governing the Guardianship of Infants (Netherlands v. Sweden)*, Merits, Judgment of 28 November 1958, (1958) ICJ Rep. 55 at 106–7; M. A. Dauses, 'The Protection of Fundamental Rights in the Community Legal Order' (1985) 10 *ELR*, 398 at 406: '... they define the structural foundation of the legal system and cannot be ignored without simultaneously bringing into question the foundations of the legal order'. B. de Witte, 'The Role of Institutional Principles in the Judicial Development of the European Union Legal Order', in F. Snyder (ed.), *The Europeanisation of Law: The Legal Effects of European Integration* (Oxford: Hart Publishing, 2000), p. 83; B. de Witte, 'Institutional Principles: A Special Category of General Principles of EC Law', in Bernitz and Nergelius, *General Principles*, p. 143.

[30] PCIJ, *Statute of Eastern Carelia (Finland v. Russia)*, Advisory Opinion of 27 April 1923 (1923) PCIJ series B, no. 5, p. 27; *Corfu Channel Case*, 35; GA, *Declaration on Principles of International Law Concerning Friendly Relations and Co-operation Among States in Accordance with the Charter of the United Nations*, UN Doc. A/RES/2625 (XXV).

[31] ECJ, Case 6/64, *Flaminio Costa v. ENEL* [1964] ECR 585; Case 106/77 *Amministrazione delle Finanze dello Stato v Simmenthal SpA* [1978] ECR 585, para. 21; Article I-6 TECE.

[32] ECJ, Case 26/62, *NV. Algemene Transporten Expeditie Onderneming van Gend en Loos* [1963] ECR 1 at 12 ; Case 41/74 *Yvonne Van Duyn v. Home Office* [1974] ECR 1337; P. Pescatore, 'The Doctrine of Direct Effect: An Infant Disease of Community Law' (1981) 8 *ELR* 155; B. de Witte, 'Direct Effect, Supremacy, and the Nature of the Legal Order', in P. Craig and G. de Búrca (eds.), *The Evolution of EU Law* (Oxford: Oxford University Press, 1999), p. 177.

[33] Article 5(2) EC; Article I-11(3) TECE.   [34] Article 5(1) EC; Article I-11(1) TECE.

It is obvious from the above that normative-ideational principles are value-laden, multi-clustered and multi-dimensional, and are consequentially incarnated in specific rules or dissected into particular behaviours. Structural principles are mono-dimensional and mediate between normative-ideational principles and specific rules. Rules, on the other hand, are individuated and individualised.[35] Truth to tell, the distinction between general principles and rules, or the distinction between normative and structural principles, is not always followed. For instance, certain rules whose content is general are referred to as principles. As the ICJ said:

> [T]he association of the terms 'rules' and 'principles' is no more than the use of the dual expression to convey one and the same idea, since in this context 'principles' clearly means principles of law, that is, it also includes rules of international law in whose case the use of the term 'principle' may be justified because of their more general and more fundamental character.[36]

It may also be recalled that in the *Nicaragua* case the ICJ treated 'non-intervention' both as a principle and as a legal rule, without proffering any cogent jurisprudential reason for such differentiated treatment.[37] According to the template discussed here, non-intervention is a structural principle that derives from the normative-ideational principle of peace and is individuated as a rule in Article 2(4) UN Charter. To use another example, from the normative principle of humanity one may deduct the structural principle of 'unnecessary suffering' individuated in the specific prohibitions of certain weapons or methods.[38]

---

[35] G. Fitzmaurice, 'The General Principles of International Law Considered from the Standpoint of the Rule of Law' (1957 II) 91 *RC* 1 at 7: 'By a principle or a general principle, as opposed to a rule, even a general rule of law is meant chiefly something which is not itself a rule, but which underlies a rule and explains or provides the reason for it. A rule answers the question "what"; a principle in effect answers the question "why".' R. M. Dworkin, 'The Model of Rules', (1967–8) 35 *University of Chicago Law Review (U Chi L Rev)* 14 at 25–8; Dworkin, *Taking Rights Seriously*, pp. 22–6.

[36] *Case Concerning Delimitation of the Maritime Boundary in the Gulf of Maine Area (Canada v. United States of America)*, Merits, Judgment of 12 October 1984 (1984) ICJ Rep. 246 at 288–90, para. 79. It went on to say that 'the principle of international law – that delimitation must be affected by agreement – and ... the implicit rule it enshrines, are principles already clearly affirmed by customary international law, principles which, for that reason, are undoubtedly of general application, valid for all States and in relation to all kinds of maritime delimitation', 292–3, para. 90.

[37] ICJ, *Military and Paramilitary Activities In and Against Nicaragua* (1986), at 106, para. 202.

[38] *Ibid.*, at 114, para. 218.

The principle *pacta sunt servanda*, a structural principle, derives from the principle of justice, a normative principle.[39] From the normative-ideological principle of union derive the principles of primacy and direct effect in the EU which are structural principles and are individuated in specific rules.

From the above, it transpires that the debate over the meaning and role of general principles of law can be placed within the wider debate about constitutionalism because the latter is about the substantive and structural premises of political spaces.[40] General principles of law are part and parcel of the constitutional debate, not only as encoded messages about the organisational and axiological premises of such orders or about actors, institutional settings and mechanisms, but also as congealing agents that provide a sense of unity and direction. Also, their open textured nature implies – like constitutionalism – a dynamic process of becoming. Thus, in the sections that follow, I will focus on the constitutive principles and explore their appeal in constitution-building. In this context I shall discuss the role of courts in introducing or interpreting general principles of law. Before I do this, it is necessary to consider the particularities of the international and EU constitutional setting, their underlying principles and the institutions at play.

The constitutional characteristics of the international and European Union political orders

Constitutional orders are defined by their constituent members. The international is the political space beyond states whose original constituents are the sovereign states. The main vocation of the international is

---

[39] E. de Vattel, *Le Droit Des Gens ou Principes de la Loi Naturelle, appliqués à la Conduite et aux Affaires des Nations et des Souverains*, C. G. Fenwick (trans.), in *Classics of International Law* (Washington D. C.: Carnegie Institution of Washington, 1916), Bk II, ch. VII, para. 163: 'It is a principle of the natural law that one who makes a promise to another confers upon him a valid right to require the thing promised, and that, in consequence, a failure to keep a valid promise is a violation of a right belonging to the promisee and is a clearly an act of injustice as it would be to deprive him of his property. The basis of the peace, welfare and safety of the human race is justice, the obligation of respecting the rights of others.'

[40] J. Bengoetxea, 'Principles in the European Constitutionalising Process' (2001) *King's College Law Journal* (*KCLJ*) 100; R. Gavison, 'What Belongs in a Constitution', (2002) 13 *Constitutional Political Economy* 89; A. von Bogdandy, 'Constitutional Principles', in A. von Bogdandy and J. Bast, *Principles of European Constitutional Law* (Oxford, Hart Publishing, 2006), p. 3; and see the Introduction to this volume, above.

to cater for the physical and moral integrity of its members, the states, and to furnish the mechanisms whereby states can channel their legislative will and reach commonly agreed outcomes.[41] As a consequence, sovereign equality, consent and non-intervention become its composite general principles. Although the international appears to be a total order if looked from outside, internally it is a disaggregated order. This is because of the institution of sovereignty.[42] Sovereignty is not asocial. It can facilitate cooperation between states and even lead to the formation of a polity with its own institutions and rules. However, sovereignty makes a claim to individuality and exclusivity; and consent is instrumental in introducing these qualities to the international constitutive process.

Thus, the scope, content and obligatory character of international norms is under the control of those who create them, and this affects their authority or meaning. Furthermore, atomism manifests itself in derogations, reservations, exceptions or in parochial actions. As a result the international constitutive process is erratic and unstable because it remains dependent on the wavering will of states. It is because of this that it cannot show patterns of entrenchment, a cherished constitutional feature. Often such entrenchment is sought in the concept of *jus cogens*; but as we shall see later this is more a juridical fiction than reality. In sum, the international constitutive process is derivative; it is not an autonomous one but it has been appropriated by its constituents, the states. It is for this reason that judicial mechanisms have also limited reach in the international order. Courts operate within a constitutionally weak environment and cannot antagonise states, the masters of the constitutive process. This state of affairs is best captured by the amount of time or effort spent in international litigation to establish jurisdiction,

---

[41] 'A State has the right to live its life in its own way, so long as it keeps itself rigidly to itself, and refrains from interfering with the equal rights of other states to live their own life in the manner which commends itself to them ...' W. E. Hall, *International Law*, 8th edn, A. P. Higgins (ed.) (Oxford, 1924), p. 50. *Military and Paramilitary Activities In and Against Nicaragua* (1986), 135, para. 269: 'in international law there are no rules, other than such rules as may be accepted by the State concerned, by treaty or otherwise ...' F. Berman, 'What does "Change" Mean? International Law vs. the International Legal System' (2003) 8 *Austrian Review of International and European Law* 11 at 16: '... the foundations of the international legal system are sound. They provide ample protection for States against the imposition of new rules or doctrines without their consent.'

[42] W. G. Werner, 'State Sovereignty and International Legal Discourse', in I. F. Dekkker and W. G. Werner, *Governance and International Legal Theory* (Leiden: Martinus Nijhoff, 2004), p. 125.

or identify the applicable law and the obligations of the parties. In the same vein, the jurisdictional constraints imposed on the ICJ with regard to *locus standi* and the limited legal effect of its judgments[43] reveal not only the limitations of the international constitutional order but also its weak normative integration. The international is not characterised by any enveloping and cohesive ideology of the common good, because it is an aggregation of individual agents whose understandings or interpretations of the public good are commensurate with their own manifold understandings or interpretations. Thus, it cannot produce a full and coherent set of normative-ideological principles, nor does it possess the instruments and authority to impress its will on its members.

Instead, the international champions minimalism with regard to the number and scope of normative-ideological principles and agnosticism as to their value. Take, for example, the normative-ideological principle of peace which is one of the two most fundamental principles, the other being the principle of humanity. As the debate on the merits of intervention in cases of human rights abuses reveals,[44] peace is prioritised but at the same time it is denied any axiological meaning. Instead, it is equated to the second order structural principle of non-intervention, regardless of the implications that this may have on the physical survival of people or the long-term peace of the referent society or the world at large.

From the above it transpires that international constitutionalism is more structural than normative. It focuses on the organisational structure of the international public space, and it defines its subjects, regulates their external relations and where possible establishes mechanisms for mutual communication. This also means that if there is any *telos* it is rather unintelligible due to the limitations imposed by the principles of

---

[43] Article 7(1) and Chapter XIV of the Charter of the UN; Article 59 of the Statute of the ICJ. *Interpretation of Peace Treaties with Bulgaria, Hungary and Romania*, Advisory Opinion, 1st Phase, 30 March 1950, (1950) ICJ Rep. 65 at 71; *Anglo-Iranian Oil Case*, Preliminary Objection, 22 July 1952 (1952) ICJ Rep. 92 at 103: '... the jurisdiction of the Court to deal with and decide a case on the merits depends on the will of the Parties. Unless the Parties have conferred jurisdiction on the court in accordance with Article 36, the Court lacks such jurisdiction.' *Monetary Gold Removed from Rome in 1943 (Italy v. France, United Kingdom and United States of America)*, Jurisdiction and Merits, Judgment of 15 June 1954 (1954) ICJ Rep. 18 at 32; *Case Concerning the Aerial Incident of 27 July 1955 (Israel v. Bulgaria)*, Preliminary Objections, Judgment of 26 May 1959 (1959) ICJ Rep. 127 at 142; *East Timor (Portugal v. Australia)*, Merits, Judgment of 30 June 1995, (1995) ICJ Rep. 102 at 105, para. 34.

[44] N. Tsagourias, *Jurisprudence of International Law: The Humanitarian Dimension* (Manchester: Manchester University Press, 2000), pp. 64–79.

sovereignty and consent. Moreover, such *telos* cannot be deduced from the international's normative principles because the latter do not constitute an organic body of principles but rather a diffused one. Is its *telos*, for example, only peace; or peace with justice, humanity and development? Even if it is said, rather intemperately, that the *telos* of international constitutionalism is a combination of all of the above, there is still little agreement on their meaning, or on how to attain them.

That said, the international's openness and structural looseness are not only constraining and disabling in the sense that they do not permit the international to carry itself autonomously and perhaps proceed as a whole towards a common purpose; but also, those particular features of the international are liberating and enabling, to the extent that they permit its subjects to embark on their own journeys – either individually or in groups. In other words, the international allows members who share common symbols to come together and form their own political clusters, which can be geographic or thematic or in other combinations.[45] Because they are anchored on mutual identifications and on shared perceptions of the good, these clusters grow their own version of constitutionalism and constitution. Thus, the international forms a transit political space placed between the bounded and autonomous state polities on the one hand, and those more- or less-bounded and autonomous meta-state polities formed by states on the other. This means that the international cannot claim internal or external authority, and cannot exercise political or legal power; whereas the state or state-formed mini-orders can do so. The EU is such a mini-order constructed by states that inhabit the international, but which share common patrimony of principles such as the principles of peace, human rights, democracy, and the rule of law. These principles define the EU as a micro-order within the international, attribute legitimacy, ensure legal coherence, foster unity and provide orientation. Furthermore, they endow the Union with its structural principles that regulate relations between itself, its member states and individuals. There is in the Union an interactive network of normative and structural principles that applies to internal or external relations,[46] which also projects the

---

[45] N. Tsagourias, 'International Community, Recognition of States, and Political Cloning', in C. Warbrick and S. Tierney (eds.), *Towards an 'International Legal Community'?* (London: BIICL, 2006), p. 211 at pp. 212–17.

[46] This is evident in the EU's accession policies. See Article 49 TEU, according to which 'any European State which respects the principles set out in Article 6(1) may apply to

Union towards its *telos*. In other words, they allow the Union to grow an indigenous constitution and claim constitutional autonomy.

There are some other features that set the EU apart from the international. The European order is 'subjectivised',[47] in contrast to the international, where individuals are mainly reached through their states; and, furthermore, there is strong cross-pollination between the national and the European order, as the dialogue between the national orders and the EU on the status and scope of human rights reveals.[48] Such mutual interaction leads to the Europeanisation of national law and domestication of European law.[49] The international, on the contrary, tries to seal itself from national influences because of its fear that this may weaken its legitimacy as a total order. This may explain the ICJ's hesitation to engage in any substantive discussion of human rights; and the prospect of the ICJ borrowing human rights from domestic jurisdictions is so remote, that it is almost absurd.

The next issue that we shall consider at this juncture is the relation between the EU and the international. In the European political and legal mythology the EU constitutes an autonomous order, in the sense of being a proto-normative order. As the ECJ put it, the European legal

become a member state of the Union'. See also the criteria as set out by the Copenhagen Council: '... the associated countries ... that so desire shall become members of the European Union. Accession will take place as soon as an associated country is able to assume the obligations of membership by satisfying the economic and political conditions required. Membership requires that the candidate country has achieved stability of institutions guaranteeing democracy, the rule of law, human rights and respect for and protection of minorities, the existence of a functioning market economy as well as the capacity to cope with competitive pressure and market forces within the Union. Membership presupposes the candidate's ability to take on the obligations of membership including adherence to the aims of political, economic and monetary union. The Union's capacity to absorb new members, while maintaining the momentum of European integration, is also an important consideration in the general interest of both the Union and the candidate countries.' *Presidency Conclusions: Copenhagen European Council* (1993) 6 EC Bull. European Commission, 'Agenda 2000', Bull. EU, Suppls 5-15/97 (1997).

[47] Even in some of the first cases it was stated that 'the subjects of "Community" comprise not only member States but also their nationals'. Case 26/62, *Van Gend en Loos*, 12; E. Stein, 'Lawyers, Judges and the making of a Transnational Constitution', (1981) 75 *AJCL* 1.

[48] Case 11/70, *Internationale Handelsgesellschaft* 1125; Bundesverfassungsgericht, decision of 12 October 1993, *Treaty of Maastrict* (Brunner), 89 BverfGE 155; [1994] 1 CMLR 57.

[49] Snyder, *The Europeanisation of Law*, pp. 1–11; M. Poiares Maduro, 'The Importance of Being Called a Constitution: Constitutional Authority and the Authority of Constitutionalism' (2005) 3 *ICON* 332 at 338–9.

order is a new and indeed a *sui generis* order.[50] One may argue that the EU is nothing more than an entity subject to international law, because it has been formed by states and established by treaties which are international law instruments. More than that, it was only by legal fiat and judicial pre-emption that the umbilical cord with the international was cut and the treaties were elevated to the apex of the European lego-political pyramid, something – as the argument goes – that was completely unwarranted. There are two lines of reasoning that show the erroneousness of the aforementioned arguments. First, how the treaties have become the *Grundnorm*, or who performed such an act, is completely irrelevant. What matters is that there is a new order which is liberated from its contingent historical, legal and political origins and which does not derive its existence or legitimacy from external sources. In the EU it was the ECJ that performed the act of severance; an act analogous to patricide which, coincidentally, in ancient Greek tragedy is about usurpation of power and the introduction of a new order.[51] What the ECJ did was to separate and shield the European order from its progenitor and to project a self-contained, self-referential and autochthonous order, having its own epistemic validity.[52]

It is a logical expectation, then, and this is our second point, that a new and autonomous order will introduce its own constitutional culture using its own institutions and mechanisms. The EU not only has its own

[50] Case 26/62, *Van Gend en Loos*, 12; Case 6/64, *Flaminio Costa*, 593–4; Opinion 1/91, *Re the Draft Treaty on a European Economic Area* [1991] ECR I-6079 at 6102, para. 21. As A-G Lagrange said: '... my Court is not an international tribunal, but is concerned with a community which ... resembles more a federation than an international organisation ... The Treaty ... although concluded in the form of international treaties and undoubtedly being one, nevertheless also constitutes, from a substantive point of view, the charter of the community and as a consequence the legal provisions derived from the Treaty must be viewed as the internal law of the Community ...' For an opposing viewpoint, see the Polish Constitutional Court's Judgment on Poland's membership to the EU, according to which the treaties are international agreements: *K 18/04, Poland's membership in the European Union (The Accession Treaty)*, Judgment of 11 May 2005, paras. 6–14a, available at www.trybunal.gov.pl/eng/summaries/documents/K_18_04_GB.pdf. Also see T. Schilling, 'The Autonomy of the Community Legal Order: An Analysis of Possible Foundations' (1996) 37 *Harvard Int LJ* 389; J. H. H. Weiler and U. R. Haltern, 'The Autonomy of the Community Legal Order – Through the Looking Glass', *ibid.*, 411.

[51] Aeschylus, *Prometheus Bound*, J. Scully and C. J. Herington (trans.) (New York: Oxford University Press, 1975), pp. 3–6.

[52] Case 6/64, *Flaminio Costa*, at 594; H. Lindahl, 'Sovereignty and Representation in the European Union', in N. Walker (ed.), *Sovereignty in Transition* (Oxford: Hart Publishing, 2003), p. 87 at pp. 105–12.

political logic, but its own mechanisms for law-production and enforce-ment and its own processes for producing legitimacy. Even if instru-ments or concepts are similar to the ones used in the international or state orders, their role and meaning is particular to the European. For example, in drafting the Charter of Fundamental Rights and the Constitutional Treaty, a mixture of methods was used, some of which are akin to the way states formulate their own constitutional documents; whereas others are more akin to international methods, such as inter-governmental conferences or treaties. However, these methods have acquired a different meaning in the EU and become part and parcel of its constitutional culture. To give another example, even if the Council's practices are reminiscent of international law, as Walter Hallstein put it, 'the Council is not a conference of governments but an institution of the Community'.[53] In the same vein, the principles of *pacta sunt servanda* and direct effect are not external to the EU legal order, but function from within this order.[54] In other words, the EU's constitutional culture cannot be pinned down to any known categories, such as that of the state or the international, but is distinct to the EU.

Our contention, then, is that the EU is a separate entity, having an indigenous constitutional culture. This point can be understood better if we consider the following scenarios. One is to compare the behaviour of member states within the EU and their behaviour outside the EU. Within the EU, states behave according to the Union's 'rules of the game', whereas the same states outside the EU behave according to the international 'rules of the game'. For example, if a rule is breached within the EU, states do not resort to countermeasures or renounce the treaties, as is the case in the international. Second, if, for argument's sake, the Union were dissolved, states would return to the international fold and interact with each other according to international rules even on those matters that were previously part of the EU. These scenarios prove the point that there are two separate polities, each having their particular constitutional ethos.

---

[53] W. Hallstein, *Europe in the Making* (London: Allen and Unwin, 1972), p. 77.

[54] Case 11/70, *Internationale Handelsgesellschaft*, at 1134, para. 3: 'The validity of a Community measure or its effects within a Member State cannot be affected by the constitution of that State or the principles of the national constitutional structure.' Whereas direct effect or supremacy is a matter of national law according to interna-tional law, it becomes a rule of European law in the EU. P. Pescatore, 'International Law and Community Law – A Comparative Analysis' (1970) 7 *CMLR* 167.

The preceding discussion also reveals that the EU as a separate entity has rejected principles found in the international which are at odds with its overall rationale.[55] The most characteristic example is the principle of sovereignty, with its propensity for detachment and disengagement. Sovereignty is mentioned nowhere in the treaties; something which prompted the ECJ to declare that the founding treaty 'is more than an agreement which creates mutual obligations' and that the member states have 'limited their sovereign rights'.[56] Even if the EU order accommodates state interests and occasionally member states or courts have reclaimed some of their powers,[57] these events should be seen as part of a network of interweaving relations and of the changing notions of self-identification between states and the EU.[58]

Moreover, the principle of primacy shields the Union treaties from external challenges, and thus supports and preserves the Union's autonomy. Related to the above is the fact that the validity of treaty provisions cannot become the object of preliminary rulings.[59] Otherwise, this may invite external sources of validation and thus challenge the internal coherence and autonomy of the European order. Furthermore, when it comes to human rights, the EU excluded sources of legitimacy that are external to the EU.[60] Instead, the human rights included in Article 6(2) TEU or in the Charter of Fundamental Rights and the TECE are simply the human rights of the EU.[61] Although this does not rule out dialogue

---

[55] For the relationship between International Law and EU general principles of law, see Case 8/55, *Fedechar* [1954–1956] ECR 245, 292 and Case 6/54, *Netherlands v. High Authority* [1954–56] ECR 103.

[56] Case 26/62, *van Gend en Loos*, at 12; Case 6/64, *Flaminio Costa v. ENEL* [1964] ECR 585; N. Maziau, 'L'internationalisation du pouvoir constituant. Essai de typologie: le point de vue heterodoxe du constitutionliste' (2002) *RGDIP* 549 at 550.

[57] Case 11/70, *Internationale Handelsgessllschaft*, para. 3; Case C-280/93, *Germany v. Commission* [1994] ECR I-4873; *Brunner v. European Union Treaty* [1994] 1 CMLR 57.

[58] G. De Búrca, 'Sovereignty and the Supremacy Doctrine of the European Court of Justice', in N. Walker (ed), *Sovereignty in Transition* (Oxford: Hart Publishing, 2003), p. 449 at pp. 455–60; M. Kumm, 'The Jurisprudence of Constitutional Conflict: Constitutional Supremacy in Europe before and after the Constitutional Treaty' (2005) 11 *ELJ* 262.

[59] Article 234 EC.

[60] Opinion 2/94, *Accession by the Community to the Convention for the Protection of Human Rights and Fundamental Freedoms* [1996] ECR I-1759. With regard to the World Trade Organization (WTO), see Case C-149/96, *Portugal v. Council* [1999] ECR I-8395.

[61] For example, see the different interpretations of the right to a fair trail: ECJ, Case 374/87, *Orkem v. Commission* [1989] ECR 3283; Case C-280/93, *Germany v. Council* [1994] ECR I-4973 at 5065, para. 78; contrasting with the European Court of Human Rights (ECHR), *Funke v. France*, Decision of 27 January 1993 (1993) ECHR (Ser. A, No. 256A).

with other human rights bodies, this 'other' law remains an external source which becomes internal only to the extent that it is permitted by the EU organs.[62]

In conclusion, the main contention here is that the international and the EU are separate polities, with different constitutional qualities and mindsets.

General principles of law and the courts

A. The role of the ICJ and the ECJ in identifying and interpreting general principles of law

The identification, interpretation or application of general principles of law raises important questions about the role of courts in constitutional affairs. Whether courts – for our purposes the ICJ and the ECJ – can play such a role, depends on the idiosyncrasy of the international and EU constitutional orders, respectively.[63] On the basis of what has been said above about the separation of the EU from the international, the ECJ was able to seize the opportunity offered by the EU's autonomous and *sui generis* character to play a central role in constitution-building.[64] It streamlined and unified the legal order and fleshed out its principles. There are also a number of other factors which have assisted the ECJ in its constitutional endeavours.[65] The ECJ is the only dispute settlement

---

[62] G. de Búrca and O. Gerstenberg, 'The Denationalization of Constitutional Law' (2006) 47 *Harvard Int LJ* 242 at 258. See also Case T-347/94, *Mayr-Melnhof v. Commission* [1998] ECR II-1751, para. 311: 'The Court of First Instance has no jurisdiction to apply the ECHR when reviewing an investigation under competition law, because the ECHR is not itself part of Community law'; and Case T-112/98, *Mannesmannrohrenwerke AG v. Commission* [2001] ECR II-729, para. 59.

[63] Judge Alvarez in *Corfu Channel Case*, 40. L. V. Prott, *The Latent Power of Culture and the International Judge* (Abingdon: Professional Books, 1979), pp. 78–80; V. Gowlland-Debbas, 'Judicial Insights into the Fundamental Values and Interests of the International Community', in A. S. Muller, D. Raič and J. M. Thuránszky (eds.), *The International Court of Justice: Its Future Role after Fifty Years* (The Hague: Martinus Nijhoff, 1997), p. 327.

[64] Opinion 1/91, *Re a Draft Treaty on a European Economic Area* at 6102, paras. 20–21; Case 294/83, *Parti écologiste 'Les Verts' v. European Parliament* [1986] ECR 1339 at 1365. Case 9/73, *Schluler v. Hauptzolamt Lorrach* [1973] ECR 1135, 1157: '... the validity of acts of the institutions within the meaning of EC Article 177 of the treaty cannot be tested against a rule of international law.'

[65] 'The prominent place occupied by the Court of Justice in the European institutional system, finds no parallel in the international system where courts are generally confined to a marginal role' Dehousse, *The European Court of Justice*, p. 5; A. Shapiro, 'The

organ in the EU, and for this reason it was often called upon to perform the functions of a constitutional court; for example, to adjudicate on the relations between institutions, states and individuals, and on the standing or interpretation of legal provisions or principles.[66] Furthermore, individuals have access to the EU courts[67] and the relation between national and EU courts is cooperative. Overall, the ECJ identified itself with the Union's political and legal culture and acted as a constitutional court but, truth to tell, it was often supported in its pursuits by the EU political institutions and the member states who endorsed its pronouncements.

Turning now to the ICJ, it cannot claim such a constitutional role, even by fiat, because the international constitutional architecture is not accommodating to this end.[68] As observed above, the international is a compendium of parallel orders and its constitutive process is horizontal. It resembles a legal patchwork superficially seamed at the edges. In such an acentric system, there is no place for a central court to authoritatively adjudicate international disputes. Instead, the international contains a motley number of dispute settlement mechanisms which are not necessarily judicial and which lack overall unity. Furthermore, the principle of consent constitutes an important constraint on the scope of ICJ jurisdiction. This became evident in the *East Timor* case, where the ICJ dismissed Portugal's application because Indonesia, an interested party, did not consent to its jurisdiction; although the case invoked the principle of self-determination which, according to the Court, is a principle of *erga omnes* standing.[69] Its decision also reveals its nervousness when confronted with general principles. Even if certain general principles such as the principle of self-determination enjoy

European Court of Justice', in P. Craig and G. de Búrca (eds.), *The Evolution of EU Law* (Oxford: Oxford University Press, 1999), p. 321; M. Poiares Maduro, *We, The Court. The European Court of Justice and the European Economic Constitution* (Oxford: Hart Publishing, 1998), pp. 7–34.

[66] Cases 188–190/80, *France, Italy and UK v. Commission* [1982] ECR 2545, at 2573.

[67] For example, Article 230 EC, Article 234 EC.

[68] M. Koskenniemi, 'Police in the Temple Order, Justice and the UN: A Dialectical View' (1995) 6 *EJIL* 325 at 341–2; *Case Concerning Questions of Interpretation and Application of the 1971 Montreal Convention Arising from the Aerial Incident at Lockerbie (Libya v. United Kingdom)*, Preliminary Objections, Judgment of 27 February 1998, (1998) ICJ Rep. 9 at 164 (Judge Schwebel, Dissenting Opinion); S. Rosenne, *The World Court: What it is and How it Works*, 5th edn (Dordrecht/London: Martinus Nijhoff, 1994), p. 36; *Legal Consequences for States of the Continued Presence of South Africa in Namibia (South West Africa) Notwithstanding Security Council Resolution 276 (1970)*, Advisory Opinion of 21 June 1971, (1971) ICJ Rep. 16 at 132–3 (Judge Peteren, Separate Opinion).

[69] *East Timor* 102; *Case Concerning Oil Platforms (Islamic Republic of Iran v. United States of America)* Judgment of 6 November 2003 (2003) ICJ Rep. 160 at 182–183, para. 42.

some vague universal appeal, their application to a particular case can be resisted in the absence of an integrated political and legal system.[70] It is not only that different understandings of the same principle may exist, but also the fact that the ICJ does not have the supporting mechanisms to enforce its judgments. It may be recalled that the ECJ often antagonises states, but it is able to assert its authority because it aligns itself with domestic actors, and appeals directly to the people. The ICJ cannot circumvent states and assert its authority because it does not enjoy such links with national courts[71] and even if it appeals to people, it can only reach them through states. Thus it cannot mobilise internal actors to force compliance. It is because of the above that the ICJ rarely mentions general principles of law in substantive terms; or when it applies them, it disguises them as legal rules.[72]

The normative fragmentation that exists at the international level is also reflected in the Court's internal organisation. One may trace, for example, in the institution of *ad hoc* judges[73] some degree of mistrust in the international judicial process.[74] On the other hand, dissenting or separate opinions,[75] often presented by *ad hoc* judges, confirm the fact that the international is normatively patchy. By saying this we do not question the

---

[70] As Root commented during the drafting of Article 38: 'it is inconceivable that a Government would agree to allow itself to be arraigned before a court which bases its sentences on its subjective conceptions of the principles of justice.' *Procès-Verbaux*, p. 309.

[71] M. S. M. Amir, *The Role of the International Court of Justice as the Principal Judicial Organ of the United Nations* (The Hague: Kluwer International, 2003), pp. 27–31.

[72] *South West Africa Case* (1966), p. 35; *North Sea Continental Shelf Cases*, 48; *Case Concerning the Continental Shelf (Tunisia v. Libya)*, 60; *Case Concerning the Continental Shelf (Libya v. Malta)*, Merits, Judgment of 2 June 1985, (1985) ICJ Rep. 13 at 39–40; *Case Concerning Maritime Delimitation in the Area between Greenland and Jan Mayen (Denmark v. Norway)*, Merits, Judgment of 14 June 1993 (1993) ICJ Rep. 38, at 120 (Judge Schwebel, Dissenting Opinion); Dissenting Opinion of Judge Koretsky in *North Sea Continental Shelf Cases*, 166.

[73] Article 31 of the Statute of the ICJ. See also S. M. Schwebel, 'National Judges and Judges Ad Hoc of the International Court of Justice', (1999) 48 *ICLQ* 889; *Application of the Convention on the Prevention and Punishment of the Crime of Genocide (Bosnia and Herzegovina v. Yugoslavia)*, Provisional Measures, Order of 13 September 1993 (1993) ICJ Rep. 325 at 408–9 (Judge Lauterpacht, Separate Opinion).

[74] As Mr Root said during the drafting of the PCIJ Statute, 'the instinctive mistrust felt by nations for a Court composed of foreign judges . . .' in Schwebel, 'National Judges', 890. For an opposing viewpoint, see T. R. Hensley, 'Bloc Voting on the International Court of Justice', (1978) 22 *Journal of Conflict Resolution* 39.

[75] R. P. Anand, 'The Role of Individual and Dissenting Opinions in Adjudication' (1965) 14 *International and Comparative Law Quarterly* (*ICLQ*) 788; I. Ro Suh, 'Voting Behaviour of National Judges in International Courts', (1969) 63 *AJIL*, 224; E. Brown Weiss, 'Judicial Independence and Impartiality: A Preliminary Inquiry', in

epistemic competence of such opinions or the professionalism of *ad hoc* judges.[76] The point we want to make is that such opinions, more often than not, appeal to home audiences and are in fact expressions of the different set of value communities that exist at the international.[77] An ICJ judgment followed by dissenting or separate opinions makes a valuable contribution to the market of ideas; but as a whole it often appears to be a *compromis* that accommodates the views of the parties and beyond. In contrast, the ECJ's decisions are institutional, de-nationalised[78] and de-personalised. By giving single and monolithic decisions, the ECJ maintains its authority and increases the persuasiveness of its judgment, ensures compliance and even allows the ECJ to engineer changes.[79]

Another obstacle to the ICJ playing a more robust role is that the relation between international institutions is heterarchical and unstructured. Often competences are shared, but can also merge in one institution; for example, the Security Council, which can exercise executive, legislative or judicial competences.[80] Even if the ICJ has said that litispendence does not affect its jurisdiction,[81] it has in fact bowed to

L. F. Damrosch (ed.), *The International Court of Justice at a Crossroads* (New York: Transnational Publishers, 1987), p. 123; A. M. Smith, 'Judicial Nationalism in International Law: National Identity and Judicial Autonomy at the ICJ' (2005) 40 *Texas International Law Journal* 197.

[76] Lauterpacht, *The Development*, pp. 66–70; R. G. Simmons, 'The Use and Abuse of Dissenting Opinions' (1956) 16 *Louisiana Law Review* 498; Separate Opinion. Judge Lauterpacht in *Application of the Convention on the Prevention and Punishment of the Crime of Genocide (Bosnia and Herzegovina v. Yugoslavia)*, Provisional Measures, Order of 13 September 1993 (1993) ICJ Rep. 325 at 408–9, paras. 4–6; Dis. Op. Judge Franck in *Case Concerning Sovereignty over Pulau Litigan and Pulau Sipadan (Indonesia/ Malaysia)*, Judgment 17 December 2002 (Merits) (2002) ICJ Rep. paras. 9–12.

[77] Anand, 'The Role of Individual and Dissenting Opinions', 804–6.

[78] National representation is important if one considers the relation between the ECJ and national courts, but this does not fragment the authority of the court. Dehousse, *The European Court of Justice*, pp. 6–15.

[79] K. Alter, 'Who Are the "Masters of the Treaty"?: European Governments and the European Court of Justice' (1998) 52 *International Organization* 121.

[80] *Certain Expenses of the United Nations*, 168; *Military and Paramilitary Activities In and Against Nicaragua (Nicaragua v. United States of America)*, Jurisdiction and Admissibility, Judgment of 26 November 1984 (1984) ICJ Rep. 433; *Case Concerning Questions of Interpretation and Application of the 1971 Montreal Convention Arising from the Aerial Incident at Lockerbie (Libya v. United Kingdom)*, Provisional Measures, Order of 14 April 1992 (1992) ICJ Rep. 3 at 26 (Judge Lachs, Separate Opinion); E. Lauterpacht, *Aspects of the Administration of International Justice* (Cambridge: Cambridge University Press, 1991), pp. 37–48.

[81] *Aegean Sea Continental Shelf (Greece v. Turkey)*, Jurisdiction, Judgment of 19 December 1978 (1978) ICJ Rep. 1, at 12; *Case Concerning US Diplomatic and Consular Staff in Tehran (United States of America v. Iran)*, Provisional Measures, Order of 15 December

the authority of the Security Council (SC).[82] This highlights the fact that the international law-making or adjudicative process is mainly shaped by political rather then judicial forces. It also highlights another issue, which is the nature of disputes brought before the ICJ. According to its Statute, the Court should deal only with 'legal disputes'[83] and these are 'a disagreement on a point of law or fact, a conflict of legal views or of interests between two persons'.[84] The ICJ has often acknowledged the 'inherent limitations on the exercise of the judicial function'[85] but has not dismissed a case because of its political nature. As was said in the *South West Africa* case, '[l]aw exists ... to serve a social need; but precisely for that reason it can do so only through and within the limits of its own discipline'.[86] The Court then went on to say in the *Namibia* case that it 'acts only on the basis of the law, independently of all outside influence or interventions whatsoever, in the exercise of the judicial

---

1979, (1979) ICJ Rep. 7 at 15–6; *Case Concerning US Diplomatic and Consular Staff in Tehran (United States of America v. Iran)*, Merits, Judgment of 24 May 1980 (1980) ICJ Rep. 3 at 29; *Military and Paramilitary Activities In and Against Nicaragua* (1984), 433, paras. 93 and 435, para. 96. D. Ciobanu, 'Litispendence between the International Court of Justice and the Political Organs of the United Nations', in L. Gross (ed.), *The Future of the International Court of Justice* (Dobbs Ferry, N.Y: Oceana Publications, 1976), p. 209.

[82] *Case Concerning Questions of Interpretation and Application of the 1971 Montreal Convention Arising from the Aerial Incident at Lockerbie (Libya v. United Kingdom)*, Provisional Measures, Order of 14 April 1992 (1992) ICJ Rep. 3; *Application of the Convention on the Prevention and Punishment of the Crime of Genocide (Bosnia and Herzegovina v. Yugoslavia)*, Provisional Measures, Order of 13 September 1993 (1993) ICJ Rep. 325. For an opposing viewpoint, see O. Schachter, 'Disputes Involving the Use of Force', in L. F. Damrosch (ed.), *The International Court*, p. 241.

[83] Article 36(2) of the Statute of the International Court of Justice.

[84] *The Mavrommatis Palestine Concessions (Greece v. United Kingdom)*, Merits, Judgment of 30 August 1924 (1924) PCIJ series A, no. 2, p. 11. According to Higgins *'the terms "political dispute" and "legal dispute" refer to the decision-making process which is to be employed in respect of them and not to the nature of the dispute itself'* (italics in the original). R. Higgins, 'Policy Considerations and the International Judicial Process', (1968) 17 *ICLQ* 74; E. Gordon, 'Legal Disputes Under Article 36(2) of the Statute', in L. F. Damrosch (ed.), *The International Court*, p. 183; Lauterpacht, *The Function of Law*, pp. 158, 164. For an opposing viewpoint, see H. H. W. Verzijl, *International Law in Historical Perspective* (Leyden: A. W. Sijhoff, 1976), vol. VIII, pp. 18–19; D. P. Forsythe, 'The International Court of Justice at Fifty', in Muller *et al.* (eds.), *The International Court*, p. 385 at pp. 387–93.

[85] *Northern Cameroons (Cameroon v. United Kingdom)*, Merits, Judgment of 2 December 1963 (1963) ICJ Rep. 15 at 29.

[86] *South West Africa Case* (1966), at 34; Dissenting Opinions of Judges Fitzmaurice and Spender in *South West Africa Cases (Ethiopia v. South Africa; Liberia v. South Africa)* (1962), at 466.

function entrusted to it alone by the Charter and its Statute. A Court functioning as a court of law can act in no other way'.[87] All that this means is that the Court needs to decode the legal aspects of each case before it can adjudicate. However, this is a daunting exercise because international disputes are often multidimensional;[88] they invoke political, social or economic questions where the legal issues, if not marginal or secondary, are placed in a wider context. Because the scope of international law is also limited due to consent, most questions seem to fall outside legal regulation and into the 'political' realm.[89] Recalling for a moment the *Nicaragua* case, it was not only about the use of force but also about acceptable forms of government and national security. The *Bosnia Genocide* case[90] was not only about genocide, but also about self-defence and self-determination. Dispute settlement in this context demands political initiatives and adjustments that the Court is not able to offer.[91] It is for

---

[87] ICJ, *Legal Consequences for States of the Continued Presence of South Africa in Namibia*, 23; see also *Northern Cameroons*, 33–4; PCIJ, *"Haute Savoie" Free zones of Upper Savoy and the district of Gex (France v. Switzerland)*, Judgment of 7 June 1932 (1932) PCIJ series A/B, no. 46, p. 162.

[88] *Border and Transborder Armed Actions (Nicaragua v. Honduras)*, Jurisdiction and Admissibility, Judgment of 20 December 1988 (1988) ICJ Rep. 69 at 91: 'The Court is aware that political aspects may be present in any legal dispute brought before it. The Court as a judicial organ, is however only concerned to establish, first, that the dispute before it is a legal dispute, in the sense of a dispute capable of being settled by the application of principles and rules of international law . . .' *United States Diplomatic and Consular Staff in Tehran* (1980), 20; *Aegean Sea Continental Shelf* (1978), 13; *Case Concerning Questions of Interpretation and Application of the 1971 Montreal Convention Arising from the Aerial Incident at Lockerbie* (1992), 27 (Judge Lacks, Separate Opinion); *Legal Consequences of the Construction of a Wall in the Occupied Palestinian Territory*, Advisory Opinion of 9 July 2004 (2004) ICJ Rep. 136, para. 37.

[89] J. W. Halderman, *The United Nations and the Rule of Law* (Dobbs Ferry, New York: Oceana Publications Inc., 1966), pp. 8, 216.

[90] *Case Concerning Application of the Convention on the Prevention and Punishment of the Crime of Genocide (Bosnia and Herzegovina v. Yugoslavia)*, Preliminary Objections, Judgment of 11 July 1996, (1996) ICJ Rep. 14.

[91] Separate Opinion of Judge Gros in *Nuclear Tests Case (Australia v. France)*, Merits, Judgment of 20 December 1974 (1974) ICJ Rep. 253 at 297: 'there is a certain tendency to submit essentially political conflicts to adjudication in the attempt to open a little door to judicial legislation and, if this tendency were to persist, it would result in the institution, on the international plane, of government by judges; such a notion is so opposed to the realities of the present international community that it would undermine the very foundations of jurisdiction.' C. de Visscher, *Theory and Reality in Public International Law*, P. E. Corbett (trans.), revised edn (Princeton, New Jersey: Princeton University Press, 1968), p. 96; M. Norton, 'The *Nicaragua* Case: Political Question Before the International Court of Justice' (1987) 27 *Virginia Journal of International Law (VaJIL)* 469 at 499–501.

this reason that judicial settlement of international disputes is often peripheral or part of a package deal that also addresses the other issues.[92] Even if the ICJ decides to proceed with the case, it needs to heed the views of other actors involved in the dispute. For example, in Bosnia, it was not only the Court but also the United Nations – among others – that was involved. Thus, in the *Bosnia Genocide* case, the ICJ sided with the rest of the UN organs and their overall policy towards Bosnia; which, at the time, was to preserve the peace at all costs. The ICJ could have ignored them and, by prioritising the principle of humanity, proclaim that genocide was being committed. This would have put it on a collision course with the rest of the UN and any victory for the victims would have been moral but ineffective on the ground. The insistence of the ICJ on dividing disputes into the legal and the political reveals, more than anything else, its existential angst.

We shall now turn to a cherished subject of international constitutionalism; the *jus cogens* principles. A constitutional reading of these principles contends that they represent fundamental principles whose aim is to provide continuity and anchoring to the international; two qualities jeopardised by the omnipotence of consent.[93] In other words, *jus cogens* principles rise above the capriciousness of state consent[94] and introduce a number of stable and permanent coordinates into the international order. It would then seem natural for the ICJ to play a constitutional role, as guardian of such principles. However, this is 'too good to be true' and the view described above is not free from difficulties. *Jus cogens* are structural-organisational principles that derive from normative-ideological principles. Because there is tension between the normative principles and no authoritative and final decision-maker exists, their application is less than self-evident. The tensions we referred to above were apparent in the cases that dealt with the prohibition of genocide, a *jus cogens* principle. In the

---

[92] *Case Concerning US Diplomatic and Consular Staff in Tehran* (1979), 21–2, para. 40: 'It is for the Court, the principal organ of the United Nations, to resolve any legal questions that may be in issue between parties to a dispute; and the resolution of such legal questions by the court may be an important, and sometimes decisive, factor in promoting the peaceful settlement of the dispute.'

[93] See Chapters 9 and 10 below.

[94] *Reservations to the Convention on the Prevention and Punishment of the Crime of Genocide*, 23; *Alvarez-Machain v. United States*, 331 F.3d 604, 613 (9th Cir. 2003): '. . . jus cogens embraces customary laws considered binding on all nations and is derived from values taken to be fundamental by the international community, rather than from the fortuitous or self interested choices of nations. Whereas customary international law derives solely from the consent of states, the fundamental and universal norms constituting *jus cogens* transcend such consent.'

Reservations to Genocide case the ICJ resorted to the normative principle of humanity, whereas in the *Bosnia Genocide* case to the normative principle of peace; and the Court reached different outcomes.[95] Furthermore, the content of *jus cogens* principles is not settled and is subject to further changes. This is true not only for those, who ascribe to the consensual rule behind *jus cogens*,[96] but also for those who ascribe to a more transcendental view. In short, *jus cogens* fails the task of providing stability and continuity. Instead, it can sponsor further individualism, in particular when the question of its enforcement is brought to the fore.[97]

Turning now to another aspect of *jus cogens*, it seems that it is endowed with special power to invalidate treaties.[98] Although there is no relevant practice with regard to treaties, with regard to secondary rules, the jurisprudence is rather undecided. *Jus cogens* has not always been successful in trumping international rules, particularly those that invoke state prerogatives such as immunities.[99] It is probably because of the aforementioned uncertainties that the ICJ has behaved prudently by not explicitly employing *jus cogens* principles to settle disputes. However, the Court of First Instance of the European Communities (CFI) has lately ventured into reviewing SC resolutions against *jus cogens* principles.[100] The cases involved sanctions that allegedly violated the human rights of natural persons.

---

[95] *Reservations to the Convention on the Prevention and Punishment of the Crime of Genocide* and *Application of the Convention on the Prevention and Punishment of the Crime of Genocide (Bosnia and Herzegovina v. Yugoslavia)*, Provisional Measures, Order of 13 September 1993 (1993) ICJ Rep. 325. Also see Separate Opinion of Judge Lauterpacht, *ibid.*, at 440. M. Toufayan, 'The World Court's Distress when Facing Genocide: A Critical Commentary on the Application of the *Genocide Convention Case (Bosnia and Herzegovina v. Yugoslavia (Serbia and Montenegro)*' (2005) 40 *Texas International Law Journal* 233.

[96] See Article 53 VCLT, according to which the norm should be 'accepted and recognised'.

[97] See Articles 40 and 41 of the International Law Commission (ILC) Draft Articles on State Responsibility (2000).

[98] Article 53 of the 1969 Vienna Convention on the Law of Treaties; Individual Opinion of Judge Schucking in *The Oscar Chinn Case (United Kingdom v. Belgium)*, Merits, Judgment of 12 December 1934 (1934) PCIJ series A/B, no. 63, p. 63, at 150. Dissenting Opinion of Judge Schwebel in *Military and Paramilitary Activities In and Against Nicaragua* (1984), 196.

[99] For example, compare Appl. No. 35763/97, *Al-Adsani v. UK* (Judgment of 21 November 2001) (2002) 34 EHRR 11, paras. 61 and 66, *R. v Bow Street Magistrate, ex p. Pinochet (No. 3)* [2000] 1 AC 147; *Case Concerning the Arrest Warrant of 11 April 2000 (Democratic Republic of the Congo v. Belgium)* Judgment of 14 February 2002 (2000) ICJ Rep. 11.

[100] Case T-315/01, *Ahmed Ali Yusuf and Al Barakaat International Foundation v. Council and Commission*, Judgment of 21 September 2005, paras. 260–82. Also Case T-315/01, *Yassin Abdullah Kadi v. Council and Commission*, Judgment of 21 September 2005.

Because the sanctions were instituted by the SC and implemented by EC Regulations, the CFI had to incidentally review the enabling SC resolutions. What is interesting in these cases is that the CFI has in fact used the Union's human rights charter, couched in the language of international *jus cogens*; but, as was noted above, the content of *jus cogens* is contested, and certainly not all human rights are included therein. This, far from being a misrepresentation, is another example of internalising an international law concept, of giving it a European content and, again, of dis-applying international law.[101]

This brings us to another point, that of judicial review. Judicial review is primarily a constitutional act performed by judges and it is about the respect of 'a system or its ideals'.[102] Courts can exercise review if they are recognised as legitimate participants in the constitutional dialogue that takes place within the political order.[103] As mentioned above, the international order is essentially disjointed and therefore the ICJ cannot become a legitimate participant in such a dialogue. For one thing, international law-making is controlled by states and thus no dialogue exists between actors other than states. Second, because there are no identifiable constitutional boundaries and benchmarks and no integrated political system, it is difficult for the ICJ to exercise review. For example, the ICJ cannot override the Security Council's findings as to what is a threat to, or breach of, the peace; not only because there are no set criteria, or because the SC's powers are discretionary,[104] or because its jurisprudence is unpredictable, but more importantly because it does not have any express or implicit authority.[105] Even if the ICJ 'rises to the bait', its pronouncements will have no effect on states because SC

---

[101] There is probably a misrepresentation or confusion when the CFI referred to the ICJ's dictum in *Legality of the Threat or Use of Nuclear Weapons* that there are certain 'intransgressible principles'; the ICJ was referring to humanitarian rather than to human rights principles, however. Case T-315/01, *Ahmed Ali Yusuf*, para. 282.

[102] S. A. Scheingold, *The Rule of Law in European Integration* (New Haven: Yale University Press, 1965), p. 6.

[103] L. B. Tremblay, 'The Legitimacy of Judicial Review: The Limits of Dialogue Between Courts and Legislatures' (2005) 3 *ICON* 617.

[104] See Articles 39 and 24(2) of the 1945 Charter of the United Nations.

[105] *Legal Consequences for States of the Continued Presence of South Africa in Namibia*, 45, para. 89; H. Kelsen, *The Law of the United Nations* (London: Stevens, 1951), pp. 294–5; K. Skubiszewski, 'The International Court of Justice and the Security Council', in V. Lowe and M. Fitzmaurice (eds.), *Fifty Years of the International Court of Justice: Essays in Honour of Sir Robert Jennings* (Cambridge: Cambridge University Press, 1996), p. 606. For opposing viewpoints, see Dissenting Opinion of Judge Weeramantry in *Case Concerning Questions of Interpretation and Application of the*

resolutions under Chapter VII are presumptively binding on all states[106] and, furthermore, the ICJ's decisions have no *erga omnes* character. Turning to the EU, although judicial review is functioning[107] and the constitutive documents recognise the remedial power of judicial decisions, the European courts are equally cautious when it comes to reviewing legislative acts, where the institutions enjoy discretionary power, and involve intergovernmental or institutional bargaining.[108] In this respect, it seems that European and international courts ascribe in different degrees to the view that they are not competent to assess the political reasoning behind legislation, or second-guess the volition of those who have a larger stake in law-making.

B. General principles of law and judicial legislation

It is often said that general principles of law fill in the lacunae found in legislation; where no law exists, judges can employ them in order to avoid pronouncing a *non liquet*.[109] However, as we indicated above, principles are open-textured; thus, their application to a particular case

1971 Montreal Convention Arising from the Aerial Incident at Lockerbie (1992), 66, 175; Dissenting Opinion of Judge Fitzmaurice in *Legal Consequences for States of the Continued Presence of South Africa in Namibia*, 294; *Conditions of Admission of a State to Membership in the United Nations (Article 4 of Charter)*, Advisory Opinion of 28 May 1948 (1947–8) ICJ Rep. 64; ICTY, Case No. IT-94-1-AR72, *The Prosecutor v. Dusko Tadic a/k/a 'Dule'*, Decision on the Defence Motion of Interlocutory Appeal on Jurisdiction (2 October 1995), para. 28.

[106] Article 25 of the UN Charter; *Certain Expenses of the United Nations*, 163.

[107] Article 230 EC and Article III-365 TECE; K. Lenaerts and T. Corthaut, 'Judicial Review as a Contribution to the Development of European Constitutionalism' (2003) 22 *Yearbook of European Law* 1; C. Koch, '*Locus Standi* of Private Applicants under the EU Constitution' (2005) 30 *ELR* 511.

[108] Case 78/74, *Deuka, Dutsche Kraftfutter GmbH, B. J. Stolp v. Einfuhr- und Vorratsstelle fur Zucker* [1975] ECR 421 at 432: '... the Commission enjoys a significant freedom of evaluation ... when examining the lawfulness of the exercise of such freedom the courts cannot substitute their own evaluation of the matter for that of the competent authority ...' For exceptions, see Case C-49/88, *Al-Jubail Fertilizer Company (Samad) and Saudi Arabian Fertilizer Company (Safco) v. Council* [1991] ECR I-3187; Case C-364/95, *T. Port GmbH & Co. v. Hauptzollamt Hamburg-Jonas* [1998] ECR I-1023. With regard to international treaties such as the treaty establishing the WTO see Case C-149/96, *Portugal v. Council* [1999] ECR I-8395, paras. 40–6.

[109] D. Anzilotti, *Cours de droit international* (Paris: Recueil Sirey, 1929), I, p. 117; H. Lauterpacht, 'Some Observations on the Prohibiton of "*Non Liquet*" and the Completeness of the Law', in *Symbolae Verzijl* (Leyden, 1958), p. 196; J. Stone, '*Non Liquet* and the Function of Law in the International Community', (1959) 35 *British Yearbook of International Law* (*BYBIL*) 124; M. Bogdan, 'General Principles of Law and

may give rise to paradoxical results. Judge Higgins' reasoning in the *Legality of the Threat or Use of Nuclear Weapons* Advisory Opinion is an eloquent exposition of the dilemmas facing judges. She begins by noting that 'the role of the judge [is] to resolve, in context, and on grounds that should be articulated, why the application of one norm rather than another is to be preferred in the particular case'.[110] In order to answer this question, she resorts to normative principles but privileges only one such principle. As she says, 'the judicial lodestar . . . must be those values that international law seeks to promote and protect. In the present case, it is the physical survival of people that we must constantly have in view'; but she could not give a clear answer as to whether pronouncing the

the Problem of Lacunae in the Law of Nations' (1977) 46 *Nordisk Tidsskrift for International Ret* 37; L. V. Prott, *The Latent Power of Culture*, pp. 77–8 and 88–98; Lauterpacht, *The Development*, pp. 155–72; A. Cassese, 'The Contribution of the International Criminal Tribunal for the Former Yugoslavia to the Ascertainment of General Principles of Law Recognised by the Community of Nations', in S. Yee and W. Tieya (eds.), *International Law in the Post-Cold War World: Essays in Memory of Li Haopei* (London: Routledge, 2001), p. 43; I.F. Dekker and W. G. Werner, 'The Completeness of International Law and Hamlet's Dilemma: *Non Liquet*, the Nuclear Weapons Case, and Legal Theory', in I. F. Dekker and H. H. G. Post (eds.), *On the Foundations and Sources of International Law* (The Hague: T. M. C. Asser Press, 2003), p. 5. *South West Africa (Ethiopia v. South Africa; Liberia v. South Africa)* (1966), 277 (Dissenting Opinion of Judge Tanaka): 'Undoubtedly a court of law declares what is the law, but does not legislate. In reality, however, where the borderline can be drawn is a very delicate and difficult matter. Of course, judges declare the law, but they do not function automatically. We cannot deny the possibility of some degree of creative element in their judicial activities. What is not permitted to judges is to establish law independently of an existing legal system, institution or norm. What is permitted to them is to declare what can be logically inferred from the *raison d'être* of a legal system, legal institution or norm. In the latter case the lacunas in the intent of legislation or parties can be filled.' ICTY, *Prosecutor v Kupreskic*, Judgment, Case No. IT-95-16T 14 January 2000, para. 591, para. 677: 'It is now clear that to fill possible gaps in international customary and treaty law, international and national criminal courts may draw upon general principles of criminal law as they derive from the convergence of the principal systems of the world. Where necessary, the trial Chamber shall use such principles to fill any *lacunae* in the Statute of the International Tribunal and in customary law.' For an opposing viewpoint, see ICJ, *South West Africa (Ethiopia v. South Africa; Liberia v. South Africa)* (1966), 48: 'the Court is not a legislative body. Its duty is to apply the law as it finds it, not to make it.' F. Castberg, 'La méthodologie du droit international public' (1933 I) 43 *RC* 309 at 342–45; Sir Humphrey Waldock, 'General Course on Public International Law' (1962 II) 106 *RC* 1 at 56–7. Joint Cases C-46/93 and C-48/93, *Brasserie du Pêcheur SA v. Federal Republic of Germany* and *R v. Secretary of State for Transport, ex p. Factortame Ltd and others* [1996] ECR I-1029 at 1144, paras. 27–8.

[110] *Legality of the Threat or Use of Nuclear Weapons*, 592, para. 40 (Judge Higgins, Dissenting Opinion).

legality or illegality of the use of nuclear weapons can achieve such objective.[111] From what was said it transpires that, in the absence of rules, general principles can be used, but which particular principle is to be so employed is a matter of 'weight' or 'importance'.[112]

The question that follows is whether the choice should be political or judicial. When the importance of a certain principle has been reaffirmed in the political process, judges tend to prioritise the said principle. For example, the ICJ prioritises the normative principle of peace, even in a decanted form, because that is what the UN Charter and UN politics advocate. As its former President put it, 'the Court as the principal judicial organ of the United Nations has to promote peace, and cannot refrain from moving in that direction'.[113] This was the guiding principle in the *Corfu*[114] and *Nicaragua*[115] cases. In the *Legality of the Threat or Use of Nuclear Weapons* opinion, however, the ICJ was not only faced with a lacuna, but also with a situation where peace as the controlling principle could give rise to conflicting results. It was thus forced to acknowledge that, in the 'current state of international law', there are no conventional or customary rules proscribing the threat or use of nuclear weapons.[116] Instead, the Court deferred to the legislative primacy of the states. It identified a nascent legislative activity[117] and pleaded with states to 'pursue in good faith and bring to a conclusion negotiations leading to nuclear disarmament in all its aspects under strict and effective international control'.[118] Had the ICJ acted as a surrogate legislature, it would have displaced states as the masters of the legislative process. Similarly, in the *South West Africa* case it rejected the argument that *actio popularis* is a principle of international law in the

---

[111] *Ibid.*, 593, para. 41. But see 576–8 (Judge Koroma, Dissenting Opinion), where he criticises the Court for not taking into consideration the principles of state sovereignty enshrined in the UN Charter as well as the principles of human rights, the prohibition of genocide and the protection of the environment. Also 270–2 (Judge Bedjaoui, Declaration).

[112] Dworkin, *Taking Rights Seriously*, p. 26.

[113] *Military and Paramilitary Activities In and Against Nicaragua* (1986), 153 (Judge Singh, Separate Opinion). Also *Arbitral Award of 31 July 1989 (Guinea-Bissau v. Senegal)*, Merits, Judgment of 12 November 1991, (1991) ICJ Rep. 121 (Judges Mawdsley and Ravena, Dissenting Opinions).

[114] *Corfu Channel Case*, 35.

[115] *Military and Paramilitary Activities In and Against Nicaragua* (1986), 107.

[116] *Legality of the Threat or Use of Nuclear Weapons*, para. 74, p. 34. For an opposing viewpoint, see Judge Schwebel, *ibid.*, p. 101.

[117] *Ibid.*, paras. 62, 73.   [118] *Ibid.*, para. 2F.

absence of a clear provision;[119] and, more strongly, in the *Fisheries* case, it said that 'the court, as a court of law, cannot render judgment *sub specie legis ferendae*, or anticipate the law before the legislator has laid it down'.[120] In sum, the ICJ is hesitant to use general principles, particularly when derivative rules do not exist or are not clear. This attitude can be contrasted to that of the ECJ, which pre-empted legislation and acted as a surrogate legislature in those cases where it decided on the direct effect of community legislative acts;[121] or when it found that a treaty provision such as Article 141 (former 119) on equal pay has direct effect, even if it is formulated in vague terms;[122] or when it decided on the direct effect of unimplemented directives; or when it introduced human rights. The ECJ was able to act as surrogate legislature because it can borrow from national orders, legitimate its pronouncements through the Union citizenry, and enforce them through national courts.

That being said, it is maintained that where lacunae exist, the principle of freedom of action precludes judicial legislation.[123] The syllogism is rather simple; what has not been regulated has been deliberately left unregulated. In the *Legality of the Threat or Use of Nuclear Weapons* opinion, Judge Guillaume adopted this principle in order to overcome the legal impasse expressed in the majority opinion. He consequently reached the conclusion that a state can resort to the threat or use of nuclear weapons in extreme

---

[119] As the ICJ said, 'although a right of this kind may be known to certain municipal systems of law, it is not known to international law as it stands at present, nor is the Court able to regard it as imported by the "general principles of law" referred to in Article 38, paragraph 1(c), of its Statute'. *South West Africa* (1966), p. 47; Dissenting Opinion of Judge Jessup, *ibid.*, pp. 387–8; *Northern Cameroons*, 32–6.

[120] *Fisheries Jurisdiction Case (United Kingdom v. Iceland)*, Merits, Judgment of 25 July 1974 (1974) ICJ Rep. 3, at 23–4, para. 53.

[121] *Van Gend*, 12; P. Craig, 'Once Upon a Time in the West: Direct Effect and the Federalisation of EEC Law' (1992) 12 *Oxford Journal of Legal Studies (OJLS)* 453.

[122] Case 43/75, *Defrenne*, 478, paras. 56–65.

[123] This principle was enunciated in the *Lotus* case, where the PCIJ said that 'international law governs relations between independent states' and the 'rules of law binding upon states . . . emanate from their own free will' whereas 'restrictions upon the independence of states cannot therefore be presumed': *The Lotus Case*, p. 18. See also *Interpretation of the Statute of Memel Territory*, PCIJ Series A/B, no. 48, 293 at 314; *Military and Paramilitary Activities In and Against Nicaragua* (1986), 135; Dissenting Opinion of Judge Shahabuddeen in *Legality of the Threat or Use of Nuclear Weapons* 866–8; Kelsen, *Principles of International Law*, p. 305; P. Weil, 'The Court Cannot Conclude Decisively . . . Non Liquet Revisited' (1997) 36 *Columbia J Trans L* 109 at 112–13.

circumstances of self-defence.[124] Freedom of action derives from the principle of sovereignty but, as indicated above, sovereignty is both enabling
and disabling.[125] States may decide to act or to refrain from acting.
Consequently, one may question whether the specific principle, or the
outcome pronounced by Judge Guillaume, is inevitable. In fact, a number
of judges disputed the specific reach of this principle and challenged its
underlying normative context.[126]

Similar arguments have been advanced in relation to the legal gaps found
in EU legislation. Often the ECJ has been criticised for 'adjudicative law
making' when the law is silent.[127] For Hartley, one of the most critical
reviewers, no gaps exist because in the absence of a specific provision, 'the
normal assumption would be that the authors of the Treaty had not
intended the Community to enter into them'.[128] Accordingly, freedom of
action applies to areas left outside specific regulation or in order to
complement gaps found in legislative instruments. Hartley employs the
residual presumption of freedom of state action in order to present a
complete legal system and to curb the power of the Court, because his
underlying hypothesis is that member states have consented to transfer
powers to the Community, and this sets the limits as to what this
Community will become and what the ECJ can claim.[129]

From the above, two consequential and interrelated questions arise; one
factual and the other constitutional. The factual question is whether the
international or European order is a complete order where courts are
presented with fewer opportunities to legislate. Post-state orders are often
incomplete because of their limited scope or weak law-making mechanisms. The international law-making process is dependent on states and the
law is composed mainly of rules established by express or implied consent.
It may then be said with reason that there remain areas or phenomena

---

[124] *Legality of the Threat or Use of Nuclear Weapons*, pp. 291–2 (Dissenting Opinion of
Judge Guillaume).
[125] *Fisheries Case (United Kingdom v. Norway)*, Merits, Judgment of 18 December 1951
(1951) ICJ Rep. 115 at 132; *North Sea Continental Shelf Cases*, 46, para. 83; *Fisheries
Jurisdiction Case* (1974), 59 (Dis. Op. of Judge Dillard); Kelsen, *Principles of
International Law*, pp. 438–40.
[126] Dissenting Opinion of Judge Weeramanty in *Legality of the Threat or Use of Nuclear
Weapons* p. 495 and Declaration of Judge Bedjaoui, *ibid.*, p. 270, para. 10.
[127] H. Rasmussen, *On Law and Policy in the European Court of Justice* (Dordrecht:
Martinus Nijhoff, 1986), pp. 507–12.
[128] T. C. Hartley, *Constitutional Problems of the European Union* (Oxford, Hart, 1999),
p. 45.
[129] *Ibid.*, pp. 43–4.

outside legal control because no agreement has been formed. In contrast, the Union has mechanisms that habitually produce legislation.[130] Consequently, they can address such gaps more easily than is the case in the international. It then follows that there are more opportunities for judicial legislation in the international than the EU.

The second question is constitutional: that is, whether courts can legitimately legislate.[131] This is closely linked to the nature of the referent order and the courts' place therein. The international constitutive process does not exhibit to a sufficient degree the level of integration that would bestow judges with the requisite legitimacy to remove such gaps by legislating. In a polity where state activity in its different guises enjoys legislative primacy, and where strong normative mechanisms to enforce compliance and absorb dissent are lacking, the ICJ cannot overstep its jurisdictional limits and challenge the legitimate expectations of states as law creators.[132] This will definitely have destabilising effects.[133] Thus gaps are addressed by states via legal or non-legal mechanisms and processes.[134] That is why, in the *Legality of the Threat or Use of Nuclear Weapons* Advisory Opinion, the ICJ acknowledged the existence of a legal vacuum, but felt that it should be addressed via

[130] P. J. Slot, 'A Contribution to the Constitutional Debate in the EU in the Light of the *Tobacco* Judgment – What Can be Learned from the USA' (2002) *Electronic Business Law Review (EBLR)* 3, at 16.

[131] 'It is not possible to admit a declaration of *non-liquet* by an international court; denial of justice must be excluded from the international court just as from national courts.' *Procès-Verbaux*, p. 312; A. Alvarez, *Le Droit International Nouveau dans ses Rapports avec la Vie Actuelle des Peuples* (Paris: Pedone, 1959), pp. 592–3; Dissenting Opinion of Judge Alvarez, *Fisheries Case* (1951), 132; Lauterpacht, *The Function of Law*, p. 65; R. Jennings and A. Watts (eds.), *Oppenheim's International Law*, 9th edn. (London: Longman, 1996), vol. 1, pp. 12–13. Joined Cases 7/56, 3/57 and 7/57, *Dineke Algera et al v. Assembly of the European Coal and Steel Community* [1957–58] ECR 39, 55: 'unless the Court is to deny justice, it is therefore obliged to solve the problem by reference to the rules acknowledged by the legislation, the learned writing and the case law of the member States.'

[132] Judge Bedjaoui recognised this when he said that 'the Court indicates that it has reached a point in its reasoning beyond which it cannot proceed without running the risk of adopting a conclusion which would go beyond what seems to it to be legitimate'. *Legality of the Threat or Use of Nuclear Weapons* (1996), p. 272, para. 18.

[133] *Applicability of the Obligation to Arbitrate under Section 21 of the United Nations Headquarters Agreement of 26 June 1947*, Advisory Opinion of 26 April 1988 (1988) ICJ Rep. 12, at 35, para. 57; *The Greco-Bulgarian "Communities"*, Advisory Opinion of 31 July 1930 (1930) PCIJ series B, no. 17, p. 4, at 32.

[134] It is maintained that *non liquet* has not been declared in contentious cases because courts must decide on the basis of submitted legal materials. Weil, 'The Court', at 115–17.

political rather than judicial processes.[135] Similarly, in the *Haya de la Torre* case, the ICJ conceded that 'the silence of the Convention implies that it was intended to leave the adjustment of the consequences of this situation to decisions inspired by considerations of convenience or of simple political expediency'.[136] But even if the ICJ were to use general principles of law, the result would have been unsatisfactory because it would have legislated only for the particular case and parties.[137] A further remark is also in order here. The concept of judicial legislation derives from the theory of legal completeness, which frowns upon the use of non-judicial methods of dispute settlement due to legal gaps.[138] This is equivalent to judicial dereliction of duties and thus courts should construct rules in order to adjudicate. It cannot be seen how this can apply to the international, where judicial settlement of disputes is not the only available method; and, in fact, it is neither compulsory nor exclusive, or even effective. At the international, there are mechanisms to settle disputes or redeem rights which are not judicial but political, whereas judicial mechanisms satisfy only a small portion of dispute settlement.

On the other hand, where a court such as the ECJ has compulsory jurisdiction and operates from within an entrenched normative and structural system, there are more opportunities for legislative judicial 'activism'.[139] Furthermore, the thick normative and structural interconnections between the Union and member states means that their orders can become auxiliary sources of legal norms, as the case of human rights proves.

---

[135] Also in the dispute between Greece and Turkey on the continental shelf in the Aegean Sea, the ICJ directed the parties to resume negotiations over their differences as the SC indicated in resolutions on the matter. *Aegean Sea Continental Shelf Case*, at 12, para. 38.

[136] *Haya de la Torre Case (Colombia v. Peru)*, Merits, Judgment of 13 June 1951 (1951) ICJ Rep. 71 at 81. It continued by saying that 'to infer from this silence that there is an obligation to surrender a person . . . would be to disregard both the role of these extra-legal factors in the development of asylum . . . and the spirit of the Havana Convention itself'.

[137] The ICJ decisions do not create precedent. *Case Concerning Certain German Interests in Polish Upper Silesia (Germany v. Poland)*, Merits, Judgment of 25 May 1926 (1926) PCJI series A, no. 7, p. 19. R. Y. Jennings, 'The Judicial Function and the Rule of Law', in R. Ago (ed.), *International Law at the Time of its Codification; Essays in Honour of Roberto Ago* (Milan: Giuffre, 1987), vol. III, p. 139.

[138] Lauterpacht, 'Some Observations', pp. 205–6 and Lauterpacht, *The Function of Law*, pp. 63–5. For an opposing viewpoint, see Stone, '*Non Liquet*', 150.

[139] T. Tridimas, 'The Court of Justice and Judicial Activism' (1996) 21 *ELR* 199 at 209: 'Judicial activism is a term not easily susceptible to objective determination. Whether a decision is active or not depends on one's standpoint.'

The ECJ can also bypass or transect state competences[140] by appealing directly to the people. As one former judge put it: 'what citizen of Europe had not been assisted in some way by rulings of the ECJ?'[141] Often the political process takes up the mantle and this is proof of the fact that the judges' prognosis was correct.[142] Sometimes the ECJ miscalculates the situation, as happened in the *Kalancke*[143] case on positive discrimination, where the ECJ misjudged state reactions and was forced to retract later in the *Marschall* case.[144] As the ECJ has often said, it needs to take into consideration not only the interests of the parties but also the interests of the Community and of member states.[145] In other cases the ECJ appealed to legislative bodies to fill in the gaps when it has felt that consensus is lacking.[146] In sum, the ECJ can entertain legislative functions – but it is aware of who are the main political and legislative forces.

Constitutional rationale and general principles of law

The two points that emerge from the preceding discussion is that general principles of law supply the normative and structural principles that constitute a particular polity, and that both the international and the EU as post-state orders exhibit constitutional mindsets, albeit in different degrees. However, the question remains as to why states, by embracing different versions of constitutionalism, form polities in post-state spaces. By examining their motives, we can probably understand the rationale behind such constitutional principles and settings.[147]

---

[140] For example, by employing the principles of supremacy and direct effect.

[141] F. Mancini and D. T. Keeling, 'Language, Culture and Politics in the Life of the European Court of Justice' (1995) 1 *Columbia Journal of European Law* (*Col JEL*) 397 at 412. One may refer in this regard to cases of sex discrimination. M. Poiares Maduro, *We, The Court: The European Court of Justice and the European Economic Constitution* (Oxford: Hart, 1998), chs. 1 and 3.

[142] For example, Article 6(2) TEU on human rights; Article I-6 TECE recognises the principle of primacy which has been enunciated by the ECJ. Also Article 230 EC recognises the European Parliament as privileged applicant in a review case following the ECJ's previous decisions. See also Article IV-438 (4) TECE.

[143] Case C-450/93, *Kalanke v. Frei Hansestadt Bremen* [1995] ECR I-3051.

[144] Case C-409/95, *Hellmut Marschall v. Land Nordrhein-Westfalen* [1997] ECR I-6363.

[145] Case 244/80, *Pasquale Foglia v. Mariele Novello (No. 2)* [1981] ECR 3045, para. 19.

[146] Case C-249/96, *Grant v. South West Trains* [1998] ECR I-621, which led to Directive 2000/78 and Directive 2000/43.

[147] J. H. H Weiler, 'Does Europe Need a Constitution? Demos, Telos and the German Maastricht Decision' (1995) 1 *European Law Journal* (*ELJ*) 219 at 220; J. E. Fossum, 'Constitution-making in the European Union', in E. O. Eriksen and J. E. Fossum (eds.),

A basic motive behind the formation of post-state polities can be utility. States represent autonomous and complete constitutional orders that inhabit meta-state spaces where they mutually interact. It is in their interest, then, to set a code of conduct that will make their living together more predictable and secure their well-being. This code may contain rules of behaviour, and rules of communication, and also institutional arrangements; all of which are about creating an environment where material and non-material goods can be safeguarded for the states. This process of organising spaces, of setting rules or debating about welfare, even if modest, initiates a process of constitutionalisation and may set in motion constitutionalism as the conceptual prism behind the process.

We can better understand the role of utility, if we look into polities that have been created by a deliberate act of their members. The European Economic Community (EEC), the EU's precursor, is a good example. The EEC was created in order to procure a number of material and non-material goods for its members, under the banner of peace and prosperity. For this reason, common institutions were established, laws were laid down and a process of constitutionalisation was set in motion. Although the EEC was created by states which are at the same time members of the international, the two polities have different constitutional ethos because states' interpretation of utility or of the public good in general is different in the two arenas which they inhabit and in which they interact.

Even if utility can explain why particular orders embrace versions of constitutionalism, it is a weak and rather erratic rationale if other coalescing facilities do not exist to support deeper identifications. Take, for example, the international where states participate in the constitutional praxis, manage public goods and operate institutions on the basis of a formal notion of sovereignty.[148] As a result, each and every state is a legitimate interlocutor and carrier of demands and benefits because the international constitutional culture views them as formally undifferentiated and interchangeable in position. However, in real terms, states are different; they have their own constitutional ethos which means that they have different needs and demand different things from meta-state spaces. Moreover, they have different understandings

---

Democracy in the European Union: Integration Through Deliberation? (London: Routledge, 2000), p. 111; N. Walker 'Constitutionalism and the Problem of Translation', in J. H. H. Weiler and M. Wind, *European Constitutionalism Beyond the State* (Cambridge: Cambridge University Press, 2003), p. 27.

[148] Tsagourias, 'International Community, Recognition of States, and Political Cloning', pp. 218–20.

of what is their well-being and different perceptions of the good and how to achieve it. In the absence of consensus as to what are the international goods, disagreements about goods and benefits often degenerate into actual conflict. Even when such conflicts are brought before courts, no settlement on the substantive issues can be achieved, because there is no shared view as to what are the underlying principles. If a settlement is achieved, it is only because the dispute has been reduced to technical matters. For example, cases before the ICJ that raised important questions about self-determination, non-intervention or humanitarianism were either dismissed or settled on the basis of a technical rule avoiding the substance of the claim.[149]

Because states are different, they seek to forge associations with other like-minded states in order to satisfy their particular needs. Such associations can ascribe to different degrees of constitutionalism. This is the case with the EU, whose members exhibit strong political, social, economic and ideological cohesion. As a result, utility gradually lost its primacy and the Union acquired normative and organisational coherence that allowed it to identify its welfare and carry itself autonomously and independently of its subjects.[150] In other words, the Union was able to embark on a constitutional journey, develop its indigenous constitution and set the parameters of the constitutional debate. This being so, one may express some reservations as to the role of courts in direct constitution-building, because their intervention may stifle the political debate that shapes the constitution of the referent order.[151] It is my view that the objectives and organisation of any constitutional order should emerge through political praxis, and political debates or conflicts, instead of being 'given' by judges. It is only through debates about the

---

[149] In the *Bosnia Genocide* case (1993), Judge Lauterpacht pleaded with the Court that 'the circumstances call for a high degree of understanding of, and sensitivity to, the situation and must exclude any narrow or overly technical approach to the problems involved'. *Ibid.*, at 408. In the *Oil Platforms* case, the ICJ limited itself to the 1955 Treaty between Iran and the USA and did not venture very much into issues of self-defence or use of force, a decision criticised by Judge Simma in his separate opinion. *Oil Platforms Case* (2003), pp. 327–8, para. 6. Similarly, in the *East Timor* case (1995), the Court dismissed the application because it would have been required to decide on the legality of Indonesia's presence in East Timor.

[150] Walker, 'Postnational Constitutionalism and the Problem of Translation', pp. 45–54.

[151] Some commentators speak of the 'juridification of the policy process': R. Dehousse, *The European Court of Justice: The Politics of Judicial Integration* (Basingstoke: Macmillan, 1998), p. 4, or about the depoliticisation of the political process: *ibid.*, p. 115.

principles and the rationale of what is to be constituted that the end product will become meaningful. Courts may be able to solidify constitutional principles or even identify imperceptible constitutional movements; however, they cannot single-handedly erect and maintain a constitutional edifice. From the preceding discussion, it is evident that the international constitutional debate is not court-driven, whereas the ECJ has been able to play a more pioneering role in constitution-building – although within the confines of constitutional reality in the EU.[152] However, it should be noted that when the constitutional debate in the Union intensified and was mainstreamed, it became political. Participant actors, procedures, agendas and even language are clothed in constitutional verbiage and emit constitutional expectations. This does not mean that courts will cease to perform constitutional tasks. Constitutionalism is not only the particular, but also the whole; and courts position themselves in between the two. The only difference is that when constitutionalism is active, they will be able to play their role on a more sure footing, although still pitting one against the other; but in the final analysis, such conflicts or debates are what constitutionalism is about.

---

[152] L. Bengoetxea, N. MacCormick and E. Soriano, 'Integration and Integrity in the Legal Reasoning of the European Court of Justice', in G. de Búrca and J. H. H. Weiler, *The European Court of Justice* (Oxford: Oxford University Press, 2001), p. 43.

4

Proportionality and discretion in international and European law

JULIAN RIVERS

Introduction

The doctrine of proportionality presents us with a key point of disagreement between the detractors and enhancers of judicial power. For the detractors of judicial power, not least many members of the judiciary themselves, proportionality imposes too intensive a test for the legality of legislative and executive action. In a recent collection of essays on proportionality in European law, Jacobs worries that proportionality might go 'too far' and concludes with a call for flexibility.[1] Lord Hoffmann goes still further in warning of 'metaphysical problems of distinguishing different forms of irrationality which would truly be worthy of mediaeval schoolmen' and calling for a reduction of the structure of judicial review to questions of irrationality and competence.[2]

It is therefore hardly surprising that, as proportionality has been increasingly accepted as a criterion of judicial review, judiciaries have been creating various discretionary devices to soften its apparent impact. One only needs to mention terms such as 'margin of appreciation', 'margin of discretion', 'due deference', 'variable intensity of review', 'sliding scale of review' and so on. This is, of course, a matter of disappointment to the enhancers of judicial power, who had been hoping for better things. Hutchinson, writing on this topic in the context of the European Convention on Human Rights (ECHR), both issues a plea for the Court to decide matters for itself, and states that 'reliance on the margin

---

[1] F. Jacobs, 'Recent Developments in the Principle of Proportionality in European Community Law', in E. Ellis (ed.), *The Principle of Proportionality in the Laws of Europe* (Oxford: Hart, 1999), p. 20.

[2] Lord Hoffmann, 'The Influence of the European Principle of Proportionality upon UK law', in *ibid.*, p. 109.

of appreciation is . . . not coherent jurisprudential principle'.[3] Similarly, Lord Lester QC is critical both of judicial restraint and of sloppiness of reasoning.[4]

Whatever one's position on the balance of power between judiciaries and other state bodies, we should at least attempt to clarify the types of discretion that may arise in the context of proportionality review and identify the factors that affect their scopes. Thus the principal aim of this essay is simply to render the margin of appreciation and other similar doctrines if at all possible 'coherent jurisprudential principle'. One easy solution, which we can reject from the outset, is to see in proportionality a limit to legitimate discretion.[5] It is true that proportionality limits discretion, but that is not the point. What we find in the case law is that discretion is treated as an inevitable component of proportionality review, but that its extent seems to be variable, effectively taking the court from one extreme of correctness-review through to the effective abandonment of the two most intensive parts of proportionality, namely the tests of necessity and balancing. Clearly, discretion is not a marginal phenomenon, but is potentially co-extensive with proportionality.

Indeed, a theory of discretion must be co-extensive with the doctrine of proportionality if the separation of powers is not to collapse. We tend to assume that proportionality functions both as a standard for primary decision-takers and as a standard for courts to review those decisions. If proportionality delivers a 'correct answer' for primary decision-takers, and the same test is being used in judicial review, there can be no discretion. We need to show how proportionality can deliver the right answer (from the perspective of a primary decision-taker), but can also admit of a range of answers (from the perspective of the court). Of course, proportionality may admit of a range of legally acceptable answers, in which case we have to consider whether the discretion primary decision-takers enjoy is exhausted by that range, or whether there are other types of discretion as well implied by the relative roles of courts and other bodies. It will be argued that proportionality both

---

[3] M. Hutchinson, 'The Margin of Appreciation Doctrine in the European Court of Human Rights' (1999) 48 *ICLQ* 638 at 649.

[4] Lord Lester QC, 'Universality Versus Subsidiarity: A Reply' (1998) *European Human Rights Law Review (EHRLR)* 73.

[5] See, e.g., Y. Arai-Takahashi, *The Margin of Appreciation Doctrine and the Principle of Proportionality in the Jurisprudence of the ECHR* (Antwerp: Intersentia, 2002), pp. 14–15: 'it is proposed that the principle of proportionality should be deployed as a device to ascertain whether national authorities have overstepped their margin of appreciation.'

admits of a range of answers and also should be applied judicially in a way which leaves other forms of leeway in place.

Another general question which emerges in the literature on proportionality is whether we need to draw qualitative distinctions between different types of case that arise in the context of judicial review. Is the existence and extent of discretion dependent on the nature of the rights and interests concerned? In the EU context we see this in the suggestion that wide-ranging policy decisions involving multiple interests are qualitatively different from fundamental rights cases.[6] In the ECHR context it has been argued that the European Court ought to draw a clear distinction between cases in which a right is limited in pursuit of a collective good, in which democratically legitimated decision-takers should have a wider discretion, and cases in which a right is limited to protect another Convention right, or an individualisable interest, such as 'the rights and freedoms of others'.[7] It will be argued that qualitative distinctions are not necessary, since the relevant differences in the scope of discretion can be explained by reference to features that are more or less present in every case.

One other cause of confusion concerns the basic nature of judicial review, in whatever context it arises. Strictly speaking, a court is never asked if a decision, rule or policy[8] is proportionate. It is asked to decide whether it is disproportionate. If the action fails, the outcome is always that the legislative or executive action in question is 'not disproportionate'. That might be for a number of reasons: the court might think the primary decision is correct, or one that the decision-taker was entitled to take, or sufficiently plausible, or it might simply not know, and remain unconvinced by the claimant's case. The problem of discretion is the mirror-image of the problem of identifying the set of decisions which courts will find disproportionate. Even when courts defer on some matter to another branch of government, they do so on the grounds that this serves the correctness of the judicial decision. They

---

[6] The distinction between bipolar and multipolar disputes was stated classically by Lon Fuller in 'The Forms and Limits of Adjudication' (1978) 92 *Harvard Law Review* 353. Paul Craig is critical of a similar division in domestic administrative law. See P. Craig, 'Unreasonableness and Proportionality in UK Law', in E. Ellis (ed.) *The Principle of Proportionality*, p. 85, at pp. 101–2.

[7] S. Greer, *The Margin of Appreciation: Interpretation and Discretion under the European Convention on Human Rights* (Council of Europe, 2000), HR Files no. 17.

[8] Hereafter, 'policy' refers to any decision, rule or policy subject to review for proportionality.

could not plausibly rule that a matter was incorrectly decided, but still permitted. Discretion is therefore residual, and in one sense we are only interested in identifying it on account of fears that there might be none, or too little.

The discussion in this essay focuses on the law applied by three bodies: the UN Human Rights Committee (HRC), the European Court of Human Rights (ECtHR) and the Court of Justice of the European Communities (ECJ). Clearly, the latter generally deals with very different types of case than the two former bodies. However, it will be suggested that the structure of proportionality and the problems of discretion which emerge from all three are essentially similar.

The nature and contexts of proportionality

The doctrine of proportionality seems to belong most naturally in the context of fundamental rights. It provides us with a multi-part test by which limitations of those rights for common social purposes or to protect other legitimate interests may be considered legally acceptable. Such limitations must pursue a legitimate aim, the means adopted must be capable of achieving that aim, they must be the least intrusive means (they must be 'necessary'), and there must be a fair and acceptable relationship between the aim pursued and the cost to rights ('balancing' or 'proportionality in the narrow sense').[9] However, there is uncertainty both about the occasions on which proportionality review is appropriate and its basic structure.

The occasions on which proportionality review come into play in the context of the European Convention on Human Rights are not entirely clear. At first glance, proportionality review would seem to be limited to those rights which have 'clawback', 'derogation' or limitation clauses, most obviously Articles 8–11. On one side of those rights there are supposedly illimitable rights such as the right to life, prohibition of torture and degrading and inhuman treatment or punishment, the right not to be subject to slavery or forced labour, and the right not to be subject to *ex post facto* laws. These seem to be a matter of rules with definable terms. On the other side are rights which expressly incorporate a large measure of national discretion, such as the power to define the legal contours of the right to marry or the right to property.

---

[9] Many expositions of proportionality presuppose the test of legitimate aim and only include the second to fourth tests in its definition. This is a purely semantic difference.

However, proportionality tends to spill out sideways: at the point of the question of definition, the social aims of the relevant legislation get thrown into the balance, which turns it into a type of proportionality review.[10] On the other side, the wide-ranging power to define the law of marriage or property may not amount to a denial of the right, and that question of basic denial of rights also requires an analysis, a weighing, of social aims.[11] The idea that each right has a core, in the sense that its very essence may never be infringed, also finds expression in the Article 5 and 6 case law, but the clear tendency is to make its scope dependent on proportionality.[12] So proportionality review has a much wider role than at first sight appears.[13]

The other problem with the ECHR case law is that it is not clear that the standard tests for the limitation of rights ('necessary in a democratic society', 'pressing social need', 'fair balance') map onto the normal proportionality test. There is a tendency on the part of the Court to collapse 'necessity' and 'balancing' into a single test, even if academic commentators tend to disaggregate them.

International Human Rights Law outside the European context is not as developed on account of the later rise of quasi-judicial processing of individual complaints (e.g., under the First Optional Protocol to the International Covenant on Civil and Political Rights).[14] However, the ICCPR contains several articles which raise issues of proportionality, most notably in the limiting clauses to the freedoms of movement; thought conscience and religion; expression; and association.[15] Issues of proportionality easily arise in other contexts as well, for example in fulfilment of the obligation under Article 20(2) to prohibit by law any advocacy of national, racial or religious hatred. The General Comments of the Human Rights Committee provide at times classical statements of

---

[10] See, e.g., the definitions of 'forced labour' in *Van der Mussele v. Belgium* (1983) 6 EHRR 163 and 'degrading and inhuman punishment' in *Kroecher and Moeller v. Switzerland* (1982) 34 DR 24.

[11] *Hamer v. UK* (1979) 24 DR 5; *F v. Switzerland* A.128 (1987) 10 EHRR 411; *Sporrong and Lönnroth v. Sweden* A.52 (1982) 5 EHRR 35.

[12] See, e.g., *Brand v. Netherlands*-49902/99 [2004] ECHR 196 (11 May 2004).

[13] See further J. Rivers, 'Proportionality and Variable Intensity of Review', (2006) 65 *Cambridge Law Journal (CLJ)* 74.

[14] Optional Protocol to the International Covenant on Civil and Political Rights, Adopted and opened for signature, ratification and accession by General Assembly resolution 2200A (XXI) of 16 December 1966, *entry into force* 23 March 1976, in accordance with Article 9.

[15] Articles 12(3), 18(3), 19(3) and 22(2) respectively.

the three components of proportionality (capability, necessity and balancing),[16] and the Siracusa Principles (1985)[17] also suggest this as a common approach to limitation clauses. So this aspect of proportionality is arguably better rooted than under the ECHR.

As far as European law is concerned, the doctrine of proportionality has been received by the European Court of Justice as a general principle derived from the component legal cultures of the EU. Perhaps because of the more obvious influence of German administrative law, the standard threefold test is well established in the case law, although it is interesting that Article 5 EC simply reads: 'Any action by the Community shall not go beyond what is necessary to achieve the objectives of this Treaty.' Clearly, then, the 'folding back'[18] of balancing into necessity is endemic, or at least a risk, in need of both explanation and clarification.[19] Proportionality has a role in situations which involve Community fundamental rights, including the four economic freedoms. But it also has a role in reviewing penalties and policy choices in areas such as the Common Agricultural Policy, albeit with very obviously varying levels of discretion.

Robert Alexy has recently suggested that legal reasoning revolves around two basic intellectual processes: subsumption and balancing.[20] Subsumption is the process of bringing rules to bear on situations, and balancing is the process of weighing two or more competing principles or values against each other to produce a normative outcome (typically a situation-specific rule). Balancing lies at the heart of the doctrine of proportionality, so in this way review for proportionality can be seen as a fundamental type of judicial reasoning activity.

Alexy's twofold analysis of legal reasoning matches his twofold analysis of the nature of law, which depends upon a basic distinction between rules and principles. Unlike Ronald Dworkin, Alexy argues

---

[16] CCPR General Comment No. 10 (1983), para. 8: 'necessity'; CCPR General Comment No. 22, (1992), para. 8: 'proportionate'; CCPR/C/21/Rev 1/Add.9 General Comment No. 27, (1999). para. 27: 'proportionate', 'appropriate', 'least intrusive' and 'proportionate to the interest to be protected'.

[17] 7 HRQ 3. United Nations, Economic and Social Council, Siracusa Principles on the Limitation and Derogation Provisions in the International Covenant on Civil and Political Rights, U.N. Doc. E/CN.4/1985/4, Annex (1985).

[18] P. Craig and G. De Búrca, *EU Law*, 3rd edn (Oxford: Oxford University Press, 2003), p. 372.

[19] The UK Privy Council does it too in *de Freitas v. Permanent Secretary of Ministry of Agriculture, Fisheries, Lands and Housing* [1998] 3 WLR 675.

[20] R. Alexy, 'On Balancing and Subsumption. A Structural Comparison' (2003) 16 *Ratio Juris* 433.

that a principle is an optimisation requirement, which obligates us to achieve as much of the substantive good, or legal interest, protected by the principle as is factually and legally possible.[21] So to say that privacy is a principle is to call for as much privacy as is factually and legally possible. The factual constraints are given by the world and human society as it is. Legal constraints are above all else other principles. If one optimises privacy alone, one destroys freedom of expression (which being a principle one is also seeking to optimise) and so the two have to be balanced against each other and are mutually limited.

The doctrine of proportionality implies and is implied by the nature of legal principles. Imagine some principle, P, which is infringed by state action adopting means, M, to pursue end, E. First, if E is not legitimate at all, P could be optimised in the absence of M. There would be a gain to P and no legally cognisable loss. So there must be a legitimate aim. Secondly, if M is not capable of achieving E, then P could again be optimised in its absence. There would be a gain to P and no loss to E. M is unlawful. Thirdly, if M is not necessary to achieve E, there must be some other means M_2 equally capable of achieving E but less intrusive on P. P can be optimised by adopting M_2 instead. M is unlawful. Finally, if M is not proportionate in the narrow sense it means that the cost to P is not sufficiently compensated for by the gain to E. $P + E$ could be optimised by abandoning M, because the state of affairs before M was adopted in which there was less E, but proportionately more P was better overall.[22]

The virtue of Alexy's account is that on the basis of one simple idea (principles as optimisation requirements) it explains both the tendency of proportionality towards a certain basic structure, and its widespread relevance even outside the scope of fundamental rights with limitation clauses. It also explains why there seems to be a 'spillover effect' by which proportionality comes to be applied in ever wider contexts, such as the definition of basic terms. The question is whether we can build on this analysis to identify the place of discretion within that basic structure.

Three types of discretion

In the Postscript to *A Theory of Constitutional Rights*, Alexy suggests that there are two broad categories of discretion under the doctrine of

---

[21] R. Alexy, *A Theory of Constitutional Rights*, J. Rivers (trans.) (Oxford: Oxford University Press, 2002), pp. 47–8.
[22] *Ibid.*, pp. 66–9.

proportionality.[23] Structural discretion refers to the fact that proportion-ality does not deliver one right answer to any problem involving two or more competing principles. There will be a choice of proportionate, legally acceptable, alternatives. Epistemic discretion arises from the fact that we have to operate under conditions of relative ignorance. It may be permis-sible to act in limitation of rights, even when we are uncertain about the extent to which a legitimate state goal may be achieved. An attempt has been made elsewhere to critique and develop these ideas systematically.[24] For present purposes it suffices to note that the international and European case law seems to give rise to three main forms of discretion, which I will call policy-choice discretion, cultural discretion and empirical discretion. The first is structural, the second and third are epistemic. They are not the only possible sources of discretion in proportionality, but they are the most significant and can shed light on our subject-matter.

A. Policy-choice discretion

Proportionate decisions have to satisfy the tests of legitimate aim, capable or suitable means, least necessary limitation of rights and fair balance, or proportionality in the narrow sense. The first two tests are threshold conditions implicit in the last two tests. They can therefore be ignored for present purposes. Policy-choice discretion can therefore be defined as the range of possible policy options which are both necessary and balanced.

The test of necessity requires that there be no avoidable fundamental rights sacrifices. If a particular end could be equally well achieved by less intrusive means, then the decision-taker is obligated to select those less intrusive means. Two features of necessity are noteworthy. First, it does not rule out any level of achievement of any legitimate end. For example, it works even in the case of a legislature seeking near-perfect protection for national security, simply asking, *given* this level of national security, is privacy restricted to the least extent possible? Thus it still leaves as much discretion as a legislature could reasonably want. It allows every level of achievement of every permissible end. Secondly, it does not require a comparative evaluation of competing principles. We do not need to know how to relate privacy to national security. All we need to be able to

---

[23] *Ibid.*, pp. 388–425.
[24] J. Rivers, 'Proportionality, Discretion and the Second Law of Balancing', in G. Pavlakos (ed.), *Law, Rights and Discourse: Themes from the Legal Philosophy of Robert Alexy* (Oxford: Hart Publishing, 2007). (forthcoming).

do is to rank states of legal regulation according to whether they are more or less restrictive of one value. Undoubtedly, this gives rise to some problems of relative evaluation within one value, and to difficulties of prognosis and empirical evidence about the impact of norms on society. For example, we might need to know of two alternative policy options whether one does achieve as much national security as the other. But that is the only question. A court can carry out an examination of whether a policy was necessary without having to assess the relative weight of different values, which is one of the most problematic parts of the doctrine of proportionality. The necessity test therefore represents the idea of efficiency or Pareto-optimality: there can be no alternative policy which improves the level of rights-enjoyment without imposing extra costs on the level of goal-realisation.[25]

The test of balancing requires a principle to be optimised relative to another principle, which means that costs to one principle must be adequately off-set by gains to the other. This means that balancing also admits of a range of possible options, i.e. those in which the cost to one principle is offset by the gain to another. Alexy argues that the line of acceptable substitutions can be represented by an indifference curve going through a set of states of affairs in which the degree of achievement of one principle is inversely proportional to the degree of achievement of the other.[26] Putting this in a way that matches more closely the language of lawyers: the intensity of interference with one principle must be proportional to the extent of satisfaction of another.

Policy-choice discretion arises when there is more than one potential policy which satisfies both tests. The possibility of this occurring is best understood by way of example. Imagine a policy which seeks to balance the interests of national security with enjoyment of rights such as privacy and freedom of expression by giving moderate scope to both. Assuming the limitation of rights is the least necessary for the specific level of national security sought, the courts are likely to find the policy acceptable. Imagine now that the government is seeking to enhance the level of national security by ever more draconian restrictions on rights. In practice, the additional gains to national security will get progressively smaller with each additional restriction on rights. Human nature being what it is, total national security (whatever that means exactly) is unachievable, even in an Orwellian world in which rights are totally

---

[25] Alexy, *A Theory of Constitutional Rights*, p. 105, n. 222 and pp. 398–9.
[26] *Ibid.*, pp. 100–9.

P_j (e.g. Privacy)

Desirable but Impossible

Necessary/Efficient

idealism

Balanced/Indifferent

Possible but Undesirable

pragmatism

0   P_i (e.g. National Security)

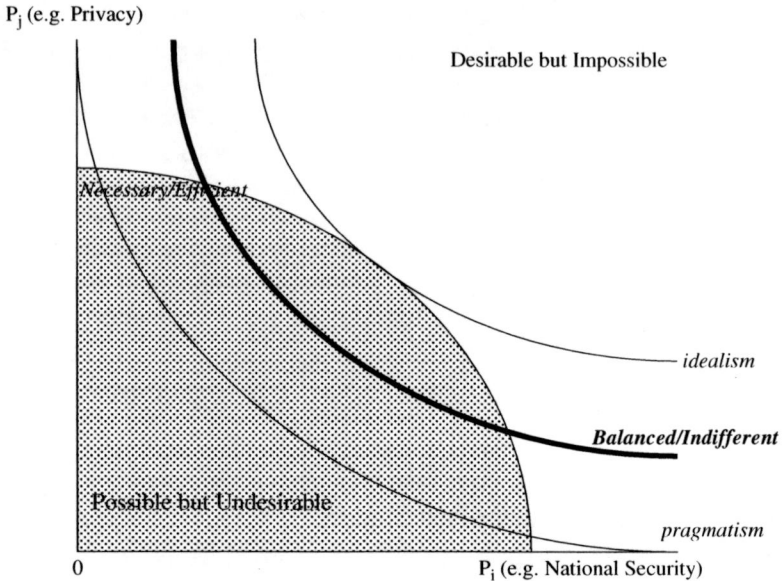

Figure 4.1: Policy-choice discretion

denied. At the same time, from the perspective of balancing, additional limitations on rights require progressively *greater* improvements to national security to justify them. If a right is already substantially limited, further restrictions require a high degree of justification before they can be countenanced. In short, as one enhances the level of national security and reduces the enjoyment of rights, there will come a point at which even the least necessary restriction of rights to achieve a certain (fairly high) level of national security becomes unjustifiable, or disproportionate. Balancing sets limits to the range of necessary policies.

It may help to illustrate this graphically (see Figure 4.1). Necessity can be illustrated by way of a convex efficiency curve; balancing can be illustrated by way of concave indifference curves. Points above the necessity curve are (by definition) impossible to achieve. Thus, where the line of balance extends above the necessity curve, the acceptable balance becomes impossible. The limits to the range of necessary policies are set by the points of intersection of the two curves.[27] This means that

---

[27] One may wonder why there is a limit for high levels of rights-enjoyment and low-levels of goal-realisation. This is only really the case if the legislature is required to optimise both principles. In practice, legislatures are merely permitted to optimise state goals, so there is no limit here.

extreme points on the necessity curve are ruled out by the proportionality test, because although possible, they impinge too intrusively on the principle which is giving way even given the gains that are admittedly being made to the other principle. They are undesirable. Observe that this is precisely the question the court asks itself, whether in spite of necessity, the cost is too great. For example, identity cards may be the least intrusive way of enhancing national security, but the additional small gain may not be worth it given the substantial cost to privacy.

It is important to note that the positioning of the indifference curve in relation to the efficiency curve is in the control of the court. The least necessary limitation of rights to achieve a certain level of some other interest is, ultimately, a question of fact. The range of acceptable trade-offs between rights and interests is not. There are thus three possibilities in the relationship between the two sets of states of legal regulation. On the first possibility, the indifference curve lies wholly above the efficiency curve. This expresses the idea that no possible satisfaction of both principles is normatively acceptable. It is the utopian position that seeks to enjoy every value to the fullest extent. It would strike down every decision as unacceptable and even castigate a failure to act. It is wholly unrealistic.

The second possibility is that the indifference curve lies wholly (or practically wholly) below the efficiency curve. Here every balanced solution is factually possible, but is not actually the best that can be done. We could call it the pragmatic position that asserts that every realisation of every value must be possible, whatever it costs, so long as it costs as little as possible. It removes the test of balancing from the field of useful controls.

The third possibility is that the two curves intersect. Within this there are two sub-possibilities. One is that the intersection takes place at just one point, where the two curves are tangential to each other. This corresponds to the one right answer thesis, namely that there is only one state of legal regulation which is simultaneously the least intrusive means to a given end and which correctly balances (i.e. maximises the product of) the competing principles. The other is that there are two points of intersection, in which case the options open to the decision-taker lie along the line of necessity (which may or may not also be the line of proportionality) between the two points of intersection.

Decision-takers have the discretion to choose from a range of efficient (Pareto-optimal) solutions to situations in which two or more principles compete, so long as such solutions are at least as good as those required by the substitution of values. The range of this discretion is determined by the relative pragmatism/idealism of the court. The set of legally possible policies will be bigger as the court inclines to pragmatism ('do whatever you think necessary'), smaller as it inclines to idealism ('get it right'), ultimately tending to one fixed point somewhere in the middle of both curves. The key question is thus about the role of the court in respect of other state organs. Note, again, that this does not affect the test of necessity; it only affects the limits to the range of necessary policies set by the requirements of balance.

By definition, the scope of policy-choice discretion cannot vary with the degree to which a right is limited. Its function is to set the permissible range of policies from low cost low gain to high cost high gain. However, it could vary according to the abstract importance of the right. For example, one might admit a smaller range of policies in respect of limitations of the right to life, while admitting a much wider range in respect of property rights.

B. Cultural discretion

Clearly, one of the major difficulties in comparing levels of satisfaction of one principle with levels of satisfaction of another principle is in assigning values according to some comparable scale. One dimension of this problem is the idea of abstract value. The seriousness of a breach of rights is a function both of the specific extent to which enjoyment is limited and the general importance of the right. We could assume that every single principle has the same abstract value. This would mean that they are all equally important, and that the most serious breaches of each principle are as serious as each other. In fact, we do not think that at all. On the contrary, there is reasonable agreement that certain values are more important than others. Life is more important than liberty, liberty than property, national security than economic prosperity. These relative abstract evaluations are not to be understood in the sense of a hierarchical ranking, or lexical priority. We do not accept that no cost to life can ever be justified by any gain to liberty, or even any gain to economic prosperity, however great. In talking of a hierarchy of values, we are simply saying that the most serious breaches of the right to life are more serious than the most serious breaches of the right to liberty and so on.

This divergence of relative abstract values has no impact on the test of necessity, which as we have seen does not compare two or more values. But it does have an impact on the test of balancing, and the indifference curve which represents normatively substitutable states of affairs. If life is worth more than liberty in the abstract, more serious breaches of liberty will be balanced by less serious breaches of life. The points of intersection between the necessity curve and the balancing curve will have shifted, such that we are less likely to say of gains to life at cost of liberty that 'it isn't worth it' and more likely to say this of gains to liberty at the cost of life.

Now the problem is, that we disagree amongst ourselves about relative abstract values. At risk of crude cultural stereotyping, the United States relatively values freedom of expression more highly than privacy, European countries the reverse. North European countries tend to value individual liberties more highly, Southern European countries common social or cultural goods.

We can assume that cultural discretion has no role in a single political community. Equality before the law requires like cases to be treated alike, and this implies a single scheme of legal values. But an international court might well want to respect that diversity by granting a cultural discretion. Note that this ought to have no impact on the question of necessity; what it will impact is the outer limits of necessity, in which one finds that even though the limitation of one principle was as unrestrictive as possible given the policy aim in view, it was too costly.

How much cultural discretion should an international court permit to a domestic system? In form this question is very similar to that of policy-choice discretion, since the court is asking what range of necessary rights-limitations it will also accept as balanced. This time though, instead of the court being faced with a range of positions from pragmatism to idealism, it is faced with a range from relativism to absolutism. A relativist court could argue that there is no right answer to the relative abstract values of principles, since objectively speaking, the values are incommensurable. Virtually any scheme of values is plausible, so long as it does not deny the minimum basis implicit in human rights instruments that the values represented there must count for something. An absolutist international court will not permit any cultural variation to the scheme of abstract values it adopts. Cultural discretion pushes the outer limits back in exactly the same way as a more pragmatic court will push those outer limits back.

Cultural discretion is invariable, in the sense that by definition it cannot rationally vary from case to case. The relative abstract weight of interests cannot be affected by the extent to which an interest is affected in any given situation. If an international court is going to admit a certain cultural discretion, the range of that discretion should be uniform and will emerge over time in its case law.

C. Evidential discretion

So far we have assumed that the value to be assigned to each side of the proportionality equation is a function of the extent of the cost or gain to the principles in question along with their abstract values. The problem is that in real life costs and gains are not always certain, so we need to factor empirical certainty into our equation as well. In fact we need to account for two dimensions of empirical certainty. First, there is the probability of any given outcome happening. Secondly, there is the reliability of our factual judgments. In practice the two are closely related.

The idea of probability is easy to build into proportionality. States are not permitted to engage in major limitations of rights unless the social gain is also major, *and certain to be major*. A small chance of a major gain is not enough to outweigh the certainty of a major cost. So we multiply the value of a gain to a social good by the chance of its realisation. In theory, this rapidly gets very complex, because we ought to take account of the different probabilities of the set of all possible scenarios. In practice, however, the problem of evidential uncertainty is reduced in various ways.

It is reduced, first, by the fact that there is usually no evidential uncertainty on the side of the infringement of an individual's right. Either an infringement has occurred (hence giving rise to the action in the first place), or, if the abstract question is asked about the compatibility of a law with fundamental rights, the court assumes that what is commanded or prohibited to the detriment of the individual, will actually happen or not happen as the case may be. So if the legislature abridges a liberty, it is no answer for the state to point out that the law will not be obeyed or fully enforced. There is an estoppel-type argument based on the Rule of Law at work here. The state is not allowed to plead that what ought to happen legally will not happen in practice. So empirical uncertainty does not usually affect the question of the cost to the right-holder.

It follows that evidential problems will play no part in a clash of rights. If an individual is given a new private law cause of action (e.g. a right under a tort of privacy) we can assume that they will do what they are permitted to do, and that individual liberties will be constrained as a result. In such circumstances we consider states of legal regulation rather than states of affairs.

What evidential problems do affect is the evaluation of the gain to be had by limiting the right. Here, we are in the realm of the social reality of law and prognosis of policy impact. If the legislature abridges freedom of expression for purposes of national security, we need to know what contribution the prohibition will in practice make to enhancing national security. Here, a general failure to obey or enforce the law is highly relevant as reducing the supposed gain to the common good. And it is at just this point that the court will feel a lack of expertise compared with national legislatures and executive bodies. By the same token, pure policy decisions which require a reconciliation of several different interests, such as we find in the Common Agricultural Policy, for example, are going to be bedevilled by evidential problems.

It is the lack of judicial expertise in empirical matters that gives rise to questions of reliability. Clearly, the primary decision-taking body will have made some assessment of the probability of the gains really being brought about by its favoured policy. It will have taken the view (if it is acting rationally) that the value of the gains factored by the chance and extent of their occurrence is sufficient to outweigh the cost to the rights affected by the policy. But how reliable are these judgments?

If there is only a minor limitation of rights, all that is needed to justify it is a minor gain, or the chance of a major gain. Either of these is inherently probable, so the court need not be excessively sceptical about claims that they are present. However, as the seriousness of the limitation of rights increases, so the inherent probability of sufficient outweighing gains decreases, and so the decision-taker has to work harder to persuade the court that the policy was justified. All the court has to do is to say that it is not yet persuaded that the legislative evaluation of the gain made or cost avoided is sufficiently reliable.

A good example of this can be found in *Palau-Martinez v. France*.[28] A French court had denied custody of a child to a mother on the grounds of her faith as a Jehovah's Witness, more precisely on the basis of general statements about what Jehovah's Witnesses do. The European Court of Human Rights held that France had not shown sufficient likelihood of impact on the children to justify the custody decision; speculative harm did not outweigh what was certainly a serious limitation of her rights under Article 14 taken together with Article 8.

We could envisage a system of court-appointed experts to answer disputed questions of fact, but in practice the resources are not available. We can go further: it is not institutionally appropriate for courts to do what is the primary function of expert executive bodies. What the court must be able to do, though, is form a view of the reliability of the processes adopted by other state organs in order to address empirical uncertainty. Judges have

---

[28] *Case of Palau-Martinez v. France*-64927/01 (2005) 41 EHRR 9.

to be able to test whether claims of expertise are made out. The deference that the court shows to primary decision-takers is thus not intrinsic and uniform, but it is a willingness to believe the decision-taker's assessment of the likelihood of gains, a willingness which should reduce with the seriousness of the limitation of the right in question and increase with the demonstration that the decision-taker adopted processes more likely to reach right answers to the relevant empirical questions.

D. Discretion and 'right answers' in proportionality

Recognition of these three main types of discretion within proportionality shows how it is possible for proportionality to function both as a structure for working towards a right answer on the part of primary decision-takers, such as legislatures and executive bodies, and also as a standard of judicial review which admits of a range of legally permissible answers. In respect of policy-choice discretion there is nothing to stop a primary decision-taker being idealistic and looking for the optimum answer – i.e. the solution which both limits relevant interests to the least possible extent and maximises their product. Courts, however, admit a range of necessary policies so long as the play-off of values is acceptable. In respect of cultural discretion, any political community will consider its hierarchy of abstract values correct (or, perhaps, correct for itself). An international court could be more sceptical and accept a range of permissible hierarchies. In respect of evidential discretion, a primary decision-taker should strive to get its facts right; a court, by contrast, will consider whether the factual prognosis is sufficiently plausible. This implies that a range of possible factual judgments will be unchallengeable.

Discretion in international and European law

We now need to consider the extent to which these three types of discretion help clarify discussions of proportionality in international and European law.

A. The Human Rights Committee

The early case of *Hertzberg v. Finland*[29] established two types of discretion in the application of proportionality by the Human Rights Committee.

---

[29] *Hertzberg v. Finland* Communication No. 61/79 2 April 1982 CCPR/C/15/D/61/1979.

The case concerned a ban on radio and TV broadcasts of discussions about homosexuality. In paras. 10.2–10.4 of its judgment, the HRC stated that it needed to assess the 'necessity' of the ban and considered whether it ought to have called for the transcripts of the proposed broadcasts. However, it rejected this option and considered that the necessity was satisfied in the light of (a) a margin of discretion accorded to the Finnish authorities in weighing freedom of expression against the protection of public morals and (b) the view of the Finnish Broadcasting Company (FBC) that live media were not appropriate forums for discussion of this issue. The former is a clear instance of cultural discretion granting the state some leeway in balancing the demands of free expression and common values in the sphere of sexual ethics. The latter consideration is slightly obscure, but seems to mean that the FBC were in a better position to judge the impact of live media broadcasts than were the HRC. In other words, it is an example of evidential discretion.

Hertzberg is still unique in its appeal to the doctrine. The margin of appreciation in the sense of a cultural discretion was rejected in the context of Article 27 (minority rights) in *Länsman v. Finland*.[30] It has also been doubted more generally whether has a place under the jurisprudence of the ICCPR.[31] The reasoning for doubting its application is curious: 'it is unwise to apply such a doctrine under the ICCPR, where a common practice would rarely be discerned among the very different States Parties to this universal treaty.' This makes two mistakes. First, it assumes that the equivalent European doctrine applies whenever there is variation in fact between different legal regimes, whereas it is more accurate to say in reverse that a margin of appreciation is unlikely to be accepted where there is a common practice. Common practice is evidence of a pan-European scale of values which renders cultural discretion redundant. Secondly, if cultural disagreement about the proper balance of competing principles is a ground for restraint on the part of international judicial bodies at European level, *a fortiori* there is a ground for restraint at a global level. Opposition to the margin of appreciation at international level seems to be a call for absolutism as regards the hierarchy of values.

---

[30] *Länsman et al. v. Finland (No. 1)*, Communication No. 511/1992, HRC 1995 Report, Annex XI, para. 9.4.

[31] S. Joseph, J. Schultz and M. Castan, *The International Covenant on Civil and Political Rights*, 2nd edn (Oxford: Oxford University Press, 2004), para. 18.24.

By contrast, evidential discretion is regularly appealed to by state parties, whenever it is alleged that they are in a better position to judge the level of the threat addressed by the state action under challenge. In general, it seems that the HRC is more likely to find that the state simply got it right, by accepting that state action was indeed necessary and proportionate, than by drawing attention to the relative expertise of the domestic state and pointing out that the international court is not in a position to judge otherwise. However, the rather fuller discussion of limitations on free expression rights in *Ross v. Canada* displays a clear sense by the Committee that the Supreme Court of Canada had approached the problem correctly and therefore deserved respect for its own judgment.[32] The Committee relied on factual findings concerning the impact of the writings in question made by lower courts, thus obviously assuming them to be sufficiently reliable.

B. European Court of Human Rights

The key doctrine by which discretion is incorporated into proportionality judgments under the ECHR is, of course, the margin of appreciation. Arai-Takahashi has recently produced a substantial analysis of the margin of appreciation case law.[33] As has already been noted, his approach is not unproblematic, since he sees proportionality as a limit to state discretion (which of course it is), rather than a formal structure which admits of discretion in its implementation (which is the real problem). Like Mahoney, he finds the best rationale for the margin of appreciation in an ongoing European value-pluralism rooted in national democracy.[34] He cites with approval the connection the Court made in *Chassagnou v. France*[35] between the fair balance of individual rights with the general interests of society on the one hand, and the proper functioning of democracy on the other, a connection which the Court described as a 'constant search'.[36] This clearly points to an understanding of the margin of appreciation as cultural discretion. Where this balancing between individual and collective interests is taking place, the question is not about the level of cost to the individual or the level

---

[32] *Malcolm Ross v. Canada* Communication No. 736/1997 U.N. Doc. CCPR/C/70/D/736/ 1997 (2000), at paras. 11.4–11.6.

[33] Arai-Takahashi, *The Margin of Appreciation*.

[34] *Ibid.*, p. 249; P. Mahoney, 'Marvellous Richness of Diversity or Insidious Cultural Relativism?' (1998) 19 *HRLJ* 1.

[35] *Chassagnou v. France* (1991) 29 EHRR 615.   [36] *Ibid.*, para. 113.

of social benefit; rather it is about how much that cost and benefit are worth, i.e. what the abstract value of the relevant legal interests are. Governments are going to argue along the lines that legislation under challenge reflects legitimate social choices about relative abstract values.

As we have already seen, cultural discretion has no place in a consideration of necessity. Either a measure is the least intrusive means of achieving a given end, or it is not. And whatever one might think of the cultural interpretation of the margin of appreciation, that is not where it has come from historically. In the early cases, when it first emerged, it is doing something quite different. *Lawless*, for example, was about the status of the UK government's determination that a state of emergency existed for the purposes of Article 15.[37] *Handyside* is about the impact of an obscene publication on the morals of young people.[38] These are complex empirical questions within the primary competence of the state. The very origin of *marge d'appréciation* in French administrative law points to this as evidential discretion. There is more expertise lower down the system, which the Court quite appropriately respects.

The judgment in the euthanasia case of *Pretty v. United Kingdom* is a good example of the margin of appreciation functioning as empirical discretion.[39] Paragraph 74 shows quite clearly that the margin of appreciation means that the states have the principal function of assessing risk and likely abuse if exceptions were to be created to a general prohibition on assisting suicide. The Court then goes on to find that the UK position is a view the state is entitled to take – i.e. it is not obviously wrong. Of particular significance in this is the possibility of flexibility in prosecution and sentencing for assisted suicide/euthanasia.

The Court also recognises that the scope of the discretion varies with the importance of the right in question. It does not think that preventing people from assisting others to commit suicide is a serious breach of rights, so the evidential leeway granted to the state is not narrow. Presumably, if the infringement of the right had been serious, the state would have had to show more to defend its refusal to create formal exceptions. The weakness here, as McBride has pointed out generally, is the lack of a clear sense of what evidence is necessary to allow the Court to assess rationally whether the policy is wrong. The approach of the Court seems to range from requiring 'expert advice', through 'general

---

[37] *Lawless v. Ireland* (1960) 1 EHRR 1.   [38] *Handyside* (1976) 1 EHRR 737.
[39] *Pretty v. United Kingdom* 2346/02 [2002] ECHR 427 (29 April 2002).

knowledge' to 'mere prejudice', and one cannot avoid the impression that it is rather uncontrolled.[40]

Apart from the presence of cultural and empirical discretion in the margin of appreciation, one can also note the impact of the abstract importance of rights on the scope of the margin of appreciation, this time understood as policy-choice discretion. By way of example, we can compare the Court's approach to the review of limitations of rights of property in which it has shown a 'markedly reticent policy',[41] with normal levels in the case of privacy and equality, and with 'heightened scrutiny'[42] in the case of Article 5. From a purely textual perspective, one ought to note also that Article 15 derogations must be 'strictly necessary' and deprivations of life under Article 2 'absolutely necessary'.[43] These too indicate a narrower range of possible circumstances in which measures are balanced, although one should not pretend that the approach of the Court is consistent with these textual indicators.

Thus the margin of appreciation functions as a general doctrine of discretion in the implementation of proportionality review, and its apparent incoherence can be explained in good measure by the way in which it conflates different types of discretion.

C. European Court of Justice

In her 1993 review of proportionality and discretion before the ECJ, de Búrca identifies two tensions which pull the Court in opposing directions.[44] On the one hand, deference is indicated by a consideration of the relative expertise, position and overall competence of the Court. On the other hand, 'the more important the particular right or the particular community interest affected, and the greater the adverse or restrictive impact upon it, the more closely the Court of Justice is likely to search for the existence of less restrictive alternatives'. This is fully in line with what a theoretical consideration of evidential discretion would lead us to expect.

One interesting development she highlights can be seen as the gradual abandonment of cultural discretion by the Court. In *R v. Henn and*

---

[40] J. McBride, 'Proportionality and the European Convention on Human Rights', in Ellis (ed.), *The Principle of Proportionality*, p. 23.

[41] Arai-Takahashi, *The Margin of Appreciation*, p. 152.   [42] *Ibid.*, p. 32.

[43] See *McCann v. United Kingdom* (1995) 21 EHRR 97, para. 149.

[44] G. de Búrca, 'The Principle of Proportionality and its Application in EC Law' (1993) 13 *Yearbook of European Law (YEL)* 105.

Derby,[45] which concerned restrictions on free movement of goods for public policy reasons, the Court stated that the question of limitation of free movement was 'for each member State to determine in accordance with its own scale of values', and a similar attitude can be found in *Van Duyn v. Home Office*.[46] But in later parallel cases such as *Conegate*[47] and *Adoui and Cornuaille*,[48] the Court has abandoned this for a stricter, uniform, scrutiny. This makes sense to the extent that the Court wants to conceive of the European Union (EU) as single political community, committed to a particular scheme of values. It also has implications for our understanding of the role of national courts when cases return after an Article 234 reference. If the ECJ simply reiterates the requirement of proportionality (as, for example, in the Sunday Trading case[49]), the purpose of national implementation is not value-diversity within the EU, but, presumably, evidential superiority. By the same token, the ECJ ought to be identifying the typical trade-offs that are acceptable as paradigm examples of a pan-European scheme of values.

Clearly, there are cases in which the court says it is engaging in proportionality review, but in which it does little more than check that the policy under review has taken account of relevant interests, and not been based on irrelevant factors. For example, in the *NIFPO* case,[50] reviewing a quota allocation under the common fisheries policy, the Court simply recalled the fact that the Council was allowed to take account of the need to ensure relative stability of fishing activities and the particular needs of regions dependent on fishing and related activities.[51] Its discretion extended beyond the nature and scope of measures to the finding of basic facts.[52] Unless the claimants could show 'manifest error or misuse of power' or that the decision was 'arbitrary or manifestly inappropriate',[53] it could not be considered disproportionate. There is nothing suspicious about this. The large range of relevant interests, the extent to which they are affected, and their relative value are all so legitimately debateable that it is practically very difficult to show that the decision is wrong, and hence disproportionate.

---

[45] Case 34/79, *R v. Henn and Derby* [1979] ECR 3795.
[46] Case 41/74, *Van Duyn v. Home Office* [1974] ECR 1337.
[47] Case 121/85, *Conegate v. Customs & Excise Commissioners* [1986] ECR 1007.
[48] Cases 115 & 116/81, *Adoui and Cornuaille v. Belgium* [1982] ECR 1665.
[49] Case 145/88, *Torfaen BC v B&Q plc* [1989] ECR 3851 at para. 17.
[50] Case C-4/96, *Northern Ireland Fish Producers' Organization Ltd v. Department of Agriculture for Northern Ireland* [1998] ECR 681.
[51] *Ibid.*, para. 46.   [52] *Ibid.*, para. 42.   [53] *Ibid.*, para. 62.

We should contrast this with the type of case in which there is a clear and quantifiable breach of a Community right on the one hand and a set of diverse, unpredictable impacts on the other. Here the court goes to great lengths to structure the proportionality review. The most recent case involving Dutch restrictions on foodstuffs fortified with added vitamins and minerals demonstrates this well.[54] The absence of harmonising law, and the potential for excessive and dangerous consumption of vitamins justifies a domestic scheme of prohibition and specific authorisation. However, restrictions must be proportionate. On the one hand, a total ban is 'the most restrictive obstacle to trade', but on the other hand, the Community policy on protecting human health aims at a 'high level of protection', and so a precautionary approach is legitimate. We might say that the protection of human health has a high abstract value, so a lack of certainty about the extent to which health is endangered is not automatically fatal to the ban. However, within human health, we can distinguish more serious 'harmful effects' from less weighty 'nutritional needs'. Absence of less weighty nutritional needs for a foodstuff could not on their own justify a total ban.[55]

Because the complete ban is serious, the evidential requirements on the Dutch government are high. A chance of harm is not enough. There must be a real risk of seriously harmful effects, based on the latest scientific data. There need not be certainty (there cannot be) but the harms must be specifically identified, in relation to each additive, in the light of other foodstuffs on the market and the possibility of substitution of the new fortified foodstuffs for other previously fortified foods. What we find here is a serious limitation of a Community right in the light of evidential uncertainty giving rise to an obligation on the State to put in place a carefully structured expert system. Since the Dutch government had assumed that anything above the recommended daily allowance was toxicologically risky, they had not done enough to satisfy the Court that the ban was not disproportionate.

However, it is still too early to tell whether Community case law on fundamental rights will accept the existence of discretion in considering the proportionality of limitations. The case law is too sparse, and much of the academic commentary depends on the contrast between

---

[54] Case C-41/02, *Commission of the European Communities v. Kingdom of the Netherlands* [2004] ECR I-11375.
[55] *Ibid.*, para. 69.

fundamental rights cases and 'policy' cases.[56] The debate about discretion has in this way been diverted by the existence of Community level review of complex, multi-polar, decisions.

Conclusion: towards a coherent jurisprudence of discretion

The first conclusion from this brief review is the obvious one. Courts should be taking more pains to distinguish the type of discretion that is at play. Particularly in the case of the margin of appreciation, which conflates all three types of discretion identified here, it would be helpful to distinguish policy-choice discretion, cultural discretion and empirical discretion.

Policy-choice discretion is a power of choice on the part of the primary decision-taker (legislature or executive) between two or more policy options, all of which are necessary and balanced. The court sets the limits to this by setting the points at which 'necessary' policies become 'unbalanced'. Its scope depends on the relative pragmatism or idealism of the court. This in turn depends on whether the court sees itself as merely a backstop for other state organs or as a substitute for failures in the state system. Some of the lack of clarity in the international and European context may well arise from a tension between the sense that the position of the court should be the same vis-à-vis every state, but that the political need for review may vary from state to state.

Cultural discretion is the right of each political community within limits to set its own scheme of abstract values of different political goods. It is essential if supranational legal systems are not to turn into monolithic schemes of value. The question is, how much diversity is compatible with a commitment to universal rights? The answer, I suggest, is actually quite a lot, since cultural diversity cannot affect the question of necessity, only the balancing of two or more principles. There would still be value in a human rights scheme which did away entirely with the test of balancing. Indeed, the test of necessity is much more easily defensible from a rational perspective than the test of balancing. This might explain the endemic tendency to collapse balancing into necessity: it enables the Court to portray itself as neutral between competing schemes of value. But the logic of the judicial protection of rights is that not every necessary limitation is acceptable; there are costs that individuals should

---

[56] See, for example, P. Craig, 'Judicial Review, Intensity and Deference in EU Law', in D. Dyzenhaus (ed.), *The Unity of Public Law* (Portland, Oregon: Hart, 2004), p. 335.

not be expected to bear for the general welfare. Balancing still has a role to play at the international level and there are still limits to the range of necessary policies states may adopt.

Evidential discretion is the power of judgment implicit in the state's right to assess the current and probable social impact of its policies. It has a particular relevance to the question of necessity. It reduces as the right affected gets more seriously limited; it increases as processes are adopted which hold out the hope of more accurately identifying social impact. The sense articulated in the literature, that certain types of case permit of more discretion, reflects situations in which empirical judgments are harder to make and require more expertise. As far as appropriate processes are concerned there would seem to be few international norms, except perhaps for an emerging consensus around the need for democratic involvement in the limitation of fundamental rights. The ECJ is far more advanced in this respect than other European and international courts.

It follows that we do not need to distinguish different categories of case to understand discretion in proportionality. Conflating the formal distinction between a true clash of rights, such as between freedom of expression and the positive obligation on the state to protect privacy, on the one hand, and the power of the state to limit a right to protect another legitimate interest on the other, will be relatively uncontroversial. In practice, the distinction is not significant, because complainants have not been able to make much progress in founding actions on breaches of positive state duties.[57]

The question is whether 'common good' cases are distinguishable from 'clash of rights' cases. Certainly in terms of policy-choice and cultural discretion, the answer is not obvious. There would seem to be a range of proportionate solutions to clashes between privacy and liberty rights just as there is a range of proportionate solutions to clashes between privacy and national security interests. Likewise, the cultural commitment to a certain scheme of values affects both the individual versus the collective, as it does the relative importance of individual interests in liberty, privacy, property and equality. One can make the

---

[57] For example, the shift in the religious hate speech case law from *Gay News* (*Gay News Ltd and Lemon v. United Kingdom* (1982) 5 EHRR 123 to *Otto-Preminger* (1994) 19 EHRR 34 and *Wingrove* (1996) 4 EHRR 1, in which the right not to be insulted moves from Article 10(2) to Article 9(1), does not seem to have had much of an impact on the substantive decisions.

case that the courts should be more pragmatic when reviewing legislative solutions in the individual-collective conflict, and more idealistic when dealing with individual-individual conflicts. Traditionally, at any rate in the common law context, the job of the legislature is to be the gatekeeper to collective limitations on rights, and only sporadically intervene in the private and criminal law of relations between individuals. But the arguments cut both ways. Surely a legislature is less likely to 'get it right' when seeking to uphold collective interests than when adjusting the balance between individual interests. It is precisely in the former case that the courts need to protect the individual and in the latter in which the courts can accept the legislature as the mouthpiece of a new social consensus around a rebalancing of interests. So it is far from clear that the scope of policy-choice discretion should be different on this account.

Where we do find differences is in the role of evidential discretion. As we have seen, considerations of rights and potential breaches of rights assume that what ought to be, actually is. So when a legislature criminalises religious hate speech it has actually limited freedom of expression. The positive duty to protect from hate speech is a duty to ensure adequate processes are in place, not a duty to ensure that hate speech never happens. There is not much scope here for questions of prognosis. By contrast, public good limitations do depend to a considerable extent on falsifiable empirical presumptions, so there is likely to be greater scope for evidential discretion here. This is even more apparent in multipolar policy-choice cases, where decision-takers are seeking to fulfil a mandate to enhance the material wellbeing of a series of diverse actors. It would seem that our intuitive sense, that review is more intensive in one case rather than another, can be adequately accounted for by evidential uncertainty and problems of institutional expertise, which are more or less present in every case. We should not be classifying according to substantive differences in the type of case.

Finally, one should note the relationship between this account of proportionality and subsidiarity. Subsidiarity is the name given to the set of reasons for allocating decision-taking capacity lower down the legal hierarchy. Those reasons may be as varied as the reasons for recognising discretion within the implementation of proportionality. They could be based on legitimacy in choosing between policy options, respect for cultural difference or evidential superiority. The countervailing formal principle is that the court should decide all questions of law. The structure of discretion in proportionality is given by the tension between these two formal principles.

PART II

Transnational constitutional interface

5

Hierarchy in organisations: regional bodies and the United Nations

NIGEL D. WHITE

Introduction

Since the inception of the United Nations, there has been a considerable tension between universalism and regionalism, especially in the field of collective security. Debates at the San Francisco conference of 1945 that led to the adoption of the UN Charter showed that even close allies, the United States of America and the United Kingdom, disagreed on the level of autonomy for regional organisations within the new institutional and normative universal framework.[1] Subsequently, debates about the hierarchy between the two levels of international organisations[2] have tended to focus on three key provisions of the UN Charter. At the insistence of regional organisations,[3] Article 51 preserves the right of individual and collective self-defence, until the Security Council has taken the necessary measures to restore peace and security.[4] Such autonomy in regional defensive matters is balanced by the apparent lack of autonomy in offensive action, in that Article 53 of the UN Charter requires that enforcement action by regional

---

[1] R. B. Russell and J. M. Muther, *A History of the United Nations Charter* (Washington: Brookings, 1958), pp. 96, 105; S. C. Schlesinger, *Act of Creation: The Founding of the United Nations* (Boulder: Westview, 2003), pp. 175–92.

[2] It is not the purpose here to debate issues of hierarchy within organisations (for example, between the executive and plenary bodies), though this is an important matter. For discussion of the different functions of organs within organisations, see P. Sands and P. Klein, *Bowett's Law of International Institutions*, 5th edn (London: Sweet and Maxwell, 2001), pp. 263–441.

[3] E. Berberg, 'Regional Organizations: A United Nations Problem' (1955) 49 *AJIL* 166 at 169.

[4] Article 51 provides in part: 'Nothing in the present Charter shall impair the inherent right of individual or collective self-defence if an armed attack occurs against a Member of the United Nations, until the Security Council has taken measures necessary to maintain international peace and security.'

bodies has to be authorised by the UN Security Council.[5] In practice, a great deal of debate has surrounded the interpretation of Article 53, concerning, for instance, issues of implicit authorisation, acquiescence amounting to authorisation, and retrospective authorisation,[6] as well as the meaning of enforcement action. Further debate focuses on Article 103 of the UN Charter, which provides that obligations of member states under the UN Charter prevail over obligations arising under any other treaties (implicitly including treaties establishing regional organisations).[7]

Whilst not dismissing the importance of such issues, this chapter will look more deeply at the relationship between the UN and regional bodies, to try to discern the underpinnings as well as the existence of any hierarchy. Hierarchies cannot readily be assumed in international relations. In an international system which is still state-dominated and horizontally constructed, there must be legitimate reasons for hierarchy between bodies set up by states. Hierarchies are antithetical to the Westphalian paradigm of sovereign, equal, nation states, recognising no superior. Even in the post-1945 era of the growth of international organisations there must be a presumption against hierarchies. As Dominicé has stated:

> The various organizations, both universal and regional, are created by autonomous international treaties, independently of each other. There only exists a legal link of subordination – in a true 'vertical' dimension – where there is a specific treaty provision to that effect, but otherwise the distinction universal-regional has merely a geographical meaning indicating that the universal organization is dealing with the whole world, whereas the regional one has merely a geographically limited field of

---

[5] Article 53(1) provides in part: 'The Security Council shall, where appropriate, utilize such regional arrangements or agencies for enforcement action under its authority. But no enforcement action shall be taken under regional arrangements or by regional agencies without the authorization of the Security Council.'

[6] See most recently U. Villani, 'The Security Council's Authorization of Enforcement Action by Regional Organizations' (2006) 6 *Max Planck UNYB* 535; E. de Wet, 'The Relationship between the Security Council and Regional Organizations during Enforcement Action under Chapter VII of the United Nations Charter' (2002) 71 *Nordic Journal of International Law* 1; C. Walter, 'Security Council Control over Regional Action' (1997) 1 *Max Planck UNYB* 129.

[7] Article 103 of the UN Charter provides that: 'In the event of a conflict between the obligations of the Members of the United Nations under the present Charter and their obligations under any other international agreement, their obligations under the present Charter shall prevail.' See R. Bernhardt, 'Article 103', in B. Simma (ed.), *The Charter of the United Nations: A Commentary*, 2nd edn (Oxford: Oxford University Press, 2002), pp. 1292–302.

action. Both are, in international law, on the same footing as autonomous entities without territorial sovereignty.[8]

Nevertheless, in two key 'constitutional' provisions, Articles 53 and 103, the founders of the UN Charter, the representatives of the international community at the time, not only created an international organisation, they provided limited legal structuring both to the relationship between the UN and regional bodies, and to the UN and its member states. The focus here will be on the nature of the relationship between the UN and regional organisations, though of necessity the relationship between organisations and their member states will also be considered.

Regionalism

It is necessary briefly to define regional organisations for the purpose of the following analysis, and to distinguish them from universal organisations. Schermers and Blokker include regional organisations within a somewhat wider category of 'closed' organisations which 'seek only membership from a closed group of states and no members from outside the group will be admitted'.[9] Of course, there may be some debate about whether an applicant country is within the group or not, as with the case of Turkey and Russia in relation to the European Union, but the contrast with universal organisations, which are normally open to all states,[10] is clear. It would seem that attempts at further refinement of the concept of a regional organisation are fraught with difficulty. To define regionalism in terms of geographical proximity is immediately appealing but in practice very difficult to judge as the endless debates about where Europe ends in a geographical sense illustrate only too well. Furthermore, 'the criterion of common cultural, linguistic, or historical relations'[11] is also imprecise and likely to cause as many disputes as it solves.[12]

[8] C. Dominicé, 'Co-ordination Between Universal and Regional Organizations', in N. M. Blokker and H. G. Schermers (eds.), *Proliferation of International Organizations: Legal Issues* (The Hague: Kluwer, 2001), p. 67.

[9] H. G. Schermers and N. M. Blokker, *International Institutional Law*, 4th edn (Leiden: Martinus Nijhoff, 2003), p. 42.

[10] See, for example, Article 4 of the UN Charter.

[11] W. Hummer and M. Schweitzer, 'Article 52', in Simma (ed.), *The Charter*, p. 821.

[12] For further discussion, see P. Taylor, *International Organizations in the Modern World* (London: Pinter, 1993), p. 7; A. Abass, *Regional Organizations in the Development of Collective Security* (Oxford: Hart, 2004), pp. 1–26; E. D. Mansfield and H. V. Milner, 'The New Wave of Regionalism', in P. F. Diehl (ed.), *The Politics of Global Governance* (Boulder: Lynne Rienner, 2001), pp. 314–16; M. P. Karns and K. A. Mingst, *International*

In reality, regional organisations are non-universal groupings of states that are essentially self-defining,[13] but generally have as their object the protection or achievement of certain values, such as peace and security or economic prosperity among their membership. The principal ones discussed in this chapter often share similar goals and values to those of the UN, ranging across peace and security, human rights and justice, to economic and social well-being, but on a regional level. Thus the potential for overlap between the functions and activities of the UN and regional organisations is considerable.

It is clear that the African Union (AU), the Organization of American States (OAS), the League of Arab States, the European Union (EU), and the Association of South East Nations (ASEAN) are leading examples of regional organisations. It is also clear that organisations such as the Economic Community of West African States (ECOWAS) and the Mercado Común Del Sur (MERCOSUR) in South America are also within the broad concept of regionalism, as sub-regional bodies. There are other organisations that should be included within the concept of regionalism, such as the Organization for Security and Co-operation in Europe (OSCE), though its membership is not confined to European states.[14] However, the North Atlantic Treaty Organization (NATO) has 'claimed for long not to be a regional organization but a collective self-defence organization based upon Article 51 of the UN Charter, in order to avoid the application of Chapter VIII'.[15] It will be argued, however, that when NATO steps beyond the confines of self-defence, it cannot be anything other than a regional organisation for 'functional purposes'.[16]

The EU is certainly a regional body in the economic sense, having a well-developed level of integration between members of the European Community. It is also developing competence with regard to foreign and security policy.[17] Unlike the established regional organisations of the Americas and Africa, which are often concerned with controlling their

---

Organizations: The Politics and Processes of Global Governance (Boulder: Lynne Rienner, 2004), pp. 145–53.

[13] See, for instance, Article 1 of the OAS Charter, which provides that the Organization is a regional one within the meaning of the UN Charter.

[14] See the 'Budapest Document of the OSCE' (1994) 15 *HRLJ* 459–62, when the Conference on Security and Cooperation in Europe (CSCE), established since the Helsinki Final Act of 1975, was declared to be the OSCE. The CSCE had already declared in 1992 that it was a regional arrangement in the sense of Chapter VIII of the UN Charter.

[15] Dominicé, 'Co-ordination', p. 69.   [16] *Ibid.*, p. 70.

[17] See R. A. Wessel, 'The State of Affairs in EU Security and Defence Policy: The Breakthrough in the Treaty of Nice' (2003) 8 *JCSL* 265.

membership, the EU's security policy is principally external to its membership, relating to threats to, or breaches of, the peace within or by states that are not members of the EU. This, though, does not disqualify it as a regional organisation. The relatively harmonious state of European affairs means that its main concern in security matters is external, though one should not underestimate the propensity of the continent towards violence, as history shows. The election of an extreme right-wing government in Austria in 2000 and the reaction of the EU to that event,[18] as well as the threat from terrorism (as illustrated by the Madrid bombings of 11 March 2004 and London of 7 July 2005), show that European security is as much an internal issue as an external one.

NATO in its inception in 1949 was an externally driven defensive alliance reflected in Article 5 of its treaty,[19] which in turn is based on Article 51 of the UN Charter. In its original form NATO seems to lack some of the features of a regional organisation in that its sole concern was external threats to its members, it was weak institutionally, and it had an ill-defined 'region' to defend.[20] However, with the end of the Cold War NATO has become a regional body in its practice and its recent policy statements though it has not expressly declared itself to be such.[21] In particular, its willingness to take offensive actions either under UN mandate,[22] or on its own authority,[23] to deal with a widening concept of security has led to it having overlapping competence with the

---

[18] M. Happold, 'Fourteen Against One: The EU Member States' Response to Freedom Party Participation in the Austrian Government' (2000) 49 *ICLQ* 953.

[19] Article 5 provides in part: 'The parties agree that an armed attack against one or more of them in Europe or North America shall be considered an attack against them all; all consequently agree that, if such an armed attack occurs, each of them, in the exercise of the right of individual or collective self-defence recognized by article 51 of the Charter of the United Nations, will assist the party or parties so attacked by taking forthwith, individually, and in concert with the other parties, such action as it deems necessary, including the use of armed force, to restore and maintain the security of the North Atlantic area . . .'

[20] For early discussion, see H. Kelsen, 'Is the North Atlantic Treaty a Regional Arrangement?'(1951) 45 *AJIL* 162; A. L. Goodhart, 'The North Atlantic Treaty of 1949' (1951) 88 *Hague Recueil* 187; E. W. Beckett, *The North Atlantic Treaty, the Brussels Treaty and the Charter of the United Nations* (London: Stevens, 1950).

[21] See *The Alliance's Strategic Concept*, NATO doc. NAC-s(99) 65, 24 April 1999, paras. 29, 41 and 48, in which NATO claimed to be able to take, in effect, 'Non-Article 5' enforcement actions.

[22] See, for example, UN Doc. S/Res/770 (1992) re Bosnia.

[23] There was no authority given by the Security Council for NATO's bombing of the FRY in the Kosovo crisis of 1999 – see UN Doc. S/Res/1199 (1999); UN Doc. S/Res/1203 (1999).

UN, as well as the EU and the OSCE. In relation to the UN this potentially brings it into conflict with the hierarchy provisions of the Charter much to the annoyance of those NATO politicians who boldly declare that NATO enforcement action is not subject to a veto in the UN Security Council.[24] Article 53's core means precisely the opposite.

Hierarchy

The term 'hierarchy' is being used in this chapter in a general sense. The nature of the hierarchical relationship is illustrated in subsequent discussion. Terms such as 'primacy', 'complementarity', and indeed 'subsidiarity', are not deployed here though they are found in the literature to describe the UN's relationship with other institutions.[25] Practice may follow different forms of hierarchy or may not be based on hierarchy but on cooperation as equals. Further, such practice may (have) become normative.[26] Nevertheless, the formal legal relationships laid down in the Charter in Articles 53 and 103 have to be addressed and they appear to be ones of constitutional hierarchy, in the sense of supremacy. As Bernhardt identifies, Article 103 means that 'the Charter has a higher rank and that obligations derived from the Charter shall prevail', being part of the Charter's aspiration to 'be the "constitution" of the international community accepted by the great majority of States'.[27] Ress and Brohmer state that under Article 53 a 'regional organization functions as a subsidiary organ of the UN'.[28]

The distinctive features of the hierarchy provisions in the UN Charter must also be borne in mind. While Article 53 is referring to enforcement action within a collective security context, and places the power in the hands of the executive body, Article 103 refers more widely to any inconsistent obligations under international agreements. In considering

---

[24] See N. D. White, 'The Legality of Bombing in the Name of Humanity' (2000) 5 *JCSL* 27 at 36.

[25] See, for example, D. O'Brien, 'The Search for Subsidiarity: The UN, African Regional Organizations and Humanitarian Action', (2000) 7(3) *International Peacekeeping* 57; see UN Doc. A/Res/49/57 (1994): 'the efforts made by regional arrangements or agencies in their respective fields of competence, in cooperation with the United Nations can usefully *complement* the work of the Organization in the maintenance of international peace and security.'

[26] See generally, N. D. White, *The UN System: Toward International Justice* (Boulder: Lynne Rienner, 2002), pp. 38–44.

[27] Bernhardt, 'Article 103', in Simma (ed.), *The Charter*, p. 1295.

[28] G. Ress and J. Brohmer, 'Article 53', in Simma (ed.), *The Charter*, p. 860.

Article 103, Bernhardt thinks that the character of the Charter as 'the basic document or "constitution" of the international community' signifies that this superiority extends beyond treaty obligations,[29] though this is not clear in practice. Furthermore, there is no clear institutional arbiter of this provision, though the Security Council is relying increasingly on its effect to drive through its anti-terrorist legislation, first against Libya in 1992,[30] and then more widely after the terrorist attacks against the United States of 11 September 2001.[31]

The deliberate use by the Security Council of the combined effect of Article 25 (which provides that Council decisions are binding),[32] and Article 103 of the UN Charter to override or supplement existing treaty obligations was certainly not fully realised in earlier commentaries on the Charter. In these, Article 103 was seen as being merely 'designed to exclude the possibility of a Member State being impeded in carrying out its obligations or enforcing its rights under the Charter by conflicting obligations which it may have accepted under other international agreements'.[33] Nevertheless, the intent was not to confine the effects of Article 103 to the 'primary' obligations of the Charter. The drafters certainly seem to envisage the effects of Article 103 applying to the 'secondary' obligations imposed by the Security Council under Articles 25 and 41 in the case of sanctions regimes,[34] where member states must accept the obligations imposed by the UN Charter and the Security Council over conflicting obligations in trade agreements for instance. Goodrich, Hambro and Simons assert that this overriding effect applies to all binding decisions of the Security Council.[35] Earlier commentaries on the Charter agree, however, that Article 103 only came into play in particular cases of conflict 'between the two categories of obligation',

---

[29] Bernhardt, 'Article 103', in Simma (ed.), *The Charter*, p. 1299.

[30] UN Doc. S/Res/748 (1992). [31] UN Doc. S/Res/1373 (2001).

[32] Article 25 provides that: 'The Members of the United Nations agree to accept and carry out the decisions of the Security Council in accordance with the present Charter.'

[33] N. Bentwich and A. Martin, *A Commentary on the Charter of the United Nations* (London: Routledge & Kegan Paul, 1950), p. 179.

[34] Article 41 of the 1945 United Nations Conference on International Organisation (UNCIO), Vol. XIII 707, provides that: 'The Security Council may decide what measures not involving the use of armed force are to be deployed to give effect to its decisions, and it may call upon the Members of the United Nations to apply such measures. These may include complete or partial interruption of economic relations and of rail, sea, air, postal, telegraphic, radio and other means of communication, and the severance of diplomatic relations.'

[35] L. M. Goodrich, E. Hambro and P. Simons, *Charter of the United Nations*, 3rd edn (New York: Columbia University Press, 1969), p. 616.

in contrast to the much wider provision in the League's Covenant that purported to automatically abrogate obligations inconsistent with those arising from the constituent treaty.[36]

The 'primary' obligations imposed on states under the UN Charter, and thus those that prevail over other treaty (and arguably customary) obligations are in reality quite limited. The primary obligations are contained in Article 2: the duties of good faith, the peaceful settlement of disputes, not to threaten or use force, and to assist the UN. Other significant ones include the pledge in Article 56 of the Charter to promote higher standards of living, conditions of economic and social progress and development; solutions to international economic, social, and health problems; cooperation on cultural and educational matters; and respect for and observance of human rights and fundamental freedoms. The normative content of these obligations in the field of economic, social and human rights matters has been developed by significant UN constitutional laws since the Universal Declaration of Human Rights in 1948.[37] In addition, as has been seen, there are also important 'secondary' obligations arising out of Security Council resolutions binding under the UN Charter by virtue of Article 25.

Thus, in practice, the hierarchy provisions of the UN Charter are being moulded by the Security Council. This is explicitly provided for in Article 53 regarding regional bodies and enforcement action, while the combination of Articles 25 and 103 has in practice given the Security Council crude supranational powers over member states.[38] There is some debate to be had about whether these supranational powers relate only to enforcement as befits an executive body, or whether the Council has legitimately extended them to acquire more of a legislative competence.[39] In its executive function of restoring peace and security, the Security Council has temporary and specific powers, but in its more

---

[36] *Ibid.*, p. 615; Bentwich and Martin, *A Commentary on the Charter*, p. 180. See Article 20 of the 1919 Covenant of the League of Nations, para. 1 of which provided that 'members of the League severally agree that this Covenant is accepted as abrogating all obligations and understandings *inter se* which are inconsistent with the terms thereof, and solemnly undertake that they will not hereafter enter into any engagements inconsistent with the terms thereof'.

[37] UN Doc. A/Res/217 A (III) (1948).

[38] Crude in the sense of not having all the features of supranationality such as direct effect: see Schermers and Blokker, *International Institutional Law*, pp. 46–8.

[39] For discussion, see M. Happold, 'Security Council Resolution 1373 and the Constitution of the United Nations' (2003) 16 *LJIL* 593; S. Talmon, 'The Security Council as World Legislature' (2005) 99 *AJIL* 175.

controversial legislative capacity, its decisions appear to have permanency although they still relate to peace and security issues.[40]

However, there are vast areas of regional organisational activity that remain unaffected by the hierarchy provisions of the UN Charter. In these areas, it is largely a question of practical cooperation between different organisations rather than issues of legal competences. In these activities the regulatory legal framework for regional organisations, beyond their own constitutional laws, is international law. As subjects of the international legal order, regional organisations are bound by its rules. Of course, not every international organisation has international legal personality, but bearing in mind that such personality can be implied[41] as well as expressly granted,[42] it is presumptively the case that those organisations having separate organs, permanency, lawful purposes and a distinction between the rights of member states and the powers of the organisation on the international plane, have international legal personality.[43] This signifies that they not only have rights on the international plane but are also subject to duties arising from customary international law, and from any treaties to which they are a party.[44] Arguably also, the UN as promulgator of the major treaties on human rights, for instance, is bound by such treaties in a constitutional law sense, even though it is not formally a party to them.[45] On the whole, therefore, we can safely say that the UN, and those regional organisations having international legal personality, are bound by the fundamental rules of international law.

---

[40] In contrast, the EU's, or rather EC's, primacy in decision-making, which is general and permanent: see generally ECJ Case 26/62, *Van Gend & Loos v. Nederlandse Administratie der Belstingen* [1963] ECR 1.

[41] See the opinion of the International Court of Justice in *Reparation for Injuries Suffered in the Service of the United Nations*, Advisory Opinion, Judgment of 11 April 1949 (1949) ICJ Rep. 174 at 178.

[42] See, for example, 2002 Treaty establishing the European Community, Article 281.

[43] I. Brownlie, *Principles of Public International Law*, 6th edn (Oxford: Oxford University Press, 2003), p. 649. See further, C. F. Amerasinghe, *Principles of the Institutional Law of International Organizations* (Cambridge: Cambridge University Press, 1996), p. 83; R. Higgins, *Problems and Process: International Law and How We Use It* (Oxford: Clarendon Press, 1994), p. 47; R. A. Wessel, 'Revisiting the Legal Status of the EU' (2000) 5 *European Foreign Affairs Review* 507 at 517.

[44] Amerasinghe, *Principles*, p. 78.

[45] N. D. White and D. Klaasen, 'An Emerging Legal Regime?', in N. D. White and D. Klaasen (eds.), *The UN, Human Rights and Post-conflict Situations* (Manchester: Manchester University Press, 2005), p. 7.

However, we have seen that the constitutional hierarchy provisions of the UN Charter (Articles 53 and 103), formally cover, or have been applied by the Security Council to cover, security matters. Thus in economic matters – issues of social policy – regional organisations have considerable autonomy. Of course, their decisions may be subject to rules of international law governing human rights, for instance, but they cannot be blocked by the Security Council, or directed by the General Assembly or the Specialized Agencies, except perhaps in a 'soft' law sense.[46] Indeed in most areas, regional organisations are subject to the same international norms as the UN, and both types of organisations contribute to the creation of international law by their practice and by treaty making. In some areas of international law, regional organisations have become more developed, as is still the case with the European system of human rights law, and is clearly the case with European economic law.

In fact, in most areas outside of collective security matters, and subject to the still relatively rare application of Article 103, the relationship between the UN system and regional systems is not one of institutional hierarchy. Both the UN and regional institutions are subject to international law, as international legal persons. Member states of these organisations cannot create entities, whether universal or regional, that somehow evade the obligations binding on their founding members.[47] There are increasing issues of conflict of norms emerging from regional entities such as the EU, and universal organisations such as the UN Security Council and the World Trade Organization (WTO), with those of international law.[48] Such legal regimes (EU law, UN Law, WTO law) cannot evade fundamental obligations under human rights law, for

---

[46] On 'soft law-making' by international organisations, see F. Van Hoof, *Rethinking the Sources of International Law* (The Hague: Kluwer, 1983), pp. 187–9; P. Szasz, 'General Law-Making Process', in O. Schachter and C. C. Joyner (eds.), *United Nations Legal Order* (Cambridge: Cambridge University Press, 1995), p. 46; D. Shelton, 'International Law and Relative Normativity', in M. Evans (ed.), *International Law* (Oxford: Oxford University Press, 2003), pp. 166–70; C. M. Chinkin, 'The Challenge of Soft Law: Development and Change in International Law' (1998) 38 *ICLQ* 850; H. Hillgenberg, 'A Fresh Look at Soft Law' (1999) 10 *EJIL* 499; P. Weil, 'Towards Relative Normativity in International Law' (1983) 77 *AJIL* 423.

[47] See European Court of Human Rights decision in *Matthews v. UK* (1999) 28 EHRR 316, para. 32.

[48] See, for example, J. Pauwelyn, *Conflict of Norms in Public International Law: How WTO Law Relates to Other Rules of International Law* (Cambridge: Cambridge University Press, 2003).

instance, so that sanctions regimes applied by the UN Security Council, or trade regimes upheld by the WTO's Dispute Settlement Body, or anti-terrorist measures produced by the European Council, must all be compatible with basic human rights provisions found in the international and regional human rights treaties.[49] Furthermore, the relationships between regional organisations and universal organisations on trade matters, for example between the EU and the WTO, are dependent on the agreement of the regional organisation to respect the rules produced by the WTO, and furthermore, an agreement to implement those rules within the region.[50]

It is not proposed in this chapter to look in detail at the whole range of activities undertaken by regional organisations, but to consider the issues where there are disputes about hierarchy under the formal provisions of the UN Charter, regarding both non-forcible and forcible measures taken in a security context. These disputes show that there is a complex interplay between the formal provisions of the UN Charter and rules of international law to which all organisations with international legal personality are bound.

Non-forcible measures

As has been stated, regional organisations have a great deal of autonomy in economic matters internal to their regions and membership. International laws are sometimes kept at bay for policy reasons,[51] but there is an acceptance that they are applicable. However, when regional organisations start to flex their economic muscles problems arise, particularly when they may be trying to coerce non-member states into changing their behaviour.

---

[49] For decisions of the European Court of First Instance on issues of the incorporation of Security Council resolutions into the European legal order and their compatibility with fundamental human rights, see Case T-306/01, *Yusuf and Al Barakaat International Foundation v. Council and Commission*, 21 September 2005; Case T-315/01, *Kadi v. Council and Commission*, 21 September 2005. See also the European Court of Human Rights decision in *Bosphorus Hava Yollari Turizm v. Ireland* (2006) 42 EHRR 1; discussed in C. Costello, 'The *Bosphorus* Ruling of the European Court of Human Rights: Fundamental Rights and Blurred Boundaries in Europe' (2006) 6 *HRLR* 87.

[50] For discussion of the application of WTO law within the EC, see G. de Búrca and J. Scott (eds.), *The EU and the WTO: Legal and Constitutional Issues* (Oxford: Hart, 2001).

[51] S. Peers, 'Fundamental Rights or Political Whim? WTO Law and the European Court of Justice', in de Búrca and Scott (eds.), *The EU and the WTO*, p. 111 at p. 130.

It may be argued that in some of these instances of external action regional organisations are simply pooling the existing international legal rights of member states to take collective non-forcible countermeasures to combat breaches of obligations owed *erga omnes*. Normally, under international law non-forcible countermeasures are taken bilaterally, by a state that has been the victim of a violation of international law against the state in breach. They are temporary measures aimed at seeking to restore normal relations between the parties. Essentially, what would otherwise be a temporary breach of international law by the victim state is permitted as a proportionate response to the initial breach by the responsible state.[52] However, if the violation constitutes a breach of a fundamental norm, for example aggression or genocide, then it has been argued that all states have a right to take countermeasures against the state in breach.[53] If those countermeasures do not go beyond the accepted limitations upon that doctrine, then, although they are enforcing *international* community obligations, international law arguably recognises the right of *regional* organisations to do so. It is a controversial right, however.[54] While the International Law Commission (ILC) recognised the existence of *erga omnes* obligations in its 2001 Articles on State Responsibility, it was silent on how to enforce them.[55] In addition, a great deal of regional practice is not so clear. In a number of instances it goes beyond the limited doctrine of countermeasure and in reality constitutes sanctions. While countermeasures are aimed at encouraging the restoration of a legal relationship sanctions have more punitive and coercive aims.[56]

If regional organisations are exercising sanctioning powers beyond the application of collective countermeasures then they appear to be

---

[52] D. Alland, 'Countermeasures of General Interest' (2002) 13 *EJIL* 1221 at 1221.

[53] J. Crawford, *The International Law Commission's Articles on State Responsibility* (Cambridge: Cambridge University Press, 2002), p. 283.

[54] See Alland, 'Countermeasures'; P. Klein, 'Responsibility for Serious Breaches of Obligations Deriving From Peremptory Norms of International Law and United Nations Law' (2002) 13 *EJIL* 1241; E. Zoller, *Peacetime Unilateral Remedies: An Analysis of Countermeasures* (Dobbs Ferry, NY: Transnational, 1984), pp. 104–5; A. Cassese, *International Law*, 2nd edn (Oxford: Oxford University Press, 2005), p. 275.

[55] Articles 41 and 54 of the ILC's Draft Articles on Responsibility of States for Internationally Wrongful Acts (2001). See Crawford, *The International Law Commission's Articles*, p. 302.

[56] N. D. White and A. Abass, 'Countermeasures and Sanctions', in Evans (ed.), *International Law*, p. 505; Zoller, *Peacetime Unilateral Remedies*, p. 106; G. Abi-Saab, 'The Concept of Sanction in International Law', in V. Gowlland-Debbas (ed.), *United Nations Sanctions and International Law* (The Hague: Kluwer, 2001), p. 32.

claiming to have greater rights than the combined rights of the member states.[57] It could be argued that when they are exercising the power to impose economic sanctions *inter partes*, within the regional membership, then the members of the regional organisations have consented to this. But upon what basis can such organisations exercise these sanctioning powers externally, for instance in the case of the EU sanctions against Burma in 2000 and Zimbabwe in 2002, both taken without any Security Council authority?[58] From where does a regional organisation claim to get its power of global governance when imposing sanctions against third states outside its region?

In general terms, the enforcement of international law is not by any means wholly centralised in international institutions, but at the same time self-help by states has been severely restricted since 1945. The lacuna in the enforcement of fundamental rules that this process has left has arguably been filled by states taking collective countermeasures, and by regional organisations, along with the UN, when it is able to act, enforcing international law. Following this line of argument, in principle when fundamental rules of international law are being breached, regional communities of states should be able to take global action. On this basis non-forcible sanctioning power, not clearly belonging to individual states, can be claimed by a regional actor for the enforcement of fundamental rules.

Again, the argument is controversial, since the enforcement of international law by the taking of non-forcible coercive measures has been much reduced for the state, as shown by the narrow doctrine of countermeasures codified by the ILC in 2001. If this is the case, why should it be less restrictive for the regional actor? The answer must be because of the greater legitimacy that action by a regional grouping of states brings. This must then depend upon the level of constitutional development in the relevant regional organisation, for the more checks and balances and

---

[57] But see F. L. Morrison, 'The Role of Regional Organizations in the Enforcement of International Law', in J. Delbrück (ed.), *The Allocation of Law Enforcement Authority in the International System* (Berlin: Duncker and Humblot, 1995), p. 39 at pp. 46–7, where he states that organisations cannot have more powers than member states.

[58] For Burma, see Council Regulation No. 1081/2000, 22 May 2000 (OJ L 122, 24 May 2000) – covering equipment for suppression, freezing of funds of persons related to important government functions – due to human rights violations. For Zimbabwe, see Regulation 310/2002, 18 February 2002 (OJ L 050, 21 February 2002) – relating to the freezing of funds and assets of members of government and ban on export of suppression equipment, due to human rights violations. See also Regulation 313/2003 (OJ L 046, 20 February 2003).

the greater the democratic development, the more legitimate the decision, and the less likely that a regional hegemon will dominate the decision.[59]

There is certainly practice by regional organisations that suggests economic sanctions do not require the authorisation of the Security Council under Article 53,[60] but it is only the EU's practice in this matter that has been consistently external, starting in the 1980s with its measures taken against Argentina for its invasion and occupation of the Falklands.[61] The EU's ability to undertake external non-forcible enforcement action is not argued to be a unique competence, but is a product of its more advanced constitutional development, and its concern with developing an external foreign policy (which is also an issue of advanced regional development). Other organisations possessing those features may have the confidence to act externally, and have their actions accepted by the international community.

Regional organisations such as the EU are claiming external competence over international matters, competence that states do not have. Or, to put it more subtly, when the EU engages in economic coercion, it is not subject to so much criticism as when individual states engage in such activity. The UN's position on economic measures undertaken by regional bodies is equivocal – from San Francisco to the debates in the 1960s about sanctions imposed by the OAS, it has never been clear that Article 53 covers non-forcible measures, requiring the authorisation of the Security Council. It is, of course, possible that the UN (Security Council or General Assembly) could censure sanctions that it felt go beyond the Charter or the principle of non-intervention,[62] just as it has done for individual states, for example in relation to the US embargo of Cuba.[63] Many of the internal (Haiti – OAS) and external (Iraq, Federal Republic of Yugoslavia – EU) regional sanctions

---

[59] For criticisms of regional organisations in this regard, see S. N. MacFarlane and T. G. Weiss, 'Regional Organizations and Regional Security' (1992) 2 *Security Studies* 16 at 29–34.

[60] Comments by R. Wolfrum in Delbrück, *Allocation*, p. 91.

[61] Council Regulation 877/82, 16 April 1982 (OJ L 102/1, 16 April 1982).

[62] 'The principle of non-intervention is part of customary international law and founded upon the concept of respect for the territorial sovereignty of states. Intervention is prohibited where it bears upon matters which each state is permitted to decide freely by virtue of the principle of state sovereignty ... Intervention becomes wrongful when it uses methods of coercion in regard to such choices, which must be free ones.' M. N. Shaw, *International Law*, 5th edn (Cambridge: Cambridge University Press, 2003), p. 1039.

[63] See, for example, UN Doc. A/Res/56/9 (2001).

regimes imposed in the 1990s[64] have actually complemented to a large degree the UN's own measures, even though they may have technically preceded them. This signifies that the precise nature of the relationship between the UN and regional organisations on non-forcible measures has not been fully developed.

The situation seems to be that there is a presumption in favour of regional organisations possessing a power to impose economic sanctions against members and in certain circumstances (where fundamental rules are being breached) against third states. While it might have been the intention of the drafters of the UN Charter to put any coercive enforcement measures (whether forcible or not) under the authority of the Security Council, this has not been the case in practice.[65] The main reason for this is because the basic freedom to trade or to shape economic relations between states has not been prohibited, though it has been curtailed, in the post-1945 era. Against this background of international law, where there is no clear prohibition on economic coercion[66] (somewhat perversely given the very narrow doctrine of countermeasures), other international legal persons can utilise such freedoms. Or, to put it another way, the clouds of obscurity that surround economic coercion when undertaken by a state, are lifted when undertaken by an organisation. Of course, the universal organisation is endowed with such powers without any doubt,[67] but because the universal rules of the Charter do not prohibit economic coercion, it is also the case that in certain circumstances, regional organisations have a similar power.[68] Attempts to argue that the prohibition on the use of force in Article 2(4) of the Charter also covered economic force or coercion, as well as armed force, failed.[69] Thus, against the background of a lack of a clear prohibition, regional organisations have asserted a right of economic coercion.

---

[64] See White and Abass, 'Countermeasures and Sanctions', pp. 515–16. See Council Regulation 2340/90, 8 August 1990 (OJ L 213/1, 9 August 1990) re Iraq; Regulation 3300/91, 11 November 1991 (OJ L 315/1, 15 November 1991) and Regulation 1432/92, 1 June 1992 (OJ L 151/4, 3 June 1992) re the Federal Republic of Yugoslavia.

[65] Dominicé, 'Co-Ordination', p. 82.

[66] O. Y. Elagab, *The Legality of Non-forcible Counter-measures in International Law* (Oxford: Clarendon Press, 1988), pp. 212–13; White and Abass, 'Countermeasures', pp. 518–21.

[67] Article 41 of the UN Charter.

[68] Though they might be restricted by the principle of non-intervention; see White and Abass, 'Countermeasures', p. 521.

[69] J. Paust and A. P. Blaustein, 'The Arab Oil Weapon – A Threat to International Peace' (1974) 68 *AJIL* 410 at 417.

Military measures

Just as a state's right to take non-forcible measures has been restricted (but not prohibited) in the post-1945 era, a state's right to take military action has also been (more severely) restricted in the new world order of 1945. In their unilateral military actions, once states have gone beyond the right of self-defence, they are acting beyond what is clearly lawful.[70] There may be attempts to develop the law of self-defence to allow for defence of individuals in other countries,[71] or to deal with imminent or indeed latent threats,[72] but the presumption of illegality of such unilateral operations must be contrasted with the presumption of legality if the Security Council authorises them.[73] The question then becomes one of whether regional organisations have a similar competence.

Here we are no longer in an issue of debate about the interpretation of Article 53, which, as will be recalled, requires enforcement action by regional bodies to be authorised by the UN Security Council. If 'enforcement action' has any meaning at all it must cover aggressive military action, action that would otherwise be unlawful if it were not permitted. The very idea of authorisation in Article 53 assumes that otherwise the action would be illegal, a situation which applies to military enforcement action which is prohibited by Article 2(4) of the UN Charter,[74] but not economic enforcement (or at least not all of it).[75] Whilst 'enforcement' action may have been interpreted more restrictively than the 1945 consensus to exclude (at least presumptively) economic sanctions, if it still retains its core meaning, it must cover military enforcement action, thus requiring Security Council authorisation.

---

[70] Articles 2(4) and 51 of the UN Charter.
[71] For discussion of the arguments for humanitarian intervention as providing for a further lawful means of using force, see S. Chesterman, *Just War or Just Peace? Humanitarian Intervention and International Law* (Oxford: Oxford University Press, 2002); J. L. Holzgrefe and R. O. Keohane (eds.), *Humanitarian Intervention: Ethical, Legal and Political Dilemmas* (Cambridge: Cambridge University Press, 2003); B. D. Lepard, *Rethinking Humanitarian Intervention: A Fresh Legal Approach Based on Fundamental Ethical Principles* (Pennsylvania: Penn. State University Press, 2003).
[72] C. Henderson, 'The Bush Doctrine from Theory to Practice' (2004) 9 *JCSL* 3.
[73] Articles 42 and 53 of the UN Charter.
[74] Article 2(4) of the Charter provides: 'All Members shall refrain in their international relations from the threat or use of force against the territorial integrity or political independence of any state, or in any other manner inconsistent with the purposes of the United Nations.'
[75] Villani, 'The Security Council's', 539.

The continued application of Article 53 to military enforcement action by regional organisations is not just a result of the terms of the provision itself, but is underpinned by the other hierarchy provisions of the Charter. More fundamentally, it is underpinned by the peremptory nature of the prohibition on the threat or use of force.[76] Some regional military enforcement (including robust peacekeeping) practice appears contrary to Article 53, for example the action of the OAS in the Dominican Republic in 1965, the Arab League in Lebanon in 1976, and of ECOWAS in Liberia and Sierra Leone in the 1990s and beyond.[77] This might be argued to have undermined this provision if it were not part of the more fundamental hierarchies of the UN Charter (Article 103 regarding the obligation to refrain from the use of force in Article 2), and of international law (the *jus cogens* obligation to refrain from the use of force). The Security Council, by virtue of Article 42 of the UN Charter, is specifically allowed to take military action in response to threats to the peace, breaches of the peace and acts of aggression.[78] The Council's power is part of the Charter rules governing the use of force, as is the right of self-defence belonging to individual states, and both are part of the peremptory norm as well.[79] Thus it is the case that backed by the hierarchy provisions of the Charter (Articles 53, 103), and by the hierarchy provisions of international law, the Security Council has powers of military enforcement not possessed by States or by regional organisations.[80]

Simply put, there are two basic hierarchies in international law. First, those provisions in the UN Charter that provide for Council authority over non-defensive uses of force, and that provide that Charter obligations including the obligation to refrain from the threat or use of force,

---

[76] Brownlie, *Principles*, pp. 488–9; Shaw, *International Law*, pp. 117–18.

[77] N. D. White, *The Law of International Organisations* (Manchester: Manchester University Press, 1996), ch. 8.

[78] Article 42 provides in part that: 'Should the Security Council consider that measures provided for in Article 41 would be inadequate or have proved inadequate, it may take such action by air, sea, or land forces as may be necessary to maintain or restore international peace and security . . .'

[79] *Jus cogens* are not confined to customary rules according to Bernhardt, 'Article 103', p. 1294.

[80] See J. Delbrück, 'The Impact of the Allocation of International Law Enforcement Authority on the International Legal Order', in J. Delbrück (ed.), *Allocation*, p. 135 at p. 158: 'International law is increasingly developing elements of a hierarchical order as is evidenced by the way international law enforcement authority is allocated, and even more so by [the way] its exercise is conceptualised i.e. by police-like enforcement of norms of "public interest".'

prevail over other treaty obligations. Secondly, there are the recognised fundamental norms of the international community, *jus cogens* or obligations owed *erga omnes*,[81] which include the prohibition of the threat or use of force. These two combine to effectively ring-fence the rules governing the use of force from any real erosion by contrary regional practice, unlike the rules governing economic sanctions where the ambiguous term 'enforcement action' in Article 53 is not backed up by clear customary rules, and certainly not by any peremptory rules, to prohibit non-forcible measures by regional organisations.

There may be greater leeway in the case of economic measures (where a state has some freedom on trading matters), allowing a collection of states in a region powers of coercion. However, there is no real freedom in use of force matters where there is a clear prohibition on the use of force – a fundamental restriction in international law, allowing only limited exceptions. This is bolstered by Articles 103 and 53 of the Charter. In other words, it is a combination of universal international law,[82] and the powers of the universal organisation (the UN) that gives universalism a certain supremacy over regionalism in use of force matters. In military matters, regional organisations thus only have autonomy in collective self-defence (a right clearly belonging to states),[83] and peacekeeping (if consensual),[84] but not in enforcement action.

Such contentions are sometimes countered by criticism of the legitimacy of the decision-making process in the Security Council.[85] Can the

---

[81] *Jus cogens* are fundamental (peremptory) rules from which no derogation is allowed. They contain obligations upon states (and other actors) not to commit certain acts. The concept of *erga omnes* refers to the extent of the interest that other states have in seeing these rules complied with. Not only the victim state of a violation of *jus cogens*, but all states have an interest in invoking the responsibility of the state in breach. See further Shaw, *International Law*, pp. 116–18.

[82] J. Charney, 'Universal International Law', (1993) 87 *AJIL* 529.

[83] Article 51 was drafted to accommodate the rights of regional organisations to undertake actions in collective self-defence: I. Brownlie, *International Law and the Use of Force by States* (Oxford: Oxford University Press, 1963), p. 270.

[84] On the importance of consent for peacekeeping, distinguishing it from military enforcement see the International Court's advisory opinion in *Certain Expenses of the United Nations*, Advisory Opinion, Judgment of 20 July 1962, (1962) ICJ Rep. 151. For a discussion of regional peacekeeping and enforcement see C. Gray, *International Law on the Use of Force*, 2nd edn (Oxford: Oxford University Press, 2004), pp. 282–327.

[85] See N. Tsagourias, 'The Shifting Laws on the Use of Force and the Trivialization of the UN Collective Security System: The Need to Reconstitute It' (2003) 34 *Netherlands Yearbook of International Law* 55. But see comments by C. Schreuer in Delbrück, *Allocation*, at p. 86, where he argues that the Council is more representative than the Assembly where small states that contribute very little to the budget can win a vote.

authority of the UN be undermined by the undoubted selectivity and lack of representation in Security Council decision-making?[86] Furthermore, does this signify that the failure to take military enforcement measures by the Council allows states or regional bodies to take action in its stead – as occurred in the case of NATO military enforcement action to bring an end to the repression in Kosovo in 1999?[87] There seem to be some implications of this type of approach in the EU's Security Strategy of 2003,[88] the 1999 Security Protocol of ECOWAS,[89] and the 2000 Constituent Treaty of the AU.[90] Claims to take military action in these documents can be interpreted very widely indeed, and yet they are subject to much more muted criticism when compared to the US claims to use force in a wide range of situations in the National Security Strategy or 'Bush Doctrine' of 2002.[91] It seems that they have greater legitimacy because they were adopted by regional organisations representing the collective view of groups of states.

Could it not also be argued that the European Council of twenty-seven States, or the NATO Council of twenty-six states, acting in the main by consensus, is more representative than the UN Security Council of fifteen states? In answer, it must be pointed out that the European

---

[86] See N. D. White, 'The Will and Authority of the UN Security Council After Iraq' (2004) 17 *LJIL* 645.

[87] See the debate between Simma and Cassese: B. Simma, 'NATO, the UN and the Use of Force: Legal Aspects' (1999) 10 *EJIL* 1; A. Cassese, '*Ex Injuria ius Oritur*: Are We Moving Towards International Legitimation of Forcible Humanitarian Countermeasures in the World Community?' (1999) 10 *EJIL* 23.

[88] 12 December 2003. At p. 7 the Strategy states that 'we should be ready to act before a crisis occurs', tackling such threats not 'by purely military means'.

[89] See Articles 3(a), 22(c) and 25(c). Article 22(c) provides for 'humanitarian intervention in support of humanitarian disaster'.

[90] Article 4(h) provides for 'the right of the Union to intervene in a Member State pursuant to a decision of the Assembly in respect of grave circumstances, namely: war crimes, genocide and crimes against humanity'. However, it is worth noting that in the 2002 Protocol Relating to the Establishment of the Peace and Security Council of the African Union, there are provisions that show greater deference to the UN Charter rules. Article 17(1) provides that 'in the fulfilment of its mandate in the promotion and maintenance of peace, security and stability in Africa, the Peace and Security Council shall cooperate closely with the United Nations Security Council, which has primary responsibility for the maintenance of international peace and security . . .' Article 17(2) further states that 'where necessary, recourse will be made to the United Nations to provide the necessary financial, logistical and military support for the African Union's activities in the promotion and maintenance of peace, security and stability in Africa, in keeping with the provisions of Chapter VIII of the UN Charter on the role of Regional Organizations in the maintenance of international peace and security'.

[91] Henderson, 'The Bush Doctrine'.

Council represents European States only, while the Security Council, for all its defects, represents the international community.[92] At the UN's founding constitutional moment in 1945,[93] it was the international community as a whole creating something unique,[94] that only the international community (i.e. all states acting together in another constitutional moment) could subsequently take away. The founders also established fundamental universal rules such as the non-use of force, which can only remain valid if they are ultimately regulated by universal organisations. This signifies that only the UN can authorise any derogations from the prohibition of the use of force beyond a state's inherent right of individual or collective self-defence. Regional self-authorisation would be subject to too much abuse – the genie of a regional world police force would be let out of the lamp, and it would be very difficult to put back.[95] Indeed, the likelihood of competing regional police forces would be great. Consequently, instead of having universal rules governing the use of force, there would emerge potentially conflicting regional rules.

Nevertheless, the universal organisation is in need of significant improvement. The problems of legitimacy in the Security Council signifies

---

[92] Article 24(1) of the UN Charter states that 'in order to ensure prompt and effective action by the United Nations, its Members confer on the Security Council primary responsibility for the maintenance of international peace and security, and agree that in carrying out its duties under this responsibility the Security Council acts on their behalf'.

[93] See D. Sarooshi, *The United Nations and the Development of Collective Security* (Oxford: Oxford University Press, 1999), pp. 26–32.

[94] See comments by C. Schreuer in Delbrück, *Allocation*, p. 82, who states that 'the evolving regime of the United Nations now goes beyond the sum total of the powers of individual states'. It is argued here that, at least on paper, this was the case in 1945.

[95] Simma, 'NATO'. But see Abass, *Regional Organizations*, p. 204, who argues that *consent* has been given by member states to military interventions within the membership by being a party to a treaty that allows such interventions. This enables regional bodies to circumvent the *jus cogens* rule, which Abass controversially argues is confined to aggression. Rules of *jus cogens* are rules from which no derogation can be made (Article 53 of the Vienna Convention on the Law of Treaties, 1969). Article 26 of the ILC's Articles on State Responsibility (2001) specifically states that consent does not provide a defence to breaches of *jus cogens*. By arguing that certain forms of use of force are not covered by the peremptory rule, Abass circumvents its effect. However, while he has some evidence that there is a distinction between aggression and other threats or uses of force (see the *Case Concerning Military and Paramilitary Activities in and Against Nicaragua (Nicaragua v. United States of America)*, Merits, Judgment of 27 June 1986, (1986) ICJ Rep. 14 at 103–8), he has limited evidence for stating that only the former is covered by the *jus cogens* rule. For a similar view to Abass, see T. Farer, 'The Role of Regional Collective Security Arrangements', in T. G. Weiss (ed.), *Collective Security in a Changing World* (Boulder: Lynne Rienner, 1993).

the need for either a more representative/accountable Council exercising its primary responsibility for peace and security[96] in a proactive consistent manner, or a re-invigoration of the subsidiary powers of the General Assembly recognised in 1950 in the Uniting for Peace Resolution.[97] However, weaknesses in the universal organisation do not signify that regional organisations can step in to fill the gaps, at least in matters of military enforcement. The international community created a universal organisation to police universal rules, something not possessed by individual states, or even non-universal organisations. Only the international community as a whole could take this away. Until that happens, we are stuck with the Security Council, currently with its in-built selectivity, and a very limited Assembly with subsidiary powers to recommend enforcement measures that can be exercised in exceptional circumstances. But if the High Level Panel recommendations of late 2004 are adopted, then we will have a more representative, more accountable Security Council concerned with upholding fundamental rules of international law. The most significant of the Panel's recommendations would remove some of the most de-legitimating selectivity by providing:

> The Panel endorses the emerging norm that there is a collective, international responsibility to protect, exercisable by the Security Council authorising military intervention as a last resort, in the event of genocide and other large-scale killing, ethnic cleansing or serious violations of humanitarian law which sovereign Governments have proved powerless or unwilling to prevent.[98]

Unfortunately, the inability of the Security Council to deal with the crimes against humanity being committed in the Darfur region of Sudan[99]

---

[96] Article 24(1) UN Charter.

[97] UN Doc. A/Res/377 (1950). See further N. D. White, 'The Legality of Bombing in the Name of Humanity' (2000) 4 *Journal of Conflict and Security Law (JCSL)* 27; S. D. Bailey and S. Daws, *The Procedure of the UN Security Council*, 3rd edn (Oxford: Clarendon, 1998), p. 296.

[98] From Report of the High-Level Panel on Threats, Challenges and Change, 'A More Secure World: Our Shared Responsibility', UN Doc. A/59/565 (2004), recommendation 55; see also 56, 73–81. See further the Report of the Secretary General, 'In Larger Freedom: Towards Security, Development and Human Rights for All', UN Doc. A/59/2005 (2005), para. 125 of which states: 'As to genocide, ethnic cleansing and other such crimes against humanity, are they also not threats to international peace and security, against which humanity should be able to look to the Security Council for protection?' See also para. 126.

[99] That this level of abuse has occurred is determined by a commission set up by the Council itself. See Report of the International Commission of Inquiry on Violations of

from 2003–05 is evidence of the continued failure of the Council to take action in all cases of serious violations of international law. The smoke-screen sent up by its reference of the matter to the International Criminal Court in March 2005[100] should not distract from the fact that all the Council could achieve, in the sense of taking meaningful action to prevent crimes being committed, was a mere threat of non-forcible measures.[101] By locking the rules on the use of force to the matter of enforcing fundamental rules of international law in the Security Council, the drafters created an inherently selective and weak system.[102] To unlock those rules in favour of regional organisations, however, may prove to be more disastrous. The better course is for a reformed and legitimate Council to emerge out of the current pressure for change.[103]

Conclusion: the international rule of law?

It has been argued that all organisations are bound by the glue of international law, and a large part of institutional activities are subject to the same obligations. Seen in this way there is no *general* hierarchy within organisations. Hierarchy is supplied by peremptory norms which are part of international law (which may be contributed to by both UN and regional organisations), and which, as we have seen, may be enforced by regional organisations as well as the UN using non-forcible measures. The UN remains the only body that can clearly authorise military measures either by states under Chapter VII[104] or by regional organisations under Chapter VIII.[105] It has been argued in this chapter that such military action can and should be authorised to enforce fundamental rules of international law or to prevent potential breaches

---

International Humanitarian Law and Human Rights Law in Darfur, UN Doc. S/2005/60 (2005).

[100] UN Doc. S/Res/1593 (2005).

[101] UN Doc. S/Res/1556 (2004); UN Doc. S/Res/1564 (2004).

[102] The version of the responsibility to protect adopted at the World Summit in September 2005 shows, by its wording, that selectivity and discretion will still be present in the Security Council even in cases of gross human rights violations. Member states declared: 'we are prepared to take collective action, in a timely and decisive manner, through the Security Council, in accordance with the UN Charter, including Chapter VII, on a case by case basis in co-operation with relevant regional organisations as appropriate, should peaceful means be inadequate and national authorities manifestly fail to protect their populations from genocide, war crimes, ethnic cleansing and crimes against humanity.' – GA Res. 60/1, 24 Oct. 2005.

[103] See Report of the Secretary General, 'In Larger Freedom', paras. 167–70.

[104] Article 42 of the UN Charter.   [105] Article 53 of the UN Charter.

of them,[106] for to allow otherwise would be to undermine the hierarchy of norms of which non-use of force is a fundamental element.[107]

However, by the terms of the Charter the Security Council does not appear to be limited to the enforcement of fundamental norms, and has developed the concept of threat to the peace widely,[108] though its practice has been characterised as being driven by a concern to deal with international or internal situations where there is a 'danger of the use of force on a considerable scale'.[109] This is compatible with the underpinnings of several peremptory norms (the non-use of force, and the prohibitions of genocide, war crimes, crimes against humanity), and prevention of their breach. Nevertheless, it is clear that Chapter VII measures were not intended to be limited to cases of non-compliance with fundamental obligations.[110] Kelsen made this clear when he declared that the purpose of enforcement measures 'is not to maintain or restore the law but to maintain or restore peace, which is not necessarily identical with the law'.[111] Thus the Security Council is not restricted to enforcement of fundamental norms, but it is argued here that this should be the core of its activities, and should be part of its duties, rather than within its wider security discretion. As Gowlland-Debbas argues, 'the development of the concept of fundamental community norms logically calls for centralised and institution-alised mechanisms to ensure their respect and enforcement'.[112] The

---

[106] For general discussion, see V. Gowlland-Debbas, 'Security Council Enforcement Action and Issues of State Responsibility' (1994) 43 *ICLQ* 55; P. Klein, 'Responsibilities for Serious Breaches of Obligations Deriving From Peremptory Norms of International and United Nations Law' (2002) 13 *EJIL* 1241.

[107] This raises the issue of the consequences of Security Council inaction in the face of a breach of *jus cogens* that the Council has deemed to constitute a threat to international peace. Stein argues that states then have the right to take action: T. Stein, 'Decentralized International Law Enforcement: The Changing Role of the State as Law Enforcement Agent', in Delbrück, *Allocation*, p. 107 at p. 117. The current writer argues that authority must then be sought from the General Assembly. The primary responsibility within the UN for peace and security is with the Security Council, subsidiary responsibility is with the General Assembly. See N. D. White, *Keeping the Peace: The United Nations and the Maintenance of International Peace and Security*, 2nd edn (Manchester: Manchester University Press, 1997), pp. 172–8.

[108] See K. Wellens, 'The UN Security Council and New Threats to the Peace: Back to the Future' (2003) 8 *JCSL* 15.

[109] J. Frowein and N. Krisch, 'Article 39', in Simma (ed.), *The Charter*, p. 726.

[110] V. Gowlland-Debbas, 'Introduction', in Gowlland-Debbas (ed.), *United Nations Sanctions*, p. 8.

[111] H. Kelsen, *The Law of the United Nations* (London: Stevens, 1950), p. 294.

[112] Gowlland-Debbas, 'Introduction', p. 27.

convergence of fundamental community norms of international law and the constitutional hierarchies of international law is not inevitable but highly desirable if we are to take these obligations seriously, and if we want to have a Council driven to protect community values as opposed to selective action motivated out of national concerns. The credibility of universal international law and the legitimacy of the United Nations are at stake.

However, one must not forget the impact of Articles 103 and 53 of the UN Charter. As has been said, if Article 103 was just confined to the original obligations of the Charter, then there would be large swathes of regional institutional activity untouched by this provision. It would only be catching obvious breaches of fundamental rules by regional organisations such as that prohibiting the use force. However, the secondary legislation found in the Council's decisions also creates binding UN Charter commitments by virtue of Article 25 and therefore effective overriding obligations under Article 103.[113] That this can override treaty obligations is shown by the *Lockerbie Cases* where the provisions of the Montreal Convention of 1971 were bypassed,[114] and it seems to have been accepted by member states that the Security Council's sanctions resolutions against individual member states and presumably against terrorism override obligations under the WTO and under regional trading regimes.[115]

This power thus gives the Security Council the potential to act in a governmental way vis-à-vis member states, and indirectly against regional organisations. It is argued that this power is limited, by the UN Charter,[116] and by fundamental rules of international law. Indeed, it has been argued, that if the Security Council wants to maintain its (admittedly shaky) monopoly over the use of non-defensive force, it

---

[113] This was at least accepted *prima facie* in the 1992 interim measures judgment of the International Court of Justice in *Questions of Interpretation and Application of the 1971 Montreal Convention Arising from the Aerial Incident at Lockerbie (Libya v. United Kingdom)*, Provisional Measures, Judgment of 14 April 1992 (1992) ICJ Rep. 3.

[114] *Ibid.* See the 1971 Convention for the Suppression of Unlawful Acts Against the Safety of Civil Aviation (the Montreal Convention).

[115] Gowlland-Debbas, 'Introduction', p. 18. On member states' acceptance of the Council's actions against terrorism, see C. A. Ward, 'Building Capacity to Combat International Terrorism: The Role of the United Nations Security Council' (2003) 8 *JCSL* 289.

[116] Article 24(2) of the UN Charter provides in part that: 'in discharging these duties the Security Council shall act in accordance with the Purposes and Principles of the United Nations . . .'

has to increase its legitimacy by taking action to combat violations or potential violations of peremptory norms, and should be very careful not to be persuaded to take military action to combat situations that are better characterised as threats to the peace of one or more of the permanent members, rather than threats to international peace. The World Summit Outcome Document of September 2005 contained a diluted commitment to protect in circumstances of gross human rights violations.[117] This should be viewed only as the first step towards a proper recognition of a duty to protect incumbent on the Security Council in cases of violations of fundamental norms.

Although the Council still has constitutional authority on its side, by dint of the Charter and by reason of the peremptory rules of international law, as with other constitutional systems it is dependent upon issues such as legitimacy, authority and loyalty, and if the UN Security Council cannot uphold the fundamental principles of the Charter and of international law, then authority may pass elsewhere leading to a degradation of the most basic rules in any legal order, namely those governing the use of force.

[117] See above, n. 102.

6

The multilevel constitution of European foreign relations

RAMSES A. WESSEL

'[T]he problem of establishing a perfect civil constitution is subordinate to the problem of a law-governed external relationship with other states, and cannot be solved unless the latter is also solved.'

Immanuel Kant, *Idea for a Universal History with
a Cosmopolitan Purpose*, 1784[1]

Introduction

My answer to the question 'Does the European Union need a Constitution?'[2] usually[3] reads something like: 'What about the Treaty on European Union?'[4] This obviously does not do justice to the legal, political and philosophical insights offered by the debate on European constitutionalism, as it has taken place ever since the launch of the European project in the 1950s.[5] For those active in international

---

[1] I. Kant, *Political Writings*, H. S. Reiss (ed.) (Cambridge: Cambridge University Press, 1991), p. 47.

[2] See, for instance, D. Grimm, 'Does Europe Need a Constitution?' (1995) 1 *ELJ* 282 and the comments by J. Habermas, 'Remarks on Dieter Grimm's "Does Europe Need a Constitution?"', *ibid.*, 303. And, J. Habermas, 'So, Why Does Europe Need a Constitution?', Hamburg Lecture of 26 June 2001: http://www.iue.it/RSCAS/e-texts/CR200102UK.pdf.

[3] Some of the arguments were already presented in my 'The Constitutional Relationship between the European Union and the European Community: Consequences for the Relationship with the Member States', in J. J. H. Weiler and A. von Bogdandy (eds.), *Jean Monnet Working Papers* 2003: www.jeanmonnetprogram.org/papers/03/030901-09.html.

[4] The Maastricht Treaty (1992) as subsequently amended.

[5] See, for an in-depth analysis of the dimensions of European constitutionalism, G. Frankenberg, 'The Return of the Contract: Problems and Pitfalls of European Constitutionalism' (2000) 3 *ELJ* 257–76. Also, on some of the inherent paradoxes of constitutionalism see J. Klabbers, 'Constitutionalism Lite' (2004) 1 *International Organizations Law Review (IOLR)* 31–58.

institutional law, however, the constituent treaty of an international organisation – a label that still fits the European Union – forms the 'constitution' of the organisation, defining the scope and content of the legal order created by it. This definition of a constitution comes close to a classic one presented by Verdross – one of the godfathers of 'international constitutional law' – who, in 1926, looked at a constitution in terms of a sustainable institutional basis of a legal community.[6] A constitution of an international organisation thus, primarily, defines an institutional framework whereby competences are being divided among institutions in a way that cannot be changed overnight. The word 'legal community' (*Rechtsgemeinschaft*), however, seems to refer to a community based on the rule of law, with a judiciary to supervise the functioning of the agreed procedures as well as an inclusion of those that are 'governed' by the international organisation, member states and – increasingly – citizens.[7] It is in particular this latter notion that is usually thought to give some substance to the primarily rather formal concept of constitution in international law, which seems to be at the heart of the debate on European constitutionalism. As Frankenberg noted:

> On closer scrutiny, the constitutional question carries a heavier political baggage than that in the overhead compartment, because it tries, not always easily, to straddle the mutually exclusive concepts of 'state' and 'international entity', and to solve the problems of legitimate authority and social integration with reference to conflicting principles such as democracy and intergovernmental co-operation, unity/centrality and subsidiarity, integration/homogeneity and diversity/heterogeneity.[8]

These two approaches to the notion of 'constitution' as applied to international organisations – the 'neutral' definition as a legal system

---

[6] A. Verdross, *Die Verfassung der Völkerrechtsgemeinschaft* (Wien/Berlin: Springer Verlag, 1926), at p. v: 'Errichtung einer dauerhaften und stabilen Grundordnung, welche eine Rechtsgemeinschaft errichtet und institutionell ausstattet.'

[7] *Cf.* Case 294/83, *Parti Ecologiste 'Les Verts' v. European Parliament* [1986] ECR 1339, para. 23, in which the Court of Justice of the European Communities (ECJ) was already referring to the EC Treaty as 'the constitutional charter of a Community based on the rule of law'. See also K. Lenaerts and M. Desomer, 'New Models of Constitution-Making in Europe: The Quest for Legitimacy' (2002) 39 *CMLR* 1217–53. Verdross himself seems to approach the concept from a more positivist angle: 'Rechtsgemeinschaft ist nur jene Gemeinschaft, die durch einen Kreis von Rechtsnormen als Einheit erfaßt und dadurch von anderen abgegrenzt wird': Verdross, *Die Verfassung*, p. 4. In that sense it should probably not be translated as 'legal community', but comes closer to 'legal system'.

[8] Frankenberg, 'The Return of the Contract', 258.

vis-à-vis the more value-orientated one – indeed form the basis of the literature on the constitutionalisation of Europe. Whereas the term 'constitutional structure' is often used to analyse the competences of the institutions and the relationship between the organisation and its member states,[9] a more substantive approach focuses on the way in which constitutional elements could be introduced to expose European governance to the checks and balances that we are familiar with in our own domestic legal systems.[10] It is obvious that this latter approach is often far from 'value-free': much of the debate not only concerns the question of how constitutional elements are to be brought into the EU legal order, but many observers are sincerely concerned about the lack of these elements in an international organisation that increasingly starts to look like a state.[11] The latter approach seems to be dominant in international constitutionalism which tends to view the international political space from the perspective of a more encompassing 'international community' and an overarching constitutional structure.[12]

An approach that seems to fit in between these two perspectives takes the more neutral definition of a constitution as a starting point, without neglecting the fact that the European Union indeed is a very special organisation, the constituent treaty of which not only concerns the 'High Contracting Parties', but also the private persons and entities within the member states. In that sense it is the prime example 'integration organisations'. An essential feature of such organisations is that competences are transferred from the member states to the organisation, or that new competences for the organisation are created, through which it becomes competent (sometimes exclusively, but often in competition) to set rules which have direct effect within the legal orders of the member states.[13]

---

[9] An example of this approach can be found in G. De Búrca, 'The Institutional Development of the EU: A Constitutional Analysis', in P. Craig and G. De Búrca (eds.), *The Evolution of EU Law* (Oxford: Oxford University Press, 1999), pp. 55–82.

[10] Some elements may be found in D. M. Curtin and R. A. Wessel (eds.), *Good Governance and the European Union: Some Reflections on Concepts, Institutions and Substance* (Antwerpen: Intersentia, 2005).

[11] An example related to the subject of the present paper is E.-U. Petersmann, 'The Moral Foundations of the European Union's Foreign Policy Constitution: Defining "European Identity" and "Community Interests" for the Benefit of EU Citizens' (1996) *Aussenwirtschaft* Heft II, pp. 151–76. See, more generally, E. de Wet, 'The International Constitutional Order' (2006) 55 *ICLQ* 51; B. Ackerman, 'The Rise of World Constitutionalism' (1997) 83 *Virginia Law Review* (*Va L Rev*) 771–97.

[12] See the contribution by Wouter Werner, Chapter 10 in this volume.

[13] I. F. Dekker and R. A. Wessel, 'Governance by International Organisations: Rethinking the Source and Normative Force of International Decisions', in I. F. Dekker and

Although states do not cease to exist by becoming members of an international (integration) organisation, it becomes difficult to view their national legal order as existing in complete isolation from the legal order of the organisation. The 'constitutional setting' in which they operate, may largely depend on general international law; and, at least, it includes the arrangements on which they have agreed, in the framework of an international organisation. And, *vice versa*, the international organisation has to deal with the Janus-faced identity of member states: member states are constituent parts of the international organisation but also its counterparts, in the sense that both occupy independent positions within the international legal order and even have obligations towards each other.[14] This relationship is indeed somewhat schizophrenic, as one scholar once observed.[15]

In that respect, Weiler's remark that '[c]onstitutionalism, more than anything else, is what differentiates the Community from other transnational systems and from the other "pillars" since 'the Community behaves as if its founding document were not a treaty governed by international law but ... a constitutional charter governed by a form of constitutional law',[16] seems to ignore the fact that 'constitutionalisation' as a process powered by the 'own dynamics' [*Eigendynamik*] of the legal orders of international organisations is not exclusively to be found in the European Community.[17] There are good reasons to apply the

W. Werner (eds.), *Governance and International Legal Theory* (Leiden/Boston: Martinus Nijhoff Publishers, 2004), pp. 215–36. Compare also Pernice's remarks regarding the direct relations between the people and the supranational institutions, through directly applicable rights and obligations for individuals: 'Although the form of an international treaty is maintained, such treaties can be regarded ... as a common exercise of constitution-making power by the peoples of the participating State.' I. Pernice, 'Multilevel Constitutionalism and the Treaty of Amsterdam: European Constitution-Making Revisited?' (1999) 36 *CMLR* 703, at 717.

[14] Cf. N. M. Blokker, 'International Organizations and Their Members' (2004) 1 *IOLR* at 139.

[15] J. Klabbers, 'The Changing Image of International Organizations', in J.-M. Coicund and V. Heishanen (eds.), *The Legitimacy of International Organizations* (Tokyo: UN University Press, 2001), pp. 221–55 at 227.

[16] J. H. H. Weiler, 'Introduction: The Reformation of European Constitutionalism', in J. H. H Weiler, *The Constitution of Europe* (Cambridge: Cambridge University Press, 1999), p. 221.

[17] This type of constitutional approach is often used by others. See, for example, W. Sauter, 'The Economic Constitution of the European Union' (1998) 4 *CJEL* 27; or B. Fassbender, 'The United Nations Charter as Constitution of the International Community' (1998) 36 *Columbia J Trans Law* 529; J. Weiler, 'The Constitution of the Common Market Place: Text and Context in the Evolution of the Free Movement of Goods' and F. Snyder, 'EMU Revisited: Are We Making a Constitution? What

same concept at least to the other 'pillars' of the European Union – 'Common Foreign and Security Policy' (CFSP) and 'Police and Judicial Cooperation in Criminal Matters' (PJCC)[18] – but maybe even to other 'integration-organisations' in the sense defined above.[19] 'Constitutional sedimentation', as one observer has called it, is a much more general phenomenon.[20] Once a treaty relationship between states is converted into a new 'legal institution'[21] through an act of legal personification, by which an 'association of states' is turned into a new separate legal entity (see below), it becomes possible to see a 'will' of the new entity as opposed to the (collective) will of the original parties to the deal and it will be easier to acknowledge that international organisations are more than a classical *agora*, a mere public realm in which international issues can be debated and, perhaps, decided.[22] The *volonté distincte* of international organisations may be congruent to the collective will of the member states, but it may very well take its own course. The notion of 'constitution', as used in the present chapter, thus owes its distinguishing characteristic to the fact that it does not merely reflect the treaty relationship between the states of an international organisation (although it is the result of this contractual process), but that it also encompasses the relationship between the newly created legal order of the organisation and the national orders of the member states. The 'european community' (no capitals) is thus understood to comprise

Constitution are We Making?', in Craig and De Búrca, *The Evolution of EU Law*, p. 349 *et seq.* and p. 417 *et seq.* respectively. Also see the concept of 'vertical constitutionalism' used by Joerges in relation to the economic constitution. C. Joerges, 'The Law in the Process of Constitutionalizing Europe', paper presented at the ARENA Conference on Democracy and European Governance, 4–5 March 2002: http://www.arena.uio.no/events/Conference2002/documents/Joerges.doc.

[18] See D. M. Curtin and I. F. Dekker, 'The Constitutional Structure of the European Union: Some Reflections on Vertical Unity-in-Diversity', in P. Beaumont, C. Lyons and N. Walker (eds.), *Convergence and Divergence in European Public Law* (Oxford: Hart, 2001), pp. 59–78.

[19] Or, in general to the international legal order; see de Wet, *The International Constitutional Order.*

[20] T. Eijsbouts, 'Constitutional Sedimentation' (1996) 1 *Legal Issues of European Economic Integration (LIEEI)* 51–60.

[21] The concept is that employed in institutional legal theory (ILT) as: 'distinct legal systems governing specific forms of social conduct within the overall legal system'. See D. W. P. Ruiter, *Legal Institutions* (Dordrecht: Kluwer Academic Publishers, 2001), p. 71.

[22] See on the different views on international organisations (a *managerial* versus an *agora* concept), J. Klabbers, 'Two Concepts of International Organization' (2005) 2 *IOLR* 277–93.

both the states and their citizens as well as the 'supranational' institution created by them.[23]

This contribution, indeed, deals with the European Union, and more particularly with the external relations of the Union. Whilst the economic external relations will occasionally be referred to, the main focus will be on the external political ('foreign affairs') relations. It is in this area in particular that the complex relationship between the Union and its member states presents itself in its full dimensions.[24] The purpose of this contribution is to present a meaningful way to analyse the constitutionalisation of the external relations of the Union on the basis of the treaty provisions, whilst acknowledging the important role of the member states in this area. Hence, I will use the language of constitutionalism not only to explain existing developments in international law in terms borrowed from domestic constitutionalism,[25] but will attempt to combine this with the notion of constitution as it is frequently used in the law of international organisations. The thematic division of powers between the Union and its member states is a central issue in the analysis. After all, the Treaty provides that the Union 'shall assert its identity on the international scene, in particular through the implementation of a common foreign and security policy' (Article 2), but that 'the Member States shall support the Union's external and security policy actively and unreservedly in a spirit of mutual solidarity' (Article 11(2)). One way of making sense of this complex development is not to focus on an emerging constitution on the EU level, but instead to take the complex relationship with the member states as well as the unity of national and supranational legal orders into account and to try and see a

---

[23] *Cf.* Fassbender, 'The United Nations Charter', 566–7: 'In principle, there cannot be a community, understood as a distinct legal entity, in the absence of a constitution providing for its own organs. Legal personality requires the actual ability to perform legal acts.'

[24] This is not to say that this phenomenon is not more general. In the words of Joerges: '*De facto*, the dependence of European governance on the collaboration of the Member States is drastically perceptible everywhere one looks. This dependence determines the EU's shaping of political programmes which are then transposed with the help of the committee system; the inclusion of non-governmental organisations, and the preference for 'soft law' and information policy measures. Equally important is the fact that the freedoms that European law guarantees are exercised outwith, or away from, one's own member State and, at the same time, can be upheld against one's own "sovereign".' Joerges, 'The Law in the Process', 33. The same line of thought can be discovered in A. Milward, *The European Rescue of the Nation State* (London: Routledge, 1992).

[25] See more extensively on the different ways to use 'constitutionalism', the contributions of Bardo Fassbender (Chapter 9) and Wouter Werner (Chapter 10) below.

constitution made up of the constitutions of the member states bound together by a complementary constitutional body consisting of the European Treaties.[26] This *Verfassungsverband* – as he calls it – was labelled by Pernice as a multilevel constitution:[27]

> This perspective views the Member States' constitutions and the treaties constituting the European Union, despite their formal distinction, as a unity in substance and as a coherent institutional system, within which competence for action, public authority or, as one may also say, the power to exercise sovereign rights is divided among two or more levels ... This concept treats European integration as a dynamic process of constitution-making instead of a sequence of international treaties which establish and develop an organization of international cooperation. The question 'Does Europe need a Constitution' is not relevant, because Europe already has a 'multilevel constitution' ... According to the concept of 'multilevel constitutionalism', the Treaties are the constitution of the Community – or, together with the national constitutions, the constitution of the European Union – made by the peoples of the member States through their treaty-making institutions and procedures.

This approach acknowledges that one cannot simply place the different issue areas of the Union (such as the 'internal market', or 'foreign policy') under either the heading of supranationalism or intergovernmentalism, but that competences related to these issue areas are allocated between the different levels of decision-making.[28] In order to place this argument in a more general setting, I will first investigate the emergence of a 'multilevel constitution' in the area of European foreign affairs (section 1). This is followed by an analysis of the current constitutional relationship between the Union and its member states in the area of foreign and security issues (section 2). Section 3 will subsequently analyse 'flexibility' as a development that may have an effect on the constitutionalisation of the external relations of the EU. The

---

[26] Cf. Lenaerts and Desomer, 'New Models', 1219: '[t]here are no convincing legal arguments why a Constitution may not be made up of a variety of interconnected Treaty texts founding the legal order.'

[27] Pernice, 'Multilevel Constitutionalism', 706–7 and 715. The notion finds its source in the multilevel governance literature, popular in some political science approaches. See, for instance, L. Hooghe and G. Marks (eds.), *Multilevel Governance and European Integration* (Lanham, MD: Rownan & Littlefield, 2001). In legal studies the notion was picked up and applied by N. Bernard, *Multilevel Governance in the European Union* (The Hague: Kluwer Law International, 2002).

[28] See on this issue, U. Di Fabio, 'Some Remarks on the Allocation of Competences between the European Union and its Member States' (2002) *CMLR* 1289–301.

constitutional notion was of course explicitly used in the Treaty establishing a Constitution for Europe of 29 October 2004. It is believed that, irrespective of whether this treaty will ever enter into force, is does not fundamentally alter the position of foreign and security policy in the European Union. Despite the disappearance of the distinct pillars of the Union – as reflected in the Constitutional Treaty – CFSP will retain a special position in the new framework and its procedures will still be different from those in other areas. Moreover, ratification is merely one aspect of a constitutionalisation process. Hence, some observations regarding the Constitutional Treaty will be made as it is indeed believed to reflect the current stage of European constitutionalism (section 4). Finally, section 5 will be used to make some concluding observations.

1. The emergence of a multilevel constitution

A. European external relations: the 'personification' of a treaty relationship

At one moment in time the external identities of the current member states of the European Union started to coincide partly with the external identity of what we now call the European Union. This may have been at the time of the entry into force of the Treaty on European Union, but there are also good reasons to locate this moment earlier in time, for instance with the entry into force of the Single European Act in 1987 or even earlier during the European political cooperation that largely took place on the basis of custom and subsequent codification.[29] The political cooperation that took place between the members of the European Economic Community during the 1970s and 80s could not be regarded as a formal treaty relationship. Nevertheless, (codified) custom surely reflected a contractual legal relation between the participating states.[30] The procedural agreements laid down in Declarations, and later on in the Single European Act reflected the emergence of a constitution which

---

[29] The debate, of course, started earlier. See R. T. Griffiths' interesting analysis, *Europe's First Constitution: The European Political Community, 1952–1954* (London: Federal Trust, 2002). It always remains interesting to note that the originally envisaged 'supra-national European Community' was explicitly regarded as having legal personality (Article 4 of the Statute of the European Community, 1953), and that it had a clear 'foreign policy' dimension.

[30] See more extensively: R. A. Wessel, *The European Union's Foreign and Security Policy: A Legal Institutional Perspective* (The Hague: Kluwer Law International, 1999), ch. 1.

increasingly posed procedural restraints on the participating states.[31] Indeed, *participating* states; they only became *member* states after the entry into force of the EU Treaty.

From that moment on there could no longer be any doubt about the fact that there exists a legal system distinct from the legal systems of the member states in the area of foreign affairs. The possibility of viewing the European Union as a legal person was the result of what Ruiter would term a 'legal operation of personification'.[32] Where 'natural personality' is a feature of human entities, personification is not only possible for non-human entities, but even for 'incorporeal' things, that is 'mental constructs', such as 'states' or 'international organisations'. Modern law systems allow 'will' to be imputed to these incorporeal things through a legal act of personification.

In order to be able to understand what exactly happens when we allow an international organisation such as the European Union to act externally, that is vis-à-vis third parties, it is helpful to see how this modification from 'contractual relationship' to 'association' takes place. Ruiter defines an association as 'a personified alliance'.[33] But, how is a contractual legal relation turned into an association that is capable of entering into legal relationships with third parties? After all, contractual relations only have regard to parties to the contract, which implies that no party can enter into transactions with third parties on behalf of the others. Ruiter claims that what we do is in fact 'personify' the contractual relation by making four adjustments:[34]

1. Contractual consensus is abandoned in favour of collective decision-making by a general meeting of members, the outcomes of which are no longer conceived of as resulting from concordant expressions of their individual wills.

---

[31] In this respect it is interesting to take a renewed look at Weiler's remarks made in 1985 regarding the European Political Cooperation: 'Even if federations have a unitary external posture [which the EPC lacks according to Weiler – RAW], it is arguable that the federal principle may vindicate itself in the *internal process of foreign policy-making*.' This leads Weiler to conceive of EPC in 1985 already as 'a new experiment of a non-unitary foreign policy process and foreign posture which may veritably be called the federal option [as an organisational principle] of foreign affairs'. J. H. H. Weiler, 'The Evolution of Mechanisms and Institutions for a European Foreign Policy: Reflections on the Interaction of Law and Politics', *EUI Working Paper No. 85/202*, at 3.

[32] D. W. P. Ruiter, 'Types of Institutions as Patterns of Regulated Behaviour' (2004) 10 *Res Publica* 207 at 214–16. See also his *Legal Institutions* (Dordrecht: Kluwer Academic Publishers, 2001).

[33] Ruiter, *Types of Institutions*, at 215.   [34] *Ibid.*, at 216.

2. The abandonment of the idea of decisions as founded on contractual agreement is accompanied by the construction of a *generalised* will imputed to the alliance itself, which is thus accorded legal personality and thereby transformed into an association.
3. The idea of an original multilateral contractual personal legal relation between participants is replaced by that of a bundle of personal legal relations between the association and its members, entitling them to vote in the general meeting.
4. An association is treated on a par with physical persons (capacity for rights), is capable of performing legal acts (legal capacity), and is responsible for behaviour flowing from the will imputed to it (legal liability).

This means that:

> ... the idea of an original multilateral contractual personal legal relation between participants is replaced by that of a bundle of personal legal relations between the association and its members ... The *raison d'être* of an association is the collective will of its members as expressed by their genetal meeting, which substitutes for the original contractual agreement.

Thus the external possibilities and competences of an association are closely linked to its internal legal structure. The complex (constitutional) relationship – the subject of this contribution – only 'announces itself' indeed, when the external relations of the member states are complementary to and at the same time governed by the body of procedural rules through which the external behaviour of the association is formed. The current Treaty on European Union reflects this situation, in which relations with third states and organisations are simultaneously defined at the national and the European levels, by international legal persons (the member states and the Union) that are separate, but at the same time inseparable.[35]

B. *A division of external competences?*

The most fundamental basis of any multilevel constitution is the division of powers between the various levels of authority. At Philadelphia the delegates first considered dividing competencies between the centre and

[35] See on the individual international legal personality of the Union, R. A. Wessel, 'The International Legal Status of the European Union', (1997) *EFA Rev.* (1997), 109–29; and 'Revisiting the International Legal Status of the EU' (2000) *EFA Rev* 507–37.

the states according to a set of abstract principles. Eventually, however, they decided that this approach would create too much conflict, as such principles tend to be vague and open to interpretation. Instead, they created a specific list of powers belonging to the central government, the default assumption being that all other powers belonged to the states. In a similar fashion, the Canadians adopted a classic federal 'catalogue of competencies' that listed which level of government had responsibility for each area of action. This approach makes the delimitation of powers extremely clear, and therefore gives maximum protection to lower-level authorities from central interference.[36]

One would have expected the European Union to opt for a clear division of competences as well. Indeed, the notion of a *'Kompetenz Katalog'* came up during the Convention on the Future of Europe whilst drafting the Constitutional Treaty, but the idea was abandoned in the final version. Because, at least in the early days, the European Community Treaty did not devote too much space to the division of external competences between the Community and its member states, the developments in this field are to a large extent case law driven. Thus, every now and then the 'outside' of the European Community was put under the spotlight. After a pause in the 1970s, following judgments such as in *ERTA, Kramer, Haegeman, International Fruit Company* or Opinions such as Opinion 1/76,[37] Opinion 1/91, Opinion 1/92 (EEA), Opinion 2/91 (OECD) and especially Opinion 1/94 on the WTO Agreement,[38] the beginning of the new millennium seemed to herald yet another period in which the external dimension of the EC received abundant attention. This may have been triggered by some new case law, in which the Court addresses the relationship between Community law and international law proper (e.g. *Racke, Opel Austria* or *Portugal v. Council*),[39] but also reflects the problems stemming from the establishment of the European Union (introducing external relations in separate but

---

[36] P. Robinson, 'A Dodgy Constitution', *Spectator*, 8 February 2003.

[37] Case 22/70, *Commission v. Council (AERT or ERTA)* [1971] ECR 263; Case 181/73, *Haegeman v. Belgium* [1974] ECR 449 at 460, para. 2/6; Case 21–24/72, *International Fruit Company NV et al. v. Produktschap voor Groenten en Fruit* [1972] ECR 1226; Opinion 1/76, *Draft Agreement establishing a European laying-up fund for inland waterway vessels* [1977] ECR 741, paras. 3, 4.

[38] Opinion 2/92, *OECD* [1995] ECR I-521; Opinion 1/92, *EEA* [1992] ECR I-2821; Opinion 1/94, *WTO Opinion* [1994] ECR I-5267.

[39] Case C-162/96, *Racke GmbH & Co. v. Hauptzollamt Mainz* [1998] ECR I-3655, para. 45; Case T-115/94, *Opel Austria GmbH v. Council* [1997] ECR II-39, para. 77; Case C-149/96, *Portugal v. Council* [1999] ECR I-8395.

connected areas) and the subsequent modification treaties, as well as from the conclusion of the Treaty Establishing a Constitution for Europe.

In the absence of case law in the area of foreign and security policy, and departing from the notion of a unity of the constitutional regulation of the external relations of the Union and its member states, the question comes up how the competences in this field are divided among the two distinct levels. Indications can, first, be found in the Preamble and the objectives of the Treaty on European Union. In the Preamble, the Heads of State declare that they are:

> Resolved to implement a common foreign and security policy including the eventual framing of a common defence policy, which might lead to a common defence, thereby reinforcing the European identity and its independence in order to promote peace, security and progress in Europe and in the world.

The beginning of the quoted statement may convey the impression that since the Heads of State, when establishing the EU, were 'resolved to implement a common foreign and security policy', it should be regarded as an overall objective and not as something that was created by the Treaty. Does this mean that the establishment of a Common Foreign and Security Policy (CFSP) is merely an objective of the Union that does not yet exist? No. Any possible confusion as to the status of CFSP was eliminated by the original Article J of the 1992 TEU, which unconditionally stipulated that '[a] common foreign and security policy is [hereby] established'.[40] Hence, in the above-quoted provision, the emphasis should be on the 'implementation' of a CFSP. This is underlined by Article 11 in the 1997 TEU, which provides that '[t]he Union shall define and implement a common foreign and security policy . . .'[41] Thus, since 1993, there exists a Union foreign and security policy – at least in a formal institutional sense.

---

[40] The fact that *a* CFSP is established, and not *the* CFSP, for some authors was an indication of the non-exclusive character of CFSP; CFSP has not replaced all aspects of the foreign and security policies of the member states, it only exists in the areas in which the member states come to an agreement. See V. Constantinesco, R. Kovar and D. Simon, *Traité sur l'Union Européenne: Commentaire article par article* (Paris: Economica, 1995), p. 786.

[41] The former Article J, by which CFSP was established, was deleted by the Amsterdam Treaty. This phrase returns in the 2004 Constitutional Treaty (Article I-12, para. 4) in slightly different terms, with an emphasis on the Union's competence in this field: 'The Union shall have competence to define and implement a common foreign and security policy, including the progressive framing of a common defence policy.'

The purposes mentioned in the Preamble come close to the ones the Heads of State had formulated in the Preamble to the Single European Act (SEA, 1986) in which they stated that they were 'aware of the responsibility incumbent upon Europe to aim at speaking increasingly with one voice and to act with consistency and solidarity in order more effectively to protect its common interests and independence . . . so that together they may make their own contribution to the preservation of international peace and security . . .'. The inconsistencies in this statement were, however, even more striking. By 'together' making their 'own contribution' the states aimed to 'speak with one voice' and to 'act with consistency and solidarity'. The words chosen explain the absence of a reference to a *common* policy; the purpose of the SEA was, as its Article 30 stipulates, to establish a 'European Cooperation in the sphere of foreign policy'. The Union Treaty aimed to go beyond this in establishing a *common* policy, and not just an *ad hoc* adaptation of different individual policies.

The purpose set forth by the Heads of State in the Preamble of the TEU reflects their decision to implement a common foreign and security policy. But, who is responsible? While the Preamble *prima facie* hints at the states themselves as being responsible, Article 2 of the Common Provisions of the TEU repeats this purpose as an 'objective of the *Union*'. Obviously, there is a difference between the 'states', as represented by the Heads of State as the original 'contractors', and the 'European Union' they created. According to Article 1 TEU, the European Union is established between the High Contracting Parties. The concept of 'Union' is not explicitly defined by the Treaty; it is said to be 'founded on the European Communities, supplemented by the policies and forms of cooperation established by this Treaty'. Regardless of its precise definition, it follows from these descriptions that the 'Union' is not to be equated with the 'states' ('High Contracting Parties') by which it was established.[42] The objective of the *Union*, as stipulated in Article 2 TEU, is:

> . . . to assert its identity on the international scene, in particular through
> the implementation of a common foreign and security policy including
> the progressive framing of a common defence policy, which might in time
> lead to a common defence . . . .

---

[42] This seems to be confirmed by Article 6, para. 3, which provides that '[t]he Union shall respect the national identities of its Member States'.

This objective is, however, slightly different from the objective of the *states* when they created the Union.[43] For the purpose of the present contribution, the question is who is responsible for attaining objectives that are partially overlapping but not entirely phrased in identical words.

The original 1992 Article J.1 provided some insight into this issue by stipulating that 'the Union and its Member States shall define and implement a common foreign and security policy'. This provision confirmed the view that *both* the Union and the states are responsible for the implementation of a CFSP. It did not define, however, the difference between the Union and the states. It even complicated their relationship by referring to 'Member States'.[44] Regarding the European Political Cooperation (EPC), the SEA consequently spoke of 'High Contracting Parties', since the EPC was not part of the European Community and it was not considered possible to be a 'member' of the EPC. Regardless of the fact that the Union is not presented as an international organisation anywhere in the TEU, the introduction of the term 'Member States' – which is still used throughout the entire text – underlines the fact that a new entity was created, an new international legal entity of which it is possible to become a 'member'.

While careless use of terminology may of course very well be the explanation, an affirmative answer to this question seems to be supported by Article 11. This Article sheds light on the division of competences as it refers to the Union as the only responsible actor for the definition and implementation of CFSP. According to the second paragraph of that Article, the member states are to 'support' the Union in that respect. Several other provisions underline the status of the Union, not only as a separate actor, but even as the key actor in CFSP. Thus, *the Union* shall pursue objectives (Article 12), *the Union* has a (external and security) policy (Article 11, para. 1 and Article 17, para. 1),[45] *the Union* may avail itself of another organisation (Article 17, para. 3), *the Union* can have a position (Article 18, para. 2), and *the Union* can take action (Article 13, para. 3). Similar wordings return in the Constitutional Treaty (e.g. Articles I-40,

---

[43] Instead of the 'reinforcement of the European identity and independence', and through that the 'promotion of peace, security and progress in Europe and the world', the objective of the Union is to 'assert its identity on the international scene', for which the implementation of a CFSP is to be regarded as the means. The different terms used – 'reinforce' and 'assert'; 'in Europe and the world' and 'on the international scene' – are not necessarily contradictory (regardless of the question why 'Europe' does not belong to 'the world').

[44] *Cf.* also in this respect Article 6, para. 3.

[45] Article 30, para. 5 of the Single European Act only referred to 'policies agreed' within the cooperation framework of the EPC.

I-41) and it seems commonly accepted by now that the Union is not to be equated by the states by which it was established.

Most important in that respect is that CFSP decisions (regardless of their form and substance) are not merely agreed on by the EU member states, but that they are adopted by an *organ*: the Council of the European Union. The pivotal position of the Council in CFSP decision-making, as well as in decisions on national deviations from agreed policy is obvious.[46] Decision-making by the Council rests on explicit power-conferring norms. Earlier studies revealed that it would be difficult to hold the view that the Council is merely a meeting hall for 15 states.[47] Without repeating the arguments, it is clear that the Council can be seen as an institution of the European Union, which finds its direct basis as well as its competences in the TEU.

This brings us to the question of how the national legal orders of the member states are related to the EU legal order in this area. Is the latter to be conceived as a 'supranational' order which by definition sets aside any conflicting national legal norm? Does the notion of a single, albeit 'multilevel', constitution exclude the possibility of looking at the different legal orders as operating in a 'dualist' fashion? And, if this is the case, do the norms created at the European level affect the citizens and other private parties within the national legal orders?

2. The constitutional relationship between the Union and its member states in foreign policy

A. The validity relation between the two levels

The acceptance of the idea of a multilevel constitution brings about two distinct questions concerning the hierarchy between the legal orders that

---

[46] More extensively, see Wessel, *The European Union's Foreign and Security Policy*, chs. 4 and 5. In this respect, see also C. Trüe, *Verleihung von Rechtspersönlichkeit an die Europäische Union und Verschmelzung zu einer einzigen Organisation – deklaratorisch oder konstitutiv?*, Vorträge, Reden und Berichte aus dem Europa-Institut, No. 357 (Saarbrücken: Europa-Institut der Universität des Saarlandes, 1997), p. 22, who pointed to the different terms used in the EPC period (when the participating states 'acted in common') and the CFSP cooperation (which leads to 'joint actions'). However, the term 'joint action' in fact does not make sense when it is seen as a decision of the Council. The best way out in this respect is to regard 'joint actions' as decisions of the Council, in which this organ decides that the member states of the Union have to act jointly.

[47] See, for references, Wessel, *The European Union's Foreign and Security Policy*, pp. 74–6.

can be found at the two levels. The first question concerns the validity relationship between different legal orders; the second question deals with the supremacy of rules in one order over rules in another. Applied to the topic of the present chapter, these questions can be phrased as follows: Is the validity of norms issued by international organisations derived from another legal order, and if so what consequences does this have for the supremacy of norms of other legal orders over these norms or *vice versa* in case of a conflict between these norms? This question becomes relevant in particular in relation to the (direct) effect of decisions of international organisations in the legal orders of the member states and thus to the way in which both the Union and its member states (jointly or individually) may approach the 'outside world' (see section C below).

Regarding the first question, Kelsen pointed to the existence of different 'basic norms' as the ultimate 'source' of distinct legal orders, but he also argued that the source of two distinct legal orders can be the same when one order is based on the other.[48] Kelsen argued that there are four conceivable (validity) relations between two distinct orders (or 'norm systems'):[49]

1. both systems are completely divided ('*unabhängig*'), i.e. they have distinct sources of validity;
2. norm system A derives its validity from norm system B;
3. norm system B derives its validity from norm system A ('*über- und unterordnung*'); and
4. both orders are of equal value, they are (relatively) independent sub-systems, coordinated by an overarching superior order ('*Koordination*').

The above analyses on the personification of a contractual legal relationship shows that the *validity* of a treaty-based legal order is derived from the valid competence of states to establish these international orders. This, however, is not enough. States can only do this on the basis of a

---

[48] H. Kelsen, *Das Problem der Souveränität und die Theorie des Völkerrechts: Beitrage zu einer reinen Rechtslehre* (Scientia Aalen, 1928/1960) at p. 105. Despite its age, this book still serves as one of the clearest interpretations of the concept of sovereignty and the relation between the international legal order and national legal orders (or 'states' in Kelsen's line of reasoning).

[49] *Ibid*, at 104. *Cf.* also W. Werner, *Het recht geworden woord: over de geschiedenis van het rechtspositivisme en de mogelijke betekenis van het pramgmatisme voor de toekomst daarvan* (Enschede: Universiteit Twente, 1995), p. 158.

'third' norm, that is not part of their own legal order. A national legal system as such cannot be a sufficient legal basis for the establishment of a valid *international* agreement between sovereign states. There has to be an external rule according to which the expressed will by a sovereign state counts as a valid way to be bound by an international agreement.[50]

At the same time, this relationship points to the unity of the international legal system. States are only connected to each other because they form part of an overarching international – or better in this respect, 'supranational' – legal order. Returning now to Verdross, the classic question described by him is that the unity of the international legal order depends on the existence of a basic norm (*Grundnorm*), which is the source of all international legal norms and which is thus capable of tying the different norms together.[51]

Whenever associations of states (multilateral treaties) have been transformed – through a legal act of personification – into new legal entities, these international organisations would also form part of the supranational legal order. States can only create these new legal entities because a supranational legal order allows them – or makes it possible for them – to do this. The acceptance of the existence of an overarching legal order, consisting of legal sub-systems (states and international organisations) indeed depends on the acceptance of the unity of this legal system, in the sense that the *Grundnorm* of this system is at the same time the source of the norms in the subsystems. The consequence of this assumption is that once a norm is validly created anywhere in the international legal order, this *validity* cannot be denied in any of the suborders. This, in turn, causes problems for advocates of the classic dualist approach, which claims that the legal systems of international organisations and the member states are completely independent,

---

[50] See also Curtin and Dekker, 'The Constitutional Structure'.

[51] 'Von einer einheitlichen Völkerrechtsordnung kann nur die Rede sein, wenn sämtliche Völkerrechtsnormen einen Verweisungszusammenhang, einen Delegationszusammenhang von berufenden und berufenen, von delegierenden und delegierten Normen bilden. Dazu ist vor allem erforderlich, daß eine oberste Norm oder ein oberstes Normengefüge, kurz eine *Grundnorm* in Geltung steht, auf die der geltungsgrund aller übrigen Völkerrechtsnormen unmittelbar oder mittelbar zurückgeführt werden kann. Bloß der bestand einer solchen Grundnorm, die die normative Grundlage für alle übrigen Völkerrechtssätze liefert, vermag die Einheitlichkeit des Völkerrechtes zu verbürgen, da die Einheitlichkeit jedes Normensystems nur dadurch möglich ist, daß alle seine Normen aus einem einheitlichen Brennpunkte ausstrahlen, über den unde durch den sie zusammenhängen. Das Problem der Einheitlichkeit des Völkerrechtes steht und fällt daher mit dem Probleme der völkerrechtlichen Grundnorm.' Verdross, *Die Verfassung*, p. 12.

separate from each other and from the overarching legal order, in the sense that they have different legal sources and different legal subjects.[52] In this approach the legal system of the international organisation provides rules for the member states (and for the functioning of the organisation itself), whereas the legal system of the member states regulates the activities of its citizens and other private persons (and the functioning of the state itself). In other words, legally valid rights and duties of individuals can only be created under the national legal system of the member states. Apart from logical problems,[53] simple empirical tests reveal the impossibility of upholding this notion. Many rules of positive international law purport to bind private persons directly, without interference from national law. Obvious examples of such rules are those on the international criminal responsibility of individuals for international crimes. Other examples may be found in the legal system of the European Union providing a range of treaty-based rules, regulations and decisions directly creating rights and duties for individuals and other legal persons. As shown by the European Community – and increasingly by other parts of the Union (and even by other international organisations)[54] – the legal order of the member states cannot claim to be immune to norms created in another legal subsystem of the international legal order.[55]

In conclusion, both states and international organisations seem to be sub-systems of the overall supranational legal order, the existence of

---

[52] See also I. Weyland, 'The Application of Kelsen's Theory of the Legal System to European Community Law – The Supremacy Puzzle Resolved' (2002) 21 *Law and Philosophy* 1. Although dealing with Community Law, Weyland argues that: '. . . analysis based on Kelsen's theory must reject a dualist conception and will lead to the assumption of only one basic norm of a unified set of norms, where the basic norm, either of the Community or of each Member State, validates both Community and national constitutional norms. The principle of the supremacy of Community over national constitutional norms may be fitted into either model.' *Ibid.* at 23. Weyland thus does not see a basic norm in an 'overarching' legal order, but rather in either the national legal order or the legal order of the international organisation.

[53] At least when one accepts Kelsen's ideas on the unity of a legal system with the basic norm as a common source of validity for norms of both states and international organisations, and the idea that state sovereignty can only be upheld on the basis of the notion that all states form part of one legal system which also provides the norm to respect the territorial sphere of validity of other states. Weyland, 'The Application of Kelsen's Theory' at 28.

[54] See R. A. Wessel, 'The Invasion by International Organizations. *De toenemende samenhang tussen de mondiale, Europese en nationale rechtsorde*', Inaugural Lecture, University of Twente, The Netherlands, 12 January 2006 (available through the author).

[55] Curtin and Dekker, 'The Constitutional Structure'.

which is, is turn, determined by the fact that states and international organisations exist. Thus, this supranational order not only defines the existence of states, but also coordinates and makes possible the relations between these states.[56] The fact that states are allowed to conclude treaties and to create international organisations, and that they are bound by these agreements, implies the existence of a 'higher' legal order with the *pacta sunt servanda*-norm as its most obvious *Grundnorm*.[57]

B. Consistency and delimitation between the constitutional levels

The starting point of the unity of the legal order in terms of the validity of the norms in that order was to present the regulation of European foreign relations as a single (multilevel) constitution in which norms at one level cannot be isolated from norms at the other. This unity of the legal system can already be found in H. L. A. Hart's theory of law, in which the unity derives from the rules of conflict within the rule of recognition, which determine relations of supra- and subordination between rules deriving from different sources.[58] One consequence of this idea is that the external relations that are based on this constitution are consistent, in the sense that third parties are not confronted with a conflicting legal output. At the same time the constitution may provide for a delimitation of the competences of the actors on the different levels.[59] The notions of delimitation and consistency are in particular reflected in four principles underlying the cooperation between the member states and the EU, which may therefore be considered key constitutional principles in this area: the information and consultation obligation, the loyalty obligation, subsidiarity, and the procedures on external representation.

---

[56] *Cf.* Kelsen, *Das Problem der Souveränität*, pp. 204–5.
[57] Verdross, *Die Verfassung*, p. 32.
[58] See also Weyland, 'The Application of Kelsen's Theory', 33. According to Weyland, this is why it is arguable that Hart's theory also supports the monistic model.
[59] The same problems occur in a 'horizontal' dimension *within* the European Union. See R. A. Wessel, 'The Inside Looking Out: Consistency and Delimitation in EU External Relations' (2000) *CMLR* 1135–71 and 'Fragmentation in the Governance of EU External Relations: Legal Institutional Dilemmas and the New Constitution for Europe', in J. W. de Zwaan, J. H. Jans, F. A. Nelissen (eds.), *The European Union – An Ongoing Process of Integration: Liber Amicorum Fred Kellermann* (Den Haag: T.M.C. Asser Press, 2004), pp. 123–40.

(a) The information and consultation principle

The autonomous competences of the Union in relations with third parties imply the existence of procedural restraints on the member states, aiming at a consistent external policy, but at the same time fixing a vertical division of competences. The key provision in this respect is to be found in the so-called information and consultation obligation. This obligation forms part of the concept of systematic cooperation and in fact builds on the system of European Political Cooperation (EPC), in which it was agreed that the participating states 'undertake to inform and consult each other on any foreign policy matters of general interest'.[60] It is this systematic cooperation that in fact formed the core of EPC from 1970 until 1993. And in CFSP it still serves as the key notion, in the absence of which it would be impossible for the Union to define and implement a foreign and security policy. In that respect it could be seen as a necessary pre-legislative procedure. The systematic cooperation referred to in Article 12 TEU is to be established in accordance with Article 16, which contains the actual procedural obligations.[61] In principle, the scope of issues to which the systematic cooperation applies is not subject to any limitation regarding time or space: 'Member States shall inform and consult one another within the Council on any matter of foreign and security policy . . .' Nevertheless, Article 16 immediately fills this lacuna, by adding the words 'of general interest'. The European Council has not provided any further specification of 'general interest' in Article 16. This seriously limits the information and consultation obligation in the first part of this Article: on the one hand, member states are obligated to inform and consult one another, whereas on the other hand they are given the individual discretion to decide whether or not a matter is of 'general interest'. This underlines the important procedural role of the 'national level' in the arrangement.

Nevertheless, it can be asserted that the member states are indeed *obligated* to inform and consult one another. Through the information and consultation obligation the member states ordered themselves to use it as one of the means to attain the CFSP objectives in Article 11. Taking into account the nature of the information and consultation obligation, it is

---

[60] See Article 30, para. 2(a) of the Single European Act (1986).
[61] The contents of Article 16 (J.2, para. 2) were not modified throughout the negotiations of the 1992 Treaty on European Union and already formed part of the Luxembourg Draft of 18 June 1991 (Article G of the CFSP provisions).

rather unfortunate that the Treaty does not further define the obligation. In order to establish the content of the obligation it is therefore necessary to turn to general descriptions of the consultation obligation in international law. A general definition was for instance formulated by Möstl, who defined the consultation obligation in international law in terms of a duty for states and other international legal subjects on the basis of an agreement to attune their actions with a view to mutual interests.[62]

A more material obligation could be phrased as the obligation not to take a position as long as this position has not been discussed with the other partner(s).[63] There are no reasons to assume that the notion of consultation as used in Article 16 deviates from these general definitions, which leads us to conclude that the EU member states are to refrain from making national positions on CFSP issues of general interest public before they have discussed these positions in the framework of the CFSP cooperation.

With regard to the obligation itself, it seems that the mandatory way in which the provision is phrased somewhat departs from the more 'intention-oriented' approach in the Single European Act (SEA). Article 30 of the SEA stipulated that '[t]he High Contracting Parties *undertake* to inform and consult each other . . .'.[64] The chosen words may indeed call for a distinction. While 'undertake' seems to go beyond 'intend', is does not seem to be the same as 'shall'.

Informing and consulting one another should take place 'within the Council'. Keeping in mind the requirement of *systematic* cooperation, this should not be interpreted as 'only within the Council'. Cooperation within the preparatory organs (Political and Security Committee, Committee of Permanent Representatives (COREPER), and working groups), as well as bilateral and multilateral consultations are equally covered by this obligation. In fact, it is in these bodies that the actual systematic cooperation takes place. A second reason not to restrict the

---

[62] W. Möstl, 'Die Konsultationsverpflichtung im Völkerrecht', Diss.jur., Würzburg (1967), p. 68: 'Die von Staaten oder anderen Völkerrechtssubjekten durch völkerrechtlichen Vertrag vereinbarte Verplichtung zu einer auf der Grundlage der Gleichheit und Gegenseitigkeit ruhenden und von einer Gemeinsamkeit der Interessen getragenen Beratung zwischen einer den Organen der Vertragspartner mit dem Ziel der Herbeiführung einer den Interessen der Beteiligten gemäßen gemeinsamen Haltung in einer bestimmten Situation.'

[63] T. Jürgens, *Die gemeinsame Europäische Aussen- und Sicherheitspolitik*, (Köln: Carl Heymanns Verlag, 1994), p. 210: '[d]as Gebot, von der endgültigen Festlegung einer eigenen Position Abstand zu nehmen, solange nicht die Anhörung des Konsultationspartners stattgefunden hat.'

[64] Emphasis added.

cooperation to meetings of the member states in the Council, may be found in Article 19. According to this provision, member states shall coordinate their action in international organisations and at international conferences as well. Even when not all member states are represented in an international organisation or at an international conference, the ones that do participate are to keep the absent states informed of any matter of common interest (see section (d) below).

(b) The loyalty principle

These observations are supported by Article 11, para. 2, which reflects a more general 'loyalty obligation': 'The Member States shall support the Union's external and security policy actively and unreservedly in a spirit of loyalty and mutual solidarity.'[65] This obligation is not further defined. A possible interpretation could be found in one of the other Union areas, where one finds a comparable provision in Article 10 EC.[66] Like Article 10 EC, the CFSP provision contains a *positive* obligation for the member states to actively develop the Union's policy in the indicated area, which since the Amsterdam Treaty even includes the obligation to 'work together to enhance and develop their mutual political solidarity'. Moreover, the *negative* obligation not to undertake 'any action which is contrary to the interests of the Union or likely to impair its effectiveness as a cohesive force in international relations' is also comparable to Article 10 EC.[67]

A comparison of the CFSP loyalty obligation with Article 10 EC reveals its potential impact. The latter Article has proven its added value in Community law; it is often seen as the basis of the constitutional nature of Community law[68] and it has been frequently used by the Court of Justice in its case law, albeit that the materialisation of the obligation

---

[65] One could be struck by the word 'external', which in this provision replaces the familiar term 'foreign', but there are no reasons to place any particular emphasis on this inconsistency.

[66] Article 10 of the Treaty establishing the European Community: 'Member States shall take all appropriate measures, whether general or particular, to ensure fulfilment of the obligations arising out of this Treaty or resulting from action taken by the institutions of the Community. They shall facilitate the achievement of the Community's tasks. They shall abstain from any measure which could jeopardise the attainment of the objectives of this Treaty.'

[67] According to Fink-Hooijer, 'From a strictly legal point of view, the restrictive loyalty clause can only apply and have effect once a European Union interest or policy has been defined': F. Fink-Hooijer, 'The Common Foreign and Security Policy of the European Union' (1994) 5 *EJIL* 173 at 180.

[68] See, for instance, J. Temple Lang, 'Community Constitutional Law: Article 5 EEC Treaty' (1998) 25 *CMLR* 595; and K. J. M. Mortelmans, 'The Principle of Loyalty to

needs to be established in conjunction with other provisions in the Treaty or in secondary law.[69] Article 10 EC has thus been interpreted as to include:

1. the obligation to take all appropriate measures necessary for the effective application of Community law;
2. the obligation to ensure the protection of rights resulting from primary and secondary Community law;
3. the obligation to act in such a way as to achieve the objectives of the Treaty, in particular when Community actions fail to appear;
4. the obligation not to take measures which could harm the *effet utile* of Community law;
5. the obligation not to take measures which could hamper the internal functioning of the institutions; and
6. the obligation not to undertake actions which could hamper the development of the integration process of the Community.[70]

Whilst it cannot be denied that the wording of the CFSP provision provides no reasons to limit its scope in relation to Article 10 EC, the absence of any competences of the Court of Justice *within* CFSP makes the question of whether these interpretations could also apply to Article 11, para. 2 a very abstract and theoretical one. On the other hand, even when the member states cooperate outside the explicit treaty provisions, Article 10 assures their solidarity. In fact, the Court has made this abundantly clear when it established that the obligations on the basis of Article 10 EC may extend beyond the limits of Community law:

> Article 5 [now Article 10] of the treaty provides that the Member States must take all appropriate measures, whether general or particular, to ensure fulfilment of the obligations arising out of the treaty. If, therefore, the application of a provision of community law is liable to be impeded by a measure adopted pursuant to the implementation of a bilateral agreement, even where the agreement falls outside the field of application of the treaty, every member state is under a duty to facilitate the

---

the Community (Article 5 EC) and the Obligations of the Community Institutions' (1998) 5 *Maastricht Journal of European and Comparative Law* 67–88.

[69] E.g. Case 78/70, *Deutsche Grammophon Gesellschaft mbH v. Metro-SB-Großmärkte GmbH & Co.* [1971] ECR 487.

[70] See, in particular, O. Due, 'Artikel 5 van het EEG-Verdrag, een bepaling met een federaal karakter?' (1992) *SEW Tijdschrift voor Europees recht* 355–66; and J. Mégret, M. Waelbroeck and J. E. De Cockborne, *Commentaire Mégret: le driot de la CEE* (Bruxelles: Éditions de l'Université de Bruxelles, 1992) pp. 26–42.

application of the provision and, to that end, to assist every other member state whichis under an obligation under community law.[71]

The reference to cooperation outside the field of application of the EC Treaty seems to imply that the scope of Article 10 EC reaches across the Union's three main areas. This is in particular apparent when the principle of consistency is taken into account. According to Article 3 TEU, the Union shall in particular ensure the consistency of its external activities. It could be argued that irrespective of the separate CFSP loyalty obligation, a failure to comply with the consistency requirement could, at least in certain cases, be seen as a breach of Article 10 of the EC Treaty, constituting grounds for the justiciability of consistency.[72] The loyalty principle thus seems to have evolved – in the words of Curtin and Dekker – 'from a duty of cooperation on the part of the Member States to a multi-sided duty of loyalty and good faith in the vertical relationship between the Union and its Member States and also among the Member States themselves and among Union institutions themselves'.[73]

(c) The subsidiarity principle

The CFSP loyalty clause may come in conflict with another important Union principle: 'subsidiarity'.[74] However, the necessary application of this principle to CFSP matters is not obvious. The principle of subsidiarity is defined in the EC Treaty (Article 5) and only referred to in Article 2 TEU: 'The objectives of the Union shall be achieved ... while

---

[71] Case 235/87, *Annunziata Matteucci v. Communauté Française de Belgique* [1988] ECR 5589, para. 19. *Cf.* also H. G. Krenzler and H. C. Schneider, 'Die Gemeinsame Außen- und Sicherheitspolitik der Europäischen Union – Zur Frage der Kohärenz' (1997) *EuR* Heft 2 144–61 at 147, with regard to 'mixed actions': '[I]t is doubtful whether the CFSP consistency obligation can still be seen as binding only under international law. When CFSP joint actions are combined with Community measures in an operation by the Union as a whole, the Community obligation imposed by Article 5 of the EC Treaty [now Article 10] spreads into the domain of CFSP, meaning that consistency could be considered obligatory under Community law as well as international law ... A failure to comply with the consistency requirement could, at least in certain cases of joint action, be seen as a breach of Article 5 of the EC Treaty, constituting grounds for the justiciability of consistency.'

[72] Krenzler and Schneider, 'Die Gemeinsame Außen', at 147.

[73] Curtin and Dekker, 'The Constitutional Structure', 12. See also A. Verhoeven, *The European Union in Search of a Democratic and Constitutional Theory* (The Hague: Kluwer Law International, 2004), pp. 304–25.

[74] See, in general on the principle of subsidiarity, e.g. A. G. Toth, 'The Principle of Subsidiarity in the Maastricht Treaty' (1992) 6 *CMLR* 1079–106; A. Estella, *The EU Principle of Subsidiarity and its Critique* (Oxford: Oxford University Press, 2002).

respecting the principle of subsidiarity as defined in Article 5 of the Treaty establishing the European Community'.[75] According to the central part of Article 5 EC, the principle of subsidiarity entails that:

> In areas which do not fall within the exclusive competence, the Community shall take action, in accordance with the principle of subsidiarity, only if and in so far as the objectives of the proposed action cannot be sufficiently achieved by the Member States and can therefore, by reason of the scale or effects of the proposed action, be better achieved by the Community.

On the basis of the wording of Article 2 TEU and Article 5 EC, one could argue that the subsidiarity principle does not extend to any other area of the Union but the European Community. Article 2 stipulates that the objectives of the Union shall be achieved while respecting the principle of subsidiarity as defined in Article 5 EC. Article 5 EC, in turn, defines subsidiarity as the principle that the *Community* shall only act if the objectives of the proposed action cannot be achieved by the member states. Hence, if the Community abides by this principle, the Union's obligation in Article 2 TEU is fulfilled. Some support for this view can be found in the analysis of the subsidiarity principle presented by the European Council of Edinburgh in December 1992, or in the fact that the Protocol on the Application of the Principles of Subsidiarity and Proportionality was annexed to the EC Treaty only and not to the TEU.[76] Despite a few general references to a Union-wide application of subsidiarity ('[the] European Union rests on the principle of subsidiarity' and 'the principle of subsidiarity as a basic principle of the European Union'), the concrete analysis of the European Council is restricted to the application of subsidiarity by the *Community*. It even observes that 'The Treaty on European Union obliges all institutions to consider, when examining a *Community* measure, whether the provisions of Article 3B [the original Article 5; RAW] are concerned'.[77] Hence,

---

[75] L. Münch, 'Die Gemeinsame Außen- und Sicherheitspolitik (GASP): ein Schaf im Wolfspelz?' (1997) *ZÖR* 389–417 at 395.

[76] See European Council of Edinburgh, Presidency Conclusions, 11–12 December 1992, Annex 1 to Part A: Overall Approach to the Application by the Council of the Subsidiarity Principle and Article 3B of the 1992 Treaty on European Union [*sic*!], *Bull. EC* 12–1992.

[77] See Part III of the Annex: 'Procedures and Practices'. Emphasis added. *Cf.* also A. G. Toth, 'A Legal Analysis of Subsidiarity', in D. O'Keeffe and P. Twomey (eds.), *Legal Issues of the Maastricht Treaty* (London: Wiley Chancery Law, 1994), pp. 37–48 at 38: '. . . Article B [now Article 2] seems to make subsidiarity applicable across the whole

despite some confusing references to a possible Union-wide application of subsidiarity, the Treaty text, as well as an authoritative interpretation by the European Council, seem to hint at the non-applicability of the principle of subsidiarity as defined in Article 5 EC to the non-Community areas of the European Union.

Nevertheless, the opposite view is more widely held. Subsidiarity is usually regarded as a Union-wide principle. Thus, according to some authors, any CFSP decision taken by the Council has to pass a test to determine whether action on the part of the European Union, as opposed to national action, can be justified.[78] The main source of the Union-wide application of the subsidiarity principle is often found in the Preamble to the TEU, which explicitly refers to it, and in Article 1 TEU stating that decisions are taken as closely as possible to the citizen. It remains difficult, however, to bring this requirement into line with the loyalty clause of Article 11, para. 2. After all, stressing that the parties to the TEU are first and foremost 'states', and only in the last resort 'member states' is obviously contradictory to the rule that they should actively develop the Union's policy and refrain from actions which are contrary to the interests of the Union or likely to impair its effectiveness. To be able to meet the requirements of a systematic cooperation, the subsidiarity test – when accepted – is to be taken in the course of the process of decision-making, and not prior to it.[79] Any other representation of the subsidiarity principle in relation to CFSP would set aside the entire set of procedural obligations agreed upon.[80] While one cannot be sure whether any CFSP decisions have failed because of an appeal to

Union Treaty. However, these provisions are more in the nature of political statements, declarations of intent, rather than provisions with precise legal effects.'

[78] See, in particular, Fink-Hooijer, 'The Common Foreign and Security Policy', 178, and Münch, 'Die Gemeinsame Außen- und Sicherheitspolitik', 395. See also the Communication of the Commission to the Council and the European Parliament, 27 October 1992, Doc. SEC (92) 1990 final.

[79] The 1992 Treaty seemed to underline this when in this respect it referred to 'areas in which the Member States have important interests in common' (Article J.1, para. 3); 'whenever it [the Council] deems it *necessary*' (Article J.2, para. 2 – emphasis added). But the 1997 Treaty also retained the reference to 'any matter of foreign and security policy of general interest' (Article 16).

[80] In this respect, L. Tindemans, 'En guise d'introduction: considérations personelles sur le Traité de Maastricht', in J. Monar *et al.* (eds.), *The Maastricht Treaty on European Union: Legal Complexity and Political Dynamic* (Brussels: European Interuniversity Press, 1993), pp. 7–8, who labelled the principle of solidarity as being necessarily complementary to subsidiarity.

subsidiarity, practice has shown no references to the principle in the preamble of the CFSP decisions taken to date.

(d) External representation

From a legal point of view, the world order is composed of unitary actors. Even in federations foreign relations are predominantly, if not exclusively, controlled by the central government. It is obvious that the Union cannot be seen as a (federal) state and that its member states have not given up their treaty-making competence.[81] On the other hand, the whole purpose of creating a CFSP (after 20 years of a rather intergovernmental EPC) was to enable the member states to speak with one voice by creating a new entity which would do this on their behalf. Again, however, the regulation of external representation is not solely to be found in the national constitutions or in the EU, but in a sophisticated and probably unprecedented constitutional regime in which external competences are allocated over two levels. Apart from the limited areas falling under the exclusive competence of the European Community, the member states retained their external competences. At the same time, however, the European Union itself was given autonomous external capacities. Apart from a large number of implied external capacities (ranging from the representation of the Union by the High Representative or the Presidency in CFSP matters to the new defence dimension),[82] the most obvious explicit capacity concerns the treaty-making power of the Union. Article 24 TEU provides:

> When it is necessary to conclude an agreement with one or more States or international organisations in implementation of this Title, the Council, acting unanimously, may authorise the Presidency, assisted by the Commission as appropriate, to open negotiations to that effect. Such agreements shall be concluded by the Council acting unanimously on a recommendation from the Presidency.

It has been argued that such agreements are concluded by the Council not on behalf of the Union but on behalf of the member states;[83]

---

[81] See, however, on the emerging elements of a Union 'statehood', T. Tiilikainen, 'To Be or Not to Be?: An Analysis of the Legal and Political Elements of Statehood in the EU's External Identity' (2001) *European Foreign Affairs Review (EFA Rev)* 223–41.

[82] See, more extensively, Wessel, 'The Inside Looking Out', 533–6.

[83] See, in particular, N. Neuwahl, 'A Partner with a Troubled Personality: EU Treaty-Making in Matters of CFSP and JHA after Amsterdam' (1998) *EFA Rev* 177–96; M. Cremona, 'External Relations and External Competence: The Emergence of an

however, there are even more convincing arguments pointing to the Council concluding such agreements on behalf of the Union.[84] The regime of Article 24 and of the connected Declaration No. 4 adopted by the Amsterdam IGC[85] reflects the multilevel character of the constitution in this regard. Article 24 provides that the Council concludes the international agreements after its members (the member states) have unanimously agreed that it could do so.[86] No reference is made to the fact that the Council in concluding the agreement would only act on behalf of the member states. However, para. 5 of Article 24 says that such agreements shall not be binding on a member state that states that it has to comply with national constitutional procedures. This provision only makes sense when the member states themselves do not become a party to the agreement. Thus it can be inferred that the international agreements are concluded by the Council on behalf of the Union. After all, the question concerning the application of national constitutional procedures would not need to be brought up when the member states as such are parties to the agreement. Furthermore, agreements shall be binding

---

Integrated Policy', in Craig and De Búrca, *The Evolution of EU law*, pp. 137–75, at p. 168. *Cf.* also J. W. de Zwaan, 'Community Dimensions of the Second Pillar', in T. Heukels, N. Blokker and M. Brus (eds.), *The European Union After Amsterdam: A Legal Analysis* (The Hague: Kluwer Law International, 1998), p. 182, who seems to recognise that this is a legal capacity of the *Union*, but nevertheless denies the existence of a 'formal legal personality'. Also J. W. de Zwaan, 'The Legal Personality of the European Communities and the European Union' (1999) *Netherlands Yearbook of International Law (NYIL)* 75–113. It has even been argued that Article 24 agreements are 'not legally binding' and not to be viewed as treaties. See the opinion of the Dutch Government in the documents of the Second Chamber, TK 1997–1998, 25 922 (R 1613), No. 5, at 51.

[84] Without repeating all arguments, I refer to Wessel, 'The Inside Looking Out', 527–33.

[85] Declaration No. 4 reads: 'The Provisions of Article J.14 and K.10 [now Articles 24 and 38 TEU; RAW] of the Treaty on European Union and any agreements resulting from them shall not imply any transfer of competence from the Member States to the European Union.'

[86] The explicit reference to the unanimity rule (as a *lex specialis*) seems to exclude the applicability of the general regime of constructive abstention in cases where unanimity is required as foreseen in Article 23 of the 1992 Treaty on European Union. Furthermore, as indicated by G. Hafner, 'The Amsterdam Treaty and the Treaty-Making Power of the European Union: Some Critical Comments', in G. Hafner, K.-H. Böckstiegel and I. Seidl-Hohenveldern (eds.), *Liber Amicorum Professor Seidl-Hohenveldern – in honour of his 80th Birthday* (The Hague: Kluwer Law International, 1998) p. 279, the application of the constructive abstention to Article 24 would make little sense, since Article 24 already provides the possibility of achieving precisely the same effect insofar as member states, by referring to their constitutional requirements, are entitled to exclude, in relation to them, the legal effect of agreements concluded by the Council.

also on the member state that has failed to state that it has to comply with the requirements of its own constitutional procedure.[87]

Declaration No. 4 (on the absence of a transfer of competences) can therefore be understood as a statement to reassure the public in certain member states that are particularly sensitive to these issues. Declarations – in case of a conflict with Treaty provisions – can never overrule agreements reflected by the Treaty itself.[88] In any respect, the Declaration in question does not seem to conflict with Article 24 TEU. Since the right to conclude treaties is an original power of the Union itself, the treaty-making power of the member states remains unfettered. The Declaration can only mean that this right of the Union must not be understood as creating new substantive competences for it.[89]

The Nice Treaty underlines the idea that the Council has a competence to conclude treaties on behalf of the Union. According to new paras. 2 and 3 of Article 24, the Council shall still act unanimously when the agreement covers an issue for which unanimity is required for the adoption of internal decisions, but it will act by a qualified majority whenever the agreement is envisaged to implement a Joint Action or Common Position. The possibility for the Council to conclude international agreements by a qualified majority further strengthens the idea of a Council that acts as an institution of the EU rather than as a representative of twenty-five individual member states. Finally, a new para. 6 sets out that that the agreements concluded by the Council shall also be binding on the institutions of the Union. This explicitly answers the question of whether the Union may have obligations under international law apart from the obligations of the member states.

By now, the Union indeed uses Article 24 as a legal basis for the conclusion of its treaties with third parties. The first treaties were concluded in 2001 and concerned agreements with the Federal Republic of Yugoslavia and Macedonia concerning the activities of the EU observer mission in that country.[90] These have been followed by

---

[87] *Ibid.*, p. 276: '. . . the silence of [the] State amounts to an acceptance of the legal effect of the respective treaty with regard to itself already by virtue of Article 24.' See also Pernice, 'Multilevel Constitutionalism', 745: '. . . all indications point to agreements concluded in the name of the Union and not the individual Member States.' *Cf.* also A. Dashwood, 'External Relations Provisions of the Amsterdam Treaty' (1998) 25 *CMLR* 1019 at 1028.

[88] Wessel, *The European Union's Foreign and Security Policy*, pp. 37–40.

[89] As also submitted by Hafner *et al.*, *Liber Amicorum Professor Seidl-Hohenveldern*, p. 272.

[90] *Agreement between the European Union and the Federal Republic of Yugoslavia* [2001] OJ L 125. The agreement with Macedonia can be found in [2001] OJ L 241.

numerous treaties, in particular in relation to the participation of third states in EU military missions and the status of EU missions in host states.[91] Apart from agreements with states, the Union may also engage in a legal relationship with another international organisation, as shown by the agreements concluded with NATO or the International Criminal Court.[92]

In general, one can say that the constitutional division of competence – in terms of vertical power-sharing – thus boils down to a system aiming at a single external Union policy through strict procedural rules restricting the freedom of the member states in this area, whilst at the same time allowing the same member states in the decision-making procedures to prevent exactly this from happening by frequently (but not always) giving them the discretion to judge whether or not issues are fit to be dealt with at the Union level. However, whenever Union decisions have been taken in the area of foreign and security policy, they bind the member states in the external actions that they undertake. This brings us to the question of the effect of these norms within the national legal orders of the member states.

C. (Direct) effect of CFSP norms in national legal systems

It remains important to note that the unity of the legal orders of states and international organisations in terms of the validity relations of the norms, only tells us something about the existence of the norms within the respective orders. Hence, so far I have only focused on one dimension of the multilevel constitution: its existence can be assumed on the basis of the unity of the legal system of which the 'two levels' form a part. At the same time it is underlined that the term 'levels' is not meant to present the relationship between states and international organisations in an hierarchical fashion. On the contrary, the point I tried to make was that it makes more sense to view states and international organisations

---

[91] See, for recent examples, the agreements concluded between the EU and Ukraine, Argentina and Chile: Council Decision 2005/495/CFSP [2005] OJ L 128; Council Decision 2005/593/CFSP [2005] OJ L 202; and Council Decision 2005/447/CFSP [2005] OJ L 156.

[92] See, more extensively, my 'The State of Affairs in EU Security and Defence Policy: The Breakthrough in the Treaty of Nice' (2003) 2 *JCSL* 265–88 and in particular 'The European *Union* as a Party to International Agreements: Shared Competences, Mixed Responsibilities?', in A. Dashwood and M. Maresceau (eds.), *Recent Trends in the External Relations of the Union* (forthcoming, 2007).

(once the latter are established) as 'living apart together', but at least side by side within the overall supranational legal order.[93]

The other dimension of the multilevel constitution concerns the effect of norms created by the international organisation within the legal order of the member states. As claimed earlier, this dimension arguably introduces another element underlying the concept of 'constitution', since it brings in other legal subjects, in addition to the states that established the organisation. Does the fact that norms of an international organisation are valid in national legal orders as well (once it is established that they both are part of the same higher legal order), imply that norms created by international organisations are – at least theoretically – by definition, supreme over national norms? The question should be answered in the negative, as supremacy should not be equated with validity. The two concepts are of a different nature and should not be confused.[94] Different norms may have the same validity source and still be conflicting and norms in 'higher' legal orders do not necessarily overrule norms in 'lower' orders. The only way of settling the supremacy relation between norms of different legal sub-systems (such as states and international organisations) is by introducing (or recognising) either a norm in the overarching supranational legal order (e.g. 'individual citizens are responsible for violations of international humanitarian law') or by agreeing on a certain modus in an international agreement between states or in the constituent treaty of an international organisation (e.g. Article 103 UN Charter). Again on the basis of the *pacta sunt servanda* rule, this modus would take priority over national norms.[95]

Thus, while validity is a prerequisite, rules in the legal order of either the member state or the international organisation may provide for norms to be *applied* in relation to certain legal subjects only (e.g. EC Directives) or only after being transformed into national law. The notion of direct effect may be distinguished from this applicability in that it only becomes relevant when norms do not have the effect they purport to have and citizens wish to invoke a norm before a national judge. Even if a norm is directly applicable – in the sense that it has a

---

[93] Verdross, *Die Verfassung*, p. 9 points to the overarching character of the international legal order: 'Daher ist die Völkerrechtsgemeinschaft die alle positiv-rechtlichen gemeinschaften überspannende Rechtseinheit, die, gleich einer Kuppel, den ganzen großen Rechtsbau überwölbt.'

[94] See, in particular, on the importance of a division between the different possible relations between legal orders: Werner, *Het recht geworden woord*, pp. 156–9.

[95] Curtin and Dekker, 'The Constitutional Structure'.

function between the legal subjects within a national legal order – there may be reasons not to allow individuals to invoke it in a court of law. One of the dimensions of the multilevel constitution in the area of foreign policy would be that it regulates the way in which the norms that are created on the EU level would have an effect on the level of the member states.

This means that we have to look for clues in either the international order, the national legal orders, or the EU legal order indicating the direct applicability, the direct effect and the hierarchical status of CFSP norms. General international law, obviously, is silent about this issue and doctrine generally reflects the principle that states are free to decide on how they want to give effect to international law in their national legal orders.[96] The constitutions of the twenty-seven EU member states indeed differ in this respect. But, as became clear from the development of the European Community, this issue can authoritatively be settled by norms in the supranational order of an international organisation. The principles of direct applicability, direct effect and supremacy were recognised by the Court of Justice of the European Communities (European Court of Justice; ECJ) as forming part of the 'new legal order' (or in the terms of this chapter, the new constitution) regulating the relationship between the EC and its member states, as well as with the legal subjects within the states (natural and legal persons).

Unlike the EC, the non-Community parts of the Union largely fall outside the reach of the ECJ. This means that, for the time being, we cannot rely on authoritative interpretations of the Court regarding the status of CFSP norms in the national legal orders. However, the Treaty itself is not completely silent in this respect. Curtin and Dekker claim that, in principle, Union law is directly applicable in the national legal orders of the member states.[97] They base this conclusion on the fact that with regard to the new types of EU decisions introduced by the Amsterdam Treaty, the 'framework decisions' and 'decisions', the Treaty explicitly provides that they 'shall not entail direct effect' (Article 34 TEU). This provision would only make sense when these types of decision could *in principle* have direct applicability. Irrespective of the inherent danger in using *a contrario* arguments, its acceptance would provide an argument in favour of the direct applicability of EU norms in

---

[96] See, for instance, A. Cassese, *International Law* (Oxford: Oxford University Press, 2001), ch. 8.
[97] Curtin and Dekker, 'The Constitutional Structure', 11.

general, since exclusion of direct effect becomes relevant only in case of direct applicability. In any case, recent case law of the ECJ seems to put the differences between Community and Union instruments into perspective.[98]

Although this example is drawn from the provision of police and judicial cooperation and not from the provisions of foreign and security policy, there is no compelling reason to differentiate between the two substantive Union areas in this respect. The direct applicability of CFSP norms would then result in the possibility – and even the necessity – of using these norms in the relationships between all legal subjects within the national legal order. Administrative as well as judicial organs could invoke them, but the same holds true for citizens and companies in their mutual relations. This is not to say that all norms by definition could be invoked in national court proceedings. Just as with Community norms, this would depend on the nature of the norm (sufficiently clear and precise), which in this case would ultimately be decided by the national judge. Curtin and Dekker claim that Union norms, at least, could have an 'indirect effect', meaning that 'all national authorities have the obligation to interpret national legislation and other measures as much as possible in the light of the wording and purpose of valid Union law'.[99] This, however, implies an acceptance of the supremacy of Union law over national law. After all, 'indirect effect' only becomes relevant in case of a (possible) conflict between an EU and a national norm. Curtin and Dekker, more or less implicitly, base this supremacy on the principle of loyalty, as laid down in Article 10 EC as one of the leading principles in the constitution of the *Union* entailing an obligation for national authorities to interpret national law as much as possible in conformity with these decisions (only limited by the restrictions imposed by the ECJ regarding the application of the principle of indirect effect[100]).

It is probably too early to make definite statements such as these, regarding the effect of CFSP norms in the national legal orders.

---

[98] Case C-105/03, *Pupino*, 16 June 2005. See M. Fletcher, 'Extending "Indirect Effect" to the Third Pillar: the Significance of Pupino?' (2005) 30 *ELR* 862–77.

[99] Curtin and Dekker, 'The Constitutional Structure', at 11. See on the principle of indirect effect, for instance, G. Betlem, 'The Principle of Indirect Effect of Community Law' (1995) *European Review of Public Law (ERPL)* 1.

[100] In particular, the principle of non-retroactivity of criminal liability. See, for instance, P. Craig and G. De Búrca, *EU Law*, 3rd edn (Oxford: Oxford University Press, 2003), p. 216.

Nevertheless, a direct applicability in the more limited definition presented earlier (using the norms in the relationships between all legal subjects within the national legal order) seems to follow from all of the above assumptions. However, it is generally held that CFSP decisions are not directly effective, in the sense that they may be relied upon by national courts.[101] It is indeed difficult to find provisions in the CFSP decisions containing rights and/or obligations for individuals. This is not to say that individuals cannot be affected at all by CFSP decisions, as was recently shown in the cases on anti-terrorism sanctions against individuals (see below). Regardless of the undetermined status of CFSP provisions in the Treaty on European Union, national constitutional systems may offer national courts the opportunity to allow individuals to invoke directly effective provisions in cases brought before them. Thus, the Dutch Constitution, for instance, provides in Article 93 that provisions in treaties or in decisions of international organisations have binding force in the Dutch legal order when they are directly effective. The latter question is decided upon by the judge, but recent European case law seems to imply a task for national courts to at least attempt to uphold a certain level of human rights protection in the case of EU/EC decisions that are based on UN Security Council resolutions. This underlines a role of the member states on the basis of the 'multilevel constitution'.[102]

Examples of potentially directly effective provisions may be found in the sanction decisions, although the actual obligations in these cases are mostly laid down in Community Regulations (which may be invoked by individuals on the basis of the EC rules on direct effect). The problems with regard to legal protection have recently been addressed by the European Court of First Instance, when it ruled that neither national states nor the EU has the ability to remove citizens from UN sanctions lists as both the member states and the EU are bound by UN law.[103] Here, another dimension is added to the multilevel complexity. Some CFSP decisions imposing sanctions, however, do not require a follow-up

---

[101] See, for instance, D. Curtin and R. H. van Ooik, 'Een Hof van Justitie van de Europese Unie?' (1999) 1 *SEW Tijdschrift voor Europees recht* 24 at 30–1.

[102] Case T-253/02, *Chafiq Ayadi v. Council of the European Union* and Case T-49/04, *Faraj Hassan v. Council of the European Union and Commission of the European Communities*, 12 July 2006.

[103] Case T-306/01, *Ahmed Ali Yusuf and Al Barakaat International Foundation v. Council and Commission*; and Case T-315/01, *Yassin Abdullah Kadi v. Council and Commission*, 21 September 2005.

in the form of an EC Regulation, such as the decisions to impose an arms embargo on Afghanistan, Burma/Myanmar, Nigeria or Sudan.[104] In these cases it would be the CFSP decision itself that would need to be invoked before a national judge. The same holds true regarding CFSP decisions establishing criteria or exceptions with respect to sanctions imposed on third countries. Common Position 95/544/CFSP, for instance, provided, *inter alia*, for an interruption of all contacts with Nigeria in the field of sports through denial of visas to official delegations and national teams. Unlike other provisions in this Common Provision, which obligate member states to take 'in accordance with national law such measures as are appropriate,' this provision does not seem to be in need of national implementation measures. Another example is Council Decision 97/820/CFSP, allowing for member states to make exceptions to the sanctions imposed on Nigeria. On the basis of this decision and subject to certain conditions, member states may derogate from these rules. In addition, a direct consequence for individuals may, for instance, emerge on the basis of the establishment of the list of dual-use goods through a CFSP decision.[105] While the actual obligations are to be found in EC Regulation No. 3381/94,[106] the decision to include or exclude certain goods is taken by the Council on the basis of Article 14 as a CFSP Joint Action, which may have consequences for the market position of companies in that area.

A final situation in which national courts could become involved in CFSP issues would arise in cases of an (alleged) liability of member states being brought up. In cases where neither the Communities, nor the European Union could be held liable for decisions taken by the Council in the area of CFSP, third states or individuals will have to turn to the national courts of the member states to seek justice. Situations in this respect could, for instance, arise whenever member states cause damage in the course of an EU action (for example, their action in Bosnia-Herzegovina, or the administration of the city of Mostar) or when member states are held liable for breaches of an agreement concluded by the Council on the basis of Article 24 TEU.[107]

---

[104] Common Positions 96/746/CFSP; 96/635/CFSP; 95/515/CFSP; and 94/165/CFSP respectively.

[105] See Decision 94/942/CFSP of 19 December 1994 or the subsequent amending decisions.

[106] EC Regulation No. 3381/94 [1994] OJ L 267.

[107] More extensively Wessel, 'The European *Union* as a Party to International Agreements'.

The main problem, however, is that all decisions imposing sanctions – EC as well as CFSP – are normally converted into national legislation. In order to check the direct applicability of CFSP decisions, one would thus need a case in which a single CFSP decision imposed a sanction regime towards a third country, without this regime being converted into national law. Furthermore, we would need a citizen or a company from that third state to challenge the trade or travel restrictions, in which case the company in the EU member state could point to its obligations on the basis of the CFSP decision. Direct applicability only refers to this rightful reference to valid norms and the case is thus not completely incomprehensible. It is not even unthinkable that a national judge would also allow this decision to have direct effect, in the sense that it may play a role in a national court proceeding. The problem, however, seems to be that in cases such as this, one cannot avoid dealing with the question of supremacy of the CFSP norms over previously established (or maybe even future) national law. The principle of loyalty may prove to be a valuable candidate for a basis of general supremacy of EU law, but at least in the area of foreign policy the multilevel constitution has not yet grown to full stature to settle this issue.

3. The constitutional impact of flexibility

One of the major issues in the post-enlargement period of the Union will undoubtedly be that of 'flexibility'.[108] As I have defined the multilevel constitution on the basis of the notion of unity of the legal system, the question emerges what the impact of flexible forms of cooperation within this system will be on its unity.[109] Here, we deal with what has been called the sovereignty paradox: on the one hand, the member states seem to retain their sovereignty with respect to cooperation in some fields; on the other hand, the member states accept to limit themselves

---

[108] See, for a survey of the problems in this area, B. de Witte, D. Hanf and E. Vos (eds.), *The Many Faces of Differentiation in EU Law* (Antwerp: Intersentia, 2001); and G. de Búrca and J. Scott (eds.), *Constitutional Change in the EU: From Uniformity to Flexibility?* (Oxford: Hart Publishing, 2000).

[109] See, for the impact of flexibility on the '*horizontal*' unity of the Union, I. F. Dekker and R. A. Wessel, 'The European Union and the Concept of Flexibility: Proliferation of Legal Systems within International Organizations', in N. M. Blokker and H. G. Schermers (eds.), *Proliferation of International Organizations* (The Hague: Kluwer Law International, 2001), pp. 381–414. See in general on flexibility and constitutions, A. Schrauwen (ed.), *Flexibility in Constitutions: Forms of Closer Cooperation in Federal and Non-federal Settings* (Groningen: Europa Law Publishing, 2002).

by agreeing on this procedure within the framework of the European Union.[110] This, paradox is one of the dimensions of the 'schizophrenic' relationship between the EU and its member states referred to above, and forms the source of a question once posed by Jo Shaw: 'is there something inherently contradictory in considering constitutionalism in conjunction with flexibility?'[111]

The multilevel constitution of EU foreign relations, indeed provides for flexible arrangements. The idea of a possible fragmented Union played an important role during the negotiations on the Amsterdam Treaty in 1996/97. The different variations of flexibility were frequently presented as harmful to the Union's unity. Thus concepts such as *variable geometry*, *concentric circles*, a *multiple-speed Europe*, or a *Europe à la carte* all seemed to prelude the end of the Union. While concepts such as these did not make it to the final draft of the Treaty, the development towards a more flexible approach of the cooperation within the European Union is reflected in the modifications to the TEU introduced by the 1997 Amsterdam Treaty,[112] and further in the Nice Treaty.

Thus, the post-Nice Treaty on European Union, as well as the modified EC Treaty, provides for a number of general and specific arrangements allowing for forms of flexible cooperation between a limited number of member states. The Treaties contain general clauses on the possibility for further integration between some but not all member states, under the new heading of 'enhanced cooperation'. In addition, new specific examples of flexibility were introduced, in particular with regard to Title IV EC on the free movement of persons, asylum and immigration and the Protocol incorporating the Schengen *acquis* into the Union's legal system. In some cases these forms of flexible cooperation allow for even greater closer cooperation between some members of the already restricted group of member states.[113] Many view this

---

[110] See M. H. M. de Bonth, 'Sovereignty Revisited', in Schrauwen, *Flexibility in Constitutions*, pp. 99–105 at 101. De Bonth develops the argument that the member states have not lost their sovereignty by creating the European Union. Sovereignty is indivisible and is more than just the sum of sovereign rights. The member states have been able to construct the European Union because they are sovereign states.

[111] J. Shaw, 'Relating Constitutionalism and Flexibility in the European Union', in De Búrca and Scott, *Constitutional Change*, pp. 337–58.

[112] See Editorial, 'The Treaty of Amsterdam: Neither a Bang nor a Whimper' (1997) 24 *CMLR* 768.

[113] See Article 1 of the Schengen Protocol, authorising the signatories to the Schengen agreements to establish closer cooperation among themselves within the scope of the

development as an undesired, but nevertheless unavoidable, solution to problems related to the socio-economic and political differences between the EU member states.

The concept of 'flexible cooperation' or 'flexibility' in the context of the present contribution concerns the situation in which the twenty-seven member states do not necessarily participate to the same extent in every policy or activity of the Union.[114] The Treaty on European Union nowhere explicitly refers to the notion of flexibility.[115] However, one can distinguish between at least two broad categories of flexibility within the Unions' legal system. The first category contains the general *enabling clauses* on the basis of which the Council has a competence – through the adoption of secondary legislation – to decide on the establishment of 'enhanced cooperation'. The second category harbours a variety of forms of flexible cooperation linked to specific fields of EU/EC competence, including the so-called *pre-determined* forms of flexibility, i.e. forms of differential treatment of certain member states as laid down in the treaties themselves or in protocols. Pre-determined flexibility may either take the form of a permission granted by all member states to a group of member states to act together through Union institutions and legislation (e.g. the Social Protocol under the Maastricht regime), or it is reflected in the permission given to member states *not* to participate in an activity in which they should in principle participate as a matter of Union or Community law (e.g. the 1991 Protocols on the basis of which Denmark and the United Kingdom are not obliged to take part in the third phase of the EMU; the 1991 Protocol concerning Denmark's non-participation in the elaboration or implementation of measures having defence implications).[116]

Article 43 TEU states: 'Member states which intend to establish enhanced cooperation between themselves may make use of the institutions, procedures and mechanisms laid down by this Treaty and the

---

Schengen *acquis*. See also E. Wagner, 'The Integration of Schengen into the Framework of the European Union' (1998) *LIEEI* 1 at 33.

[114] *Cf.* J. A. Usher, 'Flexibility: The Amsterdam Provisions', in Heukels, Blokker and Brus (eds.), *The European Union after Amsterdam: A Legal Analysis*, p. 253.

[115] See G. Edwards and E. Philippart, 'Flexibility and the Treaty of Amsterdam: Europe's New Byzantium?', *CELS Occasional Paper* No. 3, (Cambridge, 1997), at 12: 'During the legal and linguistic revision of the text agreed in June (1997), the word 'flexibility' disappeared. The need for it was no longer important in the domestic politics of the UK.' See also J. Shaw, 'The Treaty of Amsterdam: Challenges of Flexibility and Legitimacy' (1998) 4 *ELJ* at 69.

[116] *Cf.* Usher, 'Flexibility', 254–6.

Treaty establishing the European Community . . .' Additional criteria may be found in Article 11 TEC and Article 40 TEU (on police and judicial cooperation).[117] A new Article 27A was inserted, which explicitly brings the possibility of 'enhanced cooperation' into the realm of CFSP as well.

It is interesting to note the 'constitutional' restrictions which govern the regime of enhanced cooperation in the area of foreign and security policy (military and defence policy is excluded by Article 27B). Article 27A provides that enhanced cooperation in this area 'shall be aimed at safeguarding the values and serving the interests of the Union as a whole by asserting its identity as a coherent force on the international scene'. Thus, it shall respect 'the principles, objectives, general guidelines and consistency of the common foreign and security policy and the decisions taken within the framework of that policy; the powers of the European Community; and consistency between all the Union's policies and its external activities'. This preoccupation with 'consistency' returns in the procedure to establish enhanced cooperation. According to Article 27C, member states may address the Council with a request, which will subsequently be forwarded to the Commission and the European Parliament for information. The Commission shall give its opinion particularly on whether the enhanced cooperation proposed is consistent with Union policies. This idea is strengthened by other criteria in Article 43: enhanced cooperation should be aimed at furthering the objectives of the Union and of the Community, at protecting and serving their interests and at reinforcing their progress of integration; it should respect the treaties and the single institutional framework as well as the *acquis communautaire*; it may not undermine the internal market or the economic or social cohesion. Article 43A adds that enhanced cooperation may be undertaken only as a last resort, when it has been established within the Council that the objectives of such cooperation cannot be attained within a reasonable period by applying the relevant provisions of the Treaties.

Consistency, in its more vertical dimension, returns in the provision that an established form of enhanced cooperation is open to all member states, and that both the Commission and the participating member

---

[117] G. Gaja, 'How Flexible is Flexibility Under the Amsterdam Treaty?', (1998) 25 *CMLR* 855 at 856; H. Kortenberg, 'Closer Cooperation in the Treaty of Amsterdam' (1998) 25 *CMLR* 833 at 844; C. D. Ehlermann, 'Differentiation, Flexibility, Closer Cooperation: The New Provisions of the Amsterdam Treaty' (1998) 4 *ELJ* 246 at 264.

states shall ensure that as many member states as possible are encouraged to take part (Article 43B). This may form an incentive for participating states to not completely neglect non-participants. But the national dimension of the multilevel constitution is also not entirely disregarded: the Council decides on authorisation of enhanced cooperation by a qualified majority vote, *unless* this is blocked by one member for 'important and stated reasons of national policy', in which case the matter may be referred to the European Council for decision by unanimity. Once established, however, it is above all the Union (institutions) that govern the enhanced cooperation.

What is the impact of this possibility offered by the Nice Treaty on the constitutionalisation of foreign and security policy? It is tempting to repeat the conclusion that Ige Dekker and I have reached previously with regard to forms of flexibility in general within the Union's legal system: the strict requirements for establishing and implementing closer cooperation all point in the direction of an existing legal unity and the rules on flexibility *strengthen* the notion of the unity of the Union's legal system rather than that they weaken it.[118] The focus on the principle of consistency as a returning notion underlying enhanced cooperation points to a constitutional embedding in the sense that foreign policy no longer exclusively belongs to the realm of EU member states; even initiatives between smaller groups of states will have to be based on procedures laid down in the Treaty – and are even made possible only on the basis of these provisions. This is not to say that this regime is merely laid down on the Union-level of the foreign policy constitution. The 'non-unitary' dimension can be discovered in the ultimate possibility of blocking the authorisation of enhanced cooperation in the European Council as well as in the fact that acts adopted within the framework of enhanced cooperation shall not form part of the Union *acquis* (Article 44). In addition, expenditure resulting from implementation of enhanced cooperation, other than administrative costs entailed for the institutions, shall be borne by the participating member states only, unless, all members of the Council, acting unanimously, decide otherwise (Article 44). A final point in this respect concerns the exclusion of enhanced cooperation of matters having military or defence implications (Article 27B). These matters – when one is able to disconnect them from 'security policy' – can thus only be dealt with on either a (single) national or on the Union level.

---

[118] See Dekker and Wessel, 'The European Union', 408.

The Constitutional Treaty somewhat modifies the provisions on enhanced cooperation, but more importantly for our topic: it extents enhanced cooperation to CFSP without restricting it to its implementation (Articles I-44 and III-416–423).[119] Moreover, no general exception was made in relation to the Common Security and Defence Policy (CSDP), the new name for the European Security and Defence Policy (ESDP). The current legal regime completely excludes any form of enhanced cooperation in security and defence matters and merely allows for 'closer cooperation', that is: cooperation between EU member states (and possible others) outside the EU Treaty. Irrespective of the fact that because of the requirement of unanimity, enhanced cooperation in CSDP may be hard to establish, Article I-41 of the new Constitution offers interesting alternatives. First, para. 3 acknowledges the possibility that groups of member states may make available their multinational forces to CSDP. Article III-310 (1) builds on this idea by allowing the Council to entrust the implementation of a task to a group of member states. At the same time, one has to acknowledge that even in the current era, ESDP missions operate in a flexible manner as far as the composition of the troops is concerned: not all member states participate in all missions, and some missions are even built on the commitment of one state (consider the role of France in the Congo mission).[120]

In addition to this *ad hoc* flexibility, para. 6 of Article I-41 introduces the notion of 'permanent structured cooperation' for 'those Member States whose military capabilities fulfil higher criteria and which have made more binding commitments to one another in this area with a view to the most demanding missions'.[121] Other forms of variation are foreseen by the European Defence Agency and by the half-hearted establishment of a common defence.[122]

---

[119] See, in general, J. Howorth, 'The European Draft Constitutional Treaty and the Future of the European Defence Initiative: A Question of Flexibility' (2004) *EFA Rev* 483–508; and R. A. Wessel, 'Differentiation in EU Foreign, Security and Defence Policy: Between Coherence and Flexibility', in M. Trybus and N. D. White (eds.), *European Security Law* (Oxford: Oxford University Press, 2007) (forthcoming). See in general on security and defence in the Constitution: F. Naert, 'European Security and Defence Policy in the EU Constitutional Treaty' (2005) 2 *JCSL* 187–207.

[120] See also Naert, 'European Security', 202.

[121] The permanent structured cooperation is further elaborated by Article III-312 and by the Protocol on permanent structured cooperation established by Article I-41(6) and Article III-312 of the Constitution (No. 23).

[122] More extensively, R. A. Wessel, 'Differentiation'.

The flexibility provisions thus reflect the complex constitutional relationship between the Union and its member states as well as the unity of national and supranational legal orders referred to in the introduction to this chapter. As any constitution may provide for flexibility, the latter is not by definition a 'threat' to the first even when it potentially changes the constitution in a material sense. As Kelsen claimed, a revolution (only) occurs when there has been an unconstitutional change of the constitution, i.e. when any amendment of the constitution has not been effected in accordance with existing procedures for amendment.[123] The multilevel constitution which forms the basis of the current regime of foreign and security policy allows for flexible arrangements, but at the same time it makes assurances that this regime, which was carefully built up over the past thirty years or so, has enough internal safeguards to prevent its own destruction.

4. The current state of constitutionalism in European foreign relations

It can be claimed that one of the prominent goals of the mission to draft a Constitutional Treaty has been the consolidation of external relations.[124] This is reflected in the Laeken Declaration and in the establishment of two working groups by the Convention on the Draft Constitution to address the issues of legal personality and external relations.[125] Indeed, as shown above, the Union's external relations have been strongly influenced by the case law of the ECJ and therefore reflect a piecemeal approach. In addition, personality was assigned to the different European Communities, the European Union and even to some of the sub-organisations in the Community and the Union.[126] The

---

[123] See Weyland, 'The Application of Kelsen's Theory', 24; H. Kelsen, *General Theory of Law and State* (Cambridge, Mass.: Harvard University Press, 1945), pp. 117–18.

[124] This section is partly based on A. Ott and R. A. Wessel, 'The EU's External Relations Regime: Multilevel Complexity in an Expanding Union', in S. Blockmans and A. Lazowski (eds.), *The European Union and its Neighbours* (The Hague: T.M.C. Asser Press, 2006).

[125] See further, C. Hermann, 'Die Außenhandelsdimension des Binnenmarktes im Verfassungsentwurf von der Zoll- und zur Weltordnungspolitik', in A. Hatje and J. P. Terhechte (eds.), *Das Binnenmarktziel in der europäischen Verfassung* (Baden-Baden: Nomos, 2004), p. 186.

[126] See on this subject D. M. Curtin and I. F. Dekker, 'The EU as a "Layered" International Organization: Institutional Unity in Disguise', in Craig and de Búrca (eds.), *The Evolution of EU Law*, pp. 83–136.

different legal characteristics of the three pillars as well as their diverging instruments and decision-making procedures add immensely to the complexity of the Union's external relations. In that respect the abolishment of the pillar-structure and the merger of the Communities and the current European Union can only be welcomed: we are left with one single international organisation, the Union, with competences in the former Community areas as well as in the areas of CFSP and PJCC. Also in the area of external relations, no division is made between the economic and the political (foreign affairs) issues. Title V of Part III of the Constitutional Treaty is labelled 'The Union's External Action' and covers all the Union's external policies. In addition, the external objectives of the Union are no longer scattered over different treaties. Instead, Article I-3(4) provides:

> In its relations with the wider world, the Union shall uphold and promote its values and interests. It shall contribute to peace, security, the sustainable development of the earth, solidarity and mutual respect among peoples, free and fair trade, eradication of poverty and protection of human rights and in particular children's rights, as well as to strict observance and development of international law, including respect for the principles of the United Nations Charter.

Another improvement is that the fundamental principles of external relations law, which have slowly evolved from the case law of the ECJ over the last 30 years, have all been included into Part One of the Constitutional Treaty. This can be considered the most obvious part of the process of tidying up and consolidating the external relations provisions.[127] Article I-12 defines the categories of competences in such a way that only in the case of exclusive competences may the Union adopt legally binding acts, the member states being competent only if empowered by the Union or for the implementation of Union acts. According to Article I-13, exclusive competences relate to the customs union, the establishing of the competition rules necessary for the functioning of the internal market, monetary policy for the member states whose currency is the euro, the conservation of marine biological resources under the common fisheries policy and the common commercial policy. Paragraph 2 of this provision may be seen as a

---

[127] See generally on this exercise, B. de Witte, 'Simplification and Reorganisation of the European Treaties' (2002) 39 *CMLR* 1255–87.

codification of the *ERTA*-doctrine.[128] In Part III the Union's external action is defined. Article III-292 clarifies the guiding principles of external relations, namely democracy, the rule of law, the universality and indivisibility of human rights and fundamental freedoms, respect for human dignity, the principles of equality and solidarity, and respect for the principles of the United Nations Charter and international law.

As stated before, one achievement of the Constitutional Treaty is that it codifies the external relations' *acquis*. In that respect it can indeed be said to reflect the current state of the constitutionalisation of EU external policy, irrespective of the question whether the treaty will ever enter into force. This intention to structure and simplify the existing 'bits and pieces' spread out over the EU/EC Treaty, and defined in the ECJ's case law, becomes particularly visible when the provisions regarding the treaty-making are compared.[129] When the matter of international agreement concerns the Common Foreign and Security Policy, the new Minister for Foreign Affairs shall submit recommendations to the Council. The choice between the Commission or the Foreign Minister seems to depend on the point of gravity of the issue: the Foreign Minister takes the lead in issues that exclusively or principally concern CFSP. This division will no doubt lead to questions of how to define the demarcation line between principally and marginally.

It is difficult to assess whether these overall changes infuse more coherence or consistency into the foreign policy *acquis*. Some changes, such as giving the Union explicit legal personality and codifying the 'piecemeal' of external relations competences and procedures, are a necessary exercise, and long overdue. In other matters, such as the merging of the pillars and policies, more coherence is not necessarily created when differences in the decision-making process prevail and the legal review by the European Court of Justice is still restricted. However, Common Foreign and Security Policy stays partially, and in contrast to Police and Judicial Cooperation, a *'domaine réservé'*. According to Article III-376, by and large the ECJ has no jurisdiction to rule on matters in respect of Articles I-40 and 41 and Article III-293, which involve the strategy and objectives-building on external relations by

---

[128] 'The Union shall also have exclusive competence for the conclusion of an international agreement when its conclusion is provided for in the legislative act of the Union or is necessary to enable the Union to exercise its internal competence, or insofar as its conclusion may affect common rules or alter their scope.'

[129] More extensively, A. Ott and R. A. Wessel, 'The EU's External Relations'.

the European Council. Indeed, a number of provisions indicate that the drafters of the Constitutional Treaty were not willing to go 'all the way' where the integration of the pillars is concerned. CFSP continues to have a distinct nature under the new treaty.[130] A first element concerns the kind of competence in the CFSP area. Article I-11 lists the competences of the Union in the different areas: exclusive, shared or supporting and supplementary. However, none of these competences relates to CFSP, as Article I-11 includes a separate paragraph referring to a 'competence to define and implement a common foreign and security policy, including the progressive framing of a common defence policy'. As Cremona has already indicated, it is a little difficult to see what kind of competence it could be, if not one of the other categories.[131] But the simple fact that again a special status is introduced is striking and does not add to clarity in the new multilevel foreign affairs constitution.

5. Concluding observations

For politicians and international relations experts, looking at the Union's foreign and security policy in terms of a constitution would probably be an outrage. Many still see this policy area as purely intergovernmental cooperation between states. Outcomes are based on power politics, rather than on formal legal procedures – let alone on *constitutional* procedures. However, an international lawyer could argue that the CFSP objectives, as interpreted in the present contribution, imply a clear limitation of the competences of the member states in this area, as they are geared towards a *common* policy which was to go beyond cooperation on the basis of the Single European Act in the 1980s. Despite the political power games, the same states agreed on a number of rules of the game. In that respect the European foreign affairs constitution may be seen as what Phillip Allot would term a 'legal constitution' ('a structure and system of retained acts of will'), rather than a real constitution ('the constitution as actualised in the current social process, a structure and a system of power') or an ideal constitution ('a constitution as it presents to society an idea of what society might be').[132] This 'legal' or perhaps 'formal' constitution derives its

---

[130] See, for a general evaluation of the external relations under the new Constitution, M. Cremona, 'The Draft Constitutional Treaty: External Relations and External Action' (2003) 40 *CMLR* 1347–66.

[131] Cremona, 'The Draft Constitutional Treaty' at 1353.

[132] See Chapter 10, Wouter Werner, below; P. Allot, *Eunomia: New Order for a New World Order*, 2nd edn (Oxford: Oxford University Press, 2001).

multilevel dimension from the fact that the 1992 Maastricht Treaty introduced a new player: the European Union was given an 'independent' character, through which the sovereign rights of its *member* states would be preserved vis-à-vis third states. In that sense – and irrespective of the different contexts – the opinion of the European Court of Justice in the leading case of *Van Gend en Loos* seems to be applicable to CFSP as well in the sense that it 'constitutes a new legal order of international law for the benefit of which the states have limited their sovereign rights, albeit within limited fields'.

It is these 'limited fields', in particular, that do not seem to be in line with the *prima facie* broad scope of CFSP. It follows from its purposes that the CFSP is not a common policy in the same way as the concept is used in, for instance, the Community's common agricultural policy or the common commercial policy.[133] Article 11, stating that the CFSP covers *all* areas of foreign and security policy, is misleading in the sense that it disregards the fact that Title V is only applicable to those parts of foreign and security policy that are not covered by the Community or the Police and Judicial Cooperation in Criminal Matters (PJCC), and that it accepts and even demands an active role for the member states themselves ('support'), alongside the general obligation of the Union to define and implement CFSP.

What follows from the above analysis is that competences regarding the external political relations of the Union and its member states are adjudicated to different levels of government, which not only *allows* an analysis in constitutional terms along the lines that we are used to in European Community law, but perhaps even *demands* it in order to see the uniting elements of the system. Just as in most federal constitutions, the central government should predominantly be responsible for external relations. Irrespective of the substance of the Union's external policy, the procedural arrangements indeed point in this direction. Unlike most federal systems, however, the Union's 'foreign relations constitution' is more flexible in the sense that it makes use of inherent competences for individual or bilateral actions. It is furthermore striking that in this area (security and foreign policy) a constitutional debate is virtually absent. In contrast to international constitutionalism, European constitutionalism so far seems to have largely refrained from viewing the security and

---

[133] D. Galloway, 'Common Foreign and Security Policy: Intergovernmentalism Donning the Mantle of the Community Method', in M. Westlake, *The Council of the European Union* (London: Cartermill, 1995), p. 212.

foreign affairs regime in constitutional terms. The unity of the union's legal order – as reflected in the new Constitutional Treaty – may, however, shift attention from the internal 'horizontal') delimitation problems between the Union's fields of activity to the 'vertical') dimension, focusing on the relation between the Union and its members. Recent developments – in particular related to regulation in the area of terrorism[134] – even extended the debate concerning the the position of the European Community as an intermediate between the global and the domestic legal order to the foreign and security policy of the European Union. With the coming of age of the EU's foreign, security and defence policy, the (constitutional) interplay between the global, European and domestic legal order seems increasingly recognised.

The consequences of a multilevel concept are perfectly illustrated by the following quotation, which is drawn from Weiler's analysis of European Political Cooperation in 1985 and which clearly has not lost its validity more than 20 years later:

> ... the descriptive and prescriptive trend of European foreign policy is towards a Europe singing like a choir – remembering of course that the choir concept is not meant to replace totally the one voice. Training several different voices to sing in harmony is at the best of times a most difficult task; one should not be surprised if for a long time yet the European choir will often sing out of tune. Even when successful, one should further not forget that a good choir sometimes sings in unison, other times in several voices and occasionally there is even scope for soloists.[135]

However, something has changed since 1985. The score for this European song increasingly demands a performance of the choir *as such*, not always at the cost of the beauty of individual voices, but with an ever clearer (constitutional) arrangement of their parts in the whole.

---

[134] See, for instance, the debate triggered by the Yusuf and Kadi cases referred to above. *Cf.* also R. A. Wessel, 'The UN, the EU and *Jus Cogens*' (2006) 3 *IOLR* 1–6.
[135] Weiler, 'The Evolution of Mechanisms', 25.

7

Self-determination of peoples and transnational regimes: a foundational principle of global governance

ACHILLES SKORDAS*

Introduction

In the era of globalisation, and due to the transition from 'government' to 'governance',[1] the content and function of international law and its legal principles, including self-determination, need to be reassessed. If, indeed, self-determination of peoples has been the legal avenue for achieving statehood, self-determination of international sectoral or integration regimes (transnational regimes)[2] constitutes its further development, enabling the stabilisation of regional or global governance structures. Self-determination, which was proclaimed as a political principle in the aftermath of World War I and, following the adoption of the Charter of the United Nations (UN), evolved into a legal principle,[3] is now assuming the rank of a foundational constitutional principle of global governance.

* This chapter is dedicated to my teacher, Apostolos Georgiades of the Academy of Athens, in gratitude for having taught me liberal legal thought. I would like to thank Gunther Teubner, Nicholas Tsagourias, Andreas Fischer-Lescano, Dan Sarooshi, the participants in the 2005 Bristol Forum, and my student audiences in Athens and Oxford, for their ideas, remarks and constructive critique. Maria Panezi has been, again, an excellent research assistant. The usual disclaimer applies.
[1] See J. Rosenau and E.-O. Czempiel (eds.), *Governance Without Government: Order and Change in World Politics* (Cambridge: Cambridge University Press, 1992).
[2] On transnationalism and regime theory, see A. Fischer-Lescano and G. Teubner, *Regime-Kollisionen – Zur Fragmentierung des globalen Rechts* (Frankfurt/Main: Suhrkamp, 2006); C. Joerges, I.-J. Sand and G. Teubner (eds.), *Transnational Governance and Constitutionalism* (Oxford and Portland, Oregon: Hart Publishing, 2004); A. Hasenclever, P. Mayer and V. Rittberger, *Theories of International Regimes* (Cambridge: Cambridge University Press, 1997).
[3] On the evolution of the principle, see H. Hannum, 'Rethinking Self-Determination' (1993) 34 *Virginia Journal of International Law* (*Va JIL*) 1 at 2–31.

The principle of the self-determination of peoples has transcended the limits of a group right and has become a principle for the allocation and organisation of territorial authority in global society; this subject will be addressed in the next section. Moreover, as concomitant of the fragmentation of international law, self-determination permeates the operation of transnational regimes, a development which is discussed in the section following and which is visible in the representative examples of the regional integration regime of the EU and of the global sectoral WTO regime.

The intrinsic connection between these two spheres is apparent, if we consider that the transformation of the self-determination of peoples and the emergence of the self-determination of regimes are parallel developments merging into a principle of global governance. In the context of global society, governance emerges as the 'horizon of all possibilities' for self-determination: as a structural principle of international and transnational law, self-determination represents the capacity of various territorial units and actors of the global political system and of transnational regimes to organise themselves and to stabilise their identity and operations. Indeed, it would be misleading to view self-determination as an ordinary legal principle, or right, among others; its distinct feature is that it depicts the internal dynamics of units, states and organisations in their ability to evolve, to differentiate their own functions and generate their internal order. In that sense, self-determination is literally a 'foundational' principle: its validity within a system signifies that the organisation, unit or regime has reached the evolutionary threshold that guarantees the further reproduction of its internal operations (internal self-determination), and ensures the maintenance of its distinction and separation from the environment (external self-determination). Global governance in a heterarchical world is inextricably linked to the self-determination of the basal units of the system – territories and, increasingly, transnational regimes. From the standpoint of 'societal constitutionalism',[4] self-determination is a foundational priniciple for global governance, located in the area between the social and the legal. Self-determination of peoples and self-determination of regimes constitute thus the two dimensions of the same principle.

---

[4] Joerges, Sand, and Teubner, Section I, 'Transnational Societal Constitutionalism', including the contributions of G. Teubner, T. Vesting, I.-J. Sand and A. Fischer-Lescano.

Self-determination as a complex structure has, over time, integrated diverse and eventually contradictory elements, capable of pushing the overall 'system of entitlements', which it includes, in various and unpredictable directions. Although legal analysis and legal theory find their starting point in the diagnosis of state and judicial practice, it is also true that the potentialities and dynamics of a fundamental norm need to be carefully explored and assessed. A 'second-order observation'[5] might shed a different light upon the diverse elements of the principle, in comparison to the mainstream approach.

Self-determination of peoples: allocation and organisation of territorial authority

A. Structural elements: state, people, 'self'

The principle of self-determination of peoples is built on three main structural elements: state, people and 'self'. Statehood as *telos*, realisation, and consummation of self-determination is representative of the era of decolonisation and of the New International Economic Order (NIEO). Self-determination appeared as the right of a group raising claims to the protective veil of sovereignty. Nonetheless, the 'people' as the second conceptual element signifying the group of beneficiaries or right-holders has been unsettling, as it has constantly oscillated between definition on the basis of either ethnic identity or stable residency on a given territory, and imported uncertainty into the heart of the principle. 'Self', as the third element, is decisive for the determination of the identity of a people and of the state. However, the 'self' as a set of identity-defining expectations is, for the legal system, not a fact given by history and does not precede the exercise of the right, but it emerges *through* the process of self-determination itself: it can be framed as the clash between the existential political will of the group exercising the *pouvoir constituant*, and the negative or positive response of the various actors of the international community, that leads to the recognition or non-recognition of the self-determination unit or the new state. State, people and 'self' need therefore to be seen not in isolation, but as

---

[5] On the second order observation in systems-theoretical perspective, see N. Luhmann, *Law as a Social System*, K. Ziegert (trans.) (Oxford: Oxford University Press, 2004), pp. 353–6, 448–52; N. Luhmann, 'Ich sehe was, was Du nicht siehst', in N. Luhmann, *Soziologische Aufklärung 5 – Konstruktivistische Perspektiven* (Opladen: Westdeutscher Verlag, 1990), pp. 228–34.

intertwined elements of a process that, together, construe the meaning of self-determination.

Thus, self-determination cannot be realised merely though the unilateral exercise of a right, but should be perceived as a structural principle introducing a worldwide process of communication on the terms of the establishment of authority over a territory. On this level, the links between global governance and self-determination are becoming visible.

(i) Statehood as 'telos'

The 1960 United Nations General Assembly (UN GA) Declaration on the Granting of Independence to Colonial Countries and Peoples[6] made repeated references to the objective of accession to independence and exercise of sovereignty, both in the Preamble, as well as in the operative paragraphs. The Declaration stressed the need for swift transition from the colonial administration to independence;[7] at the same time, it explicitly raised the territorial integrity of states into a major international legal interest, disapproving of secession.[8] Following an explicitly sovereigntist approach, the UN GA 'Declaration on Non-Intervention'[9] stated that '*every State* has an inalienable right to choose its political, economic, social and cultural systems, without interference in any form by another State'.[10]

The 1970 'Friendly Relations Resolution' provided for a so-called 'saving clause';[11] nonetheless, despite the opening of the principle of self-determination to the question of access of racial and religious groups to government, the statist orientation of the principle did not seem to change.[12] The same Resolution is explicit on the forms of

---

[6] Declaration on the Granting of Independence to Colonial Countries and Peoples, GA Res. 1514 –XV, 15 UN GAOR Supp. (No. 16) at 66, UN Doc. A/4684 (1961).

[7] Preamble, paras. 5, 10, 11, operative part, paras. 3–5.

[8] *Ibid.*, operative part, paras. 6 and 7.

[9] UN GA Declaration on the Inadmissibility of Intervention in the Domestic Affairs of States and the Protection of Their Independence and Sovereignty. Resolution 2131(XX), UN Doc. A/6014 (1966).

[10] *Ibid.*, para. 5 (emphasis added).

[11] Declaration on Principles of International Law Concerning Friendly Relations and Cooperation Among States in Accordance with the Charter of the United Nations, Res. 2625–XXV, UN Doc. A/8082 (1970).

[12] See, on that clause, A. Cassese, *Self-Determination of Peoples – A Legal Reappraisal* (Cambridge: Cambridge University Press, 1995), pp. 109–25. See also a broader formulation in the Vienna Declaration and Programme of Action of 25 June 1993, A/CONF.157/23, para. 2: '. . . and thus possessed of a Government representing the whole people belonging to the territory without distinction of any kind'.

statehood or political status to which self-determination may lead, including the establishment of a sovereign state; the free association or integration with an independent state; or any other political status freely determined by a people. Although the drafters of this resolution ventured a limited opening to more creative forms of association, they have not completed the turn from a statist conceptualisation of the principle. In a separate chapter devoted to the sovereign equality of states, it looks as if the sovereign state, and not the people, is the holder of the right of self-determination, in that it stresses that every state has the right freely to choose and develop its political, social, economic and cultural systems.

Furthermore, the Declaration on the Establishment of a New International Economic Order (NIEO) of 1974 recognises 'the right of every country to adopt the economic and social system that it deems the most appropriate for its own development and not to be subjected to discrimination of any kind as a result'.[13] Similarly, Article 1 of the Charter of Economic Rights and Duties of States of 1974 provides the following:

> Every State has the sovereign and inalienable right to choose its economic system as well as its political, social and cultural systems in accordance with the will of its people, without outside interference, coercion or threat in any form whatsoever.[14]

It should be noted that there is no mention of any procedures that guarantee the free expression of the 'will of the people'; the above resolutions do not include any relevant constitutional principles or limits to the power of the state. On the contrary, they disapprove of anything they consider as an 'outside interference'. Following the same line of thinking, the UN Special Rapporteur of the Sub-Commission on Prevention of Discrimination and Protection of Minorities, Héctor Gros Espiell, stressed that self-determination 'does not apply to peoples already organized in the form of a State which are not under colonial and alien domination'.[15]

The International Court of Justice (ICJ), in the *Nicaragua* judgment of 1986, finally adopted the most radical state-centred doctrine by directly submitting the principle of self-determination to the sovereignty doctrine.

---

[13] UNGA Res. 3201-S-VI, UN Doc. A/9559 (1974), para. 4(d).
[14] Res. 3281–XXIX, UN Doc. A/9631 (1975).
[15] H. G. Espiell, 'The Right to Self-Determination – Implementation of United Nations Resolutions', 1980, E/CN.4/Sub.2/405/Rev.1, para. 60.

The Court unequivocally endorsed the principle of the 'equivalence of regimes', considering that international law and human rights law do not give the democratic governance preference towards any other political system. The judgment held that even the imposition of 'a totalitarian Communist dictatorship' upon the people could constitute exercise of the right to self-determination, and that 'the whole of international law' rests upon the principle that the state enjoys the freedom of introducing any political, economic, or even cultural system, without any constraints by international law: a far-reaching conclusion, indeed, because, under this interpretive alternative, self-determination is being diluted within sovereignty.[16]

The functionally differentiated world society has been viewed with great scepticism, if not with animosity, by the NIEO project. Instead, policy-making by the international organisations at the time of that judgment was more comfortable with a hierarchically structured and interventionist global politico-economic system steered by the majorities of the UN General Assembly.[17]

(ii) The people: the *Rousseauesque* and the Hobbesean

Apart from the state, the 'people' as a parallel holder of the right of self-determination appear in most of the above resolutions.[18] The 'people' can be viewed through the lenses of either the ethno-cultural or the territorial dimension. In Koskenniemi's terms, the former approach builds upon the romantic *Rousseauesque* perception defining self-determination through the legal recognition of deeply rooted community bonds ('primitive is good'), while the Hobbesean perception identifies self-determination by linking individuals to the state through their participation in formal political decision-making procedures that permit them to participate in the conduct of common affairs.[19]

Cassese had initially defined 'peoples' in an ontological sense of the former type:

[16] *ICJ, Military and Paramilitary Activities (Nicaragua v. United States of America)*, Merits, ICJ Reports 1986, para. 263; see also paras. 257–8.
[17] For an authentic description of the philosophy and objectives of the NIEO, see M. Bedjaoui, *Pour un nouvel ordre économique international* (Paris: UNESCO, 1979).
[18] See, for instance, Res. 1514–XV, Res. 2625–XXV, 3201-S-VI, Res. 3281–XXIX. See also the common Article 1 of the two UN Covenants, on Civil and Political Rights, and on Economic, Social and Cultural Rights.
[19] M. Koskenniemi, 'National Self-Determination Today: Problems of Legal Theory and Practice' (1994) 43 *ICLQ* 241 at 249–50.

> Since in this context the term 'a people' refers to a group of human beings united by ethnic, religious, cultural and historic ties, one may legitimately ask oneself which members of such a group can act upon international rules, put forward international claims, and so on.[20]

Crawford formulated the territorial-Hobbesean approach to the principle as follows:

> International law recognizes the principle of self-determination. – It is however not a right applicable directly to any group of people desiring political independence or self-government. Like sovereignty, it is a legal principle ... It applies as a matter of right only after the unit of self-determination has been determined by the application of appropriate rules.[21]

The confusion over the definition of the right-holders has been considerable, as testified by the demeanour of the UN Special Rapporteur, who failed to reconcile the two contradictory facets in a single definition.[22]

The ICJ jurisprudence achieved a major breakthrough in the *Frontier Dispute* case of 1986,[23] which reinterpreted the principle of self-determination and defined the holders of the right on the basis of territoriality and not on the basis of ethnicity. After emphasising that *uti possidetis* is the 'principle of intangibility of the frontiers inherited from colonization', that had been 'first invoked and applied in Spanish America', the Court stressed that 'its obvious purpose is to prevent the independence and stability of new States being endangered by fratricidal struggles provoked by the challenging of the frontiers following the withdrawal of the administering power'.[24] Then the judgment focused on what looked like a strained relationship between *uti possidetis* and self-determination. Though the ICJ seemed to invoke an 'outright conflict' between *uti possidetis* and self-determination, apparently suggesting that beneficiaries of the latter principle would be normally expected

---

[20] A. Cassese, *International Law in a Divided World* (Oxford: Oxford University Press, 1988), p. 93.

[21] J. Crawford, *The Creation of States in International Law* (Oxford: Oxford University Press, 1979), p. 101.

[22] Special Rapporteur of the Sub-Commission on Prevention of Discrimination and Protection of Minorities, para. 56.

[23] *Frontier Dispute case (Burkina Faso v. Mali)*, Judgment of 22 December 1986, ICJ Reports 1986, 554.

[24] *Ibid.*, para. 20.

to be ethnic groups, it rejected 'in fact' the ethno-cultural ontology and reinterpreted self-determination on the basis of *uti possidetis*.[25] Under this, now established, jurisprudence, the 'people' are not anchored in the archetypal collective mythology of history, land, domination and law,[26] but it is through the self-determination unit that an amorphous aggregate of residents from various ethnic and religious backgrounds (population) assumes the identity of a 'people' as holder of authority and rights.

The Court's stance in the *Frontier Dispute* case is indirectly linked to the 1955 *Nottebohm* case, which can be considered as a distant precursor to the Hobbesean approach of the notion of the 'people'.[27] The ICJ defined nationality as 'a legal bond having as its basis a social fact of attachment, a genuine connection of existence, interests and sentiments, together with the existence of reciprocal rights and duties';[28] it also indicated the factors that establish the particular bond in case of dual nationality and exercise of diplomatic protection:

> Different factors are taken into consideration, and their importance will vary from one case to the next: the habitual residence of the individual concerned is an important factor, but there are other factors such as the centre of his interests, his family ties, his participation in public life, attachment shown by him for a given country and inculcated in his children, etc.[29]

The list of factors is inclusive, but the practical criteria are preponderant in the overall assessment. For deciding dual nationality cases at least, the *Rousseauesque* was reduced into the subordinate role of one factor, 'the attachment' shown by an individual to a certain country and 'inculcated' in his children; nonetheless, even this criterion is not exclusively ethno-cultural, but may be one of choice. Other factors, such as the habitual residence, or the centre of one's activities, carry much more weight in the overall balance.

---

[25] Para. 25 of the Judgment. On the application of *uti possidetis* in Latin America, see *Case Concerning the Land, Island and Maritime Frontier Dispute (El Salvador v. Honduras)*, Judgment of 11 September 1992, ICJ Rep. 1992, p. 351; for the former Yugoslavia, see the Opinions of the Badinter Arbitration Commission (1992) 31 *ILM* 1488.

[26] C. Schmitt, 'Nomos-Nahme-Name' [1959], in C. Schmitt, *Staat, Großraum, Nomos – Arbeiten aus den Jahren 1916–1959*, G. Maschke, (ed.) (Berlin: Duncker und Humblot, 1995), pp. 573–91.

[27] *Nottebohm case (Liechtenstein v. Guatemala)*, Second Phase, Judgment of 6 April 1955, ICJ Reports 1955, 4.

[28] *Ibid.*, 23.   [29] *Ibid.*, 22.

Oddly enough, the cosmopolitan *Frontier Dispute* case, which orientated the concept of the 'people' towards the inclusion of all groups resident in the self-determination unit, presents certain affinities with the *Nicaragua* case, which was adopted earlier the same year (1986), despite the latter's 'socio-political archaism': both judgments were indeed thought to be components of the same judicial project of authoritarian, but supposedly enlightened, Hobbesean sovereigntism. However, this project could not but implode in the clash between diversity, demanding equality and rights for individuals and groups, and authoritarian government as a form of exercise of self-determination. Notwithstanding the 'regressive' and obstructive impact of *Nicaragua* on subsequent legal developments, the principle of equivalence of regimes came quickly under the pressure of the principle of democratic or participatory governance.[30] It is unfortunate that, in its more recent Advisory Opinion on the *Legal Consequences of the Construction of a Wall in the Occupied Palestinian Territory*,[31] the Court avoided revisiting *Nicaragua* and reassessing the normativity of the democratic principle, although it was given ample opportunity to do so.

The inherent contradictions of the principle of self-determination are also apparent, if we take a closer look at the beneficiaries from a different observation point: if 'people' is necessarily 'self', then 'self' needs to locate itself in the clash between original constitutional authority and international recognition.

(iii) The 'self' as clash: *pouvoir constituant* v. recognition

To reduce the principle of self-determination to the mechanical application of the *uti possidetis* principle does not explain the emergence of the 'self'. Moreover, international practice shows that the territorial criterion adopted by international law is not sufficient to explain the creation of new states and the recognition of self-determination units. Pomerance sharply criticised the UN for allegedly perverting the principle instead of realising the will of the peoples affected by the policies of the Organization.[32]

The role of collective political action should be viewed through the lens of the *pouvoir constituant*. Carl Schmitt had defined the *pouvoir constituant* as the political will that determines the form of the political

---

[30] See below, B(ii).   [31] Advisory Opinion of 9 July 2004.
[32] See M. Pomerance, 'Self-Determination Today: The Metamorphosis of an Ideal' (1984) 19 *Israel Law Review* 310–39.

existence as a unity and indicates the existential validity-ground for the Constitution.[33] Seen from this perspective, state creation is the case of exercise of *pouvoir constituant par excellence*. The 'founding act' is not limited to the formal adoption of a constitutional instrument, but it may also involve violence, civil strife, revolution, liberation struggle, or armed conflict with another state. Thus, the rule-based perspective of *uti possidetis* and the 'moment of decision' inherent in the establishment of the legal order *ex nihilo* seem incompatible. Either state creation and *pouvoir constituant* are existential political decision-acts, or their validity rests upon a pre-existing norm of international law, such the *uti possidetis* principle and the ensuing recognition of a territory as a self-determination unit.

The obvious gap between self-proclamation and recognition could be legally rationalised as a form of 'division of competences' between the international community and the people as holder of the right to self-determination; namely that the former recognises the existence of the self-determination unit, thus creating a provisional polity that has the power, based upon the previous recognition, to take the political decision either to form a new state, or to merge into an already existing polity or to assume some other political status,[34] according to a procedure indicated by the provisional recognition.

The Badinter Arbitration Commission, set up to facilitate the resolution of the Yugoslav conflict through international law, even prescribed the procedure for the transformation of the provisional polity into an independent state; although the Constitution of 1990 provided that the Socialist Republic of Bosnia-Hercegovina (SRBH) comprised three constituent peoples, implying thus the possibility of a 'shared' exercise of self-determination, the Commission decided that the will of the people should be expressed 'possibly by means of a referendum of all the

---

[33] '*Verfassungsgebende Gewalt ist der politische Wille, dessen Macht oder Autorität imstande ist, die konkrete Gesamtentscheidung über die Art und Form der eigenen politischen Existenz zu treffen, also die Existenz der politischen Einheit im ganzen zu bestimmen. Aus den Entscheidungen dieses Willens leitet sich die Gültigkeit jeder weiteren verfassungsgesetzlichen Regelung ab . . . Eine Verfassung beruht nicht auf einer Norm, deren Richtigkeit der Grund ihrer Geltung wäre. Sie beruht auf einer, aus politischem Sein hervorgegangenen politischen Entscheidung über die Art und Norm des eigenen Seins. Das Wort 'Wille' bezeichnet – im Gegensatz zu jener Abhängigkeit von einer normativen oder abstrakten Richtigkeit – das wesentlich Existentielle dieses Geltungsgrundes*'. C. Schmitt, *Verfassungslehre*, 8. Auflage [1928] (Berlin: Duncker und Humblot, 1993), pp. 75–6 (emphasis in the original).
[34] UN GA 'Friendly Relations' Resolution.

citizens of the SRBH without distinction, carried out under international supervision'.[35]

This path of reasoning that attempts to 'regularize the exceptional', is not entirely satisfactory. The suspicion looms, that some structured expression of the will of the 'provisional polity-in-being' puts in motion the decision-making process of the international community and leads to the recognition of the self-determination unit as such; in other words, it seems that some political actor or formation has already voiced a will that did not exist before. For Cassese, the identity of a people and the right to self-determination are appropriated by some structure, authority or representative organisation; the author acknowledges the difficulties in prescribing criteria of representation at a pre-legal stage, when such criteria are missing, by definition.[36]

The emergence of order cannot be explained exclusively through recourse to a 'command', 'decision', or 'seizure of initiative'[37] either by a group of persons, or by a broader community of states. Although the 'moment of command' as an expression of 'hegemonic will' has high visibility, it cannot by itself dissolve or generate order. The reason is that, between the *ancien régime* and the new order, intervenes the *épokhè*, the 'moment of suspense'.[38] The 'birth' of the new constitutional order, the 'original violence' of the creation of legal order, the epochal change and the 'mystical foundation of authority' is described by Jacques Derrida as follows:

> But it is in *droit* what suspends *droit*. It interrupts the established *droit* to found another. This moment of suspense, this *épokhè*, this founding or revolutionary moment of law is, in law, an instance of non-law. But it is also the whole history of law.[39]

The *épokhè* offers, in the 'cryptic critique' of Derrida and Benjamin, the key to the semantics of self-determination. In terms of the history of a nation, the revolutionary 'moment of suspense' between the *ancien*

---

[35] *Badinter Arbitration Commission*, Opinion No. 4, (1992) 31 *ILM* 1503.

[36] Cassese, *International Law in a Divided World*, pp. 93–5.

[37] So H. Lindahl, 'Sovereignty and Representation in the European Union', in N. Walker (ed.), *Sovereignty in Transition* (Oxford and Portland: Hart Publishing, 2003), pp. 87–114.

[38] The term dates back to E. Husserl; see *The Stanford Encyclopedia of Philosophy*, available online at http://plato.stanford.edu/entries/husserl/#6 (last accessed on 31 August 2006).

[39] J. Derrida, 'Force of Law: The "Mystical Foundation of Authority"' (1990) *Cardozo Law Review* 11 at 991; see also at 989–95 (trans. Mary Quaintance).

régime of 'not any more' and the 'promised land' of 'yet-to-come', is viewed in the temporal dimension of a before/after sequence and distinction. The *épokhè* reproduces the temporal dimension of revolution as struggle between successive domestic legal orders; in global society, the before/after dimension is displaced by a 'new suspension' as struggle between the domestic *pouvoir constituant* and international law: the question is, whether the 'nation' through its alleged self-centered 'existential will', or the international community through its broader policy objectives, will 'seize the initiative', dominate the interpretation of the principle of self-determination and confer legitimacy upon an emerging territorial order. Suspension is in fact a moment in the birth of the 'self'.

The 'self' does not emanate exclusively from a nation's own history and revolutionary project, but is being reproduced and re-framed in a sequence of communications among a plurality of domestic and global actors. On a first level, the *épokhè* as suspension and transition toward the foundation of a new state can be described as the tension – that may even reach the level of outright clash – between the violence of the existential politico-constitutional decision aspiring to appropriate the 'ontology of the group', on the one hand, and the rule-orientated principle of *uti possidetis*, anxious to re-establish a 'civilized' *status quo*, through the proceduralisation of the decision on the 'self', in the form of the recognition of the 'self-determination unit', on the other. International law as *uti possidetis* constitutes the first 'line of defence' of the international community's policies to 'tame' the *pouvoir constituant*. This tension should not be conceived as a struggle between two parties, but as a clash of expectations.

The *pouvoir constituant* as an existential, and thus groundless or even arbitrary, decision represents the predominance of the style of cognitive expectations;[40] although state creation *is* generation of normativity, the *pouvoir constituant* itself as 'act of exception' is deprived of any normative foundation, but merely aspires to channel a 'pure act' of political will through *épokhè* and suspension into the realm of normativity. *Uti possidetis* represents normativity-within-change and its strength relies on its capacity to reduce complexity: whilst an existential political decision to found a state needs not only to answer the question of political authority, but is compelled to inextricably bind history with

---

[40] On the distinction between normative and cognitive expectations, see N. Luhmann, *A Sociological Theory of Law*, E. King and M. Albrow (trans.) (London: Routledge & Kegan Paul, 1985), pp. 31–40.

territory,[41] *uti possidetis* envisions the making of the latter issue irrelevant and, instead, concentrates upon the rationalisation and proceduralisation of territorial authority and territorially based decision-making. However, it seems unlikely that the unpredictability of political existentialism might be ever effectively tamed, even if 'constitutional patriotism'[42] contains its more excessive forms.

Moreover, if the people as 'self' takes shape in the clash between *pouvoir constituant* and international recognition, this does not yet explain how both dimensions merge to produce order. Under any alternative, a constituent decision on the part of the 'people' or its representative organisation is indispensable, and it is not self-evident, how its groundlessness carries through the *épokhè* into an order. An explanation is possible, only if the 'people' is not romanticised as an isolated and compact actor building its own homeland in a 'struggle for recognition'.[43] Rather, the uniqueness and 'arbitrariness' of the founding act should be seen as embedded within a broader normative/cognitive context that enables the international community to integrate multiple 'founding acts' and communications into global governance structures.

In that sense, acts related to the exercise of *pouvoir constituant* as well as the responses of global society actors assume a certain regularity as 'iterative communications' defining, stabilising and allocating territorial authority in global society. In the course of that process, the notion of 'people' assumes two different meanings. First, it represents the source of territorial authority, recognised as legitimate by the international community and armed with the legal capacity to establish a state through a founding act. Secondly, it depicts the 'self' and identity of the population of the self-determination unit as it emerges in the course of this communication sequence between the 'domestic' and the 'international': what a people hold about themselves is thus the contingent output of mutual recognition and communication between various actors as 'alter' and 'ego' respectively. International recognition seals this process.

---

[41] For the complexities of the emergence of identities, cf. T. Franck, 'Clan and Superclan: Loyalty, Identity and Community in Law and Practice' (1996) 90 *AJIL* 359–83.

[42] J. Habermas, 'Citizenship and National Identity', in J. Habermas, *Between Facts and Norms*, W. Rehg (trans.) (Cambridge, Mass.: MIT Press, 1999), Appendix II, pp. 491–515 at 500.

[43] See Hegel's interpretation by A. Kojève and F. Fukuyama in F. Fukuyama, *The End of History and the Last Man* (London: Penguin, 1992), p. 143 *et seq.*

(iv) Conclusion

We have followed how the normative conflicts inherent in the principle of self-determination are formed and expressed, but it is still unclear whether recognition of a self-determination unit is a legal or a political act. In the next section, it is argued that we face acts of a different order, which might be called 'global policy' acts: recognition policies are neither 'planned' as such, nor are they derived from a superior norm, but, as individual actors spontaneously coordinate their responses, they build 'global governance'. Thus, if 'just peace' and stability are cardinal objectives of the UN Charter and of global order,[44] then it could be assumed that recognition is linked to these objectives. Furthermore, if 'allocation of territorial authority' is framed as exercise of external self-determination, and organisation of authority is defined as internal self-determination, it is necessary to view the 'thread' that connects these two dimensions of self-determination with recognition.

B. Global policies on recognition: self-determination and peace

(i) External self-determination: allocation of territorial authority

The tension between *pouvoir constituant* and international law, the uncertainties surrounding the ethno-cultural and territorial criteria for defining the beneficiaries of self-determination, and, as a correlate, the lack of precise rules on the modalities for the expression of the will of the population, are not issues that can be resolved through recourse to adjudication. The *uti possidetis* principle is not armed with automatic application, it is therefore not capable of regulating by itself the accession of territories to independence, and it dramatically fails in the case of secession, where a new territorial entity is carved out of an existing state. Under these circumstances, the practice of recognition, that weighs all these factors, appears as the main 'line of defence' of the international interest. Two advisory opinions of the ICJ, on the *Construction of a Wall*[45] and on *Western Sahara*,[46] demonstrate that the international community uses diverse criteria for defining the beneficiaries of self-determination and the paths for implementing the principle.

---

[44] See the Preamble and Article 1 of the UN Charter. On the interpretation of these terms, see below B(ii)(a).

[45] Advisory Opinion of 9 July 2004.

[46] *Western Sahara*, Advisory Opinion of 16 October 1975, ICJ Reports 1975, 12.

The ICJ Advisory Opinion on the *Construction of a Wall* considered the recognition of a 'people' as a source of authority implicitly as a major 'moment' for the exercise of the right of self-determination. The Court ruled that the existence of a 'people' could be a matter of controversy to be settled by recognition. In that respect, recognition by the opponent (Israel), or by the UN General Assembly is of fundamental significance.[47] However, as clearly results from the *Western Sahara* Opinion and its context, the international community is not obliged to accept a certain representation of the population as genuine, nor is it bound to recognise legitimacy claims based on history, and it is even not bound by the facts created in the course of the liberation struggle. Facts may bring about a *de facto* leadership; whether this leadership has a claim to recognition, or to allocation of territorial authority, or how the collective will of the people is going to find expression, is a matter in which the international community has 'a measure of discretion with respect to the forms and procedures by which that right is to be realized'.[48]

If self-determination is not an ordinary right conferred upon groups and collectivities, but a general principle of international law linked with the fundamental interest of 'just peace', then the relevant practice needs to be assessed in the light of this interest: this can then easily explain the diverse avenues and forms the principle may assume, including, but not limited to, the right to statehood. For these reasons, self-determination cannot be reduced either to the solitary egoism of *pouvoir constituant*, or to the mechanical application of *uti possidetis*. Although this latter principle constitutes the basic pillar for the overall structuring of self-determination by the international community, a wider assessment between international law and global stability, 'law and peace' in the sense of the UN Charter, needs to be undertaken. In fact, the global stability component is immanent in the implementation of self-determination. This close relationship has already been expressed in the UN GA Declaration on the Granting of Independence to Colonial Countries and Peoples.[49] The link between self-determination and

---

[47] Para. 118 of the Advisory Opinion. On the different question of the recognition of Palestine as a 'state', see J. Crawford, *The Creation of States in International Law*, 2nd edn (Oxford: Oxford University Press 2006), pp. 434–48; F. Kirgis, 'Admission of "Palestine" as a Member of a Specialized Agency and Withholding the Payment of Assessments in Response' (1990) 84 *AJIL* 218–30.

[48] ICJ, *Western Sahara*, para. 71. See also paras. 59, 72.

[49] UN GA Res. 1514–XV, UN Doc. A/4684, Preamble, paras. 2, 3 and 9, operative part, para. 1.

world peace is, however, not always clear. There is little doubt that subjection to alien domination and colonial exploitation and the ensuing violation of human rights constitute threats to international peace;[50] access to statehood in colonial cases is obviously viewed as a right, whose exercise guarantees the maintenance of international peace.

However, self-determination is not claimed only in these clear-cut cases, and it is possible that the interests of world peace are not served by the exercise of the right. There are complex situations, in which it is not always undisputable that the *status quo* before the exercise of self-determination is necessarily the worse alternative. The complexities of the Hong Kong,[51] Taiwan[52] or Chechnya[53] cases are evidence that the exercise of an alleged right to self-determination leading to the creation of independent states might gravely endanger international peace. For various reasons, the world community has refused to support moves towards the exercise of self-determination by the population in the above territories. In the two first cases, the gains and benefits in freedom from the choice of a different political status by the inhabitants would be disproportionate to the risks of regional destabilisation. In the third case, independence would most probably result in facilitating the establishment of a radical, if not rogue, regime that could not be expected to

---

[50] See briefly on the UN practice on apartheid and the threat to the peace, K. Hailbronner and E. Klein, in B. Simma (ed.), *The Charter of the United Nations – A Commentary*, 2nd edn (Oxford: Oxford University Press, 2002), Article 10, margin numbers (MN) 13–14.

[51] On the status of Hong Kong and Macau, see Crawford, *The Creation of States in International Law*, 2nd ed, pp. 244–52. See also Cassese, *Self-Determination of Peoples*, pp. 79–80, notes 34–6.

[52] On the legal status of Taiwan and the implementation of the principle of self-determination, see J. Shen, 'Sovereignty, Statehood, Self-determination, and the Issue of Taiwan' (2000) 15 *American University International Law Review* 1101–61; V. Epps, 'Self-Determination in the Taiwan/China Context' (1998) 32 *New England Law Review* (*New Eng L Rev*) 685–93; A. Hsiu-An Hsiao, 'Is China's Policy to Use Force Against Taiwan a Violation of the Principle of Non-use of Force Under International Law?' (1998) 32 *New Eng Law Rev* 715–42; R. Heuser, 'Taiwan und Selbstbestimmungsrecht' (1980) 40 *ZaöRV* 31–75.

[53] The predominance of criminal, radical nationalist, fundamentalist and terrorist elements in the political structures of the secessionist entity complicates any policy of recognition; worth noting is that, Islamic law (*Sharia*) had already been imposed on the territory in February 1999, before the major offensive by Russia, in the late summer of the same year, took place. See M. Kramer, 'The Perils of Counterinsurgency – Russia's War in Chechnya' (2004/2005) 29:3 *International Security* 5 at 5–7; for the current tendencies within the Chechen secessionist movement, *ibid.*, 57–61. See also J. Charney, 'Self-Determination: Chechnya, Kosovo, and East Timor' (2001) 34 *Vanderbilt Journal of Transnational Law* 455 at 462–4.

respect political pluralism or the rule of law. In all three cases, it is reasonable to assume that change of the current status or accession to independence would not wind up in introducing better global governance structures.

In the 1995 *East Timor* case, the ICJ offered further clues on the nature and function of self-determination.[54] The judgment qualified the right of self-determination as an *erga omnes* norm but, at the same time, it expressed serious doubts about the legal consequences of the occupation of East Timor, refusing to consider even its unlawfulness, after the Court decided that it lacked jurisdiction with respect to Indonesia.[55] As Judge Skubiszewski stressed in his dissenting opinion, with vision and fully aware of the potentialities of an era in transition, the Court failed in practice to adequately consider the normative density of self-determination and its resistance against the realities of the Indonesian occupation.[56] Setting aside the question of the alleged *jus cogens* nature of self-determination, the *erga omnes* character of the principle to self-determination implies that the world community is bound to create conditions conducive to its implementation.

This effect is described in common Article 1 to the two UN Covenants, on Civil and Political Rights, and on Economic, Social and Cultural Rights as an obligation of the contracting parties to 'promote the realization of the right of self-determination' in conformity with the provisions of the Charter and the United Nations.[57]

The Human Rights Committee's (HRC's)[58] General Comment (GC) No. 12, on Article 1 of the International Covenant on Civil and Political Rights (ICCPR), concluded that 'all States parties to the Covenant should take *positive action* to facilitate realization of and respect for the right of peoples to self-determination'.[59] Therefore, self-determination is a principle about a process that may be completed in the course of time. This decision is narrowly linked to the establishment of a legitimate domestic legal order. As GC 12 stipulates, 'States parties should

---

[54] *Case Concerning East Timor (Portugal v. Australia)*, Judgment of 30 June 1995, ICJ Reports 1995, p. 50.

[55] *Ibid.*, paras. 33–5.

[56] *Ibid.*, dissenting opinion of Judge Skubiszewski, paras. 133 *et seq.*

[57] Article 1, para. 3, of the ICCPR (UNTS vol. 999, 171) and ICESCR (UNTS vol. 993, 3) (emphasis added).

[58] HRC, General Comment 12, Article 1 (21st session, 1984), UN Doc. HRI/GEN/1/Rev.6 at 134 (2003).

[59] GC 12, para. 6 (emphasis added).

describe the constitutional and political processes which in practice allow the exercise of this right'.[60] It also provides 'the right of self-determination is of particular importance because its realisation is an essential condition for the effective guarantee and observance of individual human rights and for the promotion and strengthening of those rights',[61] and that 'this right and corresponding obligations concerning its implementation are interrelated with other provisions of the Covenant and rules of international law'.[62]

Therefore, the international community should promote the exercise of self-determination under conditions safeguarding the broader interest of maintenance of global stability and 'just peace'. After the closure of the era of colonisation, global policies of recognition in cases of disintegration of states or secession, depend, *inter alia*, on the assessment of the prospects of the emerging domestic legal order and of its consistency with the broader values of the international community.

(ii) Internal self-determination: organisation of territorial authority

(a) Democracy as 'good governance'   For Kirgis, self-determination is a 'variable right', depending on an assessment between representativeness of government in the existing state and destabilisation from a potential secession. The author acknowledges that a variation of factors that may place a role, but he considers the above to be two of the most important.[63] These considerations need to be integrated more rigorously in the rationale of global governance and 'just peace' and to the principle of democratic governance.

Here, it is necessary to distinguish briefly the different notions of 'peace' in international law. 'Negative peace' implies the absence of armed hostilities, and 'positive peace' denotes the totality of the international political, economic and human rights order. 'Peace' is, therefore, a catch-all concept for the totality of the existing global order. 'Just peace' is a 'contingency formula', which does not indicate any essentialist set of values, but it constitutes the 'program of all programs' of international law, and the 'orientation standard' for its interpretation. This notion is of major significance for the interpretation of international law; it indicates the co-evolution between the legal, the political and the economic systems of global society, and the socio-legal processes

---

[60] GC 12, para. 4.   [61] *Ibid.*, para. 1.   [62] *Ibid.*, para. 2.
[63] F. Kirgis, 'Comment: The Degrees of Self-Determination in the United Nations Era' (1994) 88 *AJIL* 304–10.

of proliferation of 'good governance' structures, and of constitutionalisation of transnational regimes.[64] Global policies of recognition are linked to the objective of 'just peace' and stability, since the purpose of self-determination is to integrate territories in the world community. The principle of democratic governance is an expression of the quest for 'just peace' and 'good governance', and, in that sense, it constitutes a major international interest and value.[65]

The realisation of self-determination as structural change and proliferation of good governance standards does not exclude the eventuality of armed conflict; 'just peace' as long-term societal stability is therefore not necessarily inconsistent with a period of armed conflict that precipitates the transition to the new order. The 'liberation struggles' of the colonial era illustrate this case. The 'premature' recognition of the Yugoslav Republics should be assessed in this perspective: though the 'inflexibility' of the path pursued by the international community at end of 1991 has been criticised,[66] the dissolution of the former Yugoslavia and the disappearance of the Milosevic regime was the prerequisite for the integration of its various self-determination units into the European community of nations.[67]

In the present chapter, self-determination as organisation of territorial authority will be seen in the perspective of the principle of democratic governance as fundamental structure for achieving 'good governance'. Democracy is emerging as the dominant principle for the legitimate exercise of internal self-determination (see section (b) below), but its ramifications are not limited on the level of the political. The proliferation of democratic standards is but one feature of the evolution of global society towards heterarchy and functional differentiation:[68] democracy facilitates the deployment of networking activities and thus enables 'collective self-governance' and 'order-building' leading to further integration (section (c) below). The main performance of

---

[64] A. Skordas, 'Just Peace Revisited: International Law in the Era of Asymmetry', in: S. Stetter (ed.), *Territorial Conflicts in World Society – Modern Systems Theory, International Relations and Conflict Studies* (London: Routledge, 2007 (forthcoming)).

[65] On the connection between peace, justice, and democracy, see the 'Agenda for Development', Report of the UN Secretary-General, A/48/935, 6 May 1994, paras. 16–40, 118–38. See also the 'Agenda for Democratization', Report of the UN Secretary-General, A/51/761, 20 December 1996.

[66] See, for instance, Koskenniemi 'National Self-Determination Today' 266–9.

[67] On the process of dissolution of the Socialist Federal Republic of Yugoslavia, see Crawford, *The Creation of States in International Law*, pp. 395–401.

[68] See also below, pp. 241–5.

democratic governance is to contribute to 'global societal pluralism' and order-building in various co-existing and autonomous spheres of activity and communication.

This is not refuted by the conditional endorsement of 'intolerant democracy' and emergency legislation by international law: here, the limitations imposed upon political activities should be necessary and proportionate for the suppression of risks and violence directed against this underlying societal structure (section (d) below). In the concluding part of the present chapter, the advisory opinion of the Supreme Court of Canada on the purported secession of Quebec stresses the importance of stability, integration and continuation of regularity of economic activities – thus, of good governance – in the policies of secession and recognition (section (e) below).

(b) Democracy as legitimate exercise of internal self-determination

Recent international practice lends support to democratic or, more generally, participatory government, as emerging principle of international law and as legitimate exercise of internal self-determination. The principle of equivalence of regimes was progressively displaced by the principle of democratic governance in the post-Cold War era.[69] Dictatorial and authoritarian systems find themselves increasingly at odds with the values and norms of international law.

The GC 25 (1996) of the HRC formulated the general principles guiding the right to participate in public affairs, voting rights and the right to equal access to public service (Article 25 of the Covenant on Civil and Political Rights). The Comment established a clear relationship between self-determination and democratic governance.[70] The HRC stipulated for the first time that, despite their distinctiveness, the exercise of the right of self-determination is linked to democratic political processes. The choice of the political status is coupled with the right to choose the form of the constitution or government. This choice is to

---

[69] See various aspects of the debate in: T. Franck, 'The Emerging Right to Democratic Governance' (1992) 86 *AJIL* at 46–91; G. Fox and B. Roth (eds.), *Democratic Governance and International Law* (Cambridge: Cambridge University Press, 2000); L.-A. Sicilianos, *L'ONU and la démocratisation de l' Etat* (Paris: Pedone, 2000); B. Roth, *Governmental Illegitimacy in International Law* (Oxford: Oxford University Press, 2000); A. von Bogdandy, 'Demokratie, Globalisierung, Zukunft des Völkerrechts – eine Bestandsaufnahme' (2003) 63 *ZaöRV* 853–877.

[70] GC 25 (1996), para. 2.

be made through political processes whose validity must fulfill the standard of Article 25 of the Covenant.

The normativity of the principle of democratic governance is supported by state practice, *opinio juris* and *opinio necessitatis*. State practice is related to the large number of states that have adopted steps towards democratisation since late 1980s and early 1990s.[71] *Opinio necessitatis* is related to the conviction and experience that democratic governance guarantees stability and societal pluralism. The UN Secretary-General's 1995 'Agenda for Development' and the 1996 'Agenda for Democratization' stressed that democracy is the form of government which is capable of contributing to peace and security, of securing justice and human rights, and of promoting economic and social development. According to this normative project, democracy can cope effectively with social conflict, foster good governance and enhance economic, social and cultural development.[72] *Opinio juris* can be drawn from the awareness that only democracy is compatible with the international human rights order. The European Court of Human Rights formulated this comprehensive normative dimension of democratic governance in the case *United Communist Party of Turkey and others v. Turkey* of 1998.[73]

A number of UNGA resolutions and resolutions of the UN Commission on Human Rights have further specified the content of the two normative pillars of democratic governance, namely the right to participation in the political process and the rule of law. The right to participate in the political process includes the right to vote, and the rights of assembly, association and expression, including free, independent and pluralistic media. The rule of law encompasses, *inter alia*, equal protection under the law, the right to liberty and security of the person, equal access to justice, fair trial, and ensuring the independence and integrity of the judiciary.[74] In an overall assessment, democracy and the rule of law as one of its main components guarantee the regular operation of a comprehensive system of fundamental rights and freedoms, including economic freedoms.

---

[71] See the UNDP Human Development Report 2002 'Deepening Democracy in a Fragmented World'.

[72] Agenda for Development, paras. 118 *et seq.*, Agenda for Democratization, paras. 15 *et seq.*

[73] ECtHR, Case no. 133/1996/752/951, Judgment of 30 January 1998, para. 45.

[74] See in particular UNGA 55/96 of 28 February 2001, and Commission on Human Rights 2000/47 under the identical titles 'promoting and consolidating democracy'.

Democratic governance as right of participation in public affairs is based upon the establishment of mechanisms of deliberation, so that legitimate and well-thought decisions are reached by the political system; parliamentary and election procedures lie at the heart of the legal definition of democratic governance.[75]

Nonetheless, democratic governance as internal self-determination should not be conceived merely as a process for alteration in power, deliberative politics, voting rights or participation in political associations. The sociological strength and global significance of democratic governance as the form of internal self-determination, and its status under international law becomes apparent, if we consider how it increases the potentialities and self-organisational capacities of individuals, groups and networks.

Hannum, for instance, views self-determination as a vehicle for a global system of governance enabling the realisation of the rights of individuals and minorities through 'functional sovereignty'.[76] 'Functional sovereignty' describes the autonomy and self-governing capacity of transnational regimes.[77] Although Hannum used the term in a more restrictive sense, he correlated the self-limitation of centralised state powers with the self-administration of sub-state communities and groups; he made thus a major step in disconnecting self-determination from *étatisme* and re-directing the notion toward more abstract governance functions.[78]

(c) **Democracy and societal pluralism**   The constitutional significance of democracy for global governance is raised on an even more complex and abstract level by systems theory. Going further than group rights, Luhmann, Verschraegen, Teubner and Ladeur, integrate elements of the above concepts and standpoints in the paradigm of a 'network' approach.

---

[75] The operation and significance of self-determination as deliberative politics in the democratic nation-state has a prominent position in Habermas, *Between Facts and Norms*.

[76] Hannum, 'Rethinking Self-Determination' 66.

[77] For the European Union, see, for instance, N. Walker, 'Late Sovereignty in the European Union', in Walker (ed.), *Sovereignty in Transition*, pp. 3–32. See also D. Sarooshi, *International Organizations and Their Exercise of Sovereign Powers* (Oxford: Oxford University Press, 2005).

[78] On self-determination and group rights, see K. Knop, *Diversity and Self-Determination in International Law* (Cambridge: Cambridge University Press, 2002).

Verschraegen focuses on the human rights perspective of Niklas Luhmann and social systems theory.[79] Both authors consider the existent constitutional and international human order as:

> ... the dominant structure of modern society, that is, of functional differentiation. Human rights are considered as a social institution, whereby modern society protects its own structure against self-destructive tendencies. By giving inalienable and equal rights to all human beings, society ensures that the differentiation between different functional subsystems is maintained and at the same time institutionalizes specific mechanisms to increase stability and protection of the individual. ... In short, because human rights enable and legitimize the free choice of the individual, they strengthen the dominant structure of modern society, which is based upon free inclusion and individual mobility. 'Through free choice, a varied and contradictory multitude of norms, roles and institutions can be built up and tried out'. As such, *human rights constitute the unnoticed and elementary condition for participation within modern society*. Human rights enable us, without paying further heed, to take part in the richness of social roles, networks, associations, and organizations that make up modern societies.[80]

The human rights order guarantees therefore the capacity of individuals to participate in modern society's various spheres of communication and activity and, thus, supports societal pluralism and the *Eigenlogiken* of the various social systems of action.

Teubner introduced the concept of 'global private regimes' and redefined the notion of civil society in liberal democracy. He considers that 'the only realistic candidate for a dynamic civil society is a pluralism of autonomous global social subsystems', such as education, art or media. In his view, these subsystems, just like the systems of economy or politics, are structured in an organised and in a spontaneous sector. Teubner gives here the example of the US university system, 'which has by contrast with the bureaucratized and politicized European universities succeeded in combining organized and spontaneous activities in a regime that is relatively autonomous vis-à-vis politics and the economy'. He then makes the following link between democracy and global private regimes:

---

[79] N. Luhmann, *Grundrechte als Institution*, 3rd edn (Berlin: Duncker und Humblot, 1986).

[80] G. Verschraegen, 'Human Rights and Modern Society: A Sociological Analysis from the Perspective of Systems Theory' (2002) 29 *JLS* 258 at 258 (abstract) and 276 (emphasis in the original).

Democracy, understood as an organizing principle that goes beyond institutionalized politics, can work only if in different social fields on the one hand decision potentials are highly specialized, organized and rationalized, on the other hand, however, do not take over total control of their social sector, but are in turn exposed to a control process through a decentralized multiplicity of spontaneous communication processes.[81]

These thoughts are developed further by Ladeur, who describes the prospects of democracy in the era of globalisation and touches upon the fundamental constitutional feature of democratic governance. In this perspective, it is not the achievement of consensus on values that characterises democracy as principle of global governance, but the capacity of supporting the operation of autonomous spaces through global or regional networking activities:

For what follows from the interpretation of democracies sketched out is that it is not so much a consensus on democratic values that explicitly constitutes the collective order (even in Rawls' sense of an 'overlapping consensus', the core of which is fed from varying political considerations) that is needed. Instead, the concept of democracy can . . . be reformulated more to the effect not of consenting to a basic stock of rules and principles. It is instead the practical, heterarchical, distributed social network of networks among citizens producing 'overlapping consensus', in the sense that the citizens are in practice involved in differing networks in different roles, and a heterarchical organized stock of linkages and co-ordinations arises from their overlapping and permeability to each other, that enables a 'polycontexturally' distributed self-observation and observation of others by the various patterns of actions produced, continually feeding the associated 'pool of knowledge' with novelty . . .[82]

In the same direction, Jack Balkin formulates the 'democratic culture' in the following terms:

A democratic culture is more than representative institutions of democracy, and it is more than deliberation about public issues. Rather, a democratic culture is a culture in which individuals have a fair opportunity to participate in the forms of meaning making that constitute them

---

[81] G. Teubner, 'Global Private Regimes: Neo-Spontaneous Law and Dual Constitution of Autonomous Sectors?', in K.-H. Ladeur (ed.), *Public Governance in the Age of Globalization* (Aldershot: Ashgate, 2004), p. 71 at 86.

[82] K.-H. Ladeur, 'Globalization and the Conversion of Democracy to Polycentric Networks: Can Democracy Survive the End of the Nation State?', in Ladeur (ed.), *Public Governance*, p. 107.

as individuals. Democratic culture is about individual liberty as well as collective self-governance; it is about each individual's ability to participate in the production and distribution of culture.[83]

Democratic governance as a legal principle for international law should not be confused as the often futile search for political consensus through global political institutions. The call to strengthen the democratic and deliberative instances on regional and global levels is often formulated as a protest against the so-called 'democratic deficit' in supranational institutions. This strategy is driven by over-optimism about the capacity of politics to effectively steer the operation of function systems. It thus neglects both the dynamics of self-steering mechanisms of function systems and the extreme complexities of global society. Instead of construing global governance from the top down, self-determination and democracy disclose the dynamics of the bottom-up approach inherent to the overall complexity of contemporary global society. Thus, internal self-determination strengthens the capacity of decentralised 'order creation' through network activity in a socio-political environment secured by 'negative rights',[84] market freedoms and integration processes.[85]

(d) Intolerance and heterarchy   In times of strain, destabilisation or threat to security, democracy can turn intolerant. In a far-sighted essay under the title 'Intolerant Democracies', written long before 9/11 on the opportunity of the cancellation of the second round of the 1992 parliamentary elections in Algeria, Fox and Nolte concluded, that international law had opted for a substantive and not for a procedural view of democracy. They pointed out that the right of political participation might be severely restricted in cases of threat against the democratic form of government, in order to safeguard the system and broader global interests.[86]

---

[83] J. Balkin, 'Digital Speech and Democratic Culture: A Theory of Freedom of Expression for the Information Society', *Yale Law School, Public Law and Legal Theory Research Paper Series*, Research Paper No. 63, in http://papers.ssrn.com/sol3/papers.cfm? abstract_id=470842 (last accessed 31 August, 2006). I thank V. Karavas for advising me on this essay.

[84] K.-H. Ladeur, *Negative Freiheitsrechte und gesellschaftliche Selbstorganisation – Die Erzeugung von Sozialkapital durch Institutionen* (Tübingen: Mohr Siebeck, 2000).

[85] E.-U. Petersmann, 'Time for a United Nations "Global Compact" for Integrating Human Rights into the Law of Worldwide Organizations: Lessons from European Integration' (2002) 13 *EJIL* 621–50.

[86] G. Fox and G. Nolte, 'Intolerant Democracies' (1995) 36 *HILJ* 1 at 69–70.

The authors acknowledged that, under international law, and in particular under the ICCPR, states are entitled to restrict the activities of anti-democratic actors, but, furthermore, they owe also an obligation to the international community to maintain the democratic form of government. They explain that 'the democratic entitlement serves as not only a human rights right enacted "merely" in the interest of individual citizens, but as one of the important legal bulwarks of world peace'.[87] They also stress the distinction of the Covenant between 'reasonable' and 'necessary' restrictions: the political right to democratic governance and the right to take part in the conduct of public affairs can be restricted under the lenient standard of 'reasonableness', while the related civil rights of association and expression underlie restrictions only under the stricter standard of 'necessity in a democratic society'.[88] This difference mirrors the concern of the Covenant to maintain societal pluralism, even if broad restrictions have been imposed upon the political freedoms of anti-democratic actors; therefore, restrictions on the operation of the political system should not fundamentally alter the democratic and pluralistic structure of society.

In its two judgments in the *Refah v. Turkey* case, the European Court of Human Rights considered that the dissolution of a radical Islamic party, being proportionate and necessary in a democratic society, does not violate the right to association of Article 11 ECHR. It is noteworthy that the judgment of the Chamber was given on 31 July 2001, that is, five weeks before 9/11 and decided by the slim majority of 4:3 votes. The judgment of the Grand Chamber on the same subject was delivered on 13 February 2003 and reached the same conclusion, but this time, unanimously (17:0). The *Refah* judgment gives a very accurate description of the notion of the link between 'intolerant' democracy and societal pluralism.[89]

The Court considered that a political party might try to change the constitutional structure of a country under two conditions: that it employs legal and democratic means, and that 'the change proposed must itself be compatible with fundamental democratic principles'.[90] The judgment considered 'fundamentalist movements', or 'fundamentalist religious

---

[87] *Ibid.*, 63.   [88] *Ibid.*, 45–9.
[89] ECtHR, *Refah Partisi and others v. Turkey*, Judgment of 13 February 2003. For a critical commentary of this judgment, see K. Boyle, 'Human Rights, Religion and Democracy: The Refah Party Case' (2004) 1 *Essex Human Rights Review* 1–16.
[90] ECtHR, *Refah Partisi*, para. 98.

movements', as anti-democratic actors who currently constitute a serious threat to democratic government and for the system of rights instituted by the Convention. Moreover, referring to two earlier German cases,[91] it considered that it was 'not at all improbable that totalitarian movements, organised in the form of political parties, might do away with democracy, after prospering under the democratic regime, there being examples of this in modern European history'.[92]

It is clear from the judgment that the Court's concerns with respect to Islamic fundamentalist movements were not limited to the sphere of the political system and political rights alone. The Court stressed that 'by the proposals for an *overall societal model* which they put before the electorate and by their capacity to implement those proposals once they come to power, political parties differ from other organizations which intervene in the political arena'.[93] Though the judgment clearly overestimates the capacity of the political system to restructure society, it is true that this is at least the objective and program of fundamentalist movements and actors. Furthermore, the Grand Chamber adopted the Chamber's reasoning, that Refah's 'societal model cannot be considered compatible with the Convention system'.[94] The Court stressed that university authorities may regulate the manifestation of religious symbols 'to prevent certain fundamentalist religious movements from exerting pressure on students who do not practise that religion'.[95]

The ECtHR also examined whether Refah's dissolution was necessary in a democratic society. The Court considered that the plan of the above party to radically transform the Turkish legal system and replace secularism with a plurality of legal systems, depending on the religion of the individual, would violate fundamental rights under the Convention. Law would become the vehicle for the exercise of pressure by religion on all other societal spheres of activity. Considering plurality of legal systems in this sense as all-pervasive, the Grand Chamber again endorsed the Chamber's reasoning that the *Sharia* was incompatible with the Convention, 'particularly with regard to its criminal law and criminal procedure, its rules on the legal status of women and the way it intervenes in all spheres of private and public life in accordance with religious precepts'.[96] The Court noted that it was not asked to express an

---

[91] ECtHR, *Communist Party (KPD) v. Germany*, No. 250/57, Commission decision of 20 July 1957; *Petersen v. Germany* (dec.), No. 39793/98.
[92] ECtHR, *Refah Partisi*, para. 99.   [93] *Ibid.*, para. 87 (emphasis added).
[94] *Ibid.*, para. 119.   [95] *Ibid.*, para. 95.   [96] *Ibid.*, para. 123.

abstract opinion on 'legal pluralism', but that, in the concrete case, the introduction of the *Sharia*'s private law rules would clearly go 'beyond the freedom of individuals to observe the precepts of their religion, for example by organising religious wedding ceremonies before or after a civil marriage . . . and according religious marriage the effect of civil marriage'.[97]

Judge Kovler criticised the judgment in his concurring opinion as too sweeping in regard to the 'plurality of legal systems'. He advocated a more permissive attitude toward customary law and 'legal pluralism', as particular legal systems might be applicable to minorities, ethnic communities and religious groups. He also considered the Court's approach to *Sharia* as too far-fetched and pronounced himself in favour of a more flexible stance that searches for balances and compromises 'between the interests of the communities concerned and civil society as a whole'.

Though the issues surrounding legal pluralism cannot be further dealt with here, it is necessary to clarify the distinction between this term, as used above, and the concept of 'societal pluralism' employed throughout the present chapter. While 'legal pluralism/plurality of legal systems', as used in the above judgment and in the opinion of Judge Kovler, denote legal systems applicable to specific groups on the basis of their identity, 'societal pluralism' is related to the plurality of 'function systems' in global society, including 'global law'.[98] As the *Refah* judgment demonstrated, particular legal systems need to comply with the standards of international law and international human rights law. Legal pluralism should not be misconstrued as 'anything goes', because customary legal systems are elements in the heterarchical structure of global society, but they develop in a complex symbiosis with modern positive law.[99]

Conclusion   Democracy as 'good governance' establishes the appropriate legal and political framework for heterarchy and global societal pluralism, that is, for 'networking' and unobstructed deployment of activities and communications in autonomous fields of societal action within and beyond state borders. States are bound by international law to guarantee democratic governance, respect human rights and support the continuing functioning of the global societal order. 'Intolerant

---

[97] *Ibid.*, para. 127.   [98] See also below, p. 238.
[99] See, for example, P. Orebech *et al.* (eds.), *The Role of Customary Law in Sustainable Development* (Cambridge: Cambridge University Press, 2005).

democracies' may introduce 'necessary' or 'reasonable' restrictions to the exercise of some rights, as the case may be, to meet these objectives. Legal and political 'intolerance' of this kind is compatible with 'just peace'.

The transformation of internal self-determination has major implications for external self-determination, too. The existing, or prospective, domestic system of governance in a potential self-determination unit is becoming a major factor in global policies of recognition, depending on how it affects 'stability'.

(e) Secession and societal stability: the case of Quebec In its advisory opinion on the legality of the process of Quebec's secession, the Supreme Court of Canada considered the objective of 'stability' and 'integration' as major factors determining the legal obligations of the federation and of the seceding entity.[100] Rejecting the existence of a right to secession under constitutional or international law, the Court stressed that if the majority of the population in Quebec would express itself in favor of secession, then an 'obligation to negotiate' would arise for both, the province and the federal government.[101] The subject of negotiations is closely related with the Court's concerns on the overall stability and continuity of the legal and societal order. The Court stressed unequivocally that the legitimacy of secession and the recognition of the claim of the secessionist unit depends on the maintenance of societal stability, legal certainty, continuity of rights, and avoidance of major disruptions at the economic level, as well as to public and private interests.[102]

Though referring to the question of secession in a democratic industrialised state, the considerations of the Supreme Court of Canada have a more general significance for the relationship between internal and external self-determination. The opinion stressed, for instance, that if the two parties breach their obligation to negotiate under the stated constitutional principles, this would be an important factor to be considered in the international process of recognition.[103]

Even more important is the Court's focus on the issue of social stability in a process of secession. The transformation of the domestic administrative boundaries into international frontiers initiates a process of disintegration of a formerly integrated space with broad implications

---

[100] *Supreme Court of Canada: Reference re Secession of Quebec* (1998) 37 *ILM* 1340–77.
[101] *Ibid.*, paras. 88–92.   [102] *Ibid.*, para. 96.   [103] *Ibid.*, paras. 103, 155.

for all levels of the social. Economic and business interests, minority rights, national debt and the national economy are some of the areas in which established relationships will have to be reassessed and restructured, eventually with high social cost. The Supreme Court of Canada highlighted the impact of secession on the achieved level of economic integration and social cohesion. Its opinion assessed the need to balance the eventual will of the regional population for an independent state against the interests of economic and social integration. In fact, the Court weighed the 'democratic' against the other spheres of the 'social' on the domestic level of the affected state. It thus brought the disintegration cost in relationship to the question of legitimacy and lawfulness of secession. Twelve years earlier, the ICJ had stressed in the *Frontier Dispute* case the principle of the stability of borders and maintenance of the territorial *status quo* as an essential element for the consolidation of the newly independent states.[104]

The two judgments need to be read together, because they complete each other by focusing on the external and internal aspect of 'stability' as factors co-determining the global policies of recognition in cases of eventual secession, or accession of territories to independence against the will of the metropolitan power or the predecessor state. Policies of recognition should consider the ramifications of secession on both, the interstate relations and the domestic space, in the context of broader values and objectives of the international community. The exercise of external self-determination and the recognition of seceding territories needs to be embedded in the overall system of just peace, good governance and democratic governance. The act of recognition as an act of global governance has to consider, whether a new independent state advances the integration of the territory and of the region, including the predecessor, in global society.

In terms of global governance, the cost of the destabilisation resulting from secession or separation of a territory can be offset only by expected tangible benefits in terms of advancement of the objectives of 'just peace'. Thus, the cost of a state's disintegration can be counterbalanced by the increased integration of the seceding territory and of the predecessor in global societal structures. Under this prism, it might be argued with certain persuasiveness that Hong-Kong, Taiwan or Chechnya would not be eligible as self-determination units. In the first two cases, the destabilisation can be expected to be wider than the

---

[104] *Frontier Dispute (Burkina Faso v. Mali).*

benefits of independence: since these territories have already achieved a satisfactory degree of integration in global society,[105] and it cannot be reasonably expected that accession to independence as such would broaden the freedoms of the inhabitants, the international community would rather consider the destabilisation risks ensuing from such a decision. As for Chechnya, the apparent lack of prospects that independence would lead to more effective and integrated governance structures is a normative factor that should be taken into account in the self-determination debate.[106]

The need to maximise the 'integration potential' of territorial changes may require more complex solutions combining elements of international recognition with policies of economic reform and integration in a single package.[107] In that way, the conflicts may lose their sharpness through successful global governance policies.

(iii) Conclusion

The 'centre of gravity' of the principle of self-determination has moved from the claim to statehood to the internal dimension and to democratic governance. The establishment of 'good governance' structures enhances societal stability and 'just peace' and unleashes the potential of global society. Global policies of recognition of self-determination units depend on the degree of stability the territory promises under a new international status. Accession to independence does not derive its legitimacy from historical rights or wrongs, but from the territory's capacity to enhance societal pluralism and peace.

The transformation of the principle of self-determination of peoples follows the emergence of the global political system that replaced the bipolar system of the Cold War. The working hypothesis for the second part of the present chapter is that, in parallel, other 'function systems' have established themselves all over the globe and have constituted what we call 'global society'. Transnational activities and communications of all kinds and types are structured through their own semantics, systems

---

[105] Hong Kong ranks 22nd among 177 states and territories in the UNDP: 2005 Human Development Index http://hdr.undp.org/reports/global/2005/pdf/HDR05_complete.pdf. As for the economic indicators and performance of Taiwan, see the relevant WTO Trade Policy Review, Report by the Secretariat, WT/TPR/S/165, 16 May 2006.

[106] See above, note 53.

[107] See, for example, for such a proposal, A. Skordas, 'Serbia, Montenegro and Kosovo: A Benelux in the Balkans?', available on the website of the Woodrow Wilson International Centre for Scholars: http://www.wilsoncenter.org/index.cfm?fuseaction=topics.print_doc&doc_id=119891&group_id=115869&topic_id=109941&stoplayout=true (last accessed 31 August 2006).

and networks. If democratic governance guarantees societal pluralism, then self-determination emerges also as a much broader principle that empowers actors and systems within and beyond the sphere of the political, and effectively precludes states from dominating over them. Self-determination secures then the autonomy and evolution of transnational legal regimes, which 'juridify', therefore, regulate and 'enable', global societal activities. Regimes that have reached a high evolutionary threshold and exhibit a strong self-organisational capacity may consolidate further their identity through elements of self-determination: in that way, they realise 'global governance'.

Self-determination in transnational regimes: an emerging principle

Transnational regimes need to be framed in the context of fragmentation of international law, constitutionalism and emergence of global society. Here, it is necessary to give a brief account of these concepts in a socio-legal perspective, taking into consideration particularly the conceptualisation of the social systems theory (section A below). Since the principle of self-determination assumes a different shape, depending on the particularities of each regime, it is more appropriate to speak of a principle 'in emergence', or of 'elements' of self-determination. The transnational regimes have 'functional polities' broadly corresponding to the concept of 'people' as beneficiaries or right-holders. In the European Union, the *pouvoir constituant* was exercised through the (provisional?) rejection of the draft Constitution (see section A(i) below). The WTO has developed elements of internal self-determination, and the case law of the Appellate Body has set up boundaries that distinguish the operations of the global trade regime from those of other normative systems; the drawing of these regime-specific boundaries is functionally equivalent to the principle of external self-determination (section A(ii) below).

A. Transnational regimes and constitutionalism

(i) Fragmentation of international law in the ILC work

The topic of fragmentation of international law has been on the agenda of the International Law Commission (ILC) since the year 2000.[108] Both the

---

[108] ILC, Report of the Study Group on Fragmentation of International Law, A/CN.4/ L.628, 1 August 2002, para. 2.

title of the initial feasibility study (Hafner Report)[109] and the final title of the topic[110] clearly demonstrate the perplexity of legal theorists before the phenomenon of expansion and diversification of international law and the apparent lack of any judicial instance capable of steering the global legal system to a clearly defined direction. Furthermore, the multiplication of globally acting actors, as testified by the ILC's conceptual turn from the 'international community of states as a whole' to the 'international community as a whole'[111], the risk of collisions between sets of norms and regimes,[112] and the absence of an effective and legitimate political authority on the level of global society maximise the pessimism on the negative impact of globalisation upon law.[113]

Other authors are less concerned. Koskenniemi considers the 'clash of legal rationales' as 'the platform for today's politics' and suggests 'that the discourse of multiplicity should itself be redescribed in political terms, as a competition between different systems and criteria for allocating resources between social groups', between those who win and those who lose.[114] Koskenniemi also identifies two alternative responses, that of constitutionalism and that of legal pluralism. He describes constitutionalism as the call 'to organize the proliferating institutions and rationalities into firm hierarchies',[115] and stresses that

---

[109] G. Hafner, 'Risks Ensuing from Fragmentation of International Law, ILC Report on the Work of its Fifty-second Session', *Official Records of the General Assembly, Fifty-fifth Session, Supplement No. 10* (A/55/10), Annex. In the words of the report, 'the system of international law consists of erratic parts and elements which are differently structured so that one can hardly speak of a homogeneous nature of international law', p. 321.

[110] 'Fragmentation of international law: difficulties arising form the diversification and expansion of international law', ILC Report on the work of fifty-fourth session, *Official Records of the General Assembly, Fifty-seventh Session, Supplement No. 10* (A/57/10).

[111] Report of the ILC, fifty-third session, *Official Records of the General Assembly, Fifty-sixth Session, Supplement No. 10* (A/56/10), Commentary on draft articles on state responsibility, Art. 25, para. 18.

[112] ILC Report on the work of its fifty-fifth session, *Official Records of the General Assembly, Fifty-eighth Session, Supplement No. 10* (A/58/10), Chapter X.C.

[113] See for instance the comments of the former ICJ President Gilbert Guillaume at the UN General Assembly, Fifty-fifth session, A/55/PV.41, 6–8. See also the moderate statement of President Shi Jiuyong, A/60/PV.39, 7. For an overview of the debate, see the contributions to the Symposium 'Diversity or Cacophony' (2004) 25 *Michigan Journal of International Law*, and 'Proliferation of International Tribunals' (1999) 31 *New York University Journal of International Law and Politics*.

[114] M. Koskenniemi, *Global Legal Pluralism: Multiple Regimes and Multiple Modes of Thought*, paper delivered at Harvard Law School, 5 March 2005 available at http//www.valt.helsinki.fi/blogs/eci/PluralismHarvard.pdf, p. 21.

[115] *Ibid.*, p. 8.

this approach 'responds to the worry about the "unity of international law" by suggesting a hierarchical priority to institutions representing general international law (especially the ICJ)';[116] he defines legal pluralism as 'the approach that seeks to grasp all the different rationalities effective in the world'.[117]

The semantics of constitutionalism characterise in fact the transition from the community of states to the functionally differentiated 'global society'.[118] This is a development associated with the experience that, in a global society that affects all aspects of life, activity and communication, something even remotely resembling to a 'constitution' should have taken shape, or needs to take shape. The legal constructs of traditional international law appear as insufficient to confer legitimacy to the new order.

International law and governance theorists have proposed various constitutionalism models. Admittedly, a major dividing line exists between 'hierarchical/political'[119] and 'fragmented/societal' constitutionalism;[120] other distinctions and conceptualisations are situated between or within them.[121] Whether governance is possible despite, or

---

[116] *Ibid.*, p. 12.

[117] *Ibid.*, p. 16. See also M. Koskenniemi and P. Leino, 'Fragmentation of International Law? Postmodern Anxieties' (2002) 15 *Leiden Journal of International Law* (LJIL), 553–79, and the ILC's Report, A/CN.4/L.682, 13 April 2006.

[118] On the concept of 'global society', see N. Luhmann, 'Die Weltgesellschaft' (1971) 57 *Archiv für Rechts- und Sozialphilosophie*, 1–35; N. Luhmann, *Die Gesellschaft der Gesellschaft* (Frankfurt/Main: Suhrkamp 1997), pp. 145–71, 806–12.

[119] See, for instance, B. Fassbender, 'The United Nations Charter As Constitution of The International Community' (1998) 36 *Columbia J Trans Law* 529–619; B. Fassbender, 'Sovereignty and Constitutionalism in International Law', in N. Walker (ed.), *Sovereignty in Transition*, pp. 115–43; P.-M. Dupuy, 'The Constitutional Dimension of the Charter of the United Nations Revisited' (1997) 1 *Max Planck UNYB* 1–33; J. Habermas, 'Hat die Konstitutionalisierung des Völkerrechts noch eine Chance?', in J. Habermas, *Der gespaltene Westen* (Frankfurt/Main: Suhrkamp, 2004), pp. 113–93.

[120] G. Teubner, 'Globale Zivilverfassungen: Alternativen zur staatszentrierten Verfassungstheorie' (2003) 63 *ZaöRV* 1–28; A. Fischer-Lescano and G. Teubner, 'Regime-Collisions: The Vain Search for Legal Unity in the Fragmentation of Global Law' (2004) 25 *Michigan Journal of International Law* 999–1046; Fischer-Lescano and Teubner, *Regime-Kollisionen* C. Walter, 'Constitutionalizing (Inter)national Governance – Possibilities for and Limits to the Development of an International Constitutional Law' (2001) 44 *GYIL* 170–201; A. Fischer-Lescano, *Die Globalverfassung* (Weilerswist: Velbrück Wissenschaft, 2005); A. Fischer-Lescano, 'Die Emergenz der Globalverfassung' (2003) 63 *ZaöRV* 717–60.

[121] 'Weak' or 'strong' societal constitutionalism, see T. Vesting, 'Constitutionalism or Legal Theory: Comments on Gunther Teubner', in Joerges, Sand, and Teubner,

because of, the fragmentation of international law and global law, seems to be the core question in the debate.

(ii) The globalisation's big bang

The discourse on constitutionalism and international law needs still to be reviewed in terms of the full emergence of the contemporary heterarchical global society of differentiated function systems, following the breakdown, in the period 1989–1993, of the alternative communist project of a hierarchically steered global society. In a final stage, the September/October 1993 extra-constitutional developments in Moscow and the subsequent adoption of the first post-Soviet Russian Constitution on 12 December 1993, marked the formal end of the antagonism between the two global societal projects of the twentieth century: free-market capitalism and Soviet communism. The post-Soviet Russian Constitution formally guaranteed the republican and democratic form of government, fundamental freedoms, property rights, and the division of powers;[122] the terms 'self-determination' and adherence of Russia to the 'world community' are met in the preamble of the Constitution.[123] At the bottom line, the political and constitutional developments in the Russian Federation between September and December 1993 constitute a major moment in the evolution of the heterarchical global society, notwithstanding various reverse developments in Russia over time.[124] Though the linkages between law, politics and economy are fluid and take different forms in various regions of the globe, the strict hierarchical societal model of Soviet communism has not proved capable of restoration, replication or imitation.

Self-determination should thus be redefined in a broader and more 'subversive' sense than the mainstream doctrine might be willing to concede. If states, along with other actors, are constitutive of the global political system, and if global function systems, such as law, economy,

---

Transnational Governance, pp. 29–39; see also I.-J. Sand, 'Polycontextuality as an Alternative to Constitutionalism', *ibid.*, pp. 41–65.

[122] T. Schweisfurth, 'Die Verfassung Rußlands vom 12. Dezember 1993' (1994) 21 *Europäische Grundrechte-Zeitschrift (EuGRZ)* 473–91.

[123] See the text of the Constitution at http://www.departments.bucknell.edu/russian/const/constit.html (last accessed 31 August 2006). For the German translation, see (1994) 21 *EuGRZ* 519–33.

[124] As an indicator, Russia was classified 'not free' in 2005 by the Freedom House: see http://www.freedomhouse.org/template.cfm?page=47&nit=366&year=2005 (last accessed 31 August 2006).

science, religion, or mass media are expanding and structuring their rationalities in transboundary networks of state and non-state actors, then we can assume that self-determination might be a principle of more general application and reach within global society.

Integration regimes, such as the EU and the WTO, exhibit features conferring upon them a particularly dynamic role in the evolution of global societal structures and could be considered as driving forces in the globalisation process. Such regimes are 'good candidates' to test the assumption that self-determination is indeed applicable beyond the relatively narrow field of the allocation and organisation of territorial authority.

(iii) Systems and rank

In a systems-theoretical perspective, the transition to functionally differentiated society is characterised by the increasing role and predominance of cognitive and adaptive vis-à-vis normative expectations; it seems that at a certain stage of societal evolution, fields of activity, such as science, technology and economy enjoy a 'relative primacy' in the evolution of global societal structures in comparison to law and politics.[125] However, this should not be taken to mean that a rank order exists among systems, comparable to that of a stratified society. Functions cannot be put into a hierarchical relationship, since they are all important for society, and their particular significance can be ascertained only in context. Since there is no 'outpost' capable of determining societal needs from the outside of society, each system proceeds in its own assessments; the fulfilment of its own function appears, therefore, as the most important from its own perspective.[126] Luhmann's formulation here deserves attention:

> In other words, a functionally differentiated society can simultaneously permit and not permit a rank order among its functions, depending on the systems reference of the operation. Every system can and must present its own function as unyielding in comparison to all others; but from the standpoint of society as a whole, the rank relationship between systems remains unregulated. 'Unregulated' means, by all means, that it is possible, indeed probable, that not all functions should be taken as equally

---

[125] N. Luhmann, 'Die Weltgesellschaft', reprinted in N. Luhmann, *Soziologische Aufklärung 2*, 1975, 51–71, at 55.

[126] N. Luhmann, *Gesellschaftsstruktur und Semantik I*, 2nd edn (Frankfurt/Main: Suhrkamp 1998), pp. 27–8.

important, and that tendencies may exist to consider individual function areas, such as those of the economy, as particularly important.[127]

There seems to be, therefore, a certain presumption that in particular linkages of law with other function systems, economy may play a significant role and arm a regime with strong auto-constitutional structures.[128] The 'strength' should not be reified or conceived in terms of some 'ontological capacity'; it depends on the evolutionary stage of a regime and on factors such as the degree of differentiation and autonomy, its resources and institutional capacity.[129]

In that sense, international integration regimes, such as the EU, NAFTA or the WTO, could be presumed as 'stronger' in comparison to legal regimes arising from the international law of cooperation and co-existence.[130] The EU economic constitution in particular is axed upon individual market freedoms, competition rules, common currency as a separate constitutional regime, the rule of law, supremacy and direct effect of EU/EC law, with the European Convention on Human Rights and democratic governance for member states as 'supportive infrastructure' for the overall system.[131] Therefore, this regime conveys individuals the capacity of decentralised action, and has developed strong self-administration mechanisms, including an effective dispute settlement system. At least constitutional 'moments' are visible in the WTO

---

[127] *Ibid.* (my translation, emphasis added). The text in the original reads as follows: 'Ein funktional differenziertes Gesellschaftssystem kann, mit anderen Worten, eine Rangordnung unter den Funktionen zugleich zulassen und nicht zulassen je nachdem, in welche Systemreferenz die Operation fällt. Jedes System kann, ja muß, seine Funktionen im Verhältnis zu allen anderen hypostasieren; aber gesamtgesellschaftlich bleibt das Rangverhältnis der Funktionen ungeregelt. "Ungeregelt" heißt übrigens durchaus, dass es möglich, ja wahrscheinlich ist, dass nicht alle Funktionen gleich wichtig genommen werden müssen, und dass es durchaus Tendenzen geben mag, einzelne Funktionskreise, etwa die der Wirtschaft, für besonders wichtig zu halten.'

[128] On the definition, see Fischer-Lescano and Teubner 'Regime-Collisions' 1014–17.

[129] On the transition from 'quasi-system' to system: see H. Willke, *Systemtheorie I – Grundlagen*, 5th edn (Stuttgart: Lucius & Lucius, 1996), p. 72 *et seq*. On the evolution and *autopoiesis* of the legal system, see G. Teubner, *Recht als autopoietisches System* (Frankfurt/Main: Suhrkamp, 1989).

[130] Petersmann, 'Time for a United Nations "Global Compact"' 621–50.

[131] On the constitutionalism debate in the EU, see the contributions of N. Walker, 'Late Sovereignty in the European Union', G. de Búrca, 'Sovereignty and the Supremacy Doctrine of the European Court of Justice', and M. Poiares Maduro, 'Contrapunctual Law: Europe's Constitutional Pluralism in Action', in N. Walker, *Sovereignty in Transition*, pp. 3 *et seq.*, 449 *et seq.*, 501 *et seq.* respectively. See also J. Shaw, 'Process and Constitutional Discourse in the European Union' (2000) 27 *JLS* 4–37.

global trade regime.[132] Circumstances of political impasse, such as the July 2006 breakdown of the Doha round negotiations[133] or the rejection of the draft Constitution for Europe should not be overrated as 'systemic crises'. They evidence the existence of alternatives, and the need for 'fundamental decisions' on the evolutionary path the regime will take.

If integration regimes are stronger than cooperation regimes, such the WHO, or the ILO, their 'hegemonic' influence in global – and fragmented – society is not rooted within the top-down exercise of political or economic power and authority. It is rather the 'broadband capacity' of their under-lying rationality that enables them to incorporate, within the prospect of further planning and development of their own structures and functions, various elements constitutive of the 'global interest'. A report of the UN High Commissioner for Human Rights (UNHCHR)[134] dealt with the question, whether the legal categories of the WTO system can be inter-preted and implemented in a way that takes into consideration the various aspects of the non-discrimination principle. The examples of three areas of regulation, namely government procurement, agricultural trade and the so-called 'social labelling',[135] clarified the different avenues through which a human rights-friendly interpretation and further development might be internalised by the WTO system.

Transnational regimes are developing self-administration mechan-isms that progressively assume autonomy from the states that partici-pate in, or have set up, the regime or its original structure. If the regime crosses a certain evolutionary threshold and is able to ensure a certain degree of self-sufficiency, self-administration and self-generation through

---

[132] E.-U. Petersmann, 'The "Human Rights Approach" Advocated by the UN High Commissioner for Human Rights and by the International Labour Organization: Is it Relevant for WTO Law and Policy?' (2004) 7 *Journal of International Economic Law* (*JIEL*) 605 at 621–3; E.-U. Petersmann, 'Challenges to the Legitimacy and Efficiency of the World Trading System: Democratic Governance and Competition Culture in the WTO' (2004) 7 *JIEL* 583–603. On the broader constitutionalism debate on the WTO, see D. Cass, *The Constitutionalization of the World Trade Organization* (Oxford: Oxford University Press, 2005); Fischer-Lescano and Teubner, *Regime-Kollisionen*, J. Dunoff, 'Constitutional Conceits: The WTO's "Constitution" and the Discipline of International Law' (2006) 17 *EJIL* 647–75.

[133] See at http://www.wto.org/english/news_e/news06_e/gc_27july06_e.htm (last accessed 31 August 2006).

[134] Report of the High Commissioner, Analytical Study of the High Commissioner for Human Rights on the Fundamental Principle of Non-discrimination in the Context of Globalization, E/CN.4/2004/40, 15 January 2004.

[135] I.e., labeling demonstrating that an agricultural product has received a fair price, or promoted human rights in the process of production, *ibid.*, para. 43.

recourse to its own resources, it is reasonable to conclude that it is being stabilised through self-determination, which anchors itself in the realm of 'societal constitutionalism'.

B. Elements of self-determination in transnational regimes

(i) Pouvoir constituant and self-determination in the European Union

Because of its hybrid nature as a supranational legal regime, but also as an 'aspiring' political-territorial entity, the European Union creates the necessary 'bridge' between self-determination of states and self-determination of regimes. Here, the focus will be limited on *pouvoir constituant* and political integration,[136] which are novel elements in the Union's efforts to transcend the 'economic' and push the integration process deep into the realm of the 'political'.

(a) **The decision for/against political integration** The rejection of the draft Constitution by the 2005 French and Dutch referenda[137] offers the opportunity of examining the evolving dynamics of self-determination of an integration regime at crossroads.

The draft Treaty establishing a Constitution for Europe[138] was intended to establish an integrated European political system as a novel evolutionary stage of the European integration process. In that sense, the process of adoption and ratification of the Constitution was, per definition, exercise of the *pouvoir constituant*. Though not explicitly spelled out, the political unification was thought to become the motor of the European integration process, with economic integration losing its exclusiveness. This major transformation of the Union's character was possible only through the exercise of the right of self-determination – and under these circumstances, the European Union operated as a *sui generis* fragmented self-determination unit.

The 'turn to the political' and the 'existential parameters' of a common European identity were visible in the draft Constitutional Treaty. The great power vision of the draft finds its place in the preamble, where the signatories state *la mission civilisatrice* of the Union: 'Europe,

---

[136] On the theoretical foundations of self-determination and *pouvoir constituant* in the European Union, see Lindahl, 'Sovereignty and Representation' at 105–14.

[137] On 31 May and 1 June 2005, respectively.

[138] *Official Journal of the European Union* (OJEU), C 310/1, 16 December 2004.

reunited after bitter experiences, intends *to continue along the path of civilisation*, progress and prosperity, for the good of all its inhabitants, including the weakest and most deprived; that it wishes to remain a continent open to culture, learning and social progress; and that it wishes to deepen the democratic and transparent nature of its public life, *and to strive for peace, justice and solidarity throughout the world.*'[139] Moreover, the draft Constitution extended the powers of the Union 'to cover all areas of foreign policy and all questions relating to the Union's security, including the progressive framing of a common defence policy that might lead to a common defence'.[140] And more pointed: 'convinced that, thus "United in diversity", Europe offers them the best chance of pursuing, with due regard for the rights of each individual and in *awareness of their responsibilities towards future generations and the Earth, the great venture which makes of it a special area of human hope.*'[141] This is, indeed, the political, constitutional and ideological agenda of a great power *in-spe*.

(b) Self-determination unit and sub-units   Peoples, states and citizens are actors in the exercise of the *pouvoir constituant* in the European Union. According to the preamble of the draft Constitution, '*the peoples of Europe* are determined to transcend their former divisions and, united even more closely, to forge a common destiny'. Though the member states have the legal authority to ratify or reject the Constitution, they are not the single holders of the right to self-determination. The differences between the respective formulations of the Treaty on European Union (TEU) and of the draft Constitutional Treaty are indicative. According to Article 1 TEU, 'by this Treaty, *the High Contracting Parties establish among themselves* a European Union, hereinafter called "the Union"';[142] Article I-1 of the Constitutional Treaty has adopted the following formulation: '*reflecting the will of the citizens and States of Europe* to build a common future, this Constitution establishes the European Union . . .'

The draft Constitutional Treaty has to be ratified by all member states, 'in accordance with their respective constitutional requirements'.[143] The letter of this provision is identical with Article 48(3) of

---

[139] *Ibid.*, para. 2 of the Preamble (emphasis added).
[140] *Ibid.*, Article I-16, para. 1.   [141] *Ibid.*, para. 4 of the Preamble (emphasis added).
[142] OJEC C 325/5, 24.12.2002 (consolidated version) (emphasis added).
[143] Article IV-447.

the TEU, stating that amendments to the treaties should 'enter into force after being ratified by all the Member States in accordance with their respective constitutional requirements'. Despite their identical wordings, the 'normative horizon' of the two provisions is different: the latter determines the regular procedure for amending the rules of a supranational regime, while the former introduces the procedure for the exercise of original constitutional authority.

The comprehensive territory of the European Union is a single self-determination unit for the purpose of taking the decision on the establishment of a political/constitutional order. Nonetheless, since a single European people have not yet come into existence, the right to self-determination cannot be exercised either through a European Constitutional Assembly, or by a pan-European referendum. The supranational 'demos' representing Union membership and commitment to its shared values[144] has not armed itself with original constitutional authority – thus self-determination in the EU can only be exercised through citizens, acting as peoples within member states. The Union as self-determination unit is segmented in sub-units, coinciding with the territories of the member states, as the European equivalent of the principle *uti possidetis*. The transformation of the Union from a primarily economic into a political association necessitates 'coinciding wills' through popular decisions, which are taken either by the representatives of the peoples or by referenda (binding or consultative), within the sub-units. The ratification of the draft Constitution by each of the member states is a formal act sealing a decision attributable to the people.

The original constitutional authority is exercised either at the end of the process, if all peoples have consented to adopt the Constitution, or at the moment of the rejection of the draft Constitutional Treaty by one or more Union peoples. A negative decision is also an exercise of the right of self-determination, because it expresses the will of the peoples to reject the political integration and maintain both, the present form of the nation-state with its democratic legitimacy and full political authority, as well as the European Union as a primarily economic association.

(c) **The negative exercise of *pouvoir constituant*** A counter-argument could contend, that the rejection of the draft Constitution by the minority of the Union's peoples, could not be, as such, exercise of self-determination.

---

[144] J. H. H. Weiler, 'Does Europe Need a Constitution? Demos, Telos and the German Maastricht Decision' (1995) 1 *ELJ* 219–57.

It could be argued that, since no 'coincidence of wills' has taken place, there can be no exercise of original constitutional authority. As it would happen with an ordinary ratification process, if a member state fails to ratify, the treaty does not enter into force.

The 'ordinary ratification' argument disregards the particularities of *pouvoir constituant* in an integration regime. It does not explain how a treaty is transformed into a Constitution, or, alternatively, how states can adopt by ratification something other than a treaty. The 'mutation' of the contractual or conventional into the constitutional presupposes that another process is taking place as 'decision', simultaneously with the formal adoption of the draft treaty. Inversely, it disregards the hegemonic act of will that 'dissects' an alternative choice and 'commands' by rejection.

The exercise of constitutional authority is intrinsically distinct from treaty amendment, because it is exercised by the 'political society' of the self-determination unit. In the particular case of the European Union, each basal self-determination sub-unit takes a separate decision – but a decision for all. The affirmative decision takes the double form of invitation to the other peoples and states to join the political association, and of acceptance of their respective invitations. A single negative decision terminates the process and, thus, substitutes itself to a decision valid for, and binding upon, all. The 'common destiny' is not the 'output' of an ordinary bureaucratic or legislative exercise, but needs to be established through an 'original act' of 'performative violence': paradoxically, the act of rejection has uttered the 'we' of the 'self' in exercise of the *pouvoir constituant*.

If the exercise of the right of self-determination through the (provisional?) rejection of the Constitutional Treaty affirms the present form of the nation-state in Europe, the further question is, whether it has a further significance for the future of European constitutionalism. It is obvious that the rejection of the Constitution does not create any 'constitutional crisis', but rather a 'moment of suspense'. No real 'constitutional crisis' has shattered Europe and the need for the reassessment of Europe's policies is of a political rather than of a constitutional order.[145]

The various and often contradictory political interpretations of the negative votes in the above two referenda[146] have only limited legal, but

---

[145] A. Skordas, 'Is Europe an "Aging Power" with Global Vision? A Tale on Constitutionalism and Restoration' (Review Essay) (2005) 12 *Col JEL* 241–91.

[146] C. Joerges, 'On the Disregard for History in the Convention Process' (2006) 12 *ELJ* 2–5; G. de Búrca, 'After the Referenda', *ibid.*, 6.

significant political, relevance. The rejection of the draft Constitution cannot be interpreted as a denial of the European project itself and of its economic constitution, because these were not subjects of the self-determination process. The question the voters had to decide upon was whether the economic constitution would be superseded by a political constitutional order, and this question was answered in the negative. Though the negative exercise of the *pouvoir constituant* secured the legitimacy of the existing system by default, the revolt of the European voters against their own national political elites signified the emergence of a supranational 'political society' strongly supportive of reform 'beyond the Constitution'. The negative outcome was not the result of an 'accidental referendum,' but had its own intrinsic logic. As Poiares Maduro and Ladeur had argued, a formal political constitution modelled after the nation-state was largely incompatible with the overall structure and nature of the European Union.[147] Reform and further development of the economic governance in the Union is moving into the heart of the debate.

Over the last half a century, European constitutionalism emerged through consecutive constitutional moments that transformed the system of the EC/EU Treaties into a full auto-constitutional integration regime. The ECJ played a major role in this evolutionary process, in that it progressively established and stabilised the EU governance system of 'functional sovereignty', by interpreting and implementing norms and principles and by raising the treaties into constitutional instruments. A 'functional polity' has taken shape and transformed the customs union into a full-fledged regime through judicial decision, administrative practice, and treaty revision;[148] the introduction of the common currency has been a major constitutional step in that direction, even without the participation of all member states.[149]

The negative exercise of the *pouvoir constituant* generates therefore strong pull for reform in the area of economic governance.[150] The

---

[147] M. Poiares Maduro, 'Contrapunctual Law' 501 at 535–6; K.-H. Ladeur, 'Globalization and the Conversion of Democracy' at 117–18.

[148] On the process of European constitutionalism, see J. H. H. Weiler, *The Constitution of Europe* (Cambridge: Cambridge University Press, 1999), in particular ch. 2 ('The Transformation of Europe'), and ch. 6 ('Introduction: The Reformation of European Constitutionalism').

[149] Cf., for instance, the provisions on 'enhanced cooperation', Articles 43–45 TEU.

[150] I. Maher, 'Committing to Change: Economic Governance and the EU Constitution' (2006) 12 *ELJ* 9–11.

rejection of the draft Constitution has been itself an exercise of constitutional authority and another fundamental step in the evolution of the constitutional structure of the European Union. In the aftermath of the referenda, the 'loose interlinkage' of the regime's formal 'functional polity' with the spontaneous 'political society' of the 'European street' will infuse more unpredictability, more creativity and more risk in the European project.

(ii) Self-determination in the WTO: on 'self' and polity

(a) **The birth of the 'self'**   If the principle of self-determination is articulated in the WTO regime, it is necessary to define the birth of the 'self' which is the source of the regime's 'polity'. The WTO regime is 'xenonomous' in the sense that its polity 'is not contemporaneous with its own genesis', and that the original GATT 1947 contracting parties 'seized the initiative', appropriated the vision of free trade and ventured the mission of establishing what later became a global trade regime.[151] The GATT has been part of a greater hegemonic project of the US and the UK on the international economic relations dating back to 1943; despite the fact that the US Senate did not ratify the Havana Charter and the International Trade Organization never came to life, the GATT progressively emerged as the centerpiece for dispute settlement and negotiations on the liberalisation of international trade.[152] GATT was part of the postwar project of 'embedded liberalism', whose complexities as a compromise between economic liberalism and welfare state John Ruggie spelled out as follows:

> This was the essence of the embedded liberalism compromise: unlike the economic nationalism of the thirties, it would be multilateral in character; unlike the liberalism of the gold standard and free trade, its multilateralism would be predicated upon domestic interventionism ... On the side of the trade regime, the structure of trade that it has encouraged and the minimization of domestic adjustment costs that it allows have both had inflationary consequences, by sacrificing economic efficiency to social stability.[153]

---

[151] On the terminology, see H. Lindahl, 'Sovereignty and Representation' at 87–114.

[152] See R. Keohane, *After Hegemony: Cooperation and Discord in the World Political Economy* (Princeton: Princeton University Press, 1984), pp. 143–4, 147–9; cf. also *Guide to GATT Law and Practice* (Geneva: WTO, 1995), pp. 3–6.

[153] J. G. Ruggie, 'International Regimes, Transactions, and Change: Embedded Liberalism in the Postwar Economic Order' (1982) 36 *International Organization* 379 at 393, 415.

The GATT regime, as product of this compromise, was intergovernmental in character and normatively weak;[154] however, it created the
societal space for the take-off of a global integration process that was
powerful enough to withstand the politico-ideological pressure of the
NIEO and win the struggle with the communist global counter-project.
The transition from the GATT to the WTO marks the transformation
of the international into a truly global regime.[155] Coincidentally, one of
the major steps forward during the Uruguay Round negotiations was
achieved late December 1991, at the time of the breakdown of the Soviet
Union.[156] The global trade regime took two more years to complete, but,
when it did, it was endowed with the youngest international organisation, a Charter, and an adjudicatory dispute settlement system.[157] This
legal infrastructure permitted the polity of the system to articulate itself
through the operation of the principle of self-determination in the
political and dispute settlement organs of the WTO. The project of
'embedded liberalism' is fading away, to be replaced by theories of
globalisation.[158]

(b) Regime polity Instead of territorially or ethno-culturally defined
'people' as right holders, self-determination of regimes is based upon the
'functional polity' and 'community' of private and public actors whose
activities, rights and interests are regulated or affected by the regime. We
can distinguish three categories of WTO polity members, namely states,
private/corporate interests, and non-governmental organisations as
public interest groups. While state participation and membership are
highly formalised, corporate interests and NGOs participate in a rather
informal and spontaneous manner in the operation of the regime.

---

[154] GATT entered into force without formal ratification requirements, on the legal basis of
the Protocol of Provisional Application, that granted the so-called 'grandfather rights'
(Part II of the GATT was to be applied as far as it does not contradict existing national
legislation, GATT Law and Practice, *ibid.*, Vol. II, 1071, 1074–83); GATT lacked a
formal judicial dispute settlement mechanism (see Articles XXII and XXIII GATT) and
was a forum deprived of the legal personality of an international organisation.

[155] The 23 original contracting parties to the GATT 1947 had risen to 149 WTO members
by the end of 2005.

[156] J. Croome, *Reshaping the World Trading System – A History of the Uruguay Round*
(Geneva, WTO 1995), pp. 323–7.

[157] See the legal texts of the WTO system at http://www.wto.org/english/docs_e/legal_e/
legal_e.htm.

[158] For a systems theoretical analysis of the global economic system, see N. Luhmann, *Die
Wirtschaft der Gesellschaft*, 2nd edn (Frankfurt/Main: Suhrkamp, 1996).

Prima facie, the WTO looks like a classical multilateral international law regime, with states representing their 'national interest' under conditions of legal equality: only states, customs territories and the EU are members in the organisation and are entitled to participate in its organs, including the dispute settlement procedures, despite the informal 'openings' of the regime to non-state actors. At a closer look, however, the regime differentiates itself in a number of aspects from classical international law.[159] An important point of differentiation is the transition from the international interest as negotiated aggregate of 'national interests' represented by states, to the broader concept of 'global' interests, which are articulated at the core of the WTO regime.

To take an example, the WTO regime differentiates between developed, developing, and least developed states.[160] Though differentiation of membership status is not, as such, unusual in international organisations, the question of development is at the centerpiece of the WTO system and is coupled with the stage of development of domestic economies *as segments* of an asymmetrical global economy based upon open, market oriented policies and 'sustainable development' policies. The WTO system has thus established the legal framework for a worldwide economic integration process that 'will strengthen the world economy' and create 'more trade, investment, employment and income growth throughout the world', leading to a 'fairer and more open multilateral trading system for the benefit and welfare' of the peoples of the member states.[161]

Moreover, the preamble of the WTO Charter describes the features of the global and dynamic economic system, along with the expected benefits for other, non-strictly economic goods: global economic integration is expected to raise standards of living, ensure full-employment and 'a large and steadily growing volume of real income and effective demand', lead to expansion of trade in goods and services, achieve optimal allocation of the world's resources, and protect and preserve the environment.[162]

---

[159] Cf. D. McRae, 'The WTO in International Law: Tradition Continued or New Frontier?' (2000) 3 *JIEL* 27–41.

[160] M. Matshushita, T. Schoenbaum and P. Mavroidis, *The World Trade Organization – Law, Practice and Policy*, 2nd edn (Oxford: Oxford University Press, 2006), pp. 763–84.

[161] See the preamble and the main body of the Marrakesh Declaration of 15 April 1994.

[162] Para. 1 of the preamble of the WTO Charter.

Therefore, and despite the primacy of 'the economic', the WTO regime is interlinked with rule systems on the environmental protection and preservation of 'global commons', as well as with the global health and labour systems through the above 'prosperity clause'. In this way, the WTO constitution realises a primary coupling of the community of states in broad sense (including customs territories and the EU) with the global economic system, in the form of the creation of the global trade regime. Beyond the roof of state membership, societal interests articulate themselves in a legal environment that encourages decentralised initiatives and networking.

The fundamentally liberal character of the WTO regime is not refuted by the existence of asymmetries and trade-restraining elements in the system;[163] the regime rules should be interpreted following the rules of the Vienna Convention on the Law of Treaties including context and purpose of the agreements, in view of their fundamental objective to secure and promote global economic integration.[164] Furthermore, secondary couplings between global trade and other special legal regimes relating to health, labour and environment need to be established, and it is up to the WTO system itself and to its dispute settlement mechanism to progressively produce its boundaries vis-à-vis these regimes.[165]

The variety of interlinkages demonstrates that the polity question cannot be exhausted in terms of international interest, which is structured exclusively by states representing their domestic constituencies. The WTO regime extends its various benefits to globally acting corporate entities, or to transnational non-state groups acting on behalf of global public interests recognised by the regime. The argument that economic actors or NGOs under the jurisdiction of one or more states can be reduced into a politically constituted 'people' represented by individual governments is out of touch with the 'normative reality' of the WTO system in the era of globalisation. The incongruence between domestic/international political decision-making, on the one hand, and the operation of global function systems, on the other, cannot be adequately bridged through the assumption, that activities in the latter are transformed into 'national interests' at the disposition of (inter)-governmental decision-making. This formalistic approach risks losing

---

[163] See the doubts expressed by R. Steinberg, 'Judicial Lawmaking at the WTO: Discursive, Constitutional and Political Constraints' (2004) 98 *AJIL* 262.

[164] Cf. Matshushita, Schoenbaum and Mavroidis, *The World Trade Organization*, pp. 33–7.

[165] See below, (iv).

the significance of various avenues through which economic or other public interests articulate themselves as 'the WTO polity'.

(iii) Internal self-determination in the WTO

The internal self-determination of regimes is expressed through the principle of participation, indicating the capacity of the 'functional polity' to participate effectively in the regime's administration and operation. In the WTO, participation does not have the meaning of 'popular representation' in the regime decision-making through a parliamentarian assembly, nor is it related to the legitimacy the organisation might enjoy in the public opinion of the member states. These are factors or ideas external to the regime and, as such, are not directly relevant for the description of the regime-specific principle of internal self-determination – though legitimacy may have an impact on the way the WTO organs deal with specific issues, understand their jurisdiction, or deal with major political issues of concern to member states.[166]

The regime is operating under the principle of internal self-determination if it is capable to establish an internal iterative communication process through the regular operation of its organs, in particular of the dispute settlement body; again, this depends on a sufficient degree of decentralisation and spontaneity built into the system. The WTO polity is participating in the operation of the regime through various avenues, some of which are fully proceduralised, while some others are emerging through the practice of the organisation and the member states. Participation is therefore structured in three different dimensions, as participation of states, as deliberation, and as assertion of economic rights and interests.

(a) **Participation of states**   States participate in the WTO system on equal footing and decisions are taken by consensus. Although Article IX:1 WTO Charter provides for voting, if consensus cannot be arrived at, the practice of the organisation has not departed from the consensus principle. The question is whether voting or consensus corresponds more to the WTO-appropriate self-determination principle of democratic participation, given that both correspond to the principle of formal equality of states. Although consensus as GATT practice originated out of concern for the weaker contracting parties,[167] a voting

---

[166] Cf. J. Dunoff, 'The Death of the Trade Regime' (1999) 10 *EJIL* 733 at 757 *et seq.*
[167] *The Future of the WTO – Report by the Consultative Board to the Director-General* (Geneva: WTO, 2004) paras. 280–1.

scheme would currently put the most powerful members into disadvantage.[168] Moreover, the one-member one-vote system is more compatible with the operation of a political international organisation. In the WTO system, considering that the EU and the US represent about 65 per cent of the WTO GDP,[169] a politicised majority voting practice under the current WTO Charter would create inequalities inconsistent with the fair representation of societal and economic interests. Nonetheless, since consensus presents major shortcomings and may lead the system into constitutional paralysis, the Report on the Future of the WTO proposed, among others, the introduction of elements of 'variable geometry'.[170] In that sense, members wanting to pursue a deeper integration would not need to await arrival at consensus, and occasional majorities could not create obstacles or setbacks to the trade liberalisation; such a solution would enhance the overall flexibility of the system. At the bottom line, the WTO participation rationale does not rely on political majorities, and this is consistent with the regime's inner structure.

(b) Deliberation Elements of deliberation and deliberative processes are visible in the WTO system, in particular in the organs instituted by the various agreements. For instance, the WTO Committee on Sanitary and Phytosanitary Measures maintains close contact with the *Codex Alimentarius* Commission, the International Office for Epizootics and the Secretariat of the International Plant Protection Convention.[171] The specific nature of deliberative politics in a functional organisation, including the EU, is often expressed as 'technocratic deliberation' or 'comitology',[172] and it is necessary that all relevant views are being considered within the system. The 'relevance' is here the crux of the problem, since arguments of an ethical order, for example, could be barely considered by the WTO organs. Moreover, risk assessment, or the status of minority scientific opinions pushes regime organs in the role of the arbiter of political decisions of the member states. The range of deliberation in a transnational regime is not identical with that of a nation-state's public sphere, and it is constantly open to challenge, depending

---

[168] Steinberg, 'Judicial Lawmaking at the WTO' at 274.
[169] *Ibid.*, at 275, note 207, based upon assessments by the CIA and the WTO.
[170] *The Future of the WTO*, para. 291 *et seq.*
[171] Art. 12, para. 3 of the Agreement on the Application of Sanitary and Phytosanitary Measures.
[172] E. O. Eriksen and J. E. Fossum, 'Europe at Crossroads: Government or Transnational Governance?', in Joerges, Sand, and Teubner, *Transnational Govermance*, pp. 125–7.

on the evolution of the regime itself. Involvement of the 'wider public' is possible within the deliberative *fora* of the regime itself.[173]

Participation of non-governmental organisations (NGOs) in the operation of the regime is a fundamental pillar of WTO deliberative politics. Article V:5 of the WTO Charter provides that 'the General Council may make appropriate arrangements for consultation and cooperation with non-governmental organizations concerned with matters related to those of the WTO'. The General Council adopted Guidelines for Arrangements on Relations with NGOs providing for a limited participation of these organisations in the regime operation.[174] Particularly controversial has been the participation of NGOs in the dispute settlement procedures; the case law of the Appellate Body has permitted a limited access of NGOs through submission of *amicus curiae* briefs,[175] despite the open dissent expressed by the developing countries through the use of ideological and over-politicised arguments. The resistances against the further democratisation and introduction of deliberative mechanisms in the WTO regime are evidence of the fact that these countries want to reinterpret the WTO system as a purely intergovernmental contract and not as an integration regime.[176] On its part, the US, although it favours a greater transparency in the dispute settlement procedure,[177] vehemently opposes gap-filling through a dynamic-evolutive interpretation of the WTO rules.[178]

---

[173] Cf. A. Herwig, 'Transnational Governance Regimes for Foods Derived from Bio-Technology and their Legitimacy', *ibid.*, pp. 199–222; P. Nanz, 'Legitimation of Transnational Governance Regimes and Foodstuff Regulation at the WTO: Comments on Alexia Herwig', *ibid.*, pp. 223–31.

[174] *Decision* adopted by the General Council on 18 July 1996, WT/L/162, 23 July 1996.

[175] On the amicus curiae practice of the Appellate Body, see *United States – Import Prohibition of Certain Shrimp and Shrimp Products*, WT/DS58/AB/R, 12 October 1998, paras. 79–91, 99–110; *United States, Imposition of Countervailing Duties on Certain Hot-Rolled Lead and Bismuth Carbon Steel Products Originating in the United Kingdom*, WT/DS138/AB/R, 10 May 2000, paras. 36–42; *European Communities – Measures Affecting Asbestos and Asbestos-Containing Products*, WT/DS135/AB/R, 12 March 2001, paras. 50–7.

[176] See the Minutes of Meeting of the General Council on 22 November 2000, WT/GC/M/60, and the standpoints of the Informal Group of Developing Countries. On the controversy, see G. Umbricht, 'An "Amicus Curiae Brief" on Amicus Curiae Briefs at the WTO' (2001) 4 *JIEL*, 773–94.

[177] See the communications from the United States TN/DS/W/79, 13 July 2005 and TN/DS/W/13, 22 August 2002.

[178] See the communications from the United States TN/DS/W/82/Add.1, 25 October 2005 and TN/DS/W/82/Add.1/Corr.1, 27 October 2005.

The increasing participation of NGOs in the WTO processes and dispute settlement procedure can be considered as an established practice subject to the discretion of the panels and Appellate Body[179] that contributes to a better management of trade and global economic issues by the regime.[180] This is why the Report on the Future of the WTO endorsed, with some reservations, the further development of the cooperative relationship of the WTO with the NGOs.[181]

(c) **Assertion of economic rights and interests** Private economic rights and interests are asserted and realised in the WTO regime through two avenues: diplomatic protection and direct access of private parties to domestic courts. Although the diplomatic protection is the main avenue, the assertion of such rights in the WTO follows its own distinctive features and rationale that enhance the dynamics of decentralised action in the system, evidenced by 348 complaints raised by July 2006.[182]

States are the single actors that have standing to bring forward claims in the WTO dispute settlement system. The jurisprudence of the WTO dispute settlement organs has recognised a very broad discretion to the complaining member with respect to the definition of 'legal interest', amounting to the institutionalisation of '*actio popularis*'.[183] Moreover, although, in principle, the WTO rules lack direct effect in the domestic legal orders,[184] member states are often bound by internal law and practice to respond to the quest of their private/corporate constituencies for protection against WTO-inconsistent conduct of other contracting parties and even take measures on the international plane, including legally dubious forms of retaliation.[185] This legal practice demonstrates that, when states act as agents for domestic commercial

---

[179] Matshushita, Schoenbaum and Mavroidis, *The World Trade Organization*, pp. 124–5.

[180] D. Esty, 'Non-Governmental Organizations at the World Trade Organization: Cooperation, Competition, or Exclusion' (1998) 1 *JIEL* 123–47.

[181] *The Future of the WTO, ibid.*, ch. V ('Transparency and Dialogue with Civil Society').

[182] http://www.wto.org/english/tratop_e/dispu_e/dispu_status_e.htm (last accessed 31 August 2006).

[183] See the formulation of Matshushita, Schoenbaum and Mavroidis, *The World Trade Organization*, p. 114.

[184] *Ibid.*, pp. 92–4, 97–102, for the US, the EU and Japan.

[185] *Ibid.*, pp. 133–9. See also P. Mavroidis and W. Zdouc, 'Legal Means to Protect Private Parties' Interests in the WTO' (1998) 1 *JIEL International Economic Law* 407–33; J. Dunoff, 'The Misguided Debate Over NGO Participation at the WTO' (1998) 1 *JIEL* 433 at 441–51, whereby the author concentrates on the practice of lobbying by business groups in the US.

and industrial interests, they generate case law progressively developing the architecture of the global trade system; given that this is done with the requisite spontaneity, which is imported into the system by the above mechanisms, it becomes apparent that states and the diplomatic *raison d'état* only superficially exercise a control over the evolution of the regime.

At least two of the WTO agreements, the TRIPs agreement and the plurilateral Agreement on Government Procurement, provide for the obligation of states to institute domestic procedures and remedy systems, through which individuals may challenge domestic law and practice inconsistent with these agreements.[186] If states comply with these due process obligations and indeed institute these domestic guarantees, then private interests assume the capacity to gain direct access to the domestic judicial system, which then treats the provisions of the said agreements as generating individual rights. Although direct access of individual interests at the WTO dispute settlement system would enormously accelerate the global integration process,[187] this is not an issue for the time being.[188] In conclusion, the WTO regime has reached a certain degree of internal autonomy realising elements of internal self-determination. State and non-state actors participate and interact on various levels of the regime's operation, enhancing thus spontaneity and recursivity in its communications.

(iv) 'Drawing the boundaries' as external self-determination

(a) The death of the trade regime   In his well publicised essay, 'The Death of the Trade Regime', Dunoff diagnosed the increasing involvement of the WTO dispute settlement mechanism with 'trade and' issues as a factor that could jeopardise the legitimacy and capacity of the WTO.

---

[186] See Part III of the TRIPS Agreement ('Enforcement of Intellectual Property Rights', providing for civil and administrative procedures and remedies, provisional measures, border measures and criminal procedures). See also Article XX of the Agreement on Government Procurement ('challenge procedures'), and Article 4 of the Agreement on Preshipment Inspection and the Decision of the General Council of 13 December 1995 on the 'Operation of the Independent Entity Established Under Article 4 of the Agreement on Preshipment Inspection', WT/L/125/Rev. 1, 9 February 1996.

[187] G. Schleyer, 'Power to the People: Allowing Private Parties to Raise Claims Before the WTO Dispute Resolution System' (1997) 65 *Fordham Law Review* 2275–311.

[188] See, for instance, the state of negotiations on the modification of the Dispute Settlement Understanding, Report of the Chairman to the Special Session of the DSB, TN/DS/9, 6 June 2003.

As a cure, he proposed a 'policy of abstention' from the resolution of such disputes by the WTO adjudication:

> Given their very different source of jurisdiction, panels have not developed 'ripeness', 'political question' or other doctrines that are available to domestic courts. But this is not to suggest that current WTO doctrines are natural or inevitable, or that panels could not use any of the passive virtues available to domestic courts.[189]

He therefore suggested that the WTO jurisprudence should be focused on clear trade disputes and should abandon the prerogative to interpret the 'and' factor. Dunoff's proposal makes the correct diagnosis, namely that the trade regime should not overstretch itself and should not attempt to overwhelm other global interests. However, the therapy looks deficient; the proposed interpretive alternative can obviously function in a politically integrated national community anxious to implement the doctrine of separation of powers of the different branches of government, as the author recognises,[190] but has little chance of success in a fragmented global society. Moreover, it can amount to denial of the principle of external self-determination of regimes, which can be defined as 'drawing the boundaries' of the regime's own sphere of action toward the spheres of other regimes.

To determine boundaries, the regime (here: the WTO) needs to realise its own separation from the other normative systems and regimes; to fulfil this objective, the WTO cannot just abandon, or delegate, authority to other systems. It needs to activate secondary couplings with other regimes and interests, that is, select facts and events originating in these regimes, re-conceptualise alien rationalities in its own categories, and process self-referentially this basket of information. There seems no other way of achieving the necessary 'closure' that guarantees the regime identity. This modus operandi is difficult to reconcile with doctrines of judicial passivity. Even the argument on the lack of 'democratic legitimacy' that bears considerable weight in the 'political question' doctrine[191] seems less compelling here, if tested, not in the relationship 'international organisation v. state', but in the reference 'regime v. regime'. Even if one regime is more democratically organised than others – and it could be reasonably argued that integration regimes have a wider polity and, in this sense, a more democratic

---

[189] Dunoff, 'The Death of the Trade Regime' at 759. [190] *Ibid.*, at 758. [191] *Ibid.*

structure than political international organisations – this offers no basis for the restriction or delegation of authority among them.

For peoples, external self-determination means the establishment of authority on a territory in the form of a state – or attachment of the territory to another state – with full territorial and personal jurisdiction; by the ensuing act of recognition, the state is then admitted into the international community as an equal partner. Each state is being distinguished from the others through a different identity, which is visualised in its boundaries; they delineate the territorial sphere of validity of the domestic legal order.[192] The clear separation of spheres of jurisdiction and the principle of the stability of the borders are fundamental principles for the maintenance of a state's identity and for the functionality of the principle of external self-determination.

Transnational regimes implement the principle of external self-determination by drawing their meaning-boundaries vis-à-vis other regimes. Just as a state determines the sphere of validity of its legal order, the regimes need to construct boundaries that separate their jurisdiction from the jurisdiction of other regimes in their environment. The difference is that, while the global political system is segmented into qualitatively similar units, regimes are differentiated functionally or regionally, in terms of the global or regional validity of the related legal instruments (e.g. the WTO, NAFTA and the EU are integration regimes with differentiated spatial spheres of validity). Hegemonic regimes are those regimes that are capable of effectively structuring these boundaries, which guarantee the continuity of their own operations and the construction of their identity.

It may seem as a paradox that 'regime hegemony' depends on the recognition and respect of other spheres of action and communication. However, if the regime lacks this capacity, it may regularly behave as 'blind' toward the complexity of the global system, it would not distinguish itself from its environment, and would lose its capacity to produce legitimate decisions in a fragmented, *thus*, pluralistic global society. 'Ignorance' of the environment would then accelerate 'the death of the trade regime'. What is sought is not judicial activism in the form of unrestricted expansion of instrumental trade rationality, but judicial activism continuously drawing and redrawing the landscape of the WTO boundaries toward other regimes.

---

[192] On the territorial principle as basis of jurisdiction, see V. Lowe, 'Jurisdiction' in M. Evans (ed.), *International Law* (Oxford: Oxford University Press, 2003), pp. 336–9.

(b) The absence of boundaries: GATT jurisprudence The transition from the GATT to the WTO offers good examples for the progressive 'enlightenment' of the regime as evidenced by the emerging elements of external self-determination. The distinction between the global trade regime and the global regime of environmental protection, as is structured by numerous treaties, as well as in regional and global *fora*, including the UNCED, has offered the subject-matter for testing the 'hetero-referential' capacity of the GATT and WTO dispute settlement mechanisms, i.e. of regime capacity to take its own decisions in view of the rules, function and operation of the other implicated regimes and avoid unnecessary collisions. A brief comparison of the interpretive approach of the *Tuna I* and *II* panel reports under the GATT[193] and of the *Shrimp* Report of the WTO Appellate Body[194] to the exception of Article XX(g) of the GATT[195] can demonstrate the evolution of the principle of external self-determination of the trade regime. The focal point of this case law is located in the way the dispute settlement organs of the GATT and of the WTO respectively observe and define 'jurisdiction' for the protection of environmental interests.

In the *Tuna I* report, the panel had to define, whether a member state had extraterritorial jurisdiction for the protection of 'exhaustible natural resources'. Instead of defining autonomously the meaning of the above term and then proceeding to the jurisdictional issue, the panel preferred to reason on the basis of the trade-related concepts of the *chapeau* of Article XX: it concluded that, since the protection of exhaustible resources should be taken in conjunction with restrictions on domestic consumption, then 'Article XX(g) was intended to permit contracting parties to take trade measures primarily aimed at rendering effective restrictions on *production or consumption within their*

---

[193] *Tuna I, United States – Restrictions on Imports on Tuna*, ILM 30 (1991), 1594; *Tuna II, United States – Restrictions on Imports of Tuna*, ILM 33 (1994), 839.

[194] *United States – Import Prohibition of Certain Shrimp and Shrimp Products*, WT/DS58/AB/R, 12 October 1998.

[195] The provision reads as follows: 'Subject to the requirement that such measures are not applied in a manner which would constitute a means of arbitrary or unjustifiable discrimination between countries where the same conditions prevail, or a disguised restriction on international trade, nothing in this Agreement shall be construed to prevent the adoption or enforcement by any contracting party of measures: (g) relating to the conservation of exhaustible natural resources if such measures are made effective in conjunction with restrictions on domestic production or consumption.'

jurisdiction' (5.31).[196] This conclusion is a literal example of 'visual challenge' with respect to an environmental concept, since, instead of 'exhaustible natural resources', the panel sees only 'domestic consumption'!

Furthermore, the panel 'did not consider that the United States measures, even if Article XX(g) could be applied extrajurisdictionally, would meet the conditions set out in that provision'. The reason was that Mexico, which was directly affected by the US policy, would not know, owing to the alleged unpredictability of the standards of the US legislation, whether it conforms or not with the measures (5.33). The panel apparently considered the communication capacities of the two governments as non-existent.

The *Tuna I* report also made reference to the principles of interpretation of the GATT with respect to the Article XX(b) exception for the protection of human, animal or plant life or health. It recalled the drafting history of the General Agreement as part of the ITO Charter, the purpose of the specific provision and the consequences that a given interpretation would have 'for the operation of the General Agreement as a whole' (5.25). It concluded that the drafting history indicated that measures safeguarding these legal interests should be restricted within the territorial jurisdiction of the states; it also concluded that, considering their purpose and the consequences on the operation of the system, unilateral actions would undermine the multilateral trade regime and would jeopardise the rights of other states under the General Agreement (5.26–5.29).

It is evident that analysis or interpretation of environmental regulations are fully absent from the report; the panel as informal organ of the General Agreement was interested exclusively in safeguarding trade rights. It did so through 'expressive ignorance' of environmental regimes. The panel was not capable of distinguishing the identity of the trade regime from the identities of other normative systems, because only the categories of 'trade' and 'sovereignty' as 'opposing poles' were visible in the GATT dispute settlement mechanism.

In the *Tuna II* report, some movement can be observed, but it is still insufficient and cannot be characterized as 'drawing of boundaries'. The panel stressed, by interpreting Article XX(g), that the jurisdictional question was more complex than the *Tuna I* panel had suggested;

---

[196] (Emphasis added.) See also the concluding sentence of para. 5.32, stating that 'the considerations that led the Panel to reject an extrajurisdictional application of Article XX(b) therefore apply also to Article XX(g)', *Tuna I* Report, above, note 193.

other paragraphs of Article XX, in particular para. (e) on prison labour, would indicate that facts or actions beyond the territorial jurisdiction might be relevant to the GATT: 'It could not therefore be said that the General Agreement proscribed in an absolute manner measures that related to things or actions outside the territorial jurisdiction of the party taking the measure' (5.16).

The next issue concerned the link with the potential extraterritorial state jurisdiction. The panel avoided again 'seeing' any environmental link outside the trade regime that could justify extraterritorial application of measures for the protection of exhaustible resources. Instead, the panel had recourse to a surprising link from general international law:

> The Panel further observed that, under general international law, states are not in principle barred from regulating the conduct of their nationals with respect to persons, animals, plants and natural resources outside of their territory. Nor are states barred, in principle, from regulating the conduct of vessels having their nationality, or any persons on these vessels, with respect to persons, animals, plants and natural resources outside their territory. A state may in particular regulate the conduct of its fishermen, or of vessels having its nationality or any fishermen on these vessels, with respect to fish located in the high seas. (5.17)

The panel still did not recognise environmental interests, but could only perceive the existence of economic activities of the state's own nationals and vessels with respect to high seas (fisheries). The GATT regime was thus interconnected though Article XX(g) and over the link of general international law with the customary law of the sea. This has been a significant step forward; however, the panel did not link the GATT with any treaty system – including conventional regimes of the law of the sea – and outright rejected arguments of the parties on behalf of interpretations located 'on environmental and trade treaties other than the General Agreement' (5.18).

Again, the report adopted a 'strategy of ignorance' for any environmental frame of reference. It considered, following a narrow interpretation of Article 31 of the Vienna Convention on the Law of Treaties, that the practice of environmentally relevant bilateral or plurilateral treaties subsequent to the negotiation of the General Agreement 'could not be taken as practice under the General Agreement, and therefore could not affect the interpretation of it' (5.19).

Finally, the panel gave a general rule of interpretation for Article XX stressing that it needed to be interpreted narrowly, and that what actually mattered was to maintain the integrity of the multilateral trade regime by safeguarding state rights in trade issues. It is surprising that it did not even try to locate the borderline between the environmental interests and the freedom of trade.[197]

Under these circumstances, one can only wonder, what the function of Article XX is, if it could not have any relevance for the recognition of regime boundaries. Evidently, the panel reconstructed the facts and situations as taking place in an exclusive 'world of states'; it could not perceive either the category of transnational regime, or the 'collision of rationalities',[198] and, as a result, could not accommodate the ensuing tensions.

(c) **The emergence of boundaries: WTO jurisprudence** The Appellate Body reversed this path and paved the way for the drawing of the WTO boundaries in the *Shrimp Report*. Moreover, it did not frame the dispute in terms of the 'protectionism v. trade', but it established the structural couplings between 'global trade regime' and environment regime(s). This change is visible throughout the report, which succeeded in demonstrating how the regime boundaries can be drawn and how the principle of external self-determination of the WTO could be activated.[199]

Interpreting Article XX(g) GATT, the Appellate Body determined the meaning of 'exhaustible natural resources' and included in the concept not only 'non-living' or 'natural' resources, but also living resources that are considered as 'renewable'.[200] Furthermore, it justified its authority

---

[197] 'The Panel observed that Article XX provides for an exception to obligations under the General Agreement. The long-standing practice of panels has accordingly been to interpret this provision narrowly, in a manner that preserves the basic objectives and principles of the General Agreement. If Article XX were interpreted to permit contracting parties to deviate from the obligations of the General Agreement by taking trade measures to implement policies, including conservation policies, within their own jurisdiction, the basic objectives of the General Agreement would be maintained. If however Article XX were interpreted to permit contracting parties to take trade measures so as to force other contracting parties to change their policies within their jurisdiction, including their conservation policies, the balance of rights and obligations among contracting parties, in particular the right to access to markets, would be seriously impaired. Under such an interpretation the General Agreement could no longer serve as a multilateral framework for trade among contracting parties' (para. 5.26 of the Report).

[198] So the expression of Fischer-Lescano and Teubner, 'Regime-Collisions' at 1005–7.

[199] See, on that report, A. Qureshi, 'Extraterritorial Shrimps, NGOs and the WTO Appellate Body' (1999) 48 *ICLQ* 199–206.

[200] See para. 128 of the *Shrimp Report*.

by stressing the significance of the transition from the GATT system to the WTO regime; in particular, the objective of sustainable development in the preamble of the WTO Charter indicated the need to integrate the environmental dimension in the trade regime.[201] Even more importantly, the Report abandoned the narrow approach of the *Tuna I* and *II* panel reports to the interpretation of the GATT. Drawing upon the preamble of the WTO Charter, it stressed that 'the generic term "natural resources" in Article XX(g) is not "static" in its content or reference but rather, by definition evolutionary'.[202] The same provision was brought into relationships with two international regimes, the United Nations Convention on the Law of the Sea (UNCLOS) and the Convention on International Trade in Endangered Species of Wild Fauna and Flora (CITES). The Appellate Body dispensed with the issue of extraterritoriality with the remark that 'there is a sufficient nexus between the migratory and endangered marine population involved and the United States for purposes of Article XX(g)'.[203]

In the interpretation of the *chapeau* of Article XX, the Appellate Body went some steps further. It referred to the establishment of the WTO Permanent Committee on Trade and Environment, and to the resolutions of the Rio Conference on Environment and Development, stressing the need to avoid protectionist trade measures and to scrutinise trade measures used for environmental purposes.[204]

The Report interpreted then the *chapeau* as an expression of the general principle of good faith.[205] And then it continues:

> Having said this, our task here is to interpret the language of the chapeau, seeking additional interpretative guidance, as appropriate, from the general principles of international law.[206]

The Appellate Body referred then to the need to mark out a line of equilibrium between the rights of members under Art. XX, on the one hand, and the rights under the substantive provisions of the GATT, on the other; it also described the essence of the meaning of regime boundaries, as drawn through the interpretation of Article XX:

> The location of the line of equilibrium, as expressed in the chapeau, is not fixed and unchanging; the line moves as the kind and the shape of the measures at stake vary and as the facts making up the specific cases differ.[207]

---

[201] *Ibid.*, para. 129.   [202] *Ibid.*, para. 130.   [203] *Ibid.*, para. 133.   [204] *Ibid.*, para. 154.
[205] *Ibid.*, para. 158.   [206] *Ibid.*   [207] *Ibid.*, para. 159.

The Report proceeded then to the interpretation of the clause of 'unjustifiable discrimination between countries where the same conditions prevail' and drew a principle for the assessment of the conduct of member states implementing programs for the conservation of resources:

> We believe that discrimination results not only when countries in which the same conditions prevail are differently treated, but also when the application of the measure at issue does not allow for any inquiry into the appropriateness of the regulatory program for the conditions prevailing in those exporting counties.[208]

The Report gave considerable weight to obligations of cooperation among the states concerned. These obligations arise from international agreements and acts of competent international organs. The standards of the chapeau of Article XX were therefore determined through the coupling of the GATT with other international legal instruments and regimes.[209]

The *Shrimp* jurisprudence of the Appellate Body determined the WTO system's boundaries through flexible general principles marking the area of the regime's identity and the respective jurisdiction of the member states. Although the Report obviously speaks of 'state rights', a closer look reveals that these rights are integrated in the rationality of various international regimes. The conceptual horizon of the WTO is not a fuzzy trade space of infinite complexity any more. At least as far as the trade-environment relationship is concerned, the WTO regime is embedded in a structured environment of co-existing normative systems and is armed with regime-proper nodal points enabling the perception of the operation and rationality of these other systems. In that way, the WTO progressively develops elements of external self-determination, and is capable of appropriating capacities of other regimes for its own operation and for its own self-restraint. Thus, instead of self-restraint of the dispute settlement mechanism, external self-determination is developed through inventive dispute settlement.

---

[208] *Ibid.*, para. 165.

[209] *Ibid.*, paras. 166 *et seq.* In the follow-up to this Report, the Appellate Body found that the US measures were applied consistently with Article XX GATT, *United States – Import Prohibitions of Certain Shrimp and Shrimp Products*, Recourse to Art. 21.5 of the DSU by Malaysia, Report, WT/DS58/AB/RW, of 22 October 2001.

The regime-proper principle of external self-determination is not an act completed by a final act of recognition and acceptance in the international community. In the WTO, and apparently in other regimes, too, external self-determination is a continuous operation, closely related to internal self-determination, and currently draws and affirms the boundaries of the regime in global society. The WTO regime cannot be considered as the mere extension of the political arm of the member states any more. Despite statements of states on the exclusively 'intergovernmental' character of global trade agreements, this aspect is being progressively overtaken by the dynamics of the regime.

The evolution of the 'boundary structures' of the WTO cannot be considered as closed. Beyond the questions on the protection of the environment, there are other 'trade and' issues and areas of regime collisions and there is an ongoing development in these areas, in particular, in the boundary between trade and health.[210] The development of a system of fundamental rights within the WTO[211] is a process that has an impact on the principle of external self-determination of the regime. We should distinguish between fundamental freedoms that establish the continuity of the internal communications of a regime (for example, the economic freedoms in the EC Treaty, or 'trade freedoms' in the WTO), and fundamental rights and interests that mark its external boundaries (e.g. Article XX GATT). External self-determination is realised through the interpretation and implementation of this category of rights, which enable a transnational regime to exercise self-restraint through 'reconnaissance' of other regimes or other normative complexes in its environment.

Self-determination as foundational principle of global governance

Self-determination of peoples as a principle of international law enables the international community to assign authority on territorial units through recognition and facilitates the emergence of order. The same

---

[210] See the Protocol inserting Art. 31 *bis* to the TRIPs Agreement, as agreed on 8 December 2005, WT/L/641.

[211] On the significance and function of human rights guarantees within regimes, see V. Karavas, 'Digitale Grundrechte: Zur Drittwirkung der Grundrechte im Internet', Dissertation Frankfurt/Main, 2005; C. Walter, 'Constitutionalizing (Inter)national Governance' at 196–201, E.-U. Petersmann, 'The WTO Constitution and Human Rights' (2000) 3 *JIEL* 19–25. See also G. Teubner, 'The Anonymous Matrix: Human Rights Violations by "Private" Transnational Actors', (2006) 69 *MLR* 327–46.

principle articulates the capacity of transnational regimes to develop and maintain internal communication cycles through their own polity, as well as to draw the external meaning-boundaries through the development of an internal system for the protection of fundamental rights and interests. The capacity of regimes to stabilise their operations, mutually recognise each other, and reach a level of 'peaceful coexistence' among the conflicting rationalities they express, is therefore a major aspect of global governance. Self-determination embodies this 'fundamental right' of territorial units and transnational regimes to exist, operate and safeguard global pluralism; it also guarantees that the sphere of political activities will not overstretch and will not irreparably damage the spontaneity, flexibility and innovation capacity of global society and of its various actors. Democratic governance thus takes deep root in all fields of 'the social'.

Global constitutionalism does not replicate the formalism of the continental European nation-state model. Transnational constitutional moments emerge in *fragmenta* through state and societal practice, take unexpected forms and evolve through asymmetric leaps. Speaking for the English Constitution, Dicey is also instructive about global constitutionalism and self-determination as its foundational principle:

> ... no precise date could be named as the day of its birth; no definite body of persons could claim to be its creators, no one could point to the document which contained its clauses; it was in short a thing by itself ... The security which an Englishman enjoys for personal freedom does not really depend upon or originate in any general proposition contained in any written document ... This is an idea utterly alien to English modes of thought, since with us freedom of person is not a special privilege but the outcome of the ordinary law of the land enforced by the courts. Here, in short, we may observe the application to a particular case of the general principle that with us individual rights are the basis, not the result, of the law of the constitution.[212]

---

[212] A. V. Dicey, *Introduction to the Study of the Law of the Constitution*, with an introduction by E. C. S. Wade, 10th edn (London: Macmillan, 1962, first published in 1885), pp. 3, 206–7.

8

Challenges to international and European corporatism presented by deliberative trends in governance

TONIA NOVITZ

Introduction

Debates over constitutionalism have led increasingly to close analysis of forms of governance, the aim being to design a constitutional framework that will enhance the legitimacy of international and European legal orders. In this respect, there have been attempts to transpose theoretical constructs utilised at the national level to the transnational level. This chapter examines two such constructs. One is the notion of 'corporatism', namely the priority given to functional participation of management and labour in norm-setting, so as to ensure that their interests are adequately reflected in social policy (in general) and labour standards (in particular). This form of governance can be understood as being concerned with 'output' legitimacy, since legal norms formulated through this process are likely to be workable in practice. A second construct is that of 'deliberative democracy', which is more concerned with 'input' legitimacy, that is, the discursive process by which a rational decision is taken that transcends the interests of particular parties. This chapter considers whether these two forms of constitutional legitimacy are reconcilable, and how such reconciliation might be achieved within international and European institutions.

Two examples of transnational corporatism are considered. The first is the 'tripartite' constitutional foundation of the International Labour Organization (ILO), established in 1919, which ensures that employer and worker representatives share in decision-making alongside government representatives. The second is the predominantly 'bipartite' process of social dialogue between management and labour which emerged within the European Union. Both institutions have chosen to prioritise participation by trade unions and employer federations, in order to achieve output legitimacy, but have done do so in significantly different ways. Both institutions have recently confronted challenges to such modes of governance, and the adequacy of their responses is evaluated here.

My suggestion is that the primary question for the survival of corporatism is whether the representation of particular interests should ever be prioritised within a framework of deliberative governance. The argument presented in this chapter is that prioritisation is defensible, but that this is very much dependent on the subject-matter of the norms under consideration. Moreover, careful consideration needs to be paid to the potential for representation of other previously excluded interests and how this can feasibly be achieved within the institutional architecture of each organisation. In addition, close attention will still need to be paid to issues of the representative status of delegates, modes of accountability, transparency of process and transparency of results.

Corporatism and the trend towards deliberative governance

This part of the chapter examines the development of debates over legitimate forms of governance. It contains an outline of the traditional case offered in support of corporatist mechanisms and introduces the notion of deliberative democracy. It is conceded that corporatist structures are often considered antithetical to the realisation of democracy, but presents the argument that there may be scope for deliberation within functional participation. Finally, suggestions are made as to potential criteria for realisation of deliberative democracy within a corporatist framework in the context of international and regional governance.

The traditional case for corporatism: recognition of vested interests

The central pluralist idea, also associated with the notion of participatory democracy, is that diverse entrenched interests do not dissipate on the election of national or local government by majority vote, but continue to exist and can covertly influence policy-making. This idea led to the call for representation of interest groups in decision-making at many levels of government, so as to ensure that there is some balance in the voice and influence of diverse interests.[1] Such a strategy can be

---

[1] See W. A. Kelso, *American Democratic Theory: Pluralism and its Critics* (Westport/London: Greenwood Press, 1978), pp. 65–87, who provides criticism from a pluralist

understood as a means by which to secure genuine participation in the formulation of policy by the very people whom that policy affects. There have been attempts to link this notion to participation of workers in policy-making within the workplace,[2] whilst corporatism can be viewed as a manifestation of interest-based representation in matters specific to industrial relations.

Corporatism in the national industrial relations context is a system of functional participation, which gives privileged access to decision-making by representatives of management and labour. Corporatism allows management and labour to reach a bargain or deal, which can then be reflected in government policy. It may not be the outcome that all parties would most want, but it is usually one which reflects some compromise between their conflicting interests and which both sides view as preferable to being excluded from the decision-making process altogether. In this way, the output of corporatism provides a balance between two divergent sets of interests, whilst the government exercises the final check that the measure to be taken is also in the general interest.[3]

While pluralism tends to have idealistic overtones, corporatism is often understood in a more pragmatic way.[4] The involvement of both sides of industry in decision-making is likely to assist elected governments in formulating feasible industrial relations strategies, that is, a better output than would have been achievable otherwise. This is because persons who possess the relevant experience have studied the proposals and expressed their confidence that they can work in practice. It would also seem that

perspective; G. Sartori, *The Theory of Democracy Revisited* (Chatham: Chatham House Publishers, 1987), pp. 324–8, who criticises the 'rule of legislators'; and S. Lukes, *Essays in Social Theory* (London: Macmillan, 1977), p. 40, who questions whether a democratic mandate arises only from majority elections.

[2] See, for example, R. A. Dahl, *A Preface to Economic Democracy* (Cambridge: Polity Press, 1985), ch. 4, and his view of functional participation both within government and the workplace. See also C. Pateman, *Participation and Democratic Theory* (Cambridge: Cambridge University Press, 1970); G. C. Gould, *Rethinking Democracy* (Cambridge: Cambridge University Press, 1988).

[3] For two key discussions of the ways in which corporatism can be understood, see P. Schmitter, 'Still the Century of Corporatism?' (1974) 36 *The Review of Politics (Rev Pol)* 85, and O. Molina and M. Rhodes, 'Corporatism: The Past, Present and Future of a Concept' (2002) 5 *Annual Review of Political Science* 305.

[4] See S. Smismans, *Law, Legitimacy, and European Governance: Functional Participation in Social Regulation* (Oxford: Oxford University Press, 2004), pp. 64–8, who distinguishes the two, contrasting the often static corporatist representational structures with the fluid unregulated competition of interest groups often associated with certain forms of pluralism.

there is greater commitment by industrial actors to the regulatory structure and legal framework. The result appears to be a reduction in the incidence of industrial unrest and political strikes. This may also be due to incentives offered to union leaders to maintain industrial peace through hierarchical structures.[5] Indeed, in many respects, corporatism tends to be associated with top-down government.

Deliberative governance: beyond vested interests?

Enthusiasm for deliberative democracy emerged as a response to the legitimacy crisis faced by modern states. Bureaucratic systems of government have become so distant from the lives of the persons they seek to govern, that they are perceived as illegitimate and inappropriate. Law then becomes a medium by which a link can be made between distant bureaucratic institutions and the immediate 'lifeworld'.[6] In this way, top-down 'government' has come to be seen as inappropriate, and has been replaced by the notion of 'governance', which may arise in various forms and at a multitude of levels.

A key advocate of deliberative governance, Jürgen Habermas, considers that we need to find ways in which law can reflect the understandings and concerns of all persons within society. He suggests that groupings of interests will spontaneously emerge within 'civil society' and that we then need to find ways of ensuring that they inform the development of public policy.[7]

In this context, Habermas posits the 'ideal speech situation', which is not always realisable, but is something we might hope to aim towards. Its creation entails, as a minimum, the establishment of a framework of basic rights upon which citizens can rely. Protection of civil liberties and political entitlements is necessary if persons are to exchange their views freely. These

---

[5] See Pizzorno's theory of 'political exchange' as set out in C. Crouch and A. Pizzorno (eds.), *The Resurgence of Class Conflict in Western Europe Since 1909* (New York: Macmillan, 1978), vol. II. See also R. Bean, *Comparative Industrial Relations: An Introduction to Cross-national Perspectives* (London/New York: Routledge, 1985), p. 135; and C. Crouch, *Industrial Relations and European State Traditions* (Oxford: Oxford University Press, 1993).

[6] J. Habermas, *Between Facts and Norms: Contributions to a Discourse Theory of Law and Democracy*, W. Rehg (trans.) (Boston, Mass.: MIT, 1997), p. 56.

[7] *Ibid.*, p. 367: Habermas describes 'civil society' as being 'composed of those more or less spontaneously emergent associations, organizations and movements that, attuned to how societal problems resonate in the private spheres, distil and transmit such reactions in an amplified form to the public sphere'.

private rights rely on public government for their existence, but also give legitimacy to that government. The two are, Habermas tells us, co-original.[8]

Habermas does not tell us the precise role that different interest groups can expect to play in decision-making. What he envisages, at the level of the nation state, would seem to be a two stage approach. The first stage is informal communicative action in the public sphere, which raises issues pertinent to any given society. Ideally, where this is possible, communities can engage in self-regulation rather than requiring external regulation. This is a familiar principle, also known in the EU context as 'subsidiarity', namely that decisions should be taken as close as possible to the persons they affect.[9] The second stage consists of formal political processes, such as elections, legislative deliberation and judicial decision-making. The latter is informed by the earlier stage, and its legitimacy depends on being responsive to public opinion and deliberative in its orientation.[10]

Participants in the deliberative process are expected to leave behind their own vested interests and prejudices, and be persuaded potentially to act in opposition to these. The pragmatics of communication, which involves making a genuine effort to understand and relate to the words of another, is said to be what makes this process possible.[11] Each person should be able and willing to question critically and evaluate the assertions of another. The aim is a consensus-led decision-making.[12] It is this consensus, emerging from a transparent and accessible process, which is understood to be constitutive of just solutions. The outcome remains open to future challenge on rational grounds, but until it is so challenged, it remains a workable basis of policy-making and lawmaking.[13]

In this way, deliberative governance would seem to challenge some of the long-held assumptions of those who advocate corporatism. First, it

---

[8] *Ibid.*, p. 104. For further analysis of this relationship, see J. Cohen, 'Reflections on Habermas on Democracy', (1999) 12 *Ratio Juris* 385 at 391 *et seq.*

[9] See, for a discussion of the relationship between deliberative democratic governance and subsidiarity, S. Syrpis, *Legitimising European Governance: Taking Subsidiarity Seriously within the Open Method of Communication* (Florence: EUI Working Paper LAW No. 2002/10, 2002).

[10] Habermas, *Between Facts*, pp. 304–8.

[11] J. Habermas, *Communication and the Evolution of Society*, F. G. Lawrence (trans.) (Boston: Beacon Press, 1979), pp. 1–68.

[12] For a discussion of Habermas' work placed in this context, see M. Rosenfeld, 'Law as Discourse: Bridging the Gap between Democracy and Rights' (1995) 108 *Harvard Law Review (Harv L Rev)* 1163.

[13] J. Habermas, 'Struggles for Recognition in Constitutional States' (1993) 1 *European Journal of Philosophy (Eur J Phil)* 128.

suggests that 'civil society' as a whole should have a voice, thereby challenging the privilege traditionally given to management and labour under corporatist systems. Secondly, the aim of a deliberative framework is to transcend the particular interests of particular factions and reach, not a trade-off or a bargain between vested interests, but a rational consensus that is in the interests of all, which everyone can understand, and to which everyone can commit themselves. If this ideal form of governance is given practical application, bargaining between employer and worker representatives, according to their perception of their own vested interests, may come to be seen as an inappropriate basis for the generation of legal norms, which should be defensible on the grounds of 'public reasons' acceptable to all.

Habermas does recognise that there could be a need for 'bargaining' between opposing factions, such as workers and employers. He considers that, insofar as any bargain is made according to fair procedures under which the rights of all persons are respected, this will not be objectionable. He does not contemplate that there will ever be so radical a conflict of value-systems or beliefs that there will be no scope for bargaining (or compromise) and no view of an appropriate shared procedure to settle the matter.[14] In this limited bargaining scenario, one might expect at a minimum that rules concerning the selection of representatives and the manner in which participation is to occur would be publicly accessible and enforceable, being responsive to public demands for transparent fairness. Moreover, the conditions for adequate dialogue, the protection of such civil and political entitlements as freedom of association and freedom of speech, would be vital to the process.

Can deliberative values be accommodated within a corporatist framework?

Corporatism has been regarded as inherently anti-democratic by some commentators. The reason is not merely that it limits the ability of elected representatives to give effect to the preferences of the electorate,

---

[14] See T. McCarthy, 'Legitimacy and Diversity: Dialectical Reflections on Analytical Distinctions' (1996) 17 *Cardozo Law Review* 1083, who identifies this as a flaw in Habermas' theoretical framework. For a reply to such concerns, see J. Habermas, 'On Law and Disagreement: Some Comments on Interpretative Pluralism' (2003) 16(2) *Ratio Juris* 187. On this attempt to tame civil society, encompassing diversity, rather than recognising the challenges posed to the legal order, see E. Christodoulidis, 'Constitutional Irresolution: Law and the Framing of Civil Society' (2003) 9 *ELJ* 401.

or that it constrains access by other interest groups to the decision-making process, but also that it has the unwanted effect of restricting democratic engagement within trade unions. For example, in 1974, Philippe Schmitter considered that:

> Corporatism can be defined as a system of interest representation in which the constituent units are organized into a limited number of singular, compulsory, non-competitive, hierarchically ordered and functionally differentiated categories, recognized or licensed (if not created) by the state and granted a deliberative representational monopoly within their respective categories in exchange for observing certain controls on their selection of leaders and articulation of demands and supports.[15]

This definition has been given contemporary support by Lucio Baccaro, who sees corporatism as: 'A particular structure of the interest representation system, characterized by monopolistic, centralized and internally non-democratic association.'[16] Baccaro suggests that the bargaining power which unions exercise within a corporatist framework turns on their ability to ensure worker acquiescence or compliance with government policies, both via horizontal coordination and hierarchical control.[17] It follows that corporatist structures tend to inhibit freedom of association because unions take a federal form such that workers have little choice as the form of their representation. Also, freedom of expression within trade unions is inhibited, since policy is not made by those at grass roots level, but is dictated by the content of compromises made by trade union leaders with governments at a national level.[18] This view of corporatism leads Baccaro to the conclusion that recent 'social partnership' agreements in Ireland and Italy aimed at promotion of economic recovery could not be 'corporatist'. How could they be so when the representational structures within Ireland and Italy are relatively weak and fragmented, allowing choice between multiple unions and extensive representational accountability? The deliberative means used by union leaders in that context to consult with workers and to seek to persuade workers that measures taken were indeed in their (and the country's) collective interests are seen by Baccaro as antithetical to corporatism.[19] He considers that there has been 'non-corporatist concertation' in these settings.[20]

---

[15] P. Schmitter, 'Still the Century', 36.
[16] L. Baccaro, 'What is Alive and What is Dead in the Theory of Corporatism' (2003) 41 *British Journal of Industrial Relations* 683 at 683.
[17] *Ibid.*, 685. [18] *Ibid.*, 686. [19] *Ibid.*, 690–1. [20] *Ibid.*, 698–702.

However, this is a very restrictive definition of corporatism and not one taken by House and McGrath, who view Ireland's success in 'social partnership' as a new form of 'inclusive corporatism', which exhibits features of other corporatist mechanisms but develops these further.[21] They observe that under 'classical' or 'social' corporatism there tended to be involvement in policy-making by a strong federal union accompanied by centralised collective bargaining and wage constraint. This changed to 'competitive' or 'neo-corporatism' following economic challenges posed by globalisation and the perceived need for flexibility which had to be accompanied by trade union co-operation in changing regulatory structures. The inclusive form of corporatism which they have identified goes one step further.

One of the features of inclusive corporatism is the ability to move beyond the tripartite participation of employers, workers and government and consult with other interested parties, such as farmers and community organisations. The agreement between labour, business and government might be the 'cornerstone of the Programme', but wider public support is needed for it to be operational.[22] Another feature of inclusive corporatism identified by House and McGrath is the involvement of participants in a process of deliberation whereby they seek understanding through regular meetings, review of objectives, and an emphasis on problem-solving rather than the presentation of demands.[23] Moreover, long-term protections of freedom of association under the Irish constitution can be seen to provide the bedrock for free consent to this evolving partnership.[24] This suggests that, at least at the national level, there may be scope for corporatism which is consistent with deliberative democracy and regarded, thereby, as legitimate. It may be that corporatism does not only take a cyclical form, as Schmitter and Grote suggest,[25] but has the capacity to undergo a more significant metamorphosis.[26]

---

[21] J. D. House and K. McGrath, 'Innovative Governance and Development in the New Ireland: Social Partnership and the Integrated Approach' (2004) 17 *Governance: An International Journal of Policy, Administration and Institutions* 29 at 33–4.

[22] *Ibid.*, 45.   [23] *Ibid.*, 49–51.   [24] Article 40, para. 6 of the Constitution of Ireland, 1937.

[25] P. Schmitter and J. R. Grote, *The Corporatist Sisyphus: Past, Present and Future* (Florence: EUI Working Paper SPS No. 97/4, 1997).

[26] F. Traxler, 'The Metamorphosis of Corporatism: From Classical to Lean Patterns' (2004) 43 *European Journal of Political Research* 571 at 572.

The potential for transformation of global and regional corporatism

As we shall see, corporatist practices within the ILO and EC are long-standing. To some extent, their aims mirror those of national corporatist practices. There is, for example, a deliberate intention to recognise the importance of institutional symmetry which will create, at least superficially, some semblance of a balance of power between the opposing interests of workers and employers.[27] Moreover, there is the evident hope that the inclusion of representatives of management and labour will improve the quality of decision-making and commitment to the decisions taken. It has, for example, been said that tripartite decision-making gives the ILO's work 'a broader basis of social consensus' and a degree of moral authority.[28] Similarly, corporatist arrangements within the EU have been described as fulfilling 'a societal consensus function' insofar as they assemble 'all major societal forces ... behind a crucial goal'.[29]

Nevertheless, the inclusion of employer and worker participation in transnational governance cannot be explained in identical terms to national corporatist structures. It is, for example, unlikely that the inclusion of union representation would reduce the incidence of industrial action; or that somehow there could be centralised control over diverse trade union movements in various countries. There is also an important difference between the relative bargaining power of parties in an international and a European forum. Within the ILO, neither worker nor employer representatives possess the influence which they can exercise at national level. Neither can offer any credible threat of withdrawal of labour or of capital to persuade governments or the institution to adopt certain policies. By contrast, within the EU, while unions struggle to engage in European-wide action, employers retain the credible

---

[27] See, for example, provisions of the ILO Constitution, 1919, such as Articles 7 and 19; and note the parity of treatment of management and labour in the 2002 Treaty establishing the European Community, Articles 137–139.

[28] *Record of Proceedings* (Philadelphia: ILO, 1944), ILC, 26th Session, per Mr Tixier (Government delegate, France) at 48. For ongoing commitment to this principle, see *Report of the Director-General: Reducing the Decent Work Deficit – A Global Challenge* (Geneva: ILO, 2001), ILC, 89th Session, ch. 3.

[29] G. Falkner, 'European Social Policy: Towards a Multi-level and Multi-actor Governance', in B. Kohler-Koch and R. Eising (eds.), *The Transformation of Governance in the European Union* (London: Routledge, 1999), p. 188.

threat of withdrawal of capital to states outside the EU.[30] However, these differences aside, the fundamental question remains whether these long-term corporatist practices can be accommodated within a deliberative framework of governance.

It is evident that discourse theory recognises the value and importance of communication within particular communities, and thereby the significance of geographical, cultural and temporal situations in law-making. This might appear to present a barrier to the extension of deliberative democracy outside the nation state. Various commentators have argued that the adoption of a deliberative framework would require more spontaneous forms of communication at the international level and a move away from multi-lateral organisation. For example, Fung, Trubek and others have argued for a move away from regulation of labour standards by multilateral organisations and towards debate between a variety of actors in the public sphere and the development of transnational networks.[31] This is arguably a kind of subsidiarity in action.

Habermas, however, considers that communicative action can be fostered by institutions such as the EU, so as to create social solidarity in a pluralistic society.[32] Moreover, he has argued for the strengthening of world institutions in the face of globalisation. Habermas does so because he appreciates that the traditional Westphalian system is under threat, 'as a consequence of the growing interdependence of global society and transnational economy'. In this context, '[t]he traditional line between foreign and domestic economic policies, in particular, has become blurred, while both the autonomy and sovereignty of formerly independent nation States have become increasingly undermined'. This said, he is more a proponent of multilevel governance than top-down government by a new world state. He argues for regulation by not only a reformed international organisation, but also nation states and a horizontal network of transnational regimes.

---

[30] See S. Fredman, 'Social Law in the European Union: The Impact of the Law-Making Process', in P. Craig and C. Harlow (eds.), *Lawmaking in the European Union* (The Hague: Kluwer International, 1998), p. 410.

[31] A. Fung, 'Deliberative Democracy and International Labor Standards', (2003) 16(1) *Governance* 51; and D. M. Trubek, J. Mosher and J. S. Rothstein, 'Transnationalism in the Regulation of Labor Relations: International Regimes and Transnational Advocacy Networks' (2000) *Law and Social Inquiry* 1187.

[32] J. Habermas, 'The European Nation-State and the Pressures of Globalization' (1999) *New Left Review* 46 and J. Habermas, 'Why Europe Needs a Constitution' (2001) *New Left Review* 11.

Habermas appreciates that such a development is viable only to the extent that there is an expansion of communicative action and civil solidarity beyond national borders, something which transnational social movements (such as the environmental lobbyists) and international institutions themselves may promote.[33] One assumes that this is because he views engagement with civil society in international law-making to be as important as it is at the national level. However, his writings to date tell us little about how this should be achieved. Some have even accused him of deliberately avoiding the issue.[34]

If we do adopt this view of the importance of participation by civil society generally, then the selective representation of management and labour within transnational institutions would have to be reviewed and, if it cannot be justified, be modified. For example, privileged participation of management and labour in the creation of anti-discrimination law, which has broad impact on those both in and outside work, may be less appropriate than the determination by employers and workers of other norms.

We may also need to face up to the difficulties associated with wholesale inclusion of NGOs in decision-making within institutions like the ILO and EU. One such difficulty is the potential dilution of effective participation in decision-making when all members of civil society (however marginally interested) are given a voice in the process. The logistical impossibility of responding in an equivalent way to all views expressed means that this exercise of voice may come to be regarded as cosmetic or even redundant. Moreover, to merely hear *every one* may be unreasonable, given that certain people may have more immediate interests in the outcome of particular debates than do others.[35] It seems more important that those listening give (good) reasons for prioritising some participants.

Once the appropriate participants have been selected, it will then be necessary to check their credentials to check that they actually do represent those they claim. This may involve checking that there are

---

[33] J. Habermas, 'Kant's Idea of Perpetual Peace, with the Benefit of Two Hundred Years' Hindsight', in J. Bohman and M. Lutz-Bachmann (eds.), *Perpetual Peace: Essays on Kant's Cosmopolitan Ideal* (Cambridge, Mass./London: MIT Press, 1997), pp. 113, 131–3. See also J. Habermas, 'A Short Reply' (1999) 12 *Ratio Juris* 445 at 450–1.

[34] Fung, 'Deliberative Democracy', 52.

[35] For detailed discussion of these problems of scale, see J. Parkinson, 'Legitimacy Problems in Deliberative Democracy' (2003) 51 *Political Studies* 180 and J. Dryzek, 'Legitimacy and Economy in Deliberative Democracy' (2001) 29 *Political Theory* 651.

systems in place whereby so-called representatives are accountable to their constituency, just as government representatives are accountable, through elections to their citizens.

It also follows that if our aim is to achieve rational consensus on the merits of decisions, then a bargain or compromise thrashed out in a corporatist setting may not be sufficient. Ideally, parties to decision-making would not only seek to achieve a deal which reflects their own interests, but would attempt to place themselves in each others' position and seek a solution to shared problems acceptable to all. The appropriate backdrop for such dialogue would have to be effective protection of human rights, such as free speech and free association.

In this context, attention may have to be paid to the bargaining power which interested parties bring to the table. Whilst we might not want such influence to determine the final outcome of any decision, the best way of achieving this may be to acknowledge its existence and provide conditions for participation that address the problem, namely some kind of balanced representation and balanced hearing through procedures established for debate. Parity of treatment will be necessary to achieve at least a perception of fairness, even if parity of resources cannot be guaranteed.[36] Moreover, to persuade others outside the process of the merits of the decision taken, there may need to be a degree of transparency.[37] This might involve disclosure not only of the reasons for the decision, but also of the process by which it was reached.

The remainder of this chapter examines the actual corporatist models that operate within the ILO and EU. The scope for challenge to these models from a deliberative perspective is considered, alongside the implications this may have for reform. This is done with reference to the theoretical constructs outlined above, and the concerns expressed here as to their appropriate application.

---

[36] L. Baccaro, 'Civil Society Meets the State: Towards Associational Democracy' (2006) 4 *Socio-Economic Review* 185 at 197 highlights the failure to meet such conditions as a reason for the relative lack of influence of various civil society groups in Irish and South African 'social partnerships'.

[37] See for advocacy of this approach, C. Hunold, 'Corporatism, Pluralism and Democracy: Toward a Deliberative Theory of Bureaucratic Accountability' (2001) 14 *Governance* 151 at 161–3.

Challenges to corporatism within the ILO

The ILO began its life as an adjunct of the League of Nations, but survived the Second World War to emerge as an influential United Nations (UN) agency. Its mandate, set out in its original Constitution and maintained today, has been the promotion of 'social justice'. This is to be achieved by, *inter alia*, the international regulation of labour standards. Its specialist role has been recognised explicitly by the WTO and the Copenhagen Social Summit.[38] This part of the chapter examines the manner in which a tripartite form of corporatism operates within the ILO, the challenges recently made to this form of governance and evaluates the response to date.

Tripartism within the ILO

The ILO has various functions. Its secretariat, the International Labour Office, provides 'technical assistance' and engages in research, promoting the exchange of information and experience through publications, data banks, meetings and seminars. However, it is the standard-setting capacity of the ILO which has been its most prominent feature, that is, its capacity to promulgate norms through Conventions which are binding under international law. What is peculiar about this capacity is its tripartite nature. The ratification of international Conventions still requires state consent, but the drafting, adoption, monitoring and enforcement of labour standards within the ILO remain the joint responsibility of employer, worker and state representatives. It should also be noted that these procedures operate against the backdrop of a constitutional framework that recognises the fundamental importance of freedom of association and freedom of speech.[39]

Within the ILO, it is the International Labour Conference (or ILC) that determines the content of draft Conventions, which can then be adopted by a two-thirds majority vote by all delegates.[40] When a Convention is adopted by the ILC, member states are under an

---

[38] See WTO Singapore Declaration of 13 December 1996, WT/MIN96/DEC/W, para. 4; and for discussion of the Programme of Action adopted by the Copenhagen Social Summit, see GB.267/LILS/5, para. 16.

[39] See the Declaration of Philadelphia, 1944, subsequently appended to the ILO Constitution, 1919.

[40] Article 19(2), ILO Constitution, available at http://www.ilo.org/public/english/about/iloconst.htm#a17p2.

obligation to attempt its ratification and must keep the ILO Director-General informed of their attempts to secure approval from the domestic legislature. Even if the domestic legislature proves recalcitrant, all member states must report the extent to which its law and practice are consistent with the norms set out in the Convention and what difficulties might prevent or delay ratification.[41]

National delegations to the International Labour Conference (ILC) consist of one worker, one employer and two government representatives. This weighting towards government representation was done to prevent worker and employer delegates outvoting government representatives. 'It was felt that unless the preponderating voice was with the Governments, the conference might tend to become a debating society, and its resolutions would not command the official authority without which they would not be carried into practical effect.'[42] However, it also ensures that no measure can be taken by states without the support of either interest group and, usually, given inevitable divisions between states, a sizeable proportion of both groups being in favour of a measure. A similar pattern of representation is found in the constitution of the Governing Body, the ILO's executive organ, which consists of 28 government representatives, 14 employer representatives and 14 worker representatives.[43] Revision of this pattern of representation was considered in 1945, but ultimately rejected as too controversial and potentially destructive of the delicate but workable power balance that had already been established.[44]

Other Committees elected by the ILC to deal with particular matters are more truly tripartite, in that they consist of employer, employee and government representatives in equal proportions. For example, the legitimacy of credentials of representatives attending the ILC as part of a national delegation are reviewed by a Credentials Committee in which government, employer and worker representatives are equally represented and have equal voting rights.[45] Other Committees with a similar make-up include the Drafting Committee for Conventions and

---

[41] Article 19(5)(e) of the ILO Constitution.

[42] H. Butler, *The International Labour Organization* (Oxford: Oxford University Press, 1939), p. 9.

[43] Article 7 of the ILO Constitution. The tasks of the Governing Body include setting the agenda for the ILC and electing the ILO Director-General.

[44] *Record of Proceedings* (Geneva: ILO, 1945), ILC, 27th Session, 55–8, 445–9.

[45] For recent reform of the Credentials Committee system, see *Interim provisions concerning verification of credentials, effective from the 93rd Session (June 2005) to the 96th Session (June 2007) of the International Labour Conference*, available at http://www.ilo.org/public/english/bureau/leg/credentials.pdf.

Recommendations, the Resolutions Committee, and the Committee on the Application of Standards. Their task is to report back to the plenary meeting of the ILC.[46]

In these settings, employers and workers tend to vote in separate blocks, which have become known as the 'employers' group' and the 'workers' group'. They usually compete to win government representatives' votes. The employers' group receive administrative support from the Bureau for Employers' Activities (or ACT/EMP), while the workers' group tend to operate through the Bureau for Workers' Activities (ACTRAV). They therefore have the resources to research issues and develop proposals which may sway the ILC. From this perspective, one might view tripartism within the ILO as something resembling a classical form of corporatism, whereby worker and employer representatives see themselves as possessing starkly contrasting interests, which they seek to protect by winning government representatives over to vote in their favour. Nevertheless, despite the often polarised nature of these block votes, it is evident that this is an improvement on many other forms of international standard-setting, in that the standards set are not reduced to that acceptable by the least enthusiastic state party.[47] Instead, decision-making is informed by lively debates between worker, employer and government representatives, the content of which is reported verbatim and is a matter of public record.[48]

One further illustration of tripartism at work within the ILO, which perhaps diverges from the classic corporatist model, is the working of a supervisory body, the Governing Body Committee on Freedom of Association. Its special role is to consider complaints relating to breaches of freedom of association. This Committee consists of three employer, three worker and three government representatives. Led by an independent legally qualified chair, it is a body which reaches decisions by consensus, and which has created a substantial body of jurisprudence.[49] This suggests that tripartism as a principle within the ILO is not

---

[46] See *Standing Orders of the International Labour Conference*, available at http://www.ilo.org/public/english/standards/relm/ilc/ilc-so.htm.

[47] F. L. Kirgis, 'Specialized Law-Making Processes', in O. Schachter and C. C. Joyner (eds.), *United Nations Legal Order* (Cambridge: Cambridge University Press, 1995), vol. I, p. 8.

[48] See the ILO website, where minutes of debates are available: http://www.ilo.org.

[49] See, for example, *Freedom of Association: Digest of Decisions and Principles of the Governing Body Committee on Freedom of Association*, 4th edn (Geneva: ILO, 1996). For further details relating to its operations, see T. Novitz, *International and European Protection of the Right to Strike* (Oxford: Oxford University Press, 2003), pp. 188–203.

simply reducible to duels between interest blocks to secure allies amongst governments, but can lead to open-minded debate and decision by consensus. Nevertheless, the role of tripartism within the ILO is not beyond challenge.

Challenges to International Labour Organization tripartism

As the Cold War ended, the relevance of the ILC as a key debating chamber for Eastern and Western bloc factions abated. At the same time, ILO standards and the organisation's very mode of governance came under scrutiny.[50] In particular, there have been accusations that existing worker representation in the ILO protects only the interests of those participating in the formal labour market.[51] The unemployed or children, women and migrant labour in informal labour markets are allegedly left without representation. For these reasons, there are demands for the ILO to allow greater participation from civil society, namely non-governmental organisations (NGOs), in the design of programmes and setting of norms.[52] Neither the workers' nor the employers' group has voiced any great enthusiasm for such reform, which is not surprising given that their role within the ILO could be threatened by such changes.

The current ILO Director-General, Juan Somavia, has stated that 'new routes to governance of globalization must emerge', but seems to be seeking a compromise position on the inclusion of 'civil society' in ILO decision-making.[53] In a report delivered to the ILC in 2001, he indicated that tripartism 'is under no threat', and that there can be no question of any erosion of 'the constitutional and policy-making prerogatives' of workers and employers. Civil society organisations would not displace their representation in the ILC or ILO committees.[54] The

---

[50] J. R. Bellace, 'The ILO Declaration of Fundamental Principles and Rights at Work' (2001) 17 *International Journal of Comparative Labour Law and Industrial Relations* (*IJCLLIR*) 269 at 271.

[51] See S. Cooney, 'Testing Times for the ILO: Institutional Reform for the New International Political Economy' (1999) 20 *Comparative Labour Law and Policy Journal* 365; T. Fashoyin, 'Tripartism and Other Actors in Social Dialogue' (2005) 21 *IJCLLIR* 37; and also L. Vosko, '"Decent Worker": The Shifting Role of the ILO and the Struggle for Global Social Justice', (2002) 2(1) *Global Social Policy* 19.

[52] Cooney, 'Testing Times', at 371–3, 390–3; and Vosko, 'Decent Worker' at 39.

[53] *Report of the Director-General: Reducing the Decent Work Deficit: A Global Challenge* (Geneva: ILO, 2001), ch. 3.1.

[54] *Ibid.*

Director-General did, however, consider it unfortunate that 'within the ILO, there continues to be reticence and insecurity about engaging outside actors', especially since NGOs may be able to represent people and families in the informal sector. The Director-General said that he was interested in hearing the views of civil society organisations and including them in deliberation on matters in which they have expertise.[55] This is, of course, already done in relation to particular projects, such as those arising under the ILO International Programme for the Elimination of Child Labour.[56] Such a strategy has been described elsewhere as 'tripartite-plus representation', for it maintains the fundamental structure of tripartism but allows participation in deliberation to 'shift and broaden according to the issues and interests concerned'.[57]

This model of inclusive participation was evident in the constitution and mandate of the ILO World Commission on the Social Dimension of Globalization, established in 2002.[58] The World Commission was set up as a fact-finding body. Its first mission was 'to establish the facts' relating to the dynamics and effects of globalisation. In this respect, it was like many other fact-finding ILO Commissions, which have been utilised throughout the history of the ILO to analyse particular issues.[59] However, the new World Commission also had a more challenging task: 'to encourage a more focused international dialogue on the social dimension of globalization, and build consensus among key actors and

---

[55] Ibid., chs. 2.2 and 3.4.

[56] See, for a recent example, IPEC Reflections on Current Strengths and Weaknesses in the West Africa Cocoa/Commercial Agriculture Programme to Combat Hazardous and Exploitative Child Labour, 27 June 2005, http://www.ilo.org/public/english/standards/ipec/download/2005_07_wacap_en.pdf (last accessed 22 August 2005), at p. 4, which recalls collaboration with domestic and international NGOs, such as CARE International, ICI (International Cocoa Initiative) and Save the Children.

[57] A. Blackett, 'Global Governance, Legal Pluralism and the Decentered State: A Labor Law Critique of Corporate Codes of Conduct' (2001) 8 Indiana Journal of Global Legal Studies 401 at 438; see also A. Trebilcock, 'Tripartite Consultation and Cooperation in National Level Economic and Social Policy-Making: An Overview', in A. Trebilcock (ed.), Towards Social Dialogue: Tripartite Cooperation in National Economic and Social Policy-Making (Geneva: ILO, 1994), pp. 29, 35, 44.

[58] See World Commission on the Social Dimension of Globalization, A Fair Globalization: Creating Opportunities for All (Geneva: ILO, 2004).

[59] See, for example, the Nicod Committee of 1924 established to consider 'Freedom of Association and Trade Unionism', the findings of which are set out in Nicod, 'Freedom of Association and Trade Unionism: An Introductory Survey' (1924) 9 International Labour Review 467 and the work of the Ohlin Committee, outlined in Report of a Group of Experts, Social Aspects of European Economic Co-operation (1956).

stakeholders on appropriate policy responses'.[60] The Commission consisted of 21 experts, possessing an impressive array of experience in such fields as government, business, trade unions, NGOs, international trade-related matters, human development and economics. They were appointed by the ILO Director-General, in consultation with the ILO Governing Body, with an evident desire to ensure representation of different genders, geographical locations and cultural backgrounds. There was no strict numerical representation of particular groups, but balance was sought 'between economic and social perspectives, between business and labour, and between global and local concerns'. It was hoped that individuals from these divergent backgrounds with their own agendas 'would be able to bring to bear expertise, judgment and experience from different perspectives, and so deepen the knowledge base for the ILO's work'.[61]

The assumption here, which has come to be linked to deliberative theory, is that persons with very different experiences and viewpoints can be placed in a room, provided with potentially conflicting information and expected to debate matters rationally. Connected to this is the belief is that such persons can, in this sphere, put their differences aside. They will be able to reach decisions by consensus, which reflect the strength of reasons given for one point of view in preference to another, rather than the relative social or economic power of persons within or outside the debating chamber. This view was reflected in the Commission's final report of 2004, which celebrated its constitution:

> As a Commission we were broadly representative of the diverse and contending actors and interests that exist in the real world. Co-chaired by two serving Heads of State, a woman and a man, from North and South, we came from countries in different parts of the worlds and at all stages of development. Our affiliations were equally diverse: government, politics, parliaments, business and multinational corporations, organized labour, academia and civil society ... our experience has demonstrated the value and power of dialogue as an instrument for change. Through listening patiently and respectfully to diverse views and interests we found common ground.[62]

---

[60] See 'Objectives' of the World Commission on the Social Dimension of Globalization, available at http://www.ilo.org/public/english/wcsdg/commission/objectives.htm (last accessed 22 August 2005).

[61] Governing Body Working Party on the Social Dimension of Globalization, *Enhancing the Action of the Working Party on the Social Dimension of Globalization: Next Steps*, GB.282/WP/SDG/1, 282nd Session of the ILO Governing Body (2001), paras. 4 and 6.

[62] World Commission on the Social Dimension of Globalization, *A Fair Globalization*, ix.

That report also emphasised, *inter alia*, the importance of consultation with a wide range of civil society actors, but did not specify how the ILO might achieve this.[63] The Director-General and the Governing Body responded with a defence of tripartism, but also some recognition of the desirability of greater engagement with NGOs, on a less *ad hoc* basis than at present.[64] The statements of the Director-General on this issue have been tentative and no detailed plans have as yet been presented to the International Labour Conference or Governing Body on this matter.

Instead, the comments of the ILO Director-General at the 2005 ILC focused on the lack of female representation among delegates, which stood only at 22.2 per cent, observing that this percentage was even less than the previous year's already low figure.[65] So, rather than extending representation beyond government, employer and worker delegates, the emphasis was on extending representation of women within those delegations. This is a vital issue, but it also seems to have been used in a way which attracts attention away from more fundamental concerns with representational structures within the ILO. Indeed, towards the end of his closing address, the Director-General reaffirmed his commitment to tripartism in the context of 'consensus-based' industrial relations.[66]

The difficulty for the ILO is how significant change in representational structures could be achieved without sacrificing a workable structure that has achieved considerable international influence. The ILO has been so successful that it has even been posited as a model appropriate for other UN agencies, such as any environmental agency that might be established.[67] It is also worth noting some of the merits of the existing ILO system, such as the openness and transparency of its proceedings, given the extensive minutes kept relating to debates within the ILC, Governing Body and other committees. The reasons given for decisions

---

[63] *Ibid.*, para. 343, p. 77.

[64] Report of the ILO Director-General, *A Fair Globalization: The Role of the ILO* (Geneva: ILO, 2004), pp. 8 and 50; see also *Follow-up to the Report of the World Commission on the Social Dimension of Globalization: Next Steps* (2004), GB.291/WP/SDG/1, 291st Session, para. 29.

[65] Report of the ILO Director-General, *Consolidating Progress and Moving Ahead* (Geneva: ILO, 2005), p. 8; and *Reply by the Director-General to the Discussion of his Report* (2005) ILC, *Provisional Record*, 93rd Session, Geneva, 23/1.

[66] *Reply by the Director-General to the Discussion of his Report* (2005) ILC, *Provisional Record*, 93rd Session, Geneva, 23/11.

[67] G. Palmer, 'New Ways to Make International Environmental Law' (1992) 86 *AJIL* 259 at 280.

are on public record and the ILO website has made these more accessible than was hitherto possible.

There is likely to be considerable resistance to wholesale reform. Resistance may come from states who are reluctant to see their influence – diminished in any case within a tripartite framework – further reduced, as a wider range of actors are involved. Worker and employer representatives may also fear that tripartism might 'turn into quadripartism or multipartism' and that participation in decision-making will be diluted to the extent that it is thwarted.[68]

There are also other practical reasons for maintenance of something resembling the *status quo*. One is that NGOs tend to be from first world or industrialised countries;[69] and it will be important that large-scale representation of NGOs does not disrupt the current geographical balance within organs such as the ILC or Governing Body. Another is the difficulty associated with assessment of the extent to which delegates are suitably representative. To date, the credentials of employer and worker delegates, especially their independence from government, has been carefully vetted by the Credentials Committee. As the numbers of NGOs rapidly increase,[70] the choice will have to be made as to which are worthy of special standing, and reasons given for their selection. This is relatively easy to achieve on an *ad hoc* basis, when considering, for example, levels of expertise relevant to particular projects, but may be more complicated to ensure systematic selection in the context of a body such as the ILC.

In summary, it seems improbable that there will be a dramatic change in corporatist governance within the ILO. Given the sensitivity of the Director-General and the Governing Body to these issues, we may, however, expect to see a more deliberative orientation in debates within the ILC and other committees, as well as more systematic consultation with NGOs in the implementation of particular projects.

Challenges to social dialogue within the EU

The terms 'social dialogue' and 'tripartism' are used almost interchangeably within the ILO.[71] However, there remain significant differences

---

[68] See Fashoyin, 'Tripartism and Other Actors', at 38.
[69] S. Charnovitz, 'Two Centuries of Participation: NGOs and International Governance' (1997) 18 *Michigan Journal of International Law* 183 at 276.
[70] *Ibid.*, at 275.
[71] Report of the ILO Director-General, *Consolidating Progress and Moving Ahead* (Geneva: ILO, 2005), p. 3, where each is described as a 'pillar' of 'decent work'.

between processes of social dialogue pursued under the auspices of the European Community and the tripartite structures of the ILO. These are outlined below, alongside the potential challenges posed by the recent focus on reform of governance within the European Union as a whole. What emerges as curious, in this setting, is the lack of concrete proposals for reform of EC social dialogue in response to the values espoused in the *European Governance* White Paper.[72]

The evolution of EU social dialogue

The participation of management and labour in EU decision-making has been characterised in two divergent ways. According to one view, this is a regulatory strategy, which has to be understood in the context of its ability to influence the content of laws binding on member states.[73] Another view is that it amounts merely to recognition of the emergence of European-level collective bargaining, which would inevitably follow the creation of an internal market.[74] The first approach is compatible with external scrutiny and an insistence by EU institutions on democratic structures, such as particular representative structures and public transparency. The second suggests that what is vital is that employer and worker organisations are accountable to their members and that minimal bureaucratic intervention is desirable.

What should also be recognised at the outset is the sheer diversity of mechanisms through which the opinions of management and labour can influence EC social policy. An overview is provided here, not just for information, but also in order to explain the evolution of social dialogue to its current elevated and extremely influential form.

The first key involvement of management and labour in EC policy-making took place by virtue of their inclusion in membership of the Economic and Social Committee, established by Article 4 of the Treaty of Rome 1957. Since 1972, the Economic and Social Committee has had the right to form its own opinions on its own initiative in all matters relating to the EU. The opinion of the Economic and Social Committee is also requested by the Commission whenever a draft proposal is submitted to Parliament. The Commission may amend its proposals

---

[72] *European Governance: A White Paper*, COM(2001)428 final.
[73] See Fredman, 'Social Law'.
[74] B. Bercusson, 'Democratic Legitimacy and European Labour Law' (1999) 28 *Industrial Law Journal* 153.

on the basis both of Parliament's advice and that of the Committee. This is, however, a body which includes other representatives of civil society and cannot be seen as essentially corporatist, despite the role it reserves for functional representation of employer and worker interests.[75]

Sectoral social dialogue has also been a significant aspect of EC social policy. From 1963 onwards, sectoral committees were created to aid the social partners in reaching European level agreements. This practice began with the creation of such Joint Committees as those on Social Problems affecting Agricultural Workers (1963), on Road Transport (1965), and on Inland Navigation (1967). By the late 1980s, in an era of deregulatory fervour, there were complaints relating to 'the formal and bureaucratic structure of the committees, with some participants expressing a preference for a more flexible and informal arrangement'.[76] The result was the creation of more informal working parties, in such sectors as construction and cleaning. The disjuncture created by these different forms of sectoral dialogue led to the Commission's decision to reform the system in 1998, such that there are now 30 specific Sectoral Dialogue Committees. They produce a variety of opinions, guidelines, codes of conduct and agreements. Such texts are not considered to be legally binding, but are essentially collective agreements on the practical aspects of implementation of EC regulations and directives within particular sectors, as well as on supplementary matters.[77]

In 1965, the Union des Confédérations de l'Industrie et des Employers d'Europe (UNICE) and the European Trade Union Confederation (ETUC) initiated European-wide social dialogue, setting up working parties on the subject of vocational training and reform of the European Social Fund. The first working party developed the European Centre for the Development of Vocational Training (Cedafop). The second led to the creation of the Standing Committee on Employment. This was a body which allowed for consultation of the social partners, having some impact on the content of provisions

---

[75] For a critical view of the current activities of the Economic and Social Committee, see S. Smismans, 'An Economic and Social Committee for the Citizen or a Citizen for the Economic and Social Committee' (1999) 5 *European Public Law* 557; and Smismans, *Law, Legitimacy*, ch. 3.

[76] 'The Sectoral Social Dialogue' (1992) 224 *EIRR* 16.

[77] See Commission Communication, *Adapting and Promoting the Social Dialogue at Community Level*, COM(98) 322; and Commission Communication, *Partnership for Change in an Enlarged Europe – Enhancing the Contribution of European Social Dialogue*, COM(2004) 557, Annex 4.

contained in the Collective Redundancies Directive.[78] In addition, the period 1970–1978 was marked by a series of tripartite conferences in which declarations were issued, indicating that governments of member states and social partners would seek to pursue similar objectives. However, representatives of management and labour still possessed no powers of decision-making.[79]

A turning point for social dialogue occurred in 1985, with the invitation of the social partners by Jacques Delors, then President of the EC Commission, to a meeting in the Chateau de Val Duchesse on the outskirts of Brussels. His aim seems to have been to break the legislative use of veto in the Council, in particular by the UK, by devolving power to create European social policy to the social partners.[80] The partners were still UNICE and the ETUC, accompanied now by the Centre Europeen de l'Entreprise Publique (CEEP). Following agreement during talks at Val Duchesse, they began to meet with the Commission in two working parties: one, dealing with the Community's economic and social problems; the other dealing with new technologies, the organisation of work and the adaptability of work.[81] However, despite the production of numerous joint opinions, recommendations and agreements, the influence of these working groups was minimal.[82]

Co-regulation only became possible after the Treaty on European Union was signed at Maastricht in 1992. Appended to the Treaty was a Social Protocol, signed by all member states apart from the UK. The content of this Protocol was heavily based on an agreement reached by the three key social partners in 1991, and its essential aspects have now been incorporated into Articles 138 and 139 of the EC Treaty. These provisions give European-level employer and worker organisations (the 'social partners') privileged influence over the generation of norms in the field of social policy.

---

[78] Collective Redundancies Directive 75/129/EEC [1976] OJ L39/40, since replaced by Directive 98/59/EEC [1998] OJ L225/16. See European Commission, *Social Europe 2/95* (1996), 7. See also, for reform of the Standing Committee on Employment, Council Decision 1999/207/EC [1999] OJ L72/33; and its replacement by the Tripartite Summit, Council Decision 2003/174/EC [2003] OJ L 70/31.

[79] 'The Sectoral Social Dialogue' (1992) 224 *European Industrial Relations Reports* 14.

[80] See European Commission, *Social Europe 2/95* (1996), 17.

[81] J. Kenner, *EU Employment Law: from Rome to Amsterdam and Beyond* (Oxford: Hart, 2003), pp. 105–6.

[82] B. Hepple, *European Social Dialogue – Alibi or Opportunity?* (London: Institute of Employment Rights, 1993), p. 17.

Article 138(1) EC requires the European Commission to promote 'the consultation of management and labour at Community level' and requires the Commission to 'take any relevant measure to facilitate their dialogue by ensuring balanced support for the parties'. The aim then is to create a forum for debate and the resources that would enable meaningful communication between the social partners and the Commission. The notion of 'balanced support' is important, for it suggests that both sides of industry deserve some parity of treatment and assistance.

Under paras. (2) and (3) of Article 138 EC, there is to be consultation of management and labour before the Commission submits to the European Parliament and Council proposals in the social policy field. Article 137 EC demarcates the legislative competence of the EC in this sphere, listing the subject matter and the procedures to be followed. Notably, the social dialogue procedure does not come into play in relation to proposals relating to anti-discrimination law under Article 13 EC; instead the co-decision process involving participation of the European Parliament is required. There is, to this extent, selective use of the social dialogue process, its use being limited to matters which are exclusively the concern of workers and employers.

Consultation is limited to those social partner organisations which meet three criteria. These are that the organisation: (i) is cross-industry or relates to specific sectors or categories and is organised at European level; (ii) consists of organisations which are themselves an integral and recognised part of member states' social partner structures and with the capacity to negotiate agreements, and which are representative of all member states, as far as possible; and (iii) has adequate structures to ensure effective participation in the consultation process.[83] There are approximately 50 such organisations which have to be consulted in accordance with Article 138.[84]

What takes the procedure of social dialogue beyond its traditional consultative framework is para. (4) of Article 138 EC, which states that when consulted, management and labour may inform the Commission of their wish to initiate a separate process of social dialogue under Article 139 EC. This enables them to take the matter away from deliberation by the Commission (usually only for a period of nine months,

---

[83] See Commission Communications COM(93)600, COM(96)448 and COM(98)322. Note that none of these Communications were published in the Official Journal.
[84] These are listed in Annex 5 to Commission Communication COM(2004)557.

unless all parties agree that the time limit should be extended) and seek to reach an agreement on the type and content of regulation that would be appropriate in the circumstances. At this point, the social partners select those with whom they wish to negotiate, a process which has come to be known as 'mutual recognition'. While there may be over 50 social partner organisations which should be consulted, only UNICE, the ETUC and CEEP initially participated in this latter process. A legal challenge to the process came after the exclusion of Union Européenne de l'Artisan et des Petits et Moyennes Enterprises (UEAPME), which represents small and medium-sized employers, from participation in negotiations over the framework agreement on parental leave that formed the basis of Directive 96/34.[85] UEAPME did not succeed in its legal challenge, as UNICE was found to be sufficiently representative of such employers, but more recently an accommodation has evidently been reached, whereby UEAPME is represented by UNICE within the social dialogue process. Nevertheless, despite this accommodation, the 'big three' organisations remain dominant.

The social dialogue process occurring under Article 139 EC may then lead to 'contractual relations' between management and labour. One option is for the social partners to jointly request that their framework agreement has legal effect, by virtue of a Council Directive. For this they require the recommendation of the Commission, which will only do so if certain criteria are met. For example, it is at this point that the Commission will take into account the representative status of the signatory parties. This is done in accordance with criteria used for the consultation phase, but also must now take account of the guidance provided by the Court of First Instance in the UEAPME case, namely that: (i) representativeness is to be assessed in relation to the content of the agreement; (ii) there need only be 'sufficient' representativeness (organisations which might be as or more representative do not have to be parties); and (iii) there need only be 'sufficient collective representativeness', such that the representativeness of the parties is assessed as a whole.[86] The Commission will also certify its belief as to the legality of each clause of the framework agreement and that it will not unduly impose burdens on small and medium-sized undertakings. At this stage, the Commission will also inform the European Parliament and the

---

[85] Case T-135/96, *Union Européenne de l'Artisan et des Petits et Moyennes Enterprises (UEAPME) v. Council* [1998] ECR II-2335.

[86] *Ibid.*, paras. 90–110; see also Smismans, *Law, Legitimacy*, pp. 392–4.

Economic and Social Committee of its proposal to give legal effect to the social partners' framework agreement. The final decision on adoption of the directive rests with the Council, which will take the decision either by qualified majority vote or unanimous vote, depending on how the subject-matter is classified under Article 137 EC.

Should the social partners fail to agree, the Commission can re-seize the initiative, and produce its own draft directive to be approved by the Parliament and Council. There is also a third option, which is for the social partners to reach an agreement that is not to have legal effect, but is to be implemented by collective agreement in the member states. To date, this has been done in respect of the Telework Agreement 2002[87] and the Framework Agreement on Work-Related Stress 2004.[88] This practice is consistent with the scope permitted for implementation of Council Directives by collective agreement within member states under Article 137(3).

It may be worth highlighting the difference between this process of bipartite dialogue and the tripartite decision-making which takes place within the ILO. Within the ILO, government, worker and employer delegates meet together in a single forum to reach agreement on any given issue. By contrast, in social dialogue under Articles 138 and 139 EC, management and labour are given the opportunity to debate issues and formulate standards without government representatives being present. A deal is effectively struck behind closed doors, the effect of which is determined primarily by the social partners. It is only if they intend the agreement to have legal effect (and not merely implementation through collective bargaining) that there is scrutiny of its content and of the representative status of parties to the agreement.[89] This can be seen as a form of subsidiarity, with norms being formulated by those directly affected by them. The nature of this process also suggests the predominance of the view that the social dialogue process is an extension of collective bargaining rather than a regulatory process.

---

[87] Available at http://europa.eu.int/comm/employment_social/news/2002/oct/teleworking_agreement_en.pdf.

[88] Available at http://europa.eu.int/comm/employment_social/news/2004/oct/stress_agreement_en.pdf.

[89] For critiques of this procedure, see P. Syrpis, 'Social Democracy and Judicial Review in the Community Order', in C. Kilpatrick, T. Novitz and P. Skidmore (eds.), *The Future of Remedies in Europe* (Oxford: Hart, 2000), p. 253 at pp. 263–5; and N. Bernard, 'Legitimising EU Law: Is the Social Dialogue the Way Forward? Some Reflections Around the *UEAPME* Case', in J Shaw (ed.), *Social Law and Policy in an Evolving European Union* (Oxford: Hart, 2000).

There does remain some limited scope for tripartite dialogue in an EC context, as is illustrated by the Council's decision to establish an annual Tripartite Social Summit for Growth and Employment, to be held annually.[90] These meetings are intended to supplement national level consultation of the social partners under the European Employment Strategy[91] and have been held unofficially since 2000, but the first official summit took place on 20 March 2003.[92] Reports of the dialogue at the annual tripartite summit do not appear to be publicly available. Instead, it seems to be left again to the social partners themselves to produce relevant public records, the result being that ETUC, CEEP and UNICE (together with UEAPME) have now produced a joint '2004 Report on Social Partner Actions in Member States to Implement Employment Guidelines', which has been published but not co-authored by the European Commission.[93] In this respect, the social partners are again acting autonomously from government representatives or EU institutions.

Democracy and the EU project for 'good governance'

As the millennium approached, the 'democratic deficit' in governance of the EU was repeatedly called into question.[94] This can perhaps be blamed upon the incremental evolution of the Communities into a single European Union and the lack of an over-arching systematic vision of its functions and powers. EC social dialogue, having evolved in a similar piecemeal fashion, simultaneously received comparable criticism. Lammy Betten, for example, expressed her concern that the ETUC, CEEP and UNICE did not represent the majority of workers

---

[90] Council Decision 2003/174/CE of 6 March 2003 establishing a Tripartite Social Summit for Growth and Employment, Official Journal L 70 of 14.03.2003.

[91] Commission Communication, *From Guidelines to Action: The National Action Plans for Employment*, COM(98)316.

[92] See Commission Communication, *The European Social Dialogue: A Force for Innovation and Change: Proposal for a Council Decision Establishing a Tripartite Social Summit for Growth and Employment* COM(2002)341; and Council Decision 2003/174/EC [2003] OJ L 70/31.

[93] Available at http://europa.eu.int/comm/employment_social/social_dialogue/docs/300_20040305_report2004_sp_contribution_empl_guidelines.pdf.

[94] Discussed in G. Majone, 'Europe's Democratic Deficit' (1998) 4 *ELJ* 237; and D. Wincott, 'Does the European Union Pervert Democracy? Questions of Democracy in New Constitutionalist Thought on the Future of Europe' (1998) 4 *ELJ* 411. See also the symptomatic *Resolution on the Democratic Deficit* [1998] OJ C 187/229.

and employers in Europe.[95] She was, therefore, alarmed that broader participation through the European Parliament was lost as soon as the social partners 'hijacked' a Commission proposal.[96] Moreover, the weakness of accountability within social partner organisations came under scrutiny. As Tiziano Treu observed, the ETUC 'has the nature of an umbrella organization rather than a negotiating structure'.[97]

In 2001, the Commission, being well aware of such concerns, launched its campaign for 'good governance'. Its flagship was the Commission White Paper of 2001,[98] which is indicative of the concerns that typify EU governance debates. The Commission observed the legitimacy crisis facing national political institutions and recognised that these were exacerbated at the European level. Whilst the public expected Europe-wide action, there were particular concerns arising from the complexity of its governance and compelling calls for its reform. The Commission's White Paper acknowledged the broad scope for potential change:

> Reforming governance addresses the question of how the EU uses the powers given by its citizens. It is about how things could and should be done. The goal is to open up policy-making to make it more inclusive and accountable. A better use of powers should connect the EU more closely to its citizens and lead to more effective policies.[99]

Specific proposals included extending the range of participants in EU policy-making, ensuring that participants are representative, and promoting transparency. 'Better involvement', including involvement with 'civil society', was to be crucial. The scope for broad NGO involvement was canvassed, but it was also acknowledged that 'trade unions and employers' organisations have a particular role and influence' through the process of social dialogue. In this respect, social partners were to be 'further encouraged to use the powers given under the Treaty to conclude voluntary agreements'.[100] However, with 'better involvement' was to come 'greater responsibility'. Civil society itself had to 'follow the principles of good governance, which include accountability and

---

[95] L. Betten, 'The Democratic Deficit of Participatory Democracy in Community Social Policy' (1998) 23 *ELR* 20 at 32.

[96] *Ibid.*, 33.

[97] T. Treu, 'European Collective Bargaining Levels and the Competences of the Social Partners', in P. Davies *et al.*, *European Community Labour Law: Principles and Perspectives* (Oxford: Oxford University Press, 1996), p. 179.

[98] *European Governance: A White Paper* COM(2001)428.   [99] *Ibid.*, 8.   [100] *Ibid.*, 14.

openness'. There were no specific comments on how this should affect social dialogue, if at all.[101]

Whether these proposed reforms can provide the basis for democratic legitimacy of the European Union remains the subject of debate. For our purposes, more pertinent are the implications such an agenda has for reform of social dialogue. What is perhaps curious is how limited its impact has been.

It has been suggested that the EC should seek to move from bipartite to tripartite social dialogue, perhaps including committees from the European Parliament,[102] but it seems that the Commission remains committed to maintaining the privileged participation of the social partners. In a Commission Communication of 2002, it was reiterated that social dialogue was 'a key to better governance' and defended the selective participation of the social partners, as follows:

> Within civil society, the social partners have a particular role and influence which flow from the very nature of the subjects they cover and the interests they represent in connection with *the world of work*.[103]

In a Communication of 2004, the Commission went further claiming that social dialogue could be seen as:

> A pioneering example of improved consultation and the application of subsidiarity in practice and is widely recognised as making an essential contribution to better governance, as a result of the proximity of the social partners to the realities of the workplace.[104]

The apparent flexibility and subsidiarity associated with the social dialogue process, which operates on a multitude of levels, appears consistent with the spontaneous engagement with civil society advocated in deliberative democratic theory. The difficulty, however, is that it does not always work in practice to promote participation at ground level. A study on social partner participation in the European Employment Strategy suggests that national level contributions have been minimal, with the only meaningful influence being exercised by European-level associations. The result, it has been suggested, is not democracy but elitism.[105]

---

[101] *Ibid.*, 15.
[102] G. P. Cella, 'European Governance, Democratic Representation and Industrial Relations' (2003) 9 *Transfer: European Review of Labour and Research* 197 at 206.
[103] Commission Communication COM(2002)341, 7.
[104] Commission Communication COM(2004)557, 6.
[105] B. H. Casey, 'Building Social Partnership? Strengths and Shortcomings of the European Employment Strategy' (2005) 11 *Transfer* 45.

Such criticism aside, one might have expected more attention to be paid to the representative status of the social partners. This issue did receive a brief mention in the 2002 Commission Communication.[106] Reference was made to a study carried out in 1998 (and published in 1999) by the UCL-IST, the Institute of Labour Studies at the Catholic University of Louvain, which apparently confirmed that European-level representative structures had become stronger.[107] The 2002 Commission Communication also made a commitment to a further study on representativeness. In the 2004 Communication, it emerged that this study was now to be commissioned from the European Industrial Relations Observatory of the Dublin Foundation.[108] No preliminary findings are, as yet, available.

What we do know is that the ETUC does not represent the majority of workers in the EU, but does represent the vast majority of trade unions across different sectors. There is, therefore, little scope for challenge to its position at the bargaining table. UNICE has, as its members, national umbrella employer associations, which it claims are also inclusive of various sectoral interests. CEEP has been described as more problematic as it tends not to represent public employers in the civil service. Catherine Barnard has commented that 'CEEP's presence is anachronistic: it is one of the established social partners only because it was there at the beginning'.[109] Despite this, there does not seem to be any immediate impetus by the Commission to displace the dominance of the ETUC, UNICE and CEEP within the extant process.

The issue of transparency was largely neglected in the 2002 Communication, which seemed to be aimed at raising the profile of social dialogue, but not necessary public access to information. This issue only emerged in 2004, in the context of the increasingly autonomous activities of the social partners, and the emergence of framework agreements or 'new generation texts', which are to be implemented through collective agreement rather than being given legal effect. The view expressed in the 2004 Communication was that it is essential to

---

[106] Commission Communication COM(2002)341, 9.

[107] *Report on the Representativeness of European Social Partner Organisations*, Part I, coordinated by the Institut des Sciences du Travail – Université Catholique de Louvain at the request of the European Commission, Directorate-General for Employment, Industrial Relations and Social Affairs, September 1999, available at http://ec.europa.eu/employment_social/social_dialogue/docs/report_en.pdf.

[108] Commission Communication COM (2004)557, 9.

[109] C. Barnard, 'The Social Partners and the Governance Agenda' (2002) 8 *ELJ* 80 at 91.

'ensure that the results of the European social dialogue are as *transparent* as possible to all those involved with the negotiation and follow-up of texts', since 'the significance and status of the European social partners' texts is not always easy to understand to those not directly involved in their dialogue, partly because of titles and formats employed, and the rather loose use of terminology'. The Commission observed that this was likely to lead to difficulties when practical implementation is attempted.[110] Its response was to draw up a typology and drafting checklist.[111] Its preference would be for the social partners to draw up their own framework, but the Commission has proposed more extensive intervention should the social partners fail to do so.[112]

We have yet to see how the social partners respond to this attempt at guidance. What is interesting is that there is, as yet, no attempt to formalise the social dialogue process itself, to ensure that records of debate are provided. Indeed, this seems unlikely to materialise, given the Commission's statement that it 'fully recognises the negotiating autonomy of the social partners on the topics falling within their competence'.[113] In other words, the Commission acknowledges that social dialogue is an essentially bipartite, and not a tripartite process. It will therefore seek to minimise regulatory intervention in these processes. This is at least cosmetically consistent with a notion of 'horizontal' subsidiarity, with decisions being taken as close as possible to the worker and employer organisations affected, but we will have to wait for further studies on systems of representation and accountability to confirm the legitimacy of the process.

The Commission's only remaining concern appears to be that the conclusions of autonomous agreements by social dialogue on a particular topic should not altogether preclude EC directives on the same subject. The 2004 Communication is significant in that it stated that where a framework agreement concluded by the social partners 'does not succeed in meeting the Community's objectives, it will consider the possibility of putting forward, if necessary, a proposal for a legislative act', and will also act if there appears to be undue delay.[114] In other words, the process of social dialogue allows the Commission and Council to delegate regulatory powers to management and labour, but where such powers are misused for any reason, the EC institutions retain the power to act. Instead of the tripartite deliberation that we see in the ILO, there appears to be potential for contested regulatory control. This reflects concerns with the output of

[110] Commission Communication COM(2004) 557, 7.
[111] *Ibid.*, Annexes 2 and 3, respectively.   [112] *Ibid.*, 11.   [113] *Ibid.*, 10.   [114] *Ibid.*

social dialogue, which has been seen as a slow process producing diluted standards, possibly due to the relative lack of bargaining power on the trade union side.[115] There is no protection of a right to strike at European level, while employers still retain the credible threat of withdrawal of capital to states where labour standards are lower.[116]

One final aspect of a deliberative democratic approach, discussed previously, is that there are guarantees of those human rights which assist in the creation of an 'ideal speech situation'. Here there is a further difference between the ILO and the EC. Within the ILO, freedom of association is a key constitutional principle, but Article 137(5) EC expressly excludes any legislative competence of Council in respect of this matter. The result is that there is no EU directive concerning freedom of association that member states are obliged to respect, or upon which citizens can rely in national courts. Nor is there any guarantee of freedom of association in the EC Treaty. Instead, the process of social dialogue relies on less direct forms of legal protection. Freedom of association is considered to be a fundamental principle of EC law, by virtue of the status given by the European Court of Justice (ECJ) to the European Convention on Human Rights and Fundamental Freedoms of 1950, Article 11 of which contains the necessary guarantee.[117] Its importance is also acknowledged through the Community Charter of the Fundamental Rights of Workers of 1989, and the EU Charter of Fundamental Rights of 2000,[118] but for the time being these instruments remain declaratory.[119] The merits of such an approach have been consistently challenged,[120] but there is no immediate likelihood of reform. The incorporation of an EU Charter of Fundamental Rights within an

---

[115] See the output assessment conducted by Smismans, *Law, Legitimacy*, pp. 365–71; and Barnard, 'The Social Partners', 94.

[116] Discussed in P. Germanotta and T. Novitz, 'Globalisation and the Right to Strike: The Case for European-Level Protection of Secondary Action' (2002) 18 *IJCLLIR* 67. See also Fredman, 'Social Law', 409.

[117] See, for an example of the approach of the ECJ, Case C-415/93, *Union Royale Belge des Societes de Football Association and others v. Bosman and others* [1995] ECR I-4921, Judgment, para. 79.

[118] Charter of Fundamental Rights of the European Union, 2000 OJ (C 364) 1 (7 December 2000).

[119] See for a useful discussion of its current status, J. Morijn, 'Balancing Fundamental Rights and Common Market Freedoms in Union Law: Schmidberger and Omega in the Light of the European Constitution' (2006) 12(1) *ELJ* 15 at 17–23.

[120] B. Ryan, 'Pay, Trade Union Rights and European Community Law' (1997) 13 *IJCLLIR* 305; and Lord Wedderburn, 'Consultation and Collective Bargaining in Europe: Success or Ideology?' (1997) 26 *Industrial Law Journal* 1.

EU Constitution could have given freedom of association the status within EU law that many commentators have hoped for,[121] but the failure of national referenda on the Constitution means that the adoption of the Constitution in its present form is highly unlikely.[122]

The overall impression is that, even if the *European Governance* White Paper was intended to be a step towards democratic legitimacy within the European Union, there is not much evidence in favour of its realisation in the context of EC social dialogue. The chiefly bipartite (as opposed to tripartite) character of social dialogue, at least under Articles 138 and 139 EC, and its resultant autonomous quality, makes it difficult to realise a deliberative framework. Even if assisted by background guarantees of free speech and freedom of association, the autonomous choice of management and labour as to the selection of parties to any framework agreement limits scope for independent assessment of the representativeness. This is more likely to be a *fait accompli*, its adequacy being confirmed by the Commission after the fact, than a matter that the Commission can regulate. Only recently has there been any attempt to achieve transparency in respect of the texts of framework agreements and other autonomous texts concluded by management and labour, while there appears to be no question of revealing the content of their debates to the public. It is also interesting that wider scope for participation of other interest groups has not been considered through enhancement of the role of the European Parliament. That is not to say that deliberative democracy would best be achieved in the absence of social dialogue,[123] but rather that there remains a case for more thorough scrutiny of its operation and potential reform.

Conclusions: future corporatism in international and European governance

Corporatism, or the privileged representation of employer and worker interests in policy-making, has been a longstanding feature of both the ILO and EU. The ILO is predominantly 'tripartite', involving discussions between employer, worker and employer representatives in a

---

[121] 2004 Treaty Establishing the Constitution for Europe, OJ C 310, 16 December 2004.
[122] Despite the Declaration by the Heads of State or Government of the Member States of the European Union on the Ratification of the Treaty Establishing A Constitution For Europe (European Council, 16 and 17 June 2005) SN 117/05.
[123] As recognised by Barnard, 'The Social Partners', 98.

variety of fora. The EU system makes more provision for 'bipartite' dialogue between representatives of management and labour. These participatory structures have been justified on the basis that they enhance the quality of decision-making and the efficacy of standards. However, advocates of a deliberative democratic approach to governance are beginning to challenge their legitimacy. This chapter has considered the prospect for reform in response to such challenges.

It has been suggested here that, even within a deliberative framework, a case may still be made for priority to be given to participation by worker and employer organisations in decision-making on matters which are of direct concern to their members. Within both the ILO and EU there seems to be some awareness of the need to broaden participation where the subject is of genuine concern to other members of civil society. The inclusion of NGO representation on the ILO World Commission on the Social Dimension of Globalization may be regarded as indicative of this realisation; as is the limitation of the topics appropriate for EC social dialogue under Articles 138–139 EC. However, the stark differences between the corporatist models that operate within the ILO and EU indicate that each organisation will respond differently to demands for representativeness, accountability and transparency, which accompany calls for deliberative democratic governance.

Arguably, the tripartite model that operates within the ILO has the greatest chance of satisfying those three demands. This may be because it is self-consciously a public regulatory process, which already has stringent standards for assessment of representative credentials and transparent records of debate. The ILO can be criticised for lacking the flexible and spontaneous aspects of ground-level decision-making demanded by deliberative governance, but there is scope to achieve this in the more concrete design and application of particular projects. Moreover, while the organisation has tended to operate through voting mechanisms reflecting discrete blocks of employer, worker and government interests, there is scope for deliberative engagement on issues and some scope for decision-making by consensus, as demonstrated by the operation of the ILO Committee on Freedom of Association.

The autonomy of social dialogue within the EU arguably offers greater capacity for flexibility and horizontal subsidiarity, but whether this is achieved depends on its work in practice. One drawback of an autonomous process may be that the choice given to the social partners to select the parties with which they will negotiate is not conducive to scrutiny of representative status. This will only occur once the social partners request that a framework agreement forms the basis of a Council Directive, and then, arguably, according to generous criteria. Much, therefore, depends on systems of accountability which operate internally within the ETUC, UNICE, CEEP and now UEAPME. Moreover, the orientation towards bargaining within social dialogue, which takes place behind closed doors, means that requirements for transparency are likely to be concerned only with the texts agreed by the parties and not the process by which agreement is reached. Ultimately, whether EC social dialogue continues to be regarded as legitimate may depend more on its output and efficacy in shaping labour standards, rather than the procedural input usually associated with deliberative democracy.

PART III

Visions of international constitutionalism

9

The meaning of international constitutional law

BARDO FASSBENDER[*]

Two faces of a problem: sovereignty and constitutionalism in international law

At the end of an article about the concept of sovereignty in international law,[1] I quoted Hans Kelsen and Wolfgang Friedmann. In spite of all their differences both legal scholars were strong supporters of an international constitutional order. It was, in fact, Friedmann who first produced a sketch of international constitutional law as a 'new field of international law'.[2] In the late 1920s, Kelsen referred to his time as a transitional period in the history of international law, and saw this character reflected in the 'contradictions of an international legal theory which in an almost tragic conflict aspires to the height of a universal legal community erected above the individual states but, at the same time, remains a captive of the sphere of power of the sovereign state'.[3] Almost 40 years later, Friedmann arrived at a very similar conclusion when he wrote:

> In terms of objectives, powers, legal structure and scope, the present state of international organisation presents an extremely complex picture. It reflects the state of a society that is both desperately clinging to the legal and political symbols of national sovereignty and being pushed towards

---

[*] This is a revised version of an essay which appeared in: R. St. J. Macdonald and D. M. Johnston (eds.), *Towards World Constitutionalism: Issues in the Legal Ordering of the World Community* (The Hague: Nijhoff, 2005), pp. 837–51.

[1] See B. Fassbender, 'Sovereignty and Constitutionalism in International Law', in N. Walker (ed.), *Sovereignty in Transition* (Oxford: Hart, 2003), p. 115 at p. 142.

[2] See W. Friedmann, *The Changing Structure of International Law* (London: Stevens, 1964), pp. 152–9.

[3] See H. Kelsen, *Das Problem der Souveränität und die Theorie des Völkerrechts. Beitrag zu einer Reinen Rechtslehre*, 2nd edn (Tübingen: Mohr, 1928), p. 320 (my translation).

the pursuit of common needs and goals that can be achieved only by a steadily intensifying degree of international organisation.[4]

What Kelsen described as a shortcoming of legal science – its inability to climb over the mental walls of the sovereign state – Friedmann extended to the state of the international order.

The contradictions Kelsen spoke of and the dilemma outlined by Friedmann are also, I think, characteristic features of world constitutionalism as a reality and an aspiration. State sovereignty, which the two authors addressed, and constitutionalism in international law are closely related issues. To speak, in our time, about the international constitutional order means approaching the subject of sovereignty, that is, the status of independent states in international law, from another side.

But what, exactly, is international constitutional law, and to what end do we study it? That subject is not to be confused with comparative constitutional law which recently has attracted new attention. In particular, scholars compare ways and means of protecting fundamental rights of citizens in various states of the Western world, or different forms of state organisation between the poles of centralisation and federalism.[5] Instead, we are searching for a sub-discipline of public international law, namely *the constitutional law of the international community*, a law which may be influenced by constitutional ideas and practices developed in a national context, but which is 'standing on its own feet'.

The use of constitutional language in international law

To use the notion of constitution in the context of public international law is today, it seems, much less controversial than it was five or, in any case, ten years ago. When I wrote about the subject back in 1998, I devoted substantial space to showing that there is no compelling reason to reserve the term 'constitution' for the supreme law of a (sovereign) state but that, instead, the fundamental legal order of any autonomous community or body politic can be addressed as a constitution.[6] I agreed

---

[4] See Friedmann, *The Changing Structure*, p. 293 *et seq.*

[5] In 2003, a new journal was founded to study such issues: *ICON*. See also the report by A. V. Bauer and C. Mikulaschek about the 'First Vienna Workshop on International Constitutional Law' (2005) 6 *German Law Journal* 1109.

[6] See B. Fassbender, 'The United Nations Charter as Constitution of the International Community' (1998) 36 *Columbia J Trans Law* 529 at 532–8, 555–61.

with Philip Allott, a scholar who has profoundly reflected on the meaning of constitutionalism in national societies and in the international society, when he said that '[a] constitution is a structure-system which is shared by all societies'.[7] This understanding entails a certain demystification of the institution of the (etatist) constitution and, with it, of the 'sovereign state' as the former constitutional monopolist.

In the meantime, this transfer of the constitutional idea into the sphere of international law, which had had only few advocates, has become almost uncontroversial,[8] even if many different opinions exist as to how exactly such transfer should be understood or constructed. Today many writers use it as a sort of *leitmotif* to capture, name, and also promote the fundamental changes in the international legal order which we all are sensing but cannot easily express in the language of (international) law that we learned.[9]

---

[7] See P. Allott, *Eunomia: New Order for a New World* (Oxford: Oxford University Press, 1990), p. 164. See also P. Allott, 'The Concept of International Law' (1999) 10 *EJIL* 31 at 35 *et seq.*, and in M. Byers (ed.), *The Role of Law in International Politics: Essays in International Relations and International Law* (Oxford: Oxford University Press, 2000), p. 69 at pp. 72–6; and P. Allott, *The Health of Nations: Society and Law Beyond the State* (Cambridge: Cambridge University Press, 2002), ch. 12 (pp. 342–79): 'Intergovernmental Societies and the Idea of Constitutionalism'.

[8] See J. Klabbers, 'Constitutionalism Lite' (2004) 1 *International Organisations Law Review* 31; D. M. Johnston, 'World Constitutionalism in the Theory of International Law', in R. St. J. Macdonald and D. M. Johnston (eds.), *Towards World Constitutionalism: Issues in the Legal Ordering of the World Community* (The Hague: Nijhoff, 2005), p. 3; B.-O. Bryde, 'International Democratic Constitutionalism', *ibid.*, p. 103; and E. de Wet, 'The International Constitutional Order' (2006) 55 *ICLQ* 51. For a re-evaluation of issues such as the traditional dichotomy between international and constitutional law (see Fassbender, 'The United Nations', pp. 532–8 and 555–61), 'constitution' as a contested notion (*ibid.*, p. 553 *et seq.*), or the use of constitutional language (*ibid.*, p. 538 *et seq.*), see T. Cottier and M. Hertig, 'The Prospects of 21st Century Constitutionalism' (2004) 7 *Max Planck UNYB* 261. For a systematic review of scholarly efforts to understand the changed international landscape, and for the place of the idea of constitutionalism in the current debate, see A. von Bogdandy, 'Demokratie, Globalisierung, Zukunft des Völkerrechts – eine Bestandsaufnahme' (2003) 63 *Zeitschrift für ausländisches öffentliches Recht und Völkerrecht* 853 at 864 *et seq.*, 869 *et seq.*, and A. von Bogdandy, 'Constitutionalism in International Law: Comment on a Proposal from Germany' (2006) 47 *Harvard Int LJ* 223 (focusing on the work of C. Tomuschat).

[9] There is, however, still some opposition on the part of scholars of (national) constitutional law and history. See, e.g., D. Grimm, 'Ursprung und Wandel der Verfassung', in J. Isensee and P. Kirchhof (eds.), 1 *Handbuch des Staatsrechts der Bundesrepublik Deutschland*, 3rd edn (Heidelberg: C. F. Müller, 2003), p. 3 at p. 36 *et seq.* (arguing that the international order is characterised by a plurality of unconnected institutions and legal sources, and that there is so far, on the international level, no entity which could be 'constitutionalised' ('*kein konstitutionsfähiger Gegenstand*')), and U. Haltern,

To some extent, the discussion about the future legal order of the European Union (EU) has contributed to the debate on international constitutionalism. In the case of the EU, legal science identified, over the course of the past ten or fifteen years, a gradual 'constitutionalisation' of a treaty-based order,[10] and this characterisation was subsequently accepted by a broad majority of governments and politicians of member states. In the summer of 2003, the European Convention adopted by consensus the 'Draft Treaty Establishing a Constitution for Europe',[11] which in an amended version was signed by the Heads of State or Government of the EU member states on 29 October 2004 in Rome as the 'Treaty Establishing the Constitution for Europe'.[12] Even if this Treaty will not come into force due to the referenda in France and the Netherlands, and even if further changes to the EU legal order will be effected by amendments to the present treaties, it is unlikely that the general view of an inherent constitutionalisation of the EU will be abandoned. Some of the ideas developed in the context of European

'Internationales Verfassungsrecht?' (2003) 128 *Archiv des öffentlichen Rechts* 511 (arguing that there is a fundamental difference between the 'aesthetic-symbolic meaning' of national law on the one hand, and European and international law on the other, leading to fundamentally different 'imaginations of the political'). For reasons not to be discussed here, German legal culture has produced both the strongest supporters and opponents of the idea of a constitution beyond the nation-state. This is overlooked by the author of a recent review essay diagnosing a 'near obsession of German international lawyers about having the UN Charter become the Constitution of the world'; see G. R. B. Galindo, 'Martii Koskenniemi and the Historiographical Turn in International Law' (2005) 16 *EJIL* 539 at 544.

[10] Of the extensive literature, I only mention J. Gerkrath, *L'émergence d'un droit constitutionnel pour l'Europe* (Bruxelles: Editions de l'Université de Bruxelles, 1997); I. Pernice, 'Multilevel Constitutionalism and the Treaty of Amsterdam: European Constitution-Making Revisited' (1999) 36 *CMLR* 703; C. Joerges, *Das Recht im Prozess der Konstitutionalisierung Europas* (EUI Working Paper LAW No. 2001/6); A. Peters, *Elemente einer Theorie der Verfassung Europas* (Berlin: Duncker & Humblot, 2001); N. Walker, 'The EU and the WTO: Constitutionalism in a New Key', in G. de Búrca and J. Scott (eds.), *The EU and the WTO: Legal and Constitutional Issues* (Oxford: Hart, 2001), p. 31; N. Walker, 'The Idea of Constitutional Pluralism' (2002) 65 *MLR* 317; N. Walker, 'Postnational Constitutionalism and the Problem of Translation', in J. H. H. Weiler and M. Wind (eds.), *European Constitutionalism Beyond the State* (Cambridge, Cambridge University Press, 2003), p. 27; B. de Witte, 'The Closest Thing to a Constitutional Conversation in Europe: The Semi-Permanent Treaty Revision Process', in P. R. Beaumont *et al.* (eds.), *Convergence and Divergence in European Public Law* (Oxford: Hart, 2002), p. 39; A. von Bogdandy, 'Europäische Verfassung und europäische Identität' (2004) 59 *Juristen-Zeitung* 53.

[11] See European Convention Doc. 850/03 of 18 July 2003.

[12] For text, see 2004 Treaty Establishing the Constitution for Europe, *OJ* C 310, 16 December 2004.

Community law were carried over to the understanding of the law of other organisations, especially the General Agreement on Tariffs and Trade (GATT), and the World Trade Organization (WTO).[13]

Secondly, it was understood that one can apply the notion of constitution in the realm of universal international law without necessarily being a proponent of a 'world state', something which to many is still the epitome of horror.[14] Thirdly, the constitutionalisation of international law is used as a possible remedy for what is conceived of as the 'fragmentation of international law'.[15] And lastly, as it happens, some writers jumped onto a wagon which appeared to be increasingly popular, content with the interesting and progressive ring of the words 'constitution' and, especially, 'constitutionalisation'.

However, the growing popularity of the use of the constitutional language in international law has rather increased the terminological confusion. For instance, the different issues of a constitutionalisation of the law of a particular intergovernmental organisation or international regime on the one hand, and of the existence of a constitution of the international community as such, on the other, are often not sufficiently distinguished.[16] Recent scholarship based on the work of Niklas Luhmann, arguing against a 'state-centered constitutionalism' (both

---

[13] See, in particular, E. U. Petersmann, *Constitutional Functions and Constitutional Problems of International Economic Law* (Boulder: Westview Press Inc., 1991). See also D. Z. Cass, 'The "Constitutionalisation" of International Trade Law: Judicial Norm-Generation as the Engine of Constitutional Development in International Trade' (2001) 12 *EJIL* 39. For a critical discussion, see A. von Bogdandy, 'Law and Politics in the WTO – Strategies to Cope with a Deficient Relationship' (2001) 5 *Max Planck UNYB* 609 at 653–6.

[14] See, e.g., C. Tomuschat, 'International Law: Ensuring the Survival of Mankind on the Eve of a New Century' (1999) 281 *RC* 9 at 89–90: 'The notion of an international community living under a common constitution has nothing to do . . . with a super-State which could claim supremacy over States, relegating them to pure "provinces" or other autonomous entities . . . International society finds itself at a medium point between the traditional model of sovereign self-sufficient States and a world with a hierarchical structure, topped by a single command centre.'

[15] See Klabbers, 'Constitutionalism Lite', 31, 49. See also M. Koskenniemi, *Fragmentation of International Law: Difficulties Arising from the Diversification and Expansion of International Law. Report of the Study Group of the International Law Commission*, UN Doc. A/CN.4/L.682 of 4 April 2006, para. 334 (views of the effects of Article 103 of the UN Charter 'on the basis of the view of the Charter as a "constitution"').

[16] But see C. Walter, 'Constitutionalizing (Inter)national Governance – Possibilities for and Limits to the Development of an International Constitutional Law' (2001) 44 *German Yearbook of International Law* 170 at 191 *et seq.*, who understands the statutes and basic rules of such organisations and regimes as *Teilverfassungen*, or 'partial constitutions', of the international community.

on a national and an international level) and recognising a 'constitutionalisation of a multiplicity of autonomous subsystems of world society', created a new notion of 'global civil constitutions' (*globale Zivilverfassungen*).[17] Such an inflationary use of the word 'constitution' entails the danger of its devaluation. Not every increase in legal regulation or legal control, and not even every evolution of a hierarchical system of rules, equates to a 'constitutionalisation'.[18]

In my 1998 article,[19] I argued that the constitutional rhetoric I had analysed was rarely based on a coherent idea of international constitutionalism, and that only few writers had made an effort systematically to explain both the reasons and the consequences for introducing constitutional ideas and terms into international law.[20] This situation has not changed much since then, although the number of authors using such ideas and terms has multiplied – to the extent that the organisers of the 2006 Biennial Conference of the European Society of International Law in Paris could say in their programme that 'over the last few years the notions of "international constitution" and "international constitutionalism" have become real buzzwords in the legal discourse'.[21]

In that article, I identified three schools of thought to which such systematic efforts to establish a constitutional reasoning in international law can be attributed: first, the school founded by the Viennese jurist Alfred Verdross,[22] who started out from Kelsen's legal theory but later both approached and influenced the mainstream; second (and partially

---

[17] See G. Teubner, 'Globale Zivilverfassungen: Alternativen zur staatszentrierten Verfassungstheorie', (2003) 63 *Zeitschrift für ausländisches öffentliches Recht und Völkerrecht* 1. See also A. Fischer-Lescano, 'Die Emergenz der Globalverfassung', *ibid.*, 717, and A. Fischer-Lescano, *Globalverfassung: Die Geltungsbegründung der Menschenrechte* (Weilerswist: Velbrück Wissenschaft, 2005).

[18] See Grimm, 'Ursprung und Wandel', 4 and 7.   [19] Above, n. 6.

[20] See Fassbender, 'The United Nations', 538. For a thoughtful recent re-examination, focusing on the constitutional character of the UN Charter, see P. M. Dupuy, 'L'unité de l'ordre juridique international (2002) 9 *RC* at 215–44, 286 *et seq.*, 303–7.

[21] See European Society of International Law, 'International Law: Do we Need It?', Agenda of the Biennial Conference in Paris, 18–20 May 2006, Forum 6: The Constitutionalization of International Law (on file with author). See also A. Kemmerer, 'Conference Report: Global Fragmentations. A Note on the Biennial Conference of the European Society of International Law' (2006) 7 *German LJ* 729 at 731 *et seq.*

[22] See, in particular, A. Verdross, *Die Verfassung der Völkerrechtsgemeinschaft* (Wien: Springer, 1926), and A. Verdross and B. Simma, *Universelles Völkerrecht: Theorie und Praxis*, 3rd edn (Berlin: Duncker und Humblot, 1984). For an analysis of Verdross' ideas, see F. Durante, 'Die Grundlage des Völkerrechts im Denken von Alfred Verdross-Drossberg' (1991) 42 *Österreichische Zeitschrift für öffentliches Recht und Völkerrecht* 59;

influenced by the first) a group of scholars, led by the late judge of the International Court of Justice (ICJ), Hermann Mosler and by Christian Tomuschat, advocating what I named the 'doctrine of international community';[23] and thirdly the New Haven School (or 'policy-science approach')[24] with Myres McDougal and Michael Reisman being the most prolific authors on the subject under discussion. Today, in the literature of international law, in particular the European, the second-mentioned school is by far the most influential one of the three; my own efforts, emphasising the importance of the Charter of the United Nations (UN Charter), are based on it. The term 'the international community' has become commonplace, but more so in continental Europe than in the UK or the US.[25] A fourth approach, championed

B. Simma, 'The Contribution of Alfred Verdross to the Theory of International Law' (1995) 6 *EJIL* 33, and R. Walter, 'Die Rechtslehren von Kelsen und Verdross unter besonderer Berücksichtigung des Völkerrechts', in R. Walter, C. Jabloner and K. Zeleny (eds.), *Hans Kelsen und das Völkerrecht* (Wien: Manz, 2004), p. 37.

[23] See, in particular, H. Mosler, 'The International Society as a Legal Community' (1974-IV) 140 *RC* 1, a revised version published as *The International Society as a Legal Community* (Alphen aan den Rijn: Sijthoff and Noordhoff, 1980); C. Tomuschat, 'Obligations Arising for States Without or Against Their Will' (1993-IV) 241 *RC* 195; C. Tomuschat, 'Die internationale Gemeinschaft' (1995) 33 *Archiv des Völkerrechts* 1; B. Simma, 'From Bilateralism to Community Interest in International Law', (1994-VI) 250 *RC* 217.

[24] See, in particular, M. S. McDougal, H. D. Lasswell and W. M. Reisman, 'The World Constitutive Process of Authoritative Decision', in M. S. McDougal and W. M. Reisman, *International Law Essays: A Supplement to International Law in Contemporary Perspective* (Mineola, NY: Foundation Press, 1981), p. 191. See also R. A. Falk, R. C. Johansen and S. S. Kim (eds.), *The Constitutional Foundations of World Peace* (Albany, N.Y.: State University of New York Press, 1993).

[25] For respective writings see, in particular, C. Tomuschat, 'Die internationale Gemeinschaft'; D. Thürer, 'Recht der internationalen Gemeinschaft und Wandel der Staatlichkeit', in D. Thürer, J.-F. Aubert and J. P. Müller (eds), *Verfassungsrecht der Schweiz – Droit constitutionnel suisse* (Zürich: Schulthess, 2001) p. 37; and A. L. Paulus, *Die internationale Gemeinschaft im Völkerrecht* (München: Beck, 2001). See also N. Tsagourias, 'The Will of the International Community as a Normative Source of International Law', in I. F. Dekker (ed.), *Governance and International Legal Theory* (Leiden/Boston: Martinus Nijhoff, 2004), p. 97. At the founding conference of the European Society of International Law, Martti Koskenniemi critically discussed the international community school as an example of the European imagination of an international order modelled on European values and ideas. See M. Koskenniemi, 'International Law in Europe: Between Tradition and Renewal' (2005) 16 *EJIL* 113 at 117: 'We Europeans share this intuition: the international world will be how we are. And we read international law in the image of our domestic legalism: multilateral treaties as legislation, international courts as an independent judiciary, the Security Council as the police. Today, that tradition is most visibly articulated in the debate – especially vocal in Germany – about the constitutionalisation of international law under the UN Charter.'

by Ernst-Ulrich Petersmann, insists on the need for integrating human rights into the law of the United Nations:

> As long as international law and the UN Charter focus on state sovereignty without effective protection of human rights and without judicial safeguards against the frequent abuses of government powers and violations of the rule of law, it seems misleading to denote the UN Charter as the 'constitution' of 'the peoples of the United Nations'.[26]

A related critique emphasises the 'democratic deficit', or lack of democratic participation, in international organisations.[27]

Most recently, this array of approaches was supplemented by an important contribution from political philosophy. Re-examining the Kantian vision of a world republic, Jürgen Habermas outlined the structure of a 'political constitution of a decentralized world society as a multi-level system of governance'.[28] Based on a dispassionate analysis of the present global situation, Habermas sees 'a conceptual possibility of a political multi-level system which, as a whole, is not a state but nevertheless able to safeguard, without a world government, on a supranational level peace and human rights . . . and to solve on a transnational level the many practical problems of "global domestic politics" (*Weltinnenpolitik*)'.[29] He describes a 'post-national constellation' of international affairs as supportive of a constitutionalisation of public

---

[26] See E. U. Petersmann, 'Constitutionalism, International Law and "We the Peoples of the United Nations"', in H. J. Cremer *et al.* (eds.), *Tradition und Weltoffenheit des Rechts: Festschrift für Helmut Steinberger* (Berlin: Springer, 2002), p. 291 at p. 303.

[27] See H. Brunkhorst, 'Globalizing Democracy without a State' (2002) 31 *Millennium – Journal of International Studies* 675.

[28] See J. Habermas, 'Hat die Konstitutionalisierung des Völkerrechts noch eine Chance?' [Does the constitutionalisation of international law still have a chance?], in J. Habermas, *Der gespaltene Westen* (Frankfurt am Main: Suhrkamp, 2004), p. 113 at p. 134. (English translation published as *The Divided West* (Cambridge: Polity Press, 2006).) For a critical discussion of Habermas's turn to constitutionalism in the context of his cosmopolitan position, see N. Walker, 'Making a World of Difference? Habermas, Cosmopolitanism and the Constitutionalisation of International Law', in O. A. Payrow Shabani (ed.), *The Practice of Law-making and the Problem of Difference* (Oxford: Oxford University Press, forthcoming).

[29] Habermas, *Der gespaltene Westen*, p. 143, see also p. 159 *et seq*. For the possibility of a global constitution without a (global) state, see Fassbender, 'The United Nations', 558: 'Having untied the bond between state and constitution, one may also apply the term in the realm of universal international law without necessarily being a proponent of a "world state". An international constitution so understood is not bound to put an end to interstate relations based on international law.'

international law[30] and agrees with this writer that in that constitutional process the UN Charter is of central importance.[31] In Habermas' view, the constitutionalisation of international law is a complementary project of cosmopolitanism – a way to renew or sustain the cosmopolitan project itself at a time in which it is threatened by alternative visions of world order such as a US hegemonic liberalism or a global Hobbesian order.

Different constitutions: fundamental rules and principles, rules not based on state consent, *jus cogens*

In what seems to be the book that introduced the notion of constitution into the doctrine of international law, Alfred Verdross in 1926 used the word to describe 'those norms which deal with the structure and subdivision of, and the distribution of spheres of jurisdiction in, a community'.[32] Accordingly, Verdross held that the constitution of the international legal community was composed of the fundamental rules and principles of international law determining its sources, subjects and application, and the jurisdiction allocated by that law to the individual states. Similarly, Tomuschat said much later, in 1993:

> Together with the rules on discharge of the executive and the judicial functions, the rules on law-making form the constitution of any system of governance. All these sets of prescriptions can be logically characterized as meta-rules, rules on how the bulk of other rules are produced, how they enter into force, how they are implemented and who, in case of differences over their interpretation and application, is empowered to settle an ensuing dispute.[33]

[30] See Habermas, *Der gespaltene Westen*, p. 176.
[31] See text accompanying n. 68 below.
[32] See Verdross, *Die Verfassung der Völkerrechtsgemeinschaft*, v.
[33] See Tomuschat, 'Obligations', 216. See also Simma, 'From Bilateralism', 262 ('the basic norms of the Charter as the constitutional law of the universal international community'), and Allott, 'The Concept of International Law', 37 and 75 *et seq.*, respectively: '*International constitutional law* is what some older writers called the "necessary" law of nations. It contains the structural legal relations which are intrinsic to the co-existence of all kinds of subordinate societies. It confers on artificial legal persons, including the state-societies, the capacity to act as parties to international legal relations … The geographical and material distribution of constitutional authority among subordinate legal systems cannot finally be determined by those legal systems themselves, but only by a superordinate legal system, namely international constitutional law … International constitutional law determines the legal relationship of the subordinate public realms.'

Clearly, this definition was influenced by H. L. A. Hart's distinction between 'primary' and 'secondary' rules, the latter being understood as 'rules about rules'.[34]

From that perspective, international constitutional law embodies rules and principles of international law distinguished from others because of their fundamental character. Those rules and principles are either formal in nature (such as the rules defining the subjects and sources of international law), or substantive (such as the principle of sovereign equality of states, the principle of self-determination of peoples, or the ban on the use of force).[35] The exact delimitation of a constitutional law of the international community so perceived varies from author to author. More or less, the respective rules belong to what, in analogy to the structure of nineteenth-century civil codes such as the German code (*Bürgerliches Gesetzbuch*) enacted in 1896,[36] we could call the 'general part' (*allgemeiner Teil*) of international law. They address issues pertinent to the 'foundation of the law of nations', as the first chapter of the introduction to Oppenheim/Lauterpacht's treatise was entitled,[37] compared to subject specific sections such as the law of the sea, the law of diplomatic relations, or environmental law.

However, what is the specific value of such a terminology? What does it tell us apart from what we all know by intuition – that some rules of international law are of a 'basic character' and therefore more important than others? Or does the constitutional language mainly have an instructive purpose, helping us to distinguish various types of rules,

---

[34] See H. L. A. Hart, *The Concept of Law* (Oxford: Clarendon, 1961), ch. V: 'Law as the Union of Primary and Secondary Rules', at p. 92: 'Thus they [the secondary rules] may all be said to be on a different level from the primary rules [of obligation], for they are all *about* such rules; in the sense that while primary rules are concerned with the actions that individuals must or must not do, these secondary rules are all concerned with the primary rules themselves. They specify the ways in which the primary rules may be conclusively ascertained, introduced, eliminated, varied, and the fact of their violation conclusively determined.'

[35] For an authoritative description of fundamental principles of a substantive character, see the Declaration on Principles of International Law concerning Friendly Relations and Co-operation among States in accordance with the Charter of the United Nations, Annex to UN General Assembly Resolution 2625 (XXV) of October 24, 1970; *United Nations Year Book 24* (1970), p. 788. The principles in question are also being addressed as 'the founding principles of the international legal order'. See C. Tomuschat, 'International Law', 9 at 161 *et seq.*

[36] *Bürgerliches Gesetzbuch* of 18 August 1896; Reichsgesetzblatt 1896, p. 195.

[37] See L. Oppenheim, *International Law: A Treatise, Vol. I: Peace*, H. Lauterpacht (ed.), 8th edn (London: Longman, Green & Co., 1955), p. 3.

and thus better understand the substance of the international law of our time?

Some authors do not stop here but emphasise, as the principal feature of international constitutional rules, their non-consensual character. Consider this statement by Tomuschat: 'States live, as from their birth, within a legal framework of a limited number of basic rules which determines their basic rights and obligations *with or without their will* . . . One may call this framework . . . the constitution of the international community.'[38] According to that view, the international constitution is the entirety of those basic rules – whether formal or substantive – which every state is bound to observe irrespective of its own will, due to its membership in the international community. Those rules are distinguished from so-called 'contingent' (i.e. accidental or non-essential) prescriptions that 'in the same way as traffic rules on left-hand or right-hand driving, must be determined for the sake of legal clarity and avoiding disorder'.[39] In the case of 'contingent' rules, state consent is said to be still the relevant basis of obligation, whereas constitutional prescriptions are determined by community interests, which may allow for at least some degree of majoritarianism.

This concept borders on another which sees the rules of *jus cogens* (or peremptory norms of international law) as the heart of an international constitution – i.e. in the words of the Vienna Convention on the Law of Treaties, rules 'accepted and recognized by the international community of States as a whole . . . from which no derogation is permitted and which can be modified only by subsequent norm[s] of general international law having the same character'.[40] Rules of *jus cogens* are 'meta-rules' as described by Tomuschat. They are rules about rules because they control the admissibility and validity of rules states want to make part of a treaty.

At the same time, *jus cogens* rules are 'higher law' (a feature generally characteristic of national constitutional law in comparison with other, 'ordinary' law) because they place certain norms beyond the reach of states when states, bilaterally or multilaterally, exercise their treaty-making (i.e. law-making) function. In that sense, Antonio Cassese noted that with *jus*

---

[38] See Tomuschat, 'Obligations', 211 (emphasis added).

[39] *Ibid.*, 286. Similarly, Allott, 'The Concept of International Law', 37 and 75, respectively, distinguishes between 'international constitutional law' and 'international public law'.

[40] See Article 53 of the 1969 Vienna Convention on the Law of Treaties, UNTS 1155, p. 331. For a recent re-evaluation of the concept of *jus cogens*, see C. Tomuschat and J.-M. Thouvenin (eds.), *The Fundamental Rules of the International Legal Order: Jus Cogens and Obligations Erga Omnes* (Leiden/Boston: Martinus Nijhoff, 2006).

cogens, 'a body of supreme or "constitutional" principles was created'[41], and Tomuschat referred to norms of *jus cogens* as belonging to 'a class of legal precepts which is hierarchically superior to "ordinary" rules of international law, precepts which cannot even be brushed aside, or derogated from, by the sovereign will of two or more States as long as the international community upholds the values encapsulated in them'.[42]

It is well known that in recent years the concept of *jus cogens* has gained importance in fields other than the law of treaties, in particular in international criminal law,[43] the law of sovereign immunity of states and state officials,[44] the determination of universal criminal jurisdiction,[45] the recognition of states[46] and the law of state responsibility.[47] Switzerland is the first country which has incorporated the concept into its constitutional law. Articles 193 and 194 of the revised Swiss Federal Constitution of 1999 provide that amendments to the Constitution may not violate peremptory norms of international law.[48]

The *jus cogens* perspective of international constitutional law is a particularly value-orientated one because all the rules presently recognised as *jus cogens* (in the first place, the prohibitions on genocide, aggression, slavery and of trading in human beings, and the right of peoples to self-determination) are substantive in nature and have a human rights dimension, the latter accounting mainly for the use that the International Criminal Tribunals for the former Yugoslavia and for Rwanda have made of *jus cogens* arguments.[49] *Jus cogens*, one could say, is a sort of Decalogue of a secularised world, a minimal code of behaviour that can be condensed into one rule: 'Thou shalt not do other human beings terrible wrongs!' Whilst this Decalogue is in accordance

---

[41] See A. Cassese, *International Law* 2nd edn (Oxford: Oxford University Press, 2005), p. 202.

[42] See C. Tomuschat, 'Reconceptualizing the Debate on *Jus Cogens* and Obligations *Erga Omnes* – Concluding Observations', in Tomuschat and Thouvenin, *The Fundamental Rules*, p. 425

[43] Cassese, *International Law*, p. 203, p. 206 *et seq.*

[44] *Ibid.*, p. 208. See also O. Dörr, 'Staatliche Immunität auf dem Rückzug?' (2003) 41 *Archiv des Völkerrechts* 201 at 214 *et seq.*

[45] See Cassese, *International Law*, p. 208.   [46] *Ibid.*, p. 207.

[47] See Articles 26, 40, 41 and 50 of the International Law Commission (ILC) Articles on the Responsibility of States for Internationally Wrongful Acts of July 26, 2001, UN Doc. A/CN.4/L.602/Rev.1 (2001) and UN Doc. A/Res/56/83 (2001) (Annex).

[48] See *Bundesverfassung der Schweizerischen Eidgenossenschaft* of 18 April 1999.

[49] See B. Fassbender, 'Der Schutz der Menschenrechte als zentraler Inhalt des völkerrechtlichen Gemeinwohls' (2003) 30 *Europäische Grundrechte Zeitschrift* 1 at 5 *et seq.*

with contemporary 'Western' values, the criticism that it is *only* reflecting such values is unfounded. It was after all the developing countries and the socialist states who advocated the concept of *jus cogens* against the opposition or scepticism of the West.[50]

There is a partial substantive identity of *jus cogens* and obligations *erga omnes* which, as is well known, the ICJ described as obligations 'towards the international community as a whole'.[51] The category of obligations *erga omnes* was advanced to give states which according to traditional international law were not affected by a certain breach of a rule, 'a legal interest in their protection'.[52] This way, pivotal community values should be safeguarded in the absence of effective community organs. The Court gave a number of examples of such obligations *erga omnes*, including the prohibition of acts of aggression and genocide; 'the principles and rules concerning the basic rights of the human person, including protection from slavery and discrimination';[53] and the right of self-determination.[54] A related third concept, 'international crimes of states', which once had been supported by the ILC,[55] was eventually

---

[50] See Cassese, *International Law*, p. 199 *et seq.*

[51] See *Barcelona Traction, Light and Power Co. Ltd (Belgium v. Spain)*, New Application: 1962, Judgment of 5 February 1970 (1970) ICJ Rep. 3, at 32, paras. 33–4, and *East Timor (Portugal v. Australia)*, Judgment of 30 June 1995, (1995) ICJ Rep. 90 at 102, para. 29. See also Article 48, para. 1(b), and Article 54 of the ILC Articles on the Responsibility of States for Internationally Wrongful Acts of 26 July 2001, UN Doc. A/CN.4/L.602/Rev.1 (2001) and UN Doc. A/Res/56/83 (2001) (annex).

[52] See *Barcelona Traction, Light and Power Co. Ltd (Belgium v. Spain)*, New Application: 1962, Judgment of 5 February 1970 (1970) ICJ Rep. 3 at 32, para. 33.

[53] *Ibid.*, para. 34.

[54] See *East Timor (Portugal v. Australia)*, Judgment of 30 June 1995 (1995) ICJ Rep. 90 at 102, para. 29.

[55] Article 19(2) of the Draft Articles on State Responsibility (Part 1) adopted by the ILC on first reading on 25 July 1980, defined an 'international crime' as follows: 'An internationally wrongful act which results from the breach by a State of an international obligation so essential for the protection of fundamental interests of the international community that its breach is recognized as a crime by that community as a whole constitutes an international crime.' Report of the ILC, UN General Assembly Official Records, Supp. No. 10, UN Doc. A/35/10 (1980), ILC Y.B. 2 (1980), pt. 2, 30, 32. For discussion, see J. H. H. Weiler, A. Cassese, M. Spinedi, *et al.* (eds.), *International Crimes of States: A Critical Analysis of the ILC's Draft Article 19 on State Responsibility* (Berlin: De Gruyter, 1989), and A. de Hoogh, *Obligations Erga Omnes and International Crimes: A Theoretical Inquiry into the Implementation and Enforcement of the International Responsibility of States* (The Hague: Kluwer, 1996).

abandoned by the Commission when it accepted the proposals of its Special Rapporteur, Professor James Crawford.[56]

What do these different approaches have in common? The international constitutionalism supported by them is, one can say, a 'progressive' movement – 'progressive' in the sense that the UN Charter speaks of the 'progressive development of international law'[57] – which aims at fostering international cooperation by consolidating the substantive legal ties between states, as well as the organisational structures of the international community built in the past. The idea of a constitution in international law is summoned as an abbreviation for an increasingly differentiated and also hierarchical law, and as a symbol of a (political) unity which eventually shall be realised on a global scale. This implies that any person who is basically satisfied with the present state of affairs, or who insists on preserving the independence of the individual state vis-à-vis the international community as much as possible, has no reason to refer to the notion of an international constitution.[58]

The relative success of the 'international community school' (Mosler, Tomuschat, Simma) is understandable because this school (unlike, for instance, the New Haven approach) stays within the limits of 'mainstream' legal thought. Rooted in positivism and determined not to lose touch with actual state practice, but at the same time cautiously idealistic, it seeks to develop the international legal system towards greater cohesion and effectiveness. This tension causes a certain doctrinal improvisation, and even an indecisiveness, that cannot satisfy those looking for a clear and convincing theoretical foundation upon which the concept of an international constitution could rest. Characteristically, authors belonging to that school like to compare the constitution of the international community with that of the UK, which has grown in stages and cannot be found in a single document.[59] In consequence, the content of a constitutional law as part of international law remains indistinct, and so do the legal consequences, if

---

[56] For an analysis of the 2001 draft articles by the Special Rapporteur, see J. Crawford, *The International Law Commission's Articles on State Responsibility: Introduction, Text and Commentaries* (Cambridge: Cambridge University Press, 2002).

[57] Article 13(1)(a) UN Charter.

[58] These last sentences have partly been taken from my 1998 article, 'The United Nations', 552. This idea of constitutionalism as a 'progressive' movement is critically discussed by Walker, 'Making a World of Difference?', section 4(b).

[59] See, e.g., Tomuschat, 'International Law', at 88.

there are any, of characterising a specific rule as constitutional rules.[60] In particular, the supremacy of international constitutional law in a hierarchy of norms of international law is only a vague concept. Indeed, for the authors of the international community school the symbolic value of the constitutional terminology prevails; 'constitution' is a reality or, at least, a necessity deriving from the high degree of interdependence and integration between peoples and states.

Perhaps this indistinct and vague character of that which is addressed as international constitutional law is a true representation of international law as it stands, i.e. an international law characterised by the contradictions and tensions mentioned at the beginning of this chapter. Ulrich Scheuner, in the last century one of Germany's most prominent and influential scholars of constitutional and international law, once remarked that, as law has always a conservative and preserving tendency, 'the interpretation of the foundations of the international community by international law will usually lag behind real developments'. By way of example, Scheuner mentioned the long clinging of legal writers to imperial and curial ideas in the late middle ages, in spite of the real formation of a system of sovereign states. He also contrasted the contemporary attachment to the concept of equal sovereignty with the 'reality of transformed notions and diverse constellations of international power'.[61] It may well be that present-day international law is equally lagging behind the reality of the international system. In other words, the international community may in fact have advanced towards its constitutionalisation more rapidly than the doctrine of international law and the common wisdom of governments have perceived. Mainstream international law may be defending a world already gone.

The UN Charter as constitution of the international community

In my own work, I have tried to give the idea of an international constitutional law a clearer and more concrete meaning by closely

---

[60] See explicitly Tomuschat, 'International Law', at 88: '[A substantive concept of constitution] constitutes no more than an academic research tool suited to focus attention on the substantive specificities of a particular group of legal norms. *No additional legal consequences may be attached to the characterization of a rule of international law as pertaining* ratione materiae *to the constitution of humankind.*' (Emphasis added.)

[61] See U. Scheuner, 'Die grossen Friedensschlüsse als Grundlage der europäischen Staatenordnung zwischen 1648 and 1815' (1964), in *Idem, Schriften zum Völkerrecht*, C. Tomuschat (ed.) (Berlin: Duncker & Humblot, 1984), p. 349 at n. 1.

associating it with the United Nations Charter.[62] Drawing especially on the writings of Verdross, I have suggested that the Charter, although it was formally created as a treaty, is characterised by a constitutional quality which in the course of the last 50 years has been confirmed and strengthened in such a way that today the instrument must be referred to as the (substantive and formal) constitution of the international community.[63] I have argued that the Charter shows a number of strong constitutional features;[64] in particular, it includes rules about how the basic functions of governance are performed in the international community, that is to say, how and by whom the law is made and applied, and how and by whom legal claims are adjudicated.[65] The Charter also establishes a hierarchy of norms in international law (Article 103). Further, I have tried to demonstrate that by understanding the Charter as a constitution we gain a standard allowing adequate (legal) solutions of issues such as the interpretation of the Charter, the relationship between its law and 'general international law', the meaning of state sovereignty in contemporary international law,[66] UN reform, or the question of the extent to which the Security Council is bound by international law.

Thomas Franck essentially endorsed these views when he wrote, in 2003:

> Perpetuity, indelibleness, primacy, and institutional autochthony: these four characteristics of the UN Charter relate that unique treaty more proximately to a constitution than to an ordinary contractual normative arrangement. But does it make a difference? Indeed it does. Whether or not the Charter is a constitution affects the way in which the norms of systemic interaction are to be interpreted by the judiciary, the political organs and by the Secretary-General ... [T]he question – is the UN Charter a constitution? – is not one of purely theoretical interest ... Indeed, how it is answered may well determine the ability of the Organization to continue to reinvent itself in the face of new challenges,

---

[62] To borrow language from Walker, this was an effort to invoke the United Nations [Charter] 'as a point of reference for the work of reform and re-imagination of international constitutionalism' and to create, on the global level, 'a suitably focused context of action'. See 'Making a World of Difference?', section 4(b).

[63] See Fassbender, 'The United Nations', 531 *et seq.*   [64] See *ibid.*, 573–84.

[65] For an exposition of the 'main functions of governance' of the international community, see Tomuschat, 'International Law', Part III (pp. 305–433).

[66] See Fassbender, 'Sovereignty and Constitutionalism'.

thereby assuring its enduring relevance to the needs of states and the emergence of an international community.[67]

In his recent book 'The Divided West', Habermas has also taken up my analytical effort by identifying three 'normative innovations' which primarily provide the UN Charter with a constitutional quality and make it possible to interpret the Charter as a global constitution: (1) the explicit combination of the goal of safeguarding world peace and a human rights policy; (2) the connection of the prohibition of the use of force with a realistic threat of sanctions and criminal prosecution; and (3) the inclusiveness of the United Nations and the universality of UN law.[68] Habermas concluded that the UN Charter 'is a framework in which UN member states no longer *must* understand themselves exclusively as subjects bringing forth international treaties; they rather can now perceive themselves, together with their citizens, as the constituent parts of a politically constituted world society'.[69]

Today, the outstanding importance of the UN Charter in the international legal order is generally accepted in legal literature. As Macdonald had already remarked in 1988, 'the majority of international lawyers would probably classify the Charter as something more than a treaty yet less than a world constitution'.[70] Dupuy called the Charter 'un traité sans équivalent', 'un acte fondateur, constitutif d'un nouvel ordre international'.[71] In even stronger, and laconic, language, Dinstein said: 'The status of the UN Charter as the equivalent of a constitution of the international community is undeniable at the present juncture.'[72]

---

[67] See T. M. Franck, 'Is the U.N. Charter a Constitution?', in J. Abr. Frowein *et al.* (eds.), *Verhandeln für den Frieden – Negotiating for Peace: Liber Amicorum Tono Eitel* (Berlin: Springer, 2003), p. 95 at pp. 102, 106. See also R. St. J. Macdonald, 'The International Community as a Legal Community', in Macdonald and Johnston (eds.), *Towards World Constitutionalism*, p. 853 at 859–68 (describing characteristical features of the UN Charter as 'the global constitution').

[68] Habermas, *Der gespaltene Westen*, p. 159.

[69] *Ibid.* ('Nach meiner Auffassung stellt die UN-Charta einen Rahmen bereit, worin sich die Mitgliedstaaten nicht länger nur als Subjekte völkerrechtlicher Verträge verstehen *müssen*; zusammen mit ihren Bürgern können sie sich nun als die konstituierenden Träger einer politisch verfassten Weltgesellschaft erkennen.')

[70] See R. St. J. Macdonald, 'The Charter of the United Nations and the Development of Fundamental Principles of International Law', in Bin Cheng and E. D. Brown (eds.), *Contemporary Problems of International Law: Essays in Honour of Georg Schwarzenberger on his Eightieth Birthday* (London: Stevens & Sons, 1988), p. 196 at p. 197.

[71] See Dupuy, 'L'unité de l'ordre', 217.

[72] See Y. Dinstein, 'Review of *The Charter of the United Nations: A Commentary* (2nd edn, 2002)' (2004) 98 *AJIL* 371.

Almost all authors who use constitutional language refer in one way or another to the Charter; and there is a tradition in political speech and legal writing of speaking of the Charter as a constitution. Consider, for instance, the following statement by McNair in his *Law of Treaties* of 1961:

> [T]he Charter … is the nearest approach to legislation by the whole community of States that has yet been realised. Our submission is that those of its provisions which purport to create legal rights and duties possess a constitutive or semi-legislative character, with the result that member States cannot 'contract out of' them or derogate from them by treaties made between them, and that any treaty whereby they attempted to produce this effect would be void.[73]

This statement draws our attention to the problem of the legal consequences of attributing to the Charter a constitutional quality. In that respect, McNair did not go beyond what is expressly provided for in Article 103 of the Charter. He did not suggest, as in fact I do, that the Charter, as the constitution of the international community, is the supporting frame of all international law and the highest layer in a hierarchy of norms of international law leaving no room for a category of 'general international law' existing independently beside the Charter.[74]

A principal reason for my suggesting that the UN Charter must be understood as *the* constitution of the international community was the intention to get 'out of the fog' of the indistinct constitutional rhetoric by turning to one visible document as an authoritative statement of the fundamental rights and responsibilities of the members of the international community and the values to which this community is committed, a document which is also the basis of the most important community institutions.[75] I have also pointed out that there is no irreconcilable contradiction between the idea of such a written constitution and that of a more inclusive constitutional process. Additionally, I have not overlooked, or kept quiet about, the shortcomings of the Charter as a constitution, in particular its limitations with respect to a definition of the basic rights of the individual ('international bill of rights'), and the concomitant necessity to see the Charter together with other customary and treaty law of a

---

[73] See A. D. McNair, *Law of Treaties* (Oxford: Clarendon Press, 1961), p. 217. See also I. Brownlie, 'The United Nations Charter and the Use of Force, 1945–1985', in A. Cassese (ed.), *The Current Legal Regulation of the Use of Force* (Dordrecht, The Netherlands: M. Nijhoff, 1986), p. 491 at p. 495.

[74] See Fassbender, 'The United Nations', 585.   [75] See *ibid.*, 616 *et seq.*

fundamental nature which I called the 'constitutional by-laws' of the international community, such as the two International Covenants on Human Rights, the Convention on the Elimination of all Forms of Racial Discrimination, the Convention on the Prevention and Punishment of the Crime of Genocide, and the Rome Statute of the International Criminal Court (ICC).[76]

Further, I have tried to explain that addressing the UN Charter as a constitution does not mean to equate the Charter with a state constitution, such as that of the United States of America or the French Republic, but that the constitutional idea in international law must be understood as an autonomous concept rather than an extrapolation of national constitutional law, or the constitutional law of a particular state.[77] In accordance with the idea of subsidiarity as a principle regulating the allocation of competencies in a multilevel system of governance, a constitution of the international community could, and need not, replicate a national constitution. Instead, its content depends on the specific tasks and responsibilities of the international community. As those tasks and responsibilities are different from those of a national body politic as organised for civil rule and government, the respective constitutional rules must differ. In particular, the task of maintaining and restoring international peace, i.e. peace between independent political communities, is a task peculiar to the international community. Compared to national constitutionalism, international constitutionalism is not 'lite'[78] but simply different.

However, an established notion such as 'constitution' is malleable only up to a certain degree. It cannot be adapted or extended at will. Since the American and the French Revolution, and notwithstanding the

---

[76] See *ibid.*, 588 *et seq.* An important interpretation of the Charter in the wider context of such fundamental treaty law is the Declaration on Principles of International Law concerning Friendly Relations and Co-operation among States in accordance with the Charter of the United Nations (Annex to UN General Assembly Res. 2625 (XXV) of 24 October 1970) (1970) 24 *UN Year Book* 788.

[77] See Fassbender, 'The United Nations', 572. For a thoughtful analysis of the relationship of state and constitution, which reflects much of the great tradition of the German *Staatslehre* of the nineteenth and twentieth centuries, see J. Isensee, 'Staat und Verfassung', in J. Isensee and P. Kirchhof (eds.), 2 *Handbuch des Staatsrechts der Bundesrepublik Deutschland*, 3rd edn (Heidelberg: C. F. Müller, 2004), p. 3. For a brief narrative of the idea of the modern state constitution, see H. Hofmann, 'Zu Entstehung, Entwicklung und Krise des Verfassungsbegriffs', in A. Blankenagel *et al.* (eds.), *Verfassung im Diskurs der Welt: Liber Amicorum für Peter Häberle zum siebzigsten Geburtstag* (Tübingen: Mohr Siebeck, 2004), p. 157.

[78] See Klabbers, 'Constitutionalism lite'.

English exception, Western political thinking associates the notion of 'constitution' not only with a system of fundamental principles according to which a state is governed, but also with a document embodying these principles and claiming superiority over all other domestic law. Therefore, it is doubtful whether a concept of a fragmented international constitution – a constitution not unified by a central text such as the UN Charter – not enjoying a superior rank, has a chance of succeeding.

One may add that a certain gap between constitutional rules and constitutional reality is not unusual in the case of state constitutions too. For that reason, the argument that, for instance, the Security Council actually has not played the role provided for it in the Charter, or the Economic and Social Council did not become the centre of international economic and social cooperation envisaged by Chapters IX and X of the Charter, is not refuting a constitutional qualification of the Charter.

Lastly, it is a profound misunderstanding to equate the advancement of the constitutional idea in international law with a weakening of the institution of the independent state. To assume the existence of a constitution of the international community does not mean to put the state in new, and necessarily more restraining, legal chains. On the contrary, it is that constitution which protects the legal authority and autonomy of every state against unlawful interventions by other states and international organisations, similar to the protection of the fundamental rights and freedoms afforded to individual citizens by a state constitution.[79] It is the constitution of the international community which safeguards the entitlement of a state, and the people constituting it, to autonomous development and self-responsibility within the limits set by international law.

However, so far most academics favouring the idea of international constitutionalism prefer to stay in conceptually vaguer worlds. Some of them seem to suffer a sort of reality shock when encountering a United Nations so far away from their ideals. Others, whilst acknowledging the necessity of a steadily intensifying degree of international organisation, remain captives of a legal training based on the cornerstone of the 'sovereign state'; in the legal map of the world that is in their minds they cannot find a proper place for a global constitution. This is also the reason for the comparative attractiveness of *jus cogens*. In its quality as

---

[79] See Fassbender, 'Sovereignty and Constitutionalism', 128 *et seq.*

customary international law, it can easily be fitted into the traditional system of sources of international law and, what is more important, the traditional idea of international law as a system of rules based on the consent of states. Accordingly, Charter law is ranked below *jus cogens*[80] – as if those peremptory norms, all of which are based on rules and values of the Charter, could survive without the Charter. The true relationship between the UN Charter and *jus cogens* is turned on its head.[81] Besides, as Cassese reminded us, 'the fact remains that undeniably, at least at the level of state-to-state relations, peremptory norms have largely remained a potentiality'.[82]

The hesitancy to give the UN Charter a central place in a constitutional structure of the international community is, however, also politically motivated. At the beginning of the twenty-first century, both the position and the role of the United Nations in international affairs find themselves under great stress. In turbulent times, the organisation faces an environment which is partly openly hostile, partly disinterested, and partly friendly but not actively supportive. Fundamental rules of the Charter, such as the ban on the use of force, are being challenged,[83] and the legitimacy of the Security Council, as the organisation's institutional backbone, is called into question. And yet, and in my opinion deplorably, the members of the international community are far away from uniting their strength in an effort to give new life and vigour to the Charter system of international governance.[84] To many, the Charter looks more and more like a monument of a distant past – an

---

[80] See *Application of the Convention on the Prevention and Punishment of the Crime of Genocide (Bosnia and Herzegovina v. Yugoslavia)*, Order of 7 October 1993, (1993) ICJ Rep. 407 at 440, para. 100 (Judge E. Lauterpacht, Separate Opinion). For critical discussion, see Fassbender, 'The United Nations', 589 *et seq.*

[81] See also Dupuy, 'L'unité de l'ordre', 307.

[82] See Cassese, *International Law*, pp. 210, 202: 'So far no state practice proper has developed with the attendant *opinio juris* or *opinio necessitatis* (that is, legal conviction) of the peremptory character of a specific norm. In particular, no dispute has arisen between states as to the *jus cogens* nature of a specific rule. Nor have one or more states insisted on the peremptory nature of a rule in a dispute with other states . . . Nor has any international tribunal, let alone the ICJ, settled any dispute revolving around the question of whether or not a specific rule must be regarded as belonging to the corpus of norms under discussion.'

[83] See B. Fassbender, 'Die Gegenwartskrise des völkerrechtlichen Gewaltverbotes vor dem Hintergrund der geschichtlichen Entwicklung' (2004) 31 *Europäische Grundrechte-Zeitschrift* 241.

[84] See B. Fassbender, 'All Illusions Shattered? Looking Back on a Decade of Failed Attempts to Reform the UN Security Council' (2003) 7 *Max Planck UNYB* 183.

embodiment of an idea of multilateralism and collective security whose days are over. In this situation, how can one dare to regard the Charter as the foundation of the entire house of contemporary international law?

Philip Allott once remarked: 'Failing to recognize itself as a society, international society has not known that it has a constitution.'[85] The future of the constitutional understanding and effectiveness of the UN Charter – which is, I suggest, tantamount to the foreseeable future of constitutionalism in international law in general – will ultimately not depend on the interpretive and constructive efforts of legal science but on the fate of the United Nations itself. Only a strong political move, comparable to the founding of the UN in the constitutional moment of 1944–45, could reaffirm the Charter's claim to be the constitution of the international community. Perhaps the UN era is drawing to a close,[86] and only now, looking back, the peoples of the United Nations realise that they had a constitution.

The idea of a constitution of the international community will, however, survive because it is both indispensable as a legal device and unrivalled as a symbol of the unity of humankind realising its interdependent existence in *one world*. If the future landscape of international relations will know a legal order at all, as an order based on the principles of self-determination, autonomy and equality of all nations, a universal constitution will be an essential element of that order. And just as much as the idea of a constitution of the international community will survive, the contribution the UN Charter has made to this idea's development will be inextinguishable in the book of world history. As Habermas said, 'the League of Nations and the United Nations are great, even though risky and reversible, achievements on the arduous way to a political constitution of world society'.[87]

---

[85] See Allott, *Eunomia*, p. 418.

[86] For a description of possible alternatives to a constitutionalisation of international law as a continuation of the 'Kantian project', see Habermas, *Der gespaltene Westen*, p. 178 *et seq.* As such alternatives, the author identifies: (1) a US 'hegemonic liberalism'; (2) a 'neoliberal global market society' with marginalised states; (3) a 'postmarxist scenario of a scattered imperial rule without a capital'; and (4) a global *Grossraumordnung* based on the ideas of Carl Schmitt.

[87] See Habermas, *Der gespaltene Westen*, p. 145.

10

The never-ending closure: constitutionalism and international law

WOUTER WERNER

Introduction

Since the 1990s, the use of constitutional language has gained increasing popularity in international legal parlance. This increased popularity has made it difficult to come up with a single and coherent definition of 'international constitutionalism'. The vocabulary of constitutionalism has been used in different contexts and for different purposes, varying from in-depth critiques of existing international law[1] to attempts to explain the rise of international tribunals,[2] the revitalisation of international organisations,[3] the self-understanding of European organisations in terms of constitutionalism[4] or the development of a core of fundamental values in international law.[5] Moreover, well before the 1990s,

---

[1] See especially, P. Allott, *Eunomia: New Order for a New World Order*, 2nd edn (Oxford: Oxford University Press, 2001); P. Allott, *The Health of Nations, Society and Law Beyond the State* (Cambridge: Cambridge University Press, 2002). For a critique of the United Nations system from a constitutionalist perspective, see E.-U. Petersmann, 'Time for a United Nations "Global Compact" for Integrating Human Rights into the Law of World Wide Organisations: Lessons from European Integration' (2002) 13 *EJIL* 621.

[2] See, for example, the positive evaluation of the phenomenon of 'judicial globalization' by A.-M. Slaughter, in 'A Global Community of Courts', (2003) 44 *Harvard Int LJ* 191 and 'Judicial Globalization' (2000) 40 *Va JIL* 1103.

[3] M. Kumm, 'The Legitimacy of International Law: A Constitutionalist Framework of Analysis' (2004) 15 *EJIL* 907.

[4] See the current debate of the 'European Constitution' and the characterisation of the founding treaties as a 'constitutional charter' by the Court of Justice of the European Communities (ECJ) in Case 294/83, *Parti Ecologiste 'Les Verts' v. European Parliament* [1986] ECR 1357, as well as the characterisation of the European Convention of Human Rights (ECHR) as a 'constitution' by the European Court of Human Rights (ECtHR); (see section 1.2).

[5] E. De Wet, 'The Value System of the International Community', (2006) 19 *LJIL* 611.

international lawyers already used the term 'constitution' to refer to the founding treaties of international organisations.[6]

In this chapter, I will not deal with all these different ways in which the language of constitutionalism is used. Rather, I will focus on one – albeit still broad – way in which it is employed in international law: as an attempt to explain existing developments in international law in terms borrowed from domestic constitutionalism, with the aim of furthering a normative agenda of internationalism, integration and legal control of politics. This way of using the language of constitutionalism is based on two desiderata: to remain within the boundaries of positive law, and to contribute to a normative, internationalist project.[7] While international constitutionalism thus aims to uphold the distinction between 'law as it is' and 'law as it ought to be', it also tries to make sense of developments in international law from a clear normative preference: the furtherance of legal unity, international integration and fundamental human rights, an anti-nationalistic understanding of sovereignty, a relaxation of the requirement of state consent and the regulation of political power through legal institutions.[8]

The project of international constitutionalism under discussion in this chapter can be illustrated by means of Allot's distinction between three types of constitution. According to Allot, a distinction can be made between the legal constitution ('a structure and system of retained acts of will'), the real constitution ('the constitution as actualised in the current social process, a structure and a system of power') and the ideal constitution ('a constitution as it presents to society an idea of what society might be').[9] The project of constitutionalism discussed in this chapter can be understood as an attempt to (1) argue in favour of the

---

[6] H. G. Schermers and N. Blokker, *International Institutional Law: Unity Within Diversity* (The Hague: Kluwer Law International, 1995).

[7] The way in which 'mainstream' international legal methodology oscillates between facts and norms, positivism and naturalism, consent and substantive values has been discussed extensively by M. Koskenniemi, *From Apology to Utopia: The Structure of International Legal Argument* (Helsinki: Finnish Lawyers' Publishing Company, 1989). In M. Koskenniemi, *The Gentle Civilizer of Nations: The Rise and Fall of International Law, 1870–1960* (Cambridge: Cambridge University Press, 2002), Koskenniemi discusses the liberal, internationalist sensitivities that were held by some of the founding fathers of modern international law: sensitivities that are not unknown to many advocates of modern constitutionalism.

[8] For a more elaborate discussion of these (not necessarily compatible) desiderata see section 3.

[9] Allott, *Eunomia*, pp. 135, 136.

existence of a legal constitution in international law, which is (2) linked to the constitution in terms of power and social process and (3) points towards the ideals articulated in the ideal constitution. As a result one often finds – in the words of one of the strongest advocates of international constitutionalism – 'a certain improvisation that cannot satisfy those looking for a clear and convincing foundation upon which the concept of an international constitution could rest'.[10] As will be demonstrated in section 4, below, the foundational problem is indeed one of the most important challenges for international constitutionalism.

In the following sections, the project of international constitutionalism will be analysed in more detail. The first section examines some of the developments in international law that have induced writers to adopt a constitutionalist perspective. The second section discusses some trends that do not seem to fit in a constitutionalist reading of international law as well as some alternative readings of the developments sketched in section 1. The third section takes up the normative side of constitutionalism: notwithstanding the existence of anti-constitutionalist trends and notwithstanding the critiques of constitutionalism, writers have advocated a constitutionalist reading of international law on normative grounds. Adoption of a constitutionalist perspective, they argue, contributes to legal control of international politics, legal unity and a foundation for international legal arguments. In section 4, these hopes of international constitutionalism are examined on the basis of lessons from constitutionalism in the domestic context, the critique of foundationalism in international legal theory and the practice of collective security.

1. Community interests and constitutionalism

The rise of international constitutionalism can partly be understood as an attempt to make sense of some (recent) developments in international law.[11] In his 1999 general course at the Hague Academy,

---

[10] B. Fassbender, 'The UN Charter as Constitution of the International Community' (1998) 36 *Columbia J Trans Law* 529 at 552.

[11] It should be noted, however, that constitutional arguments and a discussion of emerging constitutional structures have a longer history in international law. See, for example, James Brown Scott's discussion of 'an international law still of the future, in which law and morality shall be one and inseparable, in which States are created by and for human beings, and every principle of international conduct is to be tested by the good of the international community and not by the selfish standards of its more

Tomuschat presented these developments as progressive stages in the evolution of international law: from a law of coordination via a law of cooperation towards a legal order that comprises 'a comprehensive blueprint for social life'.[12] This 'comprehensive blueprint' not only serves the interests of states, but also the interests of other members of the international community. By taking up values such as human rights, democracy and good governance, Tomuschat argues, international law has fundamentally transformed itself: 'Instead of being a set of rules limiting and guiding States in their foreign policies, international law becomes a multi-faceted body of law that permeates all fields of life, wherever governments act for promoting a public purpose.'[13]

A few years earlier, Simma had characterised developments in international law in terms of an evolution from a civil law type of order between sovereign states towards a legal order where a variety of subjects are organised under an overarching legal structure (constitution) that upholds the interests of the international community as such. Simma characterised this development as a movement from bilateralism to the protection of so-called 'community interests'.[14] Although Simma did not deny the enduring relevance of bilateralism, state sovereignty and state consent in international law, he also identified legally protected interests of the international community as a whole. Such interests are the result of a 'consensus according to which respect for certain fundamental values is not to be left to the free disposition of States individually or *inter se* . . .', because 'what these interests have in common is that they go far beyond the interests held by States as such; rather, they correspond to the needs, hopes and fears of all human beings, and attempt to cope with problems the solution of which may be decisive

---

powerful and erring members': J. Brown Scott, *The Spanish Origin of International Law: Francisco De Vitoria and his Law of Nations* (London: Humphrey Milford, 1934), p. 11. Another example of a constitutionalist reading of international law can be found in the work of Sir Hersch Lauterpacht. For a discussion see, *inter alia*, Koskenniemi, *The Gentle Civilizer of Nations*, pp. 353–413 and also Koskenniemi's discussion of the continued relevance of Lauterpacht's work for contemporary constitutionalism in: M. Koskenniemi, 'Legal Cosmopolitanism: Tom Franck's Messianistic World' (2003) 35 *New York University Journal of International Law & Politics* 471–486.

[12] C. Tomuschat, 'International Law: Ensuring the Survival of Mankind on the Eve of a New Century' (1999) 281 *Recueil des cours* 63. See also C. Tomuschat, 'Obligations Arising for States Without or Against Their Will (1993–IV) 241 *Recueil des cours* 195–374.

[13] Tomuschat, 'International Law', 70

[14] B. Simma, 'From Bilateralism to Community Interest in International Law' (1994) 250 *Recueil des cours* 217.

for the survival of entire humankind'.[15] Such community interests can be found, *inter alia*, in the sphere of international peace and security, international environmental law, or in the sphere of human rights.[16]

However, neither the recognition of community values nor the inclusion of non-state actors as subjects of international law necessarily leads to a change in the deep structure of international law. What gives these developments their specific importance from the standpoint of international constitutionalism is that they have stimulated different modes of legal reasoning; modes of reasoning that cannot – or can only with difficulty – be explained in terms of international law as an order based on the consent of states. Therefore, international constitutionalism attempts to explain these developments from a different perspective: from the perspective of a more encompassing 'international community' and an overarching constitutional structure. It would be beyond the scope of this chapter to give a complete overview of the different developments which have raised questions regarding the nature of international law. Therefore, I will leave aside some important issues such as the development of *erga omnes* obligations, the rules regarding state succession or the attempts to make sense of the notion of international crimes of states.[17] Instead, I will focus on two phenomena that

---

[15] Simma, 'From Bilateralism', at 233, 244. See also Cassese's characterisation of 'community obligations' as obligations possessing the following features: '(i) they are obligations protecting fundamental values . . .; (ii) they are obligations *erga omnes* . . .; (iii) they are attended by a correlative *right* that belongs to any State (or to any other *contracting* State, in case of obligations provided for in multilateral treaties; (iv) this right may be excercised by any other (contracting) State, whether or not it has been materially or morally injured by the violation; (v) the right is exercised *on behalf of the whole international community* (or the community of contracting States) to *safeguard fundamental values* of this community'. A. Cassese, *International Law* (Oxford: Oxford University Press, 2005), p. 16.

[16] By now, there is a rich body of literature on 'community interests' in international law. For an overview see, *inter alia*, J. Delbrück (ed.), *New Trends in International Lawmaking – International 'Legislation' in the Public Interest* (Berlin: Duncker and Humblot, 1997) and E. de Wet, 'The International Constitutional Order' (2006) 55 *ICLQ* 51.

[17] For a discussion, see Tomuschat, 'International Law'; Simma, 'From Bilateralism'; A. Peters, 'Compensatory Constitutionalism: The Function and Potential of Fundamental International Norms and Structures' (2006) 19 *LJIL* 579; S. Villapando, *L'émergence de la communauté internationale dans la responsabilité des Etats* (Paris: Presses Universitaires de France, 2005); A. de Hoogh, *Obligations Erga Omnes and International Crimes: A Theoretical Inquiry into the Implementation and Enforcement of the International Responsibility of States* (Leiden: Brill, 1996); A. Paulus, *Die Internationale Gemeinschaft Im Völkerrecht – Eine Untersuchung Zur Entwicklung Des Völkerrechts Im Zeitalter Der Globalisierung* (München: Beck, 2001).

are often invoked by advocates of a constitutionalist reading of international law: the attempts to establish a hierarchy in international law through the concept of *jus cogens*, and the creation of so-called 'world order treaties'. Both phenomena have been selected because they offer a good illustration of the essential role of the concept of the 'international community' in international constitutionalism.

A. Jus cogens

As may be recalled, the concept of *jus cogens* or peremptory norms was first introduced in the law of treaties. Its aim was to privilege some norms that protect essential community values by giving them a specific status vis-à-vis other norms of international law. According to Article 53 of the Vienna Convention on the Law of Treaties (VCLT), a treaty is void if, at the time of its conclusion, it conflicts with a peremptory norm of general international law, such as the prohibition on genocide, aggression or torture.[18] Article 64 of the same Convention adds that, if a new peremptory norm of general international law emerges, any existing treaty which is in conflict with that norm becomes void and terminates. Peremptory norms may also have other effects. It is by now generally accepted that *jus cogens* norms also invalidate other conflicting rules of international law (e.g. rules of a customary nature), whereas the impact of *jus cogens* norms has been felt in areas such as criminal law, the recognition of states, reservations to treaties and even domestic constitutional law.[19]

Peremptory norms thus limit the law-making capacity of states. This raises the question of how *jus cogens* norms are created, and how we should determine which norms have acquired the status of 'peremptory norms of general international law'. This question remains partly unresolved and, so far, it has proven difficult to come up with an exhaustive list of norms having a *jus cogens* character.

At first sight, Article 53 of the VCLT seems to give a purely consent-based answer to this question. It states:

> . . . a peremptory norm of general international law is a norm accepted
> and recognized by the international community of States as a whole as a
> norm from which no derogation is permitted and which can be modified

---

[18] For the text of Article 53 of the VCLT, see below.
[19] For a discussion of the impact of *jus cogens* norms outside the law of treaties see Cassese, 'International Law', pp. 198–212.

only by a subsequent norm of general international law having the same character.

This formulation seems to leave room for dissenting states, as it relies heavily on the free will of states. Advocates of a consensualist reading of international law, therefore, have interpreted Article 53 of the Vienna Convention as a provision that does not fundamentally challenge traditional international law. Danilenko, for example, has argued:

> [T]he acceptance of *jus cogens* by the international legal order does not automatically imply the introduction of a new international law-making technique based on majority rule. It is generally recognized that in order to acquire the quality of *jus cogens* a norm must first pass the normative tests for rules of 'general international law'. It is also established that, secondly, such a norm must be 'accepted and recognized' as a peremptory norm by 'the international community of states' as a whole. These requirements appear to provide the dissenting minority with ample opportunities to dissociate itself from both the binding quality and the peremptory character of a rule.[20]

However, advocates of a constitutional reading of international law generally take a different perspective on the creation and effect of peremptory norms. They argue that Article 53 should not be read as giving individual states the right to block the creation of *jus cogens* norms or the possibility to opt out.[21] Instead, the question, of whether a norm has obtained peremptory status, is answered in two – not necessarily compatible – ways: on the basis of the content of the norm and on the basis of the acceptance of a norm as peremptory by a majority of the 'most representative and important States'.

The importance of the *content* of a norm is emphasised by several writers, who hold that 'the superior legal force of a peremptory norm must be sought in its contents, inasmuch as it reflects common values essential for upholding peace and justice in the world'.[22] A clear illustration of this interpretation can also be found in a decision of the

---

[20] G. M. Danilenko, 'International *Jus Cogens*: Issues of Law-Making', (1991) 2 *EJIL* 42.

[21] See, for example, Simma's reading of the jurisprudence of the International Court of Justice, which leads him to the conclusion that, in the case of *jus cogens* norms: 'Persistent objection is regarded to be inadmissible or, in any case, not as leading to the effect desired by the objector.' Simma, 'From Bilateralism', 292.

[22] C. Tomuschat, 'Obligations for States without or against their Will' (1993 IV) 241 *Recueil des cours* 223. Tomuschat refers to several writers who have defended this interpretation of creation of *jus cogens* norms.

Hungarian Constitutional Court. In 1993, this court argued that the rules pertaining to the punishment of war crimes and crimes against humanity have a peremptory character, because 'these crimes threaten mankind and international co-existence in their foundations', whilst states that refuse to accept these norms 'may not participate in the international community'.[23]

The *recognition* of a norm as peremptory was stressed during the drafting of Article 53 of the VCLT. Thus the chair of the Drafting Committee argued that the creation of *jus cogens* norms is not conditional upon acceptance by all states. What is necessary, he argued, is that a very large majority of states, reflecting the 'essential components' of the international community, accepts the peremptory nature of a norm.[24] Similarly, the International Law Commission (ILC), in its 1976 report argued that Article 53 was not meant to give each state the power to block the emergence of a peremptory norm of international law. Rather, the development of a peremptory norm would require recognition 'by all the essential components of the international community'.[25]

The requirements of content and recognition reflect two different approaches to international law: an approach based on substantive values and an approach based on law-making by a privileged group of states. Yet, both approaches are often taken together in the notion of the 'international community'.[26] This notion then serves both as the embodiment of the fundamental values that peremptory norms aim to protect

---

[23] Quoted in Cassese, 'International Law', p. 203.

[24] See also his statement that: 'there was not question of requiring a rule to be accepted and recognized as peremptory by all States. It would be enough if a very large majority did so; that would mean that, if one State in isolation refused to accept the peremptory character of the rule, or if that State was supported by a very small number of States, the acceptance and recognition of the peremptory character of the rule by the international community as a whole would not be affected.' (1969) 50 *United Nations Conference on the Law of Treaties, Official Records*, First Session at 472.

[25] (1976) *YILC* 119. Note, however, that in its 1966 Report, the ILC also stressed the importance of the content of a norm. The *jus cogens* character of a norm, the ILC argued, does not lie in its form, but rather follows from 'the particular nature of the subject matter with which it deals ...'. Quoted in P. Weil, 'Towards Relative Normativity' (1983) 77 *AJIL* 413 at 425.

[26] A good example is Simma's discussion of *jus cogens* norms. In his 1994 general lecture, Simma first argues that *jus cogens* norms are based on 'recognition by the international community' and subsequently argues that the peremptory character of norms is derived from the elementary considerations of humanity: Simma, 'From Bilateralism', 292–3.

and as the entity that recognises those values; as the *idea* of humanity as well as the society that recognises the validity of this idea.[27]

B. World order or regional order treaties

World order or regional order treaties are characterised by two elements: a broad – and sometimes quasi-universal – membership, and the fact that they aim to protect community values that transcend the interests of individual states. Just as in the case of *jus cogens* norms, the idea of the international community thus plays a decisive role in the characterisation of world order treaties. Such treaties are accepted by a community of states (and non-state entities) and aim to protect fundamental community values such as peace and security, human dignity, the environment or economic development. An additional reason why world order treaties have been widely discussed by advocates of international constitutionalism is that they are increasingly enforced by international judicial or political organs and so limit the power of states to interpret their own obligations under international law.[28] These features have made it difficult to explain the creation and development of world order treaties exhaustively in terms of consensualism.

An example of this is the UN Charter. In section three, we will discuss in more detail the specific importance of the UN Charter for international constitutionalism. For now, it suffices to note that, in the words of Tomuschat, 'a State which becomes a member of the world organisation consents not just to a series of well-defined and easily identifiable obligations, it agrees to a changed status under international law'.[29] This changed status is particularly visible in the relation between member states and the Security Council (SC). Under the UN Charter, the SC enjoys powers that are akin to what Schmitt regarded as the core of the political: the determination of the public enemy as well as the means that

---

[27] As Tsagourias has argued in another context: '. . . the international community plays a normative but also empirically real constitutive function.' N. Tsagourias, 'The Will of the International Community as a Normative Source of International Law', in I. F. Dekker and W. G. Werner (eds.), *Governance and International Legal Theory* (Leiden: Brill, 2004), p. 97, at p. 100.

[28] The problem of auto-interpretation was one of the core issues in the work of one of the earlier advocates of international constitutionalism, Sir Hersch Lauterpacht. For a discussion of the importance of the problem of auto-interpretation in Lauterpacht's work see Koskenniemi, 'The Gentle Civilizer', pp. 353–411.

[29] C. Tomuschat, 'International Law', 249.

should be used to fight that enemy.[30] Of course, the wording of the Charter differs from the friend/enemy distinction used by Schmitt. The powers of the SC are not phrased in terms of a public enemy, but in terms of threats to the peace, breaches of the peace or acts of aggression. Yet, states formally endow the SC with the prerogative to determine what counts as threats to international peace and security and to determine what should be done about those threats. As a corollary of the protection formally offered by the SC, states put themselves under an obligation to carry out the decisions of the SC, even if those decisions may conflict with other international obligations (even obligations held towards non-members of the UN).[31] Moreover, the SC has successfully claimed direct authority vis-à-vis non-member states as well as vis-à-vis non-state entities. In several instances, the SC has not limited its resolutions to member states of the UN, but rather called *all* states to undertake certain actions.[32] In other instances, the SC has addressed non-state actors, either in the form of hortatory acts[33] or in the form of binding decisions.[34]

A second example of the way in which world order (or 'regional order') treaties can challenge a more traditional reading of international law can be found in the sphere of human rights. Already in 1978, the European Court of Human Rights declared the European Convention on Human Rights and Fundamental Freedoms to be of a constitutional nature.[35] In *Loizidou*, the Court once more stressed that the Convention

---

[30] For a definition of the political in terms of the friend/enemy distinction see C. Schmitt, *The Concept of the Political* (Chicago: Chicago University Press, 1996).

[31] Fassbender, 'The UN Charter', at 577, 593. However, see also the discussion as to whether UN law ranks below *jus cogens* in: *Application of the Convention on the Prevention and Punishment of the Crime of Genocide (Bosnia-Herzegovina v. Yugoslavia)*, Order of the Court on Provisional Measures, Judgment of 13 September 1993 (1993) ICJ Rep. 4 at 440, para. 100 (separate opinion of Lauterpacht).

[32] See, for example, the Resolutions imposing arms embargoes on Iraq: UN Doc. S/RES/661 (1990), UN Doc. S/RES/670 (1990); the territory of the former Yugoslavia, UN Doc. S/RES/713 (1991); or Serbia-Montenegro, UN Doc. S/RES/757 (1992).

[33] See, for example, UN Doc. S/RES/788 (1992) (on the situation in Liberia) addressed to 'all parties to the conflict and all others concerned'.

[34] See the discussion by Fassbender, 'The UN Charter', at 609. In this context it is interesting to note that already in the late ninteenth and early twentieth century constitutional arguments were linked to a move from sovereign equality to legalised hegemony, with a special role for great powers to act in the name of the common good. For a discussion see G. Simpson, *Great Powers and Outlaw States: Unequal Sovereigns in the International Legal Order* (Cambridge: Cambridge University Press, 2004), p. 123.

[35] *Ireland v. United Kingdom* (1978) 2 EHRR 25.

is more than a treaty between sovereign states. According to the Court, the Convention should rather be considered as a 'constitutional document of the European public order'.[36] This perspective on the European Convention induced the Court to deviate from some of the principles that normally apply in international law. Thus, in *Waite and Kennedy v. Germany*, it held that member states cannot grant immunity from legal proceedings to international organisations, if such immunity would jeopardise the rights protected under the European Convention. In its decision, the Court attached little value to the fact that the organisation in question, the European Space Agency, was set up after the coming into force of the European Convention.[37] Instead, the Court 'focussed on the state's responsibility for the protection of fundamental human rights norms, which is not affected by any rules of the law of treaties on the relationship between incompatible treaties'.[38]

In similar fashion, the Court deviated from the traditional rules on the effects of reservations to international treaties. Under the VCLT, reservations that go against the object and purpose of a particular (multilateral) treaty are inadmissible (Article 19). However, the law of treaties leaves it up to each state party to decide, 'individually and from its own standpoint',[39] whether it holds a reservation to be in accordance with the object and purpose of the treaty in question. In the cases of *Belilos*[40] and *Loizidou*,[41] the European Court of Human Rights set aside this approach towards the admissibility of reservations. The Court assumed the power to determine whether reservations are compatible with the object and purpose of the European Convention. Moreover, after dismissing the reservations made by Switzerland (in *Belilos*) and Turkey (in *Loizidou*), it held that both states were still bound by the Convention, irrespective of the validity of the reservation. The

---

[36] *Loizidou v. Turkey* (Preliminary Objections) – 15318/89 [1995] ECHR 10 (23 March 1995) para. 75.

[37] *Waite and Kennedy v. Germany* – 26083/94 [1999] ECHR 13 (18 February 1999). See also the discussion of this case by C. Walter, 'Constitutionalising (Inter)national Governance – Possibilities and Limits to the Development of an International Constitutional Law' (2001) 44 *GYIL* 170.

[38] For a discussion see, *inter alia*, de Wet, 'The Value System'.

[39] In the words of the ICJ: *Reservations to the Convention on the Prevention and Punishment of the Crime of Genocide*, Advisory Opinion of 28 May 1951, (1951) ICJ Rep. 26. See also Article 20 of the 1969 VCLT.

[40] *Belilos v. Switzerland*, Decision of 29 April 1988, (1988) ECHR (Ser: A.), No. 132.

[41] *Loizidou v. Turkey*, Preliminary Objections, 23 March 1995 (1995) ECHR (Ser: A.), No. 310.

underlying rationale for this deviation from the traditional approach towards reservations was spelled out by the Human Rights Committee (HRC). The HRC adopted the interpretation on the admissibility of reservations set out by the European Court, because the traditional approach was:

> ... inappropriate to address the problem of reservations to human rights treaties. Such treaties ... are not a web of inter-State exchanges of mutual obligations. They concern the endowment of individuals with rights ... Because of the special nature of human rights treaty law, the compatibility of a reservation with the object and purpose of the Covenant must be established objectively, by reference to legal principles, and the Committee is particularly well placed to perform this task.[42]

The approach propagated by the Committee is based on the special nature of human rights treaties and deviates from the inter-state perspective that underlies the Vienna Convention. Adoption of this approach, therefore, would imply significant changes in the legal regime on reservations.

However, as the ongoing discussion on the topic of reservations to (human rights) treaties demonstrates, the view of the Committee is still not generally accepted.[43] The more 'constitutionalist' reading of international human rights law is still challenged by more classical interpretations of the nature and function of international law.

2. Alternative narratives

From the foregoing, it can be inferred that international constitutionalism seeks to explain certain developments in international law in terms that deviate from a purely consensualist understanding of the international legal order. However, as was mentioned before, it would be a mistake to consider

---

[42] Human Rights Committee, General Comment 24 (52), General comment on issues relating to reservations made upon ratification or accession to the Covenant or the Optional Protocols thereto, or in relation to declarations under Article 41 of the Covenant, U.N. Doc. CCPR/C/21/Rev.1/Add.6 (1994). See also M. Koskenniemi and P. Leino, 'Fragmentation of International Law? Postmodern Anxieties', (2002) 15 *LJIL* 553. See also the rejection of the position taken by the Court and the Committee by France, the UK and the US and the discussion of this topic by the ILC, e.g. *Report of the International Law Commission, fifty-fifth session*, UN Doc. A/58/10 (2003), at ch. 8.

[43] Sixth Committee concludes consideration of report of International Law Commission, 7 November, 1997, GA/L/3085: http://www.scienceblog.com/community/older/archives/L/1997/B/un971633.html (accessed 12 July 2006). See also the discussion of this topic by the ILC, e.g. *Report of the International Law Commission, Fifty-Fifth session*, UN Doc. A/58/10 (2003), at ch. 8.

the use of constitutional language as merely an attempt to explain existing trends in international law. After all, it is also possible to point at phenomena that are difficult to reconcile with a constitutional reading of international law. Two of these phenomena will be discussed below: the continued violation of some fundamental norms of international law (including *jus cogens* norms) (section 2.A) and the position of the world's only superpower towards some world order treaties (section 2.B). Moreover, it is possible to interpret the rise of community values from a different perspective: not as a step towards the realisation of a benign international community, but as a development that offers to hegemonic powers possible justifications for the setting aside of the principles of state sovereignty and non-intervention (section 2.C).

A. Violations of fundamental norms

The most obvious challenge to a constitutional reading of international law is the fact that many of fundamental norms of international law are still violated in practice. Neither the emergence of peremptory norms nor the creation of world order treaties (including the supervisory bodies) have been able to prevent widespread violations of human rights and humanitarian law, armed conflicts, environmental degradation or even genocide. Neither has the often proclaimed official solidarity between rich and poor countries nor the adoption of social and economic rights prevented the persistence of world poverty. As the United Nations Development Programme has estimated, 831 million humans are chronically undernourished, while 1,197 million do not have access to safe water and 2,447 million do not have access to basic sanitation.[44] The endurance of world poverty and inequality is of particular relevance for international constitutionalism. It is plausible to assume that one of the causes of world poverty is the existence of a global structure that, in general, works to the advantage of rich countries and to the disadvantage of poor countries.[45] This global structure is manifested in the bargaining powers of rich and poor countries, and, consequently, in international legal rules and institutions. Thus, while some emphasise that international economic institutions rest on constitutional principles and

---

[44] T. Pogge, 'Recognised and Violated by International Law: The Human Rights of the Global Poor' (2005) 18 *LJIL* 717.

[45] For this argument, see T. Pogge, *World Poverty and Human Rights: Cosmopolitan Responsibilities and Reforms* (Cambridge: Polity Press, 2002).

aim to further community values, others have pointed out that those structures have reinforced world inequality. As Pogge has argued:

> We should expect that the design of the global institutional order reflects the shared interests of the governments, corporations and citizens of the affluent countries more than the interest in global poverty avoidance, insofar as these interests conflict . . . There is much evidence that the present rules of the game favour the affluent countries by allowing them to continue protecting their markets through quotas, tariffs, anti-dumping duties, export credits and subsidies to domestic producers in ways poor countries are not permitted, or cannot afford to match. Other important examples include the WTO regulations of cross-border investment and intellectual property rights.[46]

Although this is a far cry from the statement that 'all the existing law-making processes have been designed in such a way as to prevent any unfair outcome',[47] advocates of international constitutionalism generally do not turn a blind eye to violations of international law or the dark sides of international institutions. However, they do not believe that such violations of constitutional principles should be used to justify abandoning the project of international constitutionalism. On the contrary: they believe that such violations only show the need for further 'constitutionalisation', and also, the need to take the ideals of international constitutionalism more seriously.[48] This once more shows that international constitutionalism is located in between ideals and reality. It claims to rely on actual developments in international law, but is also a normative, programmatic project: if the facts do not match constitutional ideals, advocates of constitutionalism emphasise the need to change the facts rather than the need the need to water down the ideals of internationalism.

B. The United States position and community values

Since the end of the Cold War, the position of the United States towards the international rule of law has been a much-debated topic in academic circles.[49] The several studies, taken together, show that one should be careful not to jump to general conclusions regarding the position of the

---

[46] Pogge, 'Recognised and Violated', 6–7.   [47] Tomuschat, 'International Law', 26.
[48] Peters, 'Compensatory Constitutionalism'.
[49] For an analysis see: M. Byers and G. Nolte (eds.), *United States Hegemony and the Foundations of International Law* (Cambridge: Cambridge University Press, 2003); R. Foot, N. MacFarlane and M. Mastanduno, *US Hegemony and International Organisations* (Oxford: Oxford University Press, 2002); N. Deller, A. Makhijani and J. Burroughs (eds.), *Rule of Power or Rule of Law: An Assessment of U.S. Policies and*

US too easily. In some cases, the US has taken the lead in multilateral efforts to create legal rules and institutions and has offered considerable (financial) support. In other cases, the US has found that multilateral cooperation and acceptance of some form of international supervision are the best available options for a superpower in a uni/multipolar world.[50] However, there have also been instances in which the US attitude towards international law has been less favourable. So far, the US has refused to sign or ratify a number of multilateral treaties that aim to protect community values, such as the Kyoto Protocol on Climate Change,[51] the Rome Statute of the International Criminal Court,[52] or the Landmines Treaty.[53] Although the US does not violate international law by refusing to accept these treaties, it is difficult to maintain that this position actively contributes to a strengthening of the international rule of law. This also applies to the US reluctance to accept third party settlement in international disputes, or the possibility for its citizens to submit petitions to international supervisory bodies in the area of human rights.[54] In yet other instances, the US has simply violated international legal obligations, especially in the sphere of international pace and security, human rights and humanitarian law and UN membership.[55]

Actions Regarding Security-related Treaties (New York: Apex Press, 2003); J. Brunee, 'The United States and International Environmental Law: Living with an Elephant' (2004) 15 *EJIL* 617; J. F. Murphy, *The United States and the Rule of Law in International Affairs* (Cambridge: Cambridge University Press, 2004).

[50] In the field of environmental law, for example, Brunee concludes that, notwithstanding the high profile withdrawal from the Kyoto Protocol, 'American compliance with treaty commitments is generally good': Brunee, 'The United States', 651.

[51] For an overview of the Climate Change Convention, including the parties and observers see: http://unfccc.int/2860.php (last accessed 12 July 2006).

[52] For an overview of the ICC, including the parties to the Statute, see http://www.icc-cpi.int/ (last accessed 12 July 2006).

[53] For an overview of the Convention on the Prohibition of the Use, Stockpiling, Production and Transfer of Anti-Personnel Mines and on Their Destruction, including the parties and non-parties, see http://www.icbl.org/treaty (last accessed 12 July 2006).

[54] For a discussion see J. F. Murphy, *The United States and the Rule of Law in International Affairs* (Cambridge: Cambridge University Press, 2004).

[55] For a general overview, focusing on violations of international law by the US, see Deller, Makhijani and Burroughs (eds.), *Rule of Power*. On the illegality of the invasion in Iraq, see N. D. White, 'The Will and Authority of the Security Council after Iraq' (2004) 17 *LJIL* 645. Another example in the sphere of international peace and security is the implementation of domestic legislation in relation to the Chemical Weapons Convention. This legislation contains limitations upon the verification efforts of the OPCW that are difficult to reconcile with the obligations under the Chemical Weapons Convention. See Murphy, *The United States*, p. 350. See also P. Sands, *Lawless World: America and the Making and Breaking of Global Rules* (London: Allen Lane, 2005).

In the case of the International Criminal Court (ICC), the US has combined several strategies to prevent the Court from prosecuting US nationals. Based on their fears for political prosecutions and their concerns about insufficient bases for jurisdiction, lack of sufficient fair trial guarantees and lack of SC control, the US has so far refused to become a party to the ICC Statute. In addition, the US has acted in (at least) three other ways to check the power of the ICC: through probably the most important world order treaty, through bilateral treaties and through unilateral measures.

The US has used a *world order treaty* in its fight against the powers of the ICC. In 2002, the US used its special position in the UN to stimulate the adoption of SC Resolution 1422 (2002).[56] Resolution 1422 requests the ICC to refrain from investigations or prosecutions against peace-keepers who are nationals of states that are not party to the ICC Statute. The Resolution was adopted after the US had threatened to veto the extension of a UN peacekeeping mission in Bosnia-Herzegovina and threatened to block further UN operations. Because the US feared that its nationals working for the UN could be subject to politically motivated prosecutions by the prosecutor, it demanded permanent immunity for all peacekeeping personnel from states that are not party to the ICC Statute. Although many states opposed the US position, members of the SC felt the need to compromise in order to prevent further frustration of UN operations by the US.[57] This compromise took the form of Resolution 1422, which exempts peacekeepers from ICC proceedings, but only for a (renewable) period of 12 months. The request for exemption was renewed in 2003 (through Resolution 1487),[58] but was finally dropped in 2004.[59] Resolutions 1422 and 1478 illustrate how a world order treaty such as the UN Charter may be used to address concerns of particular, powerful states.

---

[56] Un Doc. S/RES/1422 (2002).

[57] In the open meeting of the SC held on 10 July 2002 nearly all of the 39 representatives criticised the US position, yet recognised that a compromise was necessary to prevent the blocking of further UN operations by the US. See the discussion by B. MacPherson, 'Authority of the Security Council to Exempt Peacekeepers from International Criminal Proceedings' (July 2002) *ASIL Insights* at http://www.asil.org/insights.htm (last accessed 12 July 2006).

[58] Un Doc. S/Res/1478 (2003).

[59] For a discussion, see F. L. Kirgis, 'U.S. Drops Plan to Exempt G.I.s from U.N. Court' (July 2004) *ASIL Insights* at http://www.asil.org/insights/insigh139.htm (last accessed 12 July 2006).

The US has also used *bilateral treaties* to prevent the ICC from exercising jurisdiction over US nationals. Based on a literal interpretation of Article 98(2) of the ICC Statute,[60] the US has signed so-called 'bilateral immunity agreements' with several states. Although the US has signed different types of agreements with different states, the general point of the bilateral immunity agreements is clear: to prevent states from either directly surrendering US nationals to the ICC or from cooperating with efforts from other states to do so. The conclusion of the immunity agreements indicates a development that runs counter to Simma's move from bilateralism to community interest:[61] in order to check the powers of an organ that aims to protect community values, the US makes use of the traditional method of bilateralism.

The third means by which the US has sought to fight the ICC is through *unilateral measures*.[62] The most widely discussed measure is the American Servicemembers' Protection Act of August 2002, granting the President several powers to prevent prosecution of US citizens.[63] Among the powers of the President is the power 'to use all necessary means' to free US officials, service members and government employees detained by the ICC.[64]

From the perspective of international constitutionalism, the US attitude towards some world order treaties raises serious questions. After all, notwithstanding its idealistic character, international constitutionalism claims to be more than a normative blueprint for a better society. It claims to be related to what Allot has called the 'real constitution' in a society: 'the constitution as actualised in the current social process, a structure and a system of power'.[65] Moreover, for international constitutionalism, world order treaties such as the UN Charter should

---

[60] Article 98(2) reads as follows: 'The Court may not proceed with a request for surrender which would require the requested State to act inconsistently with its obligations under international agreements pursuant to which the consent of a sending State is required to surrender a person of that State to the Court, unless the Court can first obtain the cooperation of the sending State for the giving of consent for the surrender.'

[61] Simma, 'From Bilateralism'.

[62] For an overview, see Washington working group on the ICC, *U.S. Legal Limitations to Cooperation with the ICC*, http://www.globalsolutions.org/programs/law_justice/faqs/icclaws2004.pdf.

[63] American Servicemembers' Protection Act of 2002, http://www.state.gov/t/pm/rls/othr/misc/23425.htm (last accessed 12 July 2006).

[64] Section 2008(a) states that: 'The President is authorized to use all means necessary and appropriate to bring about the release of any person described in subsection (b) who is being detained or imprisoned by, on behalf of, or at the request of the International Criminal Court.'

[65] Allott, 'Eunomia', pp. 135, 136.

safeguard a general interest and not the interests of particular, powerful states. In this context, it is not surprising to find that Habermas, in his recent plea for international constitutionalism, expresses his concern about the position of the US towards international law, and especially towards the UN system of collective security. According to Habermas, the project of 'constitutionalisation' of international politics, that started with the League of Nations and was further realised in the UN system, is now endangered by the 'liberal ethics of the remaining super-power' [*liberale Weltmachtethik*].[66] The legalisation of international politics, Habermas argues, is endangered by the combination of *real-politik* and the turn to ethics that typifies current foreign policy of the US.[67]

C. Community interests as politics

The adoption of community interests and the related notions of hier-archy and constitutionalism have not been received favourably by all commentators. Some have argued that making a distinction between different types of legal norms poses a threat to the unity and coherence of international law and undermines the principle of legal certainty.[68] Another recurring concern is that the under-determined character of notions such as *jus cogens* and 'community interests' would leave power-ful states too much leeway to assume the power to speak on behalf of the international community. Thus, Weil argued that:

> . . . as the international community still remains an imprecise entity, the normative power nominally vested in it is in fact entrusted to a directo-rate of this community, a *de facto* oligarchy. There is a danger of the implantation in international society of a legislative power enabling certain states – the most powerful or numerous – to promulgate norms that will be imposed on others . . . the concepts of 'legal conscience' and 'international community' may become code words, lending themselves

---

[66] J. Habermas, *Der Gespaltene Westen* (Frankfurt am Main: Suhrkamp, 2004), p. 145.

[67] *Ibid.*, at p. 115. According to Habermas, 'Das Kantische Projekt kann nur dann eine Fortsetzung finden, wenn die USA zu ihrem nach 1918 und nach 1945 energisch vertretenen Internationalismus zurückkehren und erneut die historische Rolle eines Schrittmachers auf dem Wege der Evolution des Völkerrechts zu einem "Weltbürgerlichen" zustand übernehmen'. *Ibid.*, p. 116. For a critique of the 'turn to ethics' in international law, see also Koskenniemi's defence of a 'culture of formalism' against the more flexible approach towards international relations advocated by some liberal and cosmopolitan scholars: Koskenniemi, 'The Gentle Civilizer', pp. 474–510.

[68] See Weil's critique on relative normativity in Weil, 'Towards Relative Normativity'.

to all kinds of manipulation, under whose cloak certain states may strive to implant an ideological system of law.[69]

However, the most incisive critique of the inclusion of universal values in international law was already formulated well before the creation of the UN or the adoption of notions such as *jus cogens*. After the First World War, Carl Schmitt agued that the adoption of universalism in international law would not do away with what he regarded as the core of the political: the determination of the public enemy and the ways to fight this enemy.[70] On the contrary: rather than setting aside politics, the application of universal values in concrete circumstances would become the new field of political struggles. According to Schmitt, the belief in universal humanitarism should be seen as just another attempt to create a neutral, non-political ground upon which human interactions could take place. In European history, similar attempts had been made in the name of religion, metaphysics and the economy. However, as Schmitt explains in 'The Age of Neutralisations and Depoliticisations', all these attempts eventually failed. The neutral grounds rather proved to be the new terrains on which the political struggle could enfold:

> In the new sphere, at first considered neutral, the antitheses of men and interests unfold with a new intensity and become increasingly sharper. Europeans always have wandered from a conflictual to a neutral sphere, and always the newly won neutral sphere has become immediately another area of struggle, once again necessitating the search for a new neutral sphere. Scientific thinking was also unable to achieve peace. The religious wars evolved into the still cultural and yet already economically determined national wars of the nineteenth century and lineally into economic wars.[71]

---

[69] *Ibid.*, at 441. See also G. Arangio-Ruiz, 'The "Federal Analogy" and UN Charter Interpretation, A Crucial Issue' (1997) 8 *EJIL* 1.

[70] See C. Schmitt, *Die Wendung zum Diskriminierenden Kriegsbegriff* (Berlin: Duncker & Humblot, 2003) (reprint from the 1938 edition).

[71] 'Auf dem neuen, zunächst für neutral gehaltenen Felde entfaltet sich sofort mit neuer Intensität der Gegensatz der Menschen und Interessen, und zwar um so stärker, je fester man das neue Sachgebiet in Besitz nimmt. Immer wandert die europäische Menschheit aus einem Kampfgebiet in neutrales Gebiet, immer wird das neu gewonnene neutrale Gebiet sofort wieder Kampfgebiet und wird es notwendig, neue neutrale Sphären zu suchen. Auch die Naturwissenschaftlichkeit konnte den Frieden nicht herbeiführen. Aus den Religionskriegen wurden die halb noch kulturell, halb bereits ökonomisch determinierten Nationalkriege des 19. Jahrhunderts und schließlich einfach Wirtschaftskriege.' C. Schmitt, 'Das Zeitalter der Neutralisierungen und Entpolitisierungen', reprinted in C. Schmitt, *Der Begriff des Politischen*, 4th edn, M. Konzett (trans.) (Berlin: Duncker & Humblot, 1963), p. 79 at p. 84; and see

Although one may question whether Schmitt's reading of European history is completely accurate[72] and although one may certainly question his alternative to liberal internationalism (the *Großraumtheorie*),[73] Schmitt's critique of universalism remains relevant for the project of international constitutionalism. As was discussed in the previous section, (powerful) states *do* use community values and world order treaties to implement their own policies. Moreover, as will be set out in more detail in section 4, below, constitutionalism is unable to provide a neutral, non-political ground for human interaction. International constitutionalism, in other words, should take the political seriously.

3. The aspirations of international constitutionalism

From the foregoing, it can be inferred that a constitutional reading of international law is by no means dictated by reality, a point also acknowledged by some advocates of international constitutionalism. Simma, for example, has wondered whether the notion of an 'international community' might exist only in the minds of cosmopolitan professionals and non-governmental organisations working for what they perceive to be the common interest.[74] Moreover, one of the recurring topics in discussions of international constitutionalism is the relation between ideal and reality, norm and fact, or law and power. In this context, advocates of international constitutionalism emphasise the existence of an overarching constitutional framework, the critical potential of which remains intact notwithstanding violations and misuse in practice. In this sense, international constitutionalism aims to bring about what it describes as existing: a legal order that integrates states, fosters international cooperation, checks the exercise of political power and unifies a global community. As Fassbender has argued: '[t]he

J. P. McCormick 'The Age of Neutralizations and Depoliticizations (1929)' (1993) 96 *Telos* 130 at 138).

[72] C. Brown, *From Humanised War to Humanitarian Intervention: Carl Schmitt's Critique of the Just War Tradition*, Online Paper Archive of the Fifth Pan-European International Relations Conference, The Hague, 9–11 September 2004: http://www.sgir.org/archive/index.htm (last accessed 12 July 2006).

[73] See Habermas, *Der Gespaltene Westen*, pp. 187–93. See also A. Gattini, 'Sense and Quasisense of Schmitt's *Großraum* Theory in International Law – A Rejoinder to Carty's "Carl Schmitt's Critique of Liberal International Legal Order"' (2002) 15 *LJIL* 53.

[74] 'Viewed realistically, or pessimistically, a truly worldwide sense of community might be present only with a few international civil servants or experts or, more importantly, with non-governmental organisations active on a global level'. Simma, 'From Bilateralism', at 248.

idea of a constitution is summoned as a symbol of (political) unity which eventually will be realized on a global scale.'[75]

The constitutional reading of international law, in other words, aims at the realisation of some core values borrowed from modern, domestic constitutionalism. Two values are particularly important for international constitutionalism: (1) the limitation of political power through legal rules and institutions; and (2) the creation of legal and political unity (and the corresponding notions of legal hierarchy and integration).

A. Limitation through law

The taming of political power through legal rules and institutions is one of the main aims of modern constitutionalism. As Koopmans emphasises, one of the central points of constitutionalism is that power is not 'exercised arbitrarily, reflecting the mere will of the political leaders of the day, but in accordance with the law, which creates or recognises permanent institutions and organises the powers to be exercised by them'.[76]

In this sense, the term 'constitution' has also been used in studies of (diplomatic) history to characterise the institutional arrangements that were set up after major disruptions of the international order. The Westphalian Peace Treaties, the Vienna Settlement and the Versailles Treaty have all been described as forms of an 'international constitution'.[77] These arrangements were indeed the result of a constitutive act that brought about a specific setting for the exercise of political power. The arrangements aimed to constrain politics by defining what counts as acceptable behaviour, by setting up institutions that reduced the gains of winning and by affecting the identities of those involved in the institutional structures that were established.[78]

---

[75] Fassbender, 'The UN Charter', at 552.

[76] T. Koopmans, *Courts and Political Institutions: A Comparative View* (Cambridge: Cambridge University Press, 2003), p. 245. For the idea that constitutionalism entails the limitation of power through legal institutions, see also J. E. Lane, *Constitutions and Political Theory* (Manchester: Manchester University Press, 1996); S. L. Elkin and K. E. Soltan (eds.), *A New Constitutionalism: Designing Political Institutions for a Good Society* (Chicago: Chicago University Press, 1993); L. Alexander (ed.), *Constitutionalism: Philosophical Foundations* (Cambridge: Cambridge University Press, 1998).

[77] G. J. Ikenberry, 'Constitutional Politics in International Relations' (1998) 4 *EJIR* 147 at 148.

[78] For a critique of a purely rationalistic understanding of legal institutions, see C. Reus-Smit, *The Politics of International Law* (Cambridge: Cambridge University Press, 2004).

In international legal discourse, the notion of a 'constitution' is also used to characterise the foundational treaty of an international organisation. Such treaties constitute a specific organisation, provide it with legal powers and set limits to the exercise of powers by the organisation. The limitation of powers of international organisations has gained greater importance as a result of the process of internationalisation and globalisation. The processes of globalisation and internationalisation put an increasing number of issues out of reach of the traditional bulwark of constitutionalism: the constitution of the sovereign state. Increasingly, power is exercised by non-state actors, in international networks, or in and by international organisations. In order to uphold one of the core values of constitutionalism, the regulation of power through law, an international response is required.[79] This has led to calls for constitutionalisation in a wide variety of international organisations.[80]

However, the constitutionalisation of different international organisations might have a negative effect on a second aim of constitutionalism: the creation of (legal) unity. After all, international organisations do not operate in neatly separated areas, but often have complementary or competing powers. As Klabbers has noted, in such context, constitutionalisation of international organisations may very well result in 'deeper fragmentation, as the various competing regimes and organisations will be locked firmly in constitutional place and battle with each other'.[81] In order to preserve the dual aims of constitutionalism, constraint and unity, a more comprehensive form of constitutionalism is required; a form of 'world' or 'global constitutionalism'.

B. Legal unity

Global constitutionalism goes beyond specific international organisations or regimes: it aims to express constitutional principles at a deeper level; principles that reflect the unity of international law as a whole. It rests on the belief that 'the law shuns multiplicity [and] its vocation is to

---

[79] T. Cottier and M. Hertig, 'The Prospects of 21st Century Constitutionalism' (2003) 7 *Max Planck UNYB* 261.

[80] Klabbers identifies calls for constitutionalisation in the EU, the UN, the WTO, the IMF, the World Bank, the Council of Europe and in international criminal law: J. Klabbers, 'Constitutionalism Lite', (2004) 1 *International Organizations Law Review* 1 at 3–4. See also K. Wellens, *Remedies Against International Organisations* (Cambridge: Cambridge University Press, 2002).

[81] Klabbers, 'Constitutionalism Lite', at 23.

a unified and hierarchical order, one that is unified precisely because it is hierarchical'.[82]

Traditionally, this unity was sought in the so-called general part of international law: the constitutive rules on sources and subjects, together with the foundational principles (such as sovereign equality, and *pacta sunt servanda*) and some norms reflecting the basic values of the international society at a given point in time (such as, nowadays, the peremptory norms of international law). These rules and principles were regarded as 'constitutional' because they regulate the creation and identification of other rules and cannot be changed at will by states.[83] The existence of such a 'constitution' in international law is relatively uncontroversial and even accepted by some of the most outspoken critics of contemporary international constitutionalism.[84]

Others, however, have sought to locate the unity of international law in a single, foundational document: the Charter of the United Nations. Several authors have argued that the UN Charter should be regarded as a constitutional document that regulates the international community as a whole. In this way, writers attempt to do justice to the specific characteristics of the UN Charter, such as its objective legal personality, its claim to precedence over conflicting treaty obligations, the

[82] M. Delmas-Marty, *Trois défis pour un droit mondial* (Paris : Seuil, 1998), p. 104. The quote is taken from the translation found in Koskenniemi and Leino, 'Fragmentation' at 57. In the same article, Koskenniemi and Leino also recall the spirit of Lauterpacht, who, during the Second World War, spoke of the 'Reality of the Law of Nations' and expressed his firm belief that '[t]he disunity of the modern world is a fact; but so, in a truer sense, is its unity. Th(e) essential and manifold solidarity, coupled with the necessity of securing the rule of law and the elimination of war, constitutes a harmony of interests which has a basis more real and tangible than the illusions of the sentimentalist or the hypocrisy of those satisfied with the existing *status quo*' (*ibid.*, at 556). H. Lauterpacht, *International Law, Being the Collected Papers of Sir Hersch Lauterpacht*, systematically arranged and edited by E. Lauterpacht, QC, vol. 2 (Cambridge: Cambridge University Press, 1970–1978), p. 26.

[83] See, for example, Tomuschat's characterisation of the constitution of international law in his 1993 lecture: 'States live, as from their birth, within a legal framework of a limited number of basic rules which determines their rights and obligations with or without their will ... One may call this framework, from which every State receives its legal entitlement to be respected as a sovereign entity, the constitution of the international society, or preferably, the constitution of the international community ...' C. Tomuschat, 'Obligations Arising for States Without or Against Their Will', 195–374.

[84] See, for example, Arangio-Ruiz, 'The "Federal Analogy"', at 6: 'As a legal system ... general international law has, in its way, a constitution ... This constitution probably consists of what Hart calls the "rule of recognition" (identifying primary rules) and the principle of the legal equality of states. One should add perhaps the merely negative principle reflecting the maxim *superiorem non recognoscentes.*'

exceptional powers of the SC or its universal nature. Opinions differ as
to the exact constitutional status of the UN Charter. Some cautiously use
terms such as 'quasi-constitutional',[85] 'key connector in a constitutional
order'[86] or refer to the Charter as a document in between a treaty and a
constitution.[87] Others, however, speak more frankly of the UN Charter
as the constitution of the international community. Thus, authors have
referred to the Charter as the 'constitution for the world community'[88]
or 'the constitution of the entire international community'[89] and have,
accordingly, characterised the SC as, to some degree, an 'executive of the
international community' and an 'international government'.[90] This
tradition, as Koskenniemi has pointed out, embodies 'the fulfilment of
the modernist wish to find a single, comprehensive, and consistent point
of view on the political organisation of humankind'.[91]

One of the most thorough expressions of this wish can be found in
Fassbender's 'The United Nations Charter as Constitution of the
International Community'.[92] In this article, Fassbender argues that a
constitutional reading of the Charter is preferable on both explanatory
and normative grounds. The fact that the Charter imposes obligations
on non-members,[93] Fassbender argues, can only be satisfactorily
explained if the establishment of the Charter is regarded as a revolutionary, foundational act that broke with the consent-based international system that existed in 1945.[94] At the same time, the
characterisation of the UN Charter as *the* constitution of the international community is based on normative grounds: the rejection of a

---

[85] T. Franck, *Recourse to Force, State Action Against Threats and Armed Attacks*
(Cambridge: Cambridge University Press, 2002), p. 5.

[86] De Wet, 'The Value System'.

[87] R. MacDonald, 'The Charter of the United Nations in Constitutional Perspective'
(1999) 20 *Australian YIL* 205.

[88] G. Ress, 'Interpretation of the Charter', in B. Simma *et al.* (eds.), *The Charter of the
United Nations: A Commentary*, 2nd edn (Oxford: Oxford University Press, 2002), p. 16.

[89] A. Bleckmann and B. Fassbender, 'Article 2(1)', in *ibid.*, p. 84.

[90] J. A. Frowein and N. Krisch, 'Introduction to Chapter VII', in *ibid.*, p. 702.

[91] M. Koskenniemi, 'Review of Bruno Simma (ed.), The Charter of the United Nations:
A Commentary' (1996) 17 *Australian YIL* 227; see also A. Orford 'The Gift of
Formalism' (2004) 15 *EJIL* 179.

[92] Fassbender, 'The UN Charter'.   [93] For this see also above, section 1.2.

[94] Fassbender here follows Kelsen's interpretation of the UN Charter in Kelsen's *The Law
of the United Nations* (London: Stevens, 1950); Fassbender, 'The UN Charter', 573: 'The
broad power conceded to the SC, as well as Articles 2 paragraph 6 and 103 indicate a
renunciation of the traditional concepts of state sovereignty and bilateralism.'

plurality of constitutional frameworks and the desire to establish a single basis for authority as well as 'clarity, transparency and reliability of the law'.[95] Thus, international law is portrayed as a hierarchical structure that derives its validity from a single, constitutive document. This document embraces 'all international law', leaves 'no room for a category of general international law existing independently from the Charter',[96] and assigns world order treaties such as the International Covenant on Civil and Political Rights or the Genocide Convention the status of 'constitutional by-laws of the Charter'.[97] The result of this interpretation of the UN Charter is far-reaching and yet familiar. It projects the hopes of domestic constitutionalism in the international legal order. International law is portrayed as a hierarchically organised order with a single and ultimate source of authority,[98] which unifies the community and limits the exercise of political power.

4. The never-ending closure

A. The domestic analogy

Advocates of international constitutionalism reject the assumption that constitutions can operate only within the context of the sovereign state. Although theories of constitutionalism were developed in the context of the nation state, there is no *a priori* reason why the notion of a constitution could not be transplanted to other contexts as well. This also implies that advocates of international constitutionalism do not necessarily (and, in fact, generally do not at all) favour a world state. Yet, international constitutionalism is deeply rooted in the tradition of constitutionalism as it has developed in the domestic context. It borrows from domestic constitutionalism the notion of the constitution as the foundation of a hierarchically structured legal order that unifies a community and regulates (limits) the exercise of political power.

Since international constitutionalism is based on a domestic analogy, it also incorporates some of the paradoxes and tensions inherent in domestic constitutionalism. One of these tensions was already touched upon in the previous section: the non-foundational foundation of constitutional law. It has proven to be impossible to find a coherent legal

---

[95] Fassbender, 'The UN Charter', 567.   [96] *Ibid.*, 585.   [97] *Ibid.*, 588–9.
[98] See, for example, the remark that: '[f]or its implementation and enforcement, constitutions cannot rely upon any higher law or authority. It is the structure of the constitution itself which has to ensure its effectiveness and duration.' *Ibid.*, 537.

foundation for constitutional law as the highest form of law in a polity.[99] Thus, in order to explain the ultimate source of validity of the constitution, legal theory had recourse to constructions such as hypothetical, *a priori*, or fictitious basic norms,[100] sociological observations,[101] foundational political decisions[102] or the mystical foundation of authority.[103] The openness of the constitution to non-legal elements is not confined to its foundational moment. Studies in the practice of constitutional systems have indicated that, even in well-developed constitutional systems, 'the constitution can be frustrated by politics',[104] since constitutional language has 'limited capacity ... to limit public power'.[105] Especially in times of crisis, constitutions do not provide a neutral ground beyond politics, but rather become the topic of political contestation themselves – and sometimes are simply ignored or set aside.[106] Of course, this does not mean that constitutions are unimportant. It does mean, however, that it is difficult to understand the actual functioning of a constitution as a practice in which a pre-determined normative order is realised. Therefore, it is not surprising that some important theories of constitutionalism are theories of constitutional *interpretation*.[107] Bobbitt, for example, has based his theory of the constitution on a rejection of foundationalism. He argues that

---

[99] One way out is to argue, with Kelsen, that constitutional law derives its validity from public international law: H. Kelsen, *Reine Rechtslehre* (Wien: Österreichische Staatsdruckerei, 1992, revised reprint from the 1960 edition), pp. 321–43. However, this does not solve the foundational question, but only shifts its focal point from domestic constitutional law to international law.

[100] Throughout his work, Kelsen has offered different readings of the status of the *Grundnorm*. In *Das Problem der Souveränität* (Tübingen: Mohr, 1920), p. 99, Kelsen referred to the basic norm as a hypothesis. In *Reine Rechtslehre*, pp. 196–228, Kelsen characterised the basic norm as a transcendental assumption, while in *Allgemeine Theorie der Normen* (Manz: Verlag, 1979), pp. 203–15, Kelsen understood the basic norm as an internal and external inconsistent (yet necessary) fiction.

[101] Hart, *The Concept of Law* (Oxford: Clarendon Press, 1961).

[102] C. Schmitt, *Verfassungslehre* (Berlin: Duncker & Humblot, 1928).

[103] J. Derrida, 'Force of Law: The Mystical Foundation of Authority' (1990) 11 *Cardozo Law Review* 919.

[104] S. M. Griffin, *American Constitutionalism: From Theory to Politics* (Princeton: Princeton University Press, 1996), p. 6.

[105] J. E. Lane, *Constitutions and Political Theory* (Manchester: Manchester University Press, 1996), p. 10.

[106] For this argument, see O. Tans, 'The Constitutional Theatre' (2002) 8 *Res Publica* 231.

[107] See, for example, R. Dworkin, 'Law as Interpretation' (1982) 60 *Texas Law Review* 527; R. Dworkin, *Taking Rights Seriously* (London: Duckworth, 1996); R. Dworkin, *Law's Empire* (Cambridge, Mass.: Harvard University Press, 1986). See also the – on some important points fundamentally different – approach of S. Fish, 'Doing What Comes

constitutional arguments should not be regarded as statements whose validity can be verified by their correspondence with a pre-existing constitution. Rather, they should be regarded as part of a continuous interpretative practice in which several methods of argumentation are played out.[108] One of the most important methods advanced in constitutional reasoning, Bobbitt argues, is the 'ethical argument': the argument whose force relies on the character or *ethos* of the constitution and the politic community.[109] Although legalistic approaches have tried to play down the importance of such arguments, Bobbitt argues, ethical arguments often play a major role in constitutional reasoning.[110]

The openness of constitutional discourse is also visible in international law, for example in what Brownlie has called the 'basic constitutional doctrine of the law of nations': the sovereignty and equality of states.[111] As Koskenniemi, amongst others, has demonstrated, the notions of sovereignty and equality lack a clear and determinate meaning that could serve as a foundation for other legal rules. Rather, it is the notion of sovereign equality *itself* that is the very object of endless foundational debates.[112] This does not mean that the concept of sovereignty is meaningless or superfluous for international legal discourse.[113] The concept of sovereignty is important (and perhaps even 'constitutional'), because it structures important parts of international legal discourse in terms of an unresolved tension between individuality and community. Or, as Koskenniemi has put it:

> On the one hand, we seem incapable of conceptualizing the State or whatever liberties it has without reflecting on the character of the social relations which surround it. The sphere of liberty of a member of society must, by definition, be delimited by the spheres of liberty of the other members of that society. But the delimitations of freedoms in this way

Naturally: Change, Rhetoric, and the Practice of Theory' (1989) *Literary and Legal Studies* 563.

[108] P. Bobbitt, *Constitutional Fate: Theory of the Constitution* (Oxford: Oxford University Press, 1982); P. Bobbitt, *Constitutional Interpretation* (Oxford: Blackwell, 1991).

[109] Bobbit, *Constitutional Fate*, p. 94.

[110] For an application of Bobbit's theory to judicial reasoning in international law, see J. E. Alvarez, 'Judging the Security Council' (1996) 90 *AJIL* 1.

[111] I. Brownlie, *Principles of Public International Law*, 6th edn (Oxford: Oxford University Press, 2003), p. 287.

[112] M. Koskenniemi, *From Apology*, ch. 4; D. Kennedy, *International Legal Structures* (Baden-Baden: Nomos, 1987).

[113] W. G. Werner, 'Sovereignty and International Legal discourse', in I. F. Dekker and W. G. Werner (eds.), *Governance and International Legal Theory* (The Hague: Kluwer, 2003).

requires that we do not rely on the self-definition of the members of their liberties. In other words, a State's sphere of liberty must be capable of determination from a perspective which is external to it. On the other hand, we cannot derive the State completely from its social relations and its liberty from an external (and overriding) normative perspective without losing the State's individuality as a nation and the justification for its claims to independence and self-determination.[114]

A similar tension is present in debates on the powers of international organisations. As was set out in the previous section, the founding treaties ('constitutions') of international organisations simultaneously ground and limit the legal powers of international organisations. They are, in other words, both the instruments through which common interests are served and the checks on over-ambitious international organisations. This tension is visible in the different methods of interpretation of the founding treaties of international organisations. Here, restrictive approaches – reflecting the constitutionalist aim of limiting and regulating power – compete with teleological approaches – reflecting the aims of integration and unity. Moreover, the tension is visible in the different approaches that have been developed to determine the scope of an organisation's competences, such as the doctrines of attributed powers and implied powers, functionalism or the *ultra vires* doctrine. As Klabbers has argued, none of these doctrines has been able to provide stable answers to the question of the delimitation of powers between international organisations and their member states. Underlying this difficulty is the well-known problem of sovereignty and community:

> If constitutionalism is somehow defined as having to do with limits to government . . . then the law of international organizations is not wanting for constitutional or quasi-constitutional defence mechanisms . . . The one problem, however, is that none of those mechanisms seems to work very well . . . Perhaps the main intellectual problem bedevilling the law of international organizations is that it is never quite clear who is in control: the member states, or the organization.[115]

---

[114] Koskenniemi, *From Apology*, p. 193.

[115] Klabbers, 'Constitutionalism Lite', at 37 and 43 respectively. The problem of individuality and community is also one of the threads of J. Klabbers, *An Introduction to International Institutional Law* (Cambridge: Cambridge University Press, 2002).

B. The powers of the Security Council

This problem has also framed one of the ensuing debates regarding the powers of the Security Council (SC). As has been explained above,[116] several writers used the far-reaching powers of the SC as one of the most important arguments for the constitutional nature of the UN Charter. One of the bases for these far-reaching powers is Article 24 of the UN Charter. Article 24(1) reads as follows:

> In order to ensure prompt and effective action by the United Nations, its Members confer on the Security Council primary responsibility for the maintenance of international peace and security, and agree that in carrying out its duties under this responsibility the Security Council acts on their behalf.

This provision has been read in two fundamentally different ways. The first school denies that Article 24 should be read as expressing a delegation of powers from the member states to the SC. Instead, it argues, the powers of the SC follow from the Charter as a constitutional document. As Delbrück has argued: '... an interpretation of Art. 24(1) which is based on the premise of a delegation by the member States of the powers granted to the Security Council under this provision cannot be upheld. The SC is an organ of the UN and therefore derives its powers from the UN Charter itself. As an organ of the UN, the SC acts on behalf of the organisation and not on behalf of the individual member states.'[117] The last part of Article 24(1) – the SC acts on behalf of the member states – is denounced as 'legally erroneous and superfluous'.[118]

Others, however, have read Article 24 in a different way and argued that the powers of the SC do rest on a delegation of powers by the member states. This position was expressed by the representative of Brazil during the debates preceding the establishment of the International Criminal Tribunal for the former Yugoslavia (ICTY):

> ... it should be borne in mind that the authority of the SC is not self-constituted but originates from a delegation of powers by the whole membership of the Organization. It is never too much to recall that the SC, in the exercise of its responsibilities, acts on behalf of the Members of the United Nations.[119]

---

[116] See above, sections 1.2 and 3.2.
[117] J. Delbrück, 'Article 24' in Simma, *Commentary*, p. 449.   [118] *Ibid.*
[119] Quoted in D. Sarooshi, *The United Nations and the Development of Collective Security* (Oxford: Oxford University Press, 2000), p. 45.

Although, formally speaking, the powers of the SC of course follow from the Charter, it is the member states acting collectively that have endowed the SC with those powers. Accordingly, the last part of Article 24(1) is not regarded as erroneous or superfluous. On the contrary: it is viewed as an important reminder that the powers of the SC rest on a delegation of powers by a collectivity of states.

The debate on the foundations of the powers of the SC is not only of academic interest. It is closely bound up with discussions on the account-ability of the SC, the extent to which the SC can delegate its powers, the powers of review of SC Resolutions by national courts[120] and the possible existence of residual enforcement powers by states and regional organisa-tions.[121] The latter topic gained specific relevance as a result of the increased involvement of regional organisations in matters of peace and security since the end of the Cold War. This involvement sometimes went far beyond the peaceful settlement of disputes or the establishment of peacekeeping opera-tions as, for example, the regional role assumed by NATO in the Yugoslavia crisis demonstrates.[122] Similarly, the actions taken by ECOWAS in Liberia and Sierra Leone went beyond the pacific settlement of disputes envisaged in Article 52(2) of the Charter.[123]

These actions have raised questions regarding the relationship between the SC and regional organisations. According to Article 53 of the UN Charter, regional organisations can only undertake enforcement actions under authority of the SC.[124] This Article thus seems to establish

---

[120] E. de Wet and A. Nollkaemper, 'Review of SC Decisions by National Courts' (2002) 45 *GYIL* 166.

[121] D. Sarooshi, *The United Nations*, at pp. 20–49; N. Tsagourias, 'The Shifting Laws on the Use of Force and the Trivialization of the UN Collective Security System: the Need to Reconstitute It' (2003) *NYIL* 56 at 61–70. A. Abass, *Regional Organisations and the Development of Collective Security, Beyond Chapter VIII of the UN Charter* (Oxford: Hart Publishing, 2004), especially ch. 4.

[122] Abass, 'Regional Organizations'. See also the discussion in relation to the role assumed by NATO in the 1990s in I. Dekker and E. Myjer, 'Air Strikes on Bosnian Positions: Is NATO also Legally the Proper Instrument of the UN?' (1996) 9 *LJIL* at 411–16; N. Blokker and A. Muller, 'NATO as the UN Security Council's Instrument: Question Marks From the Perspective of International Law', *ibid.* at 417–421; I. Dekker and E. Myjer, 'Postscript', *ibid.* at 422–4.

[123] Article 52(2) of the UN Charter reads as follows: 'The Members of the United Nations entering into such arrangements or constituting such agencies shall make every effort to achieve pacific settlement of local disputes through such regional arrangements or by such regional agencies before referring them to the Security Council.'

[124] Article 53(1) of the UN Charter reads as follows: 'The Security Council shall, where appropriate, utilize such regional arrangements or agencies for enforcement action

a clear hierarchy: the SC may use regional organisations if it deems necessary but regional organisations are barred from undertaking enforcement actions on their own.

However, since the late 1990s, this hierarchy has been questioned in several ways.[125] Some of the most clear and open challenges to the formal hierarchy claimed by Article 53 of the UN Charter have been the adoption of the 'Protocol Relating to the Mechanism for Conflict Prevention, Management, Resolution, Peacekeeping and Security' by the member states of ECOWAS[126] and the adoption of the Constitutive Act of the African Union.[127] Both ECOWAS and the African Union claim a right of (humanitarian) intervention, with or without the authorisation of the SC.[128] Following the example set by the ECOWAS Security Mechanism,[129] Article

under its authority. But no enforcement action shall be taken under regional arrangements or by regional agencies without the authorization of the Security Council . . .'

[125] See also the examples of *ex post facto* and implicit authorisations by the SC in the context of the ECOWAS interventions in Liberia and Sierra Leone: UN Doc. S/RES/788 (1992); UN Doc. S/RES/1260 (1999).

[126] Adopted on 10 December 1999. The text of the Protocol Relating to the Mechanism for Conflict Prevention, Management, Resolution, Peacekeeping and Security is available at http://www.iss.co.za/af/regorg/unity_to_union/pdfs/ecowas/ConflictMecha.pdf (last accessed 12 July 2006).

[127] The Constitutive Act of the African Union was adopted on 26 May 2001. For general information on the AU, see http://www.africa-union.org/ (last accessed 12 July 2006).

[128] It is interesting to contrast the justifications given for the Kosovo operation with the rights claimed by ECOWAS and the African Union. During the Kosovo operation several NATO members refused to challenge the collective security system of the UN too openly: they denied a general right of humanitarian intervention, stressed the unique and exceptional nature of the intervention or made attempts to legitimise the intervention in terms of existing resolutions of the SC. See, for example, US Secretary of State Albright who emphasised that Kosovo was a 'unique situation *sui generis* in the region of the Balkans' and warned against the danger of 'overdraw[ing] the various lessons that come out of it'. Quoted in M. Byers and S. Chesterman, 'Changing the Rules About Rules? Unilateral Humanitarian Intervention and the Future of International Law', in J. L. Holzgrefe and R. O. Keohane, *Humanitarian Intervention, Ethical, Legal and Political Dilemmas* (Cambridge: Cambridge University Press, 2003), pp. 177–204 at p. 199. See also the analysis of N. D. White, 'The Legality of Bombing In the Name Of Humanity' (2000) 5 *JCSL* 27.

[129] Article 22 charges the ECOMOG with the task of, *inter alia*, 'humanitarian intervention in support of [*sic*] humanitarian disaster'. Unless we are to believe that ECOMOG is endowed with a rather macabre task, the most plausible interpretation of Article 22 is that the term 'in support of' is the result of a mistake in the drafting and should be read as 'to prevent' or possibly 'to relieve'. Article 25 states that the Mechanism is applied, not only in cases of aggression or international conflict, but also in cases of: (a) an internal conflict that threatens to trigger a humanitarian disaster or poses a serious

4(h) of the Constitutive Act of the African Union provides for 'a right of the Union to intervene in a Member State pursuant to a decision of the Assembly in respect of grave circumstances, namely: war crimes, genocide and crimes against humanity'.[130]

The adoption of founding treaties such as the ECOWAS Security Mechanism and the Constitutive Act of the African Union have reopened debates on the relationship between the SC and the member states of the UN. In order to justify the enforcement powers claimed by regional organisations some commentators have argued that the powers of the SC are not absolute. Upon ratification of the UN Charter, they argue, states have taken up the responsibility to collectively police world affairs; a responsibility that was simultaneously contracted out, under certain conditions, to the SC.[131] If the SC fails to meet the conditions set out in the Charter, the responsibility to police would fall back on the individual states. Thus, Abass has argued that:

> ... it was states, rather than the Charter, that imbued the SC with primary responsibility for collective security. The UN is a creation of a treaty. The activities of the organs that act on its behalf must as such conform to the powers assigned to it by the parties to the treaty ... It is proposed that states, especially when operating under auspices of regional organisations, may act in the defence of collective interests where both the Security Council and the General Assembly have failed to discharge their obligations.[132]

threat to sub-regional peace and security; (b) serious and massive violations of human rights and the rule of law; and (c) an overthrow of a democratically elected government or an attempt to do so. For a discussion of the Mechanism, see A. Abass, 'The New Collective Security Mechanism of ECOWAS: Innovations and Problems' (2000) 5 *JCSL* 211.

[130] The Assembly is composed of the Heads of State and Government or their duly accredited representatives. Decision-making in the Assembly is by consensus or, failing which, by a two-thirds majority of the member states eligible to vote (Article 7). In 2003 the AU adopted an amendment to Article 4(h) that broadens the right of intervention considerably. In its amended form, Article 4(h) provides for a right of intervention also in case of 'serious threat to legitimate order to restore peace and stability to the Member State of the Union ...'. Article 4 of the Protocol on Amendments to the Constitutive Act of the African Union, 3 February 2003. The intervention under the amended Article 4(h) should be based upon recommendation of the Peace and Security Council, which is composed of 15 members of the AU. The position of the Peace and Security Council is set out in the Protocol Relating to the Establishment of the Peace and Security Council of the African Union, 9 July 2002.

[131] This argument has been developed in A. Abass, 'The New Collective Security Mechanism', at 224–6.

[132] Abass, *Regional Organisations*, p. 135.

It is not the aim of this chapter to evaluate the legal or moral appropriateness of this interpretation of the UN Charter.[133] Instead, the discussion on the relation between the SC and the UN member states has been used to illustrate how constitutional provisions, rather than providing normative closure, have a tendency to become the subject of foundational debates themselves.

This becomes even clearer if one takes into account the official debates leading up to the establishment of the ECOWAS Security Mechanism, or the Constitutive Act of the African Union. When confronted with the question of whether the right of intervention claimed by ECOWAS is compatible with the UN collective security system, a representative declared that 'whilst the subregion appreciates the importance of its obligations under the United Nations Charter, its recent experience has shown that the cost of waiting for the United Nations authorisation could be very high in terms of life and resources'.[134] Similarly, in the process of drawing up the Constitutive Act of the African Union:

> ... questions ... as to whether the Union could possibly have an inherent right to intervene other than through the SC ... were dismissed out of hand. This decision reflected a sense of frustration ... with instances in which the international community tended to focus attention on other parts of the world at the expense of Africa ... the leaders have shown

---

[133] The interpretation offered by Abass resembles earlier arguments developed by the policy school as well as in Tesón's normative individualistic theory of international law. Therefore, these justifications are also vulnerable to some of the existing critiques on the policy school and Tesón's international legal theory: the risk of a deformalised reading of international law, the blurring line between law, morality and politics and the risk that hegemonic states assume the power to act in the name of their particular interpretation of universal values. For an overview of the most important arguments of the liberal and policy school arguments see: F. R. Tesón, 'The Kantian Theory of International Law' (1991) Columbia Law Rev 53; F. R. Tesón, Humanitarian Intervention: An Inquiry into Law and Morality (New York: Transnational Publishers, 1997), pp. 141–2; W. M. Reisman, 'Sovereignty and Human Rights in Contemporary International Law', in G. H. Fox and B. R. Roth (eds.), Democratic Governance and International Law (Cambridge: Cambridge University Press, 2000), pp. 240–1; W. M. Reisman, 'Unilateral Action and the Transformations of the World Constitutive Process: The Special Problem of Humanitarian Intervention' (2000) 11 EJIL 3. For a critique of these arguments, see M. Koskenniemi, 'The Lady Doth Protest Too much: Kosovo and the Turn to Ethics in International Law' (2002) 65 MLR 159. See also B. Kingsbury, 'Sovereignty and Inequality' (1998) 9 EJIL 599.

[134] Statement by R. Laloupo, on behalf of ECOWAS, quoted in Abass, 'The New Collective Security Mechanism', 223–4.

themselves willing to push the frontiers of collective stability and security to the limit without any regard for legal niceties such as authorization of the Security Council.[135]

In this way, the creation of the Security Mechanism and the Constitutive Act are also illustrations of what Klabbers has called 'a deep paradox of constitutionalism':[136] the desire to 'constitutionalise' certain values will make it more difficult for future generations to change those constitutional provisions, which results in the paradox that:

> ... in order to escape the trappings of constitutionalism, the only resort there is, is to resort to precisely the type of behaviour that constitutionalism was deemed to prevent. If the constitution does not allow an activity which is nonetheless deemed necessary, then the most obvious way around it is, quite literally, to work around the constitution.[137]

C. Working around the constitution

'Working around the constitution' may take different forms. On occasions, it may take the form of a blunt act of power that shows little respect for the constitution in question. However, it may also take more subtle and respectful forms; forms that, for example, take seriously the special role of the UN in international affairs. In this section, I will discuss a few examples of such forms of working around the constitution (or, in this case, the UN Charter). The aim of this section is not to evaluate the different forms of working around the constitution or to determine which form (if any) is preferable. Rather, the aim is to further underline some of the points made in the previous sections: the fact that constitutions do not create a societal reality in their image but rather constitute discursive practices, the limited capacity of constitutions to contain politics and the importance of what Bobbit called 'ethical arguments'.[138]

The examples in this section are taken from the debates on humanitarian intervention that took place in the context of the Kosovo

---

[135] B. Kioko, 'The Right of Intervention Under the African Union's Constitutive Act: From Non-Interference to Non-Intervention (2003) 85 *International Review of the Red Cross* 807 at 821. See also the arguments discussed by T. Mulawi, 'Reimagining African Unity: Some Preliminary Reflections on the Constitutive Act of the African Union' (2001) 9 *African YIL* 3.

[136] Klabbers 'Constitutionalism Lite', 20.   [137] Klabbers, 'Constitutionalism Lite', 20–1.

[138] Bobbitt, *Constitutional Fate*, p. 94.

intervention. From these debates, it can be inferred that the weight of scholarly opinion and the majority of states still consider it illegal to intervene for humanitarian purposes if authorisation from the SC is lacking.[139] The rejection of a legal right to humanitarian intervention, however, does not mean that international legal discourse offers no possibilities to justify such action. After all, legal discourse is not confined to questions of legality and illegality only, but also takes into account questions of appropriateness, as well as questions regarding the function of law in society. This is clearly visible in the legal discourse on humanitarian intervention, where several discursive strategies have been developed around the concept of 'mitigation'.

The first possible strategy is to argue that humanitarian intervention is illegal, but that moral necessity and the factual situation in which a particular intervention takes place should be accepted as mitigating factors *in a concrete case*. In this way, the prohibition on the use of force is upheld and even strengthened, because the intervention is identified as a violation of this prohibition. At the same time, the focus shifts from the (il)legality of the intervention itself to the determination of the legal consequences of the intervention. The necessity to intervene in the name of humanity in a particular case could thus be invoked as a mitigating factor, just as – in a completely different context – mitigating factors were taken into consideration by the International Court of Justice (ICJ) in the *Corfu Channel* case.[140] In the strictest sense, mitigating factors in a case of humanitarian intervention are regarded as purely circumstantial. Thus, Chesterman rejects the desirability – or even the possibility – of developing *a priori* legal criteria in this context:

> ... all such criteria are doomed to redundancy. The very project assumes the possibility of an 'ideal' humanitarian intervention. That there has been no such ideal intervention is rarely taken into account. The impetus

---

[139] For a general overview of the arguments, see J. L. Holzgreve and R. O. Keohane, *Humanitarian Intervention: Ethical, Legal, and Political Dilemmas* (Cambridge: Cambridge University Press, 2003), pp. 15–52.

[140] In 1949 the UK mine-swept the Albanian waters after a British vessel was hit. The ICJ, in the *Corfu Channel* case, qualified this as a violation of the non-intervention principle, but added that the circumstances of the case should be taken into account in the evaluation of this violation of international law: 'the Albanian Government's complete failure to carry out its duties after the explosion, and the dilatory nature of its diplomatic notes, are extenuating circumstances for the action of the United Kingdom Government'. *Corfu Channel (United Kingdom v. Albania)*, Merits, Judgment of 9 April 1949 (1949) ICJ Rep. 4 at 35.

to develop some sort of normative regime is understandable but misplaced: the circumstances in which law may be violated are not themselves susceptible to legal regulation[141] ... certain acts are against the law, but ... the decision of whether to condemn them is *outside* the law ...[142]

Other commentators go beyond a purely circumstantial interpretation and consider the use of mitigating factors as part of a wider normative practice. Franck, for example, takes the quasi-constitutional nature of the UN Charter as a starting point in his examination of the rules governing the use of force in international relations.[143] His understanding of the UN as a constitutional document, however, is deeply influenced by the interpretative turn discussed in section 4.1. Accordingly, Franck discusses the use of the concept of mitigation in the context of an evolution in which international law increasingly becomes part of a broader discourse, embodied in the UN as a 'continually dynamic, evolving institution imbued with a spirit of relevance, one in which the emphasis is on practical problem-solving rather than formal doctrinal exegesis'.[144] In this discourse, UN organs weigh the violation of the prohibition on the use of force against the expected outcomes of inaction. In several cases, Franck argues, UN organs – without accepting a right to humanitarian intervention as such – have acquiesced in the outcomes of interventions or at least refused to condemn these interventions as acts of aggression.[145] As the ongoing discussion on humanitarian intervention demonstrates, the positions taken by UN organs are understood as more than answers to a unique case only. They have, in Franck's words, 'an afterlife as ... precedent'[146] and partly shape the context for the evaluation of future humanitarian interventions.

This 'discursive approach' towards humanitarian intervention is sometimes supplemented by a quest for a more coherent normative framework. An example can be found in the report on humanitarian intervention by the Dutch Advisory Council on International Affairs and Advisory Committee on Issues of Public International Law.[147] This report concludes that

---

[141] S. Chesterman, *Just War or Just Peace, Humanitarian Intervention and International Law* (Oxford: Oxford University Press, 2001), p. 230.
[142] *Ibid.*, p. 227.   [143] Franck, *Recourse to Force*, pp. 135–92.
[144] Franck, 'Interpretation and Change in the Law of Humanitarian Intervention', in Holzgreve and Keohane, *Humanitarian Intervention*, p. 204 at p. 205.
[145] Franck, *Recourse to Force*, pp. 174–92.
[146] Franck, 'Interpretation and Change', in Holzgreve and Keohane, *Humanitarian Intervention*, p. 207.
[147] http://www.aiv-advice.nl/E1000AD/E113/E113SA.htm.

humanitarian intervention has no basis in positive international law, but may nevertheless be legitimate in some cases. Subsequently, it tries to develop criteria to evaluate the derogation from the prohibition on the use of force.[148]

In legal theory, the most thorough attempt to develop such a normative framework can be found in the work of Buchanan.[149] Buchanan questions whether it is fruitful to juxtapose law and morality in international legal discourse. In the case of a humanitarian intervention, Buchanan argues, the question is not simply whether the moral obligation to protect human rights trumps the legal obligation to abstain from the use of force. After all, states and scholars defending humanitarian intervention do not refer to values that are alien to international law. On the contrary: they rely on peremptory norms such as the prohibition on genocide, torture, or grave violations of humanitarian law. The question, therefore, is not only whether a violation of international law (the use of force) is morally justified, but also whether the illegal use of force is required to prevent or stop violations of other core values of the international legal system. In this sense, Buchanan argues, the use of force might be 'lawful though illegal'.[150] This raises an important, though thorny, foundational question: under what circumstances is it morally allowed to violate existing international law in order to improve the international system according to its own constitutional aspirations? Buchanan examines this question on the basis of a specific conception of the rule of law in international affairs. He rejects the thesis that 'the rule of law' is simply shorthand for 'an absolute obligation to obey the law'. Rather, he relies on a 'normatively rich' understanding of the rule of law in international affairs; an understanding that establishes a link between

---

[148] The criteria are developed to answer the following questions: (1) Which states should be allowed to engage in humanitarian intervention? (2) When should states be allowed to engage in humanitarian intervention? (3) What conditions should states satisfy during humanitarian intervention? (4) When and in what way should states end their humanitarian intervention? For a discussion of more preventive strategies in relation to security threats, human rights violations and humanitarian disasters, see *A More Secure World: Our Shared Responsibility*, Report of the Secretary-General's High-level Panel on Threats, Challenges and Change, http://www.un.org/secureworld/ (last accessed 12 July 2006). This high-level report also discusses questions of legitimacy and attempts to provide guidelines for UN action.

[149] A. Buchanan, 'From Nuremberg to Kosovo: The Morality of Illegal International Legal Reform' (2001) 111 *Ethics* 673; A. Buchanan, *Justice, Legitimacy and Self-determination: Moral Foundations for International Law* (Oxford: Oxford University Press, 2003); A. Buchanan, 'Reforming the International Law on Humanitarian Intervention', in Holzgreve and Keohane, *Humanitarian Intervention*, pp. 130–73.

[150] A. Buchanan, 'Reforming the International Law', 132.

the obligation to respect international law and the obligation to contribute to just institutions. In this way, Buchanan heavily relies on what Bobbit has called 'ethical constitutional arguments';[151] arguments that advance the character of *ethos* of the international community as a source from which particular decisions derive.[152]

As was explained in the introduction to this section, this is not the place to discuss the merits of Buchanan's proposals for legal reform. Neither is Buchanan's approach advocated as an alternative foundation for international law that would cure the defects of other foundations. On the contrary: his approach is discussed as an example of the openness of constitutional discourse and the limited capacity of words to dictate reality. Attempts to do away with this openness will most likely result in new attempts to work around the constitution.

5. Epilogue

This chapter has interpreted international constitutionalism as a project that is situated in between facts and norms. International constitutionalism offers an explanation of some developments in international law, based on the existence of a constitution that is valid for the entire international community. At the same time, it aims to bring about what it describes: the existence of a hierarchically structured international legal order that unifies the international community and regulates the exercise of political power. International constitutionalism has much to offer: it draws attention to new developments in international law and expresses faith in the critical potential of the ideals set out in the Charter and in human rights documents.[153] Yet, as has been explained in this chapter, one should not raise one's hopes too high. International constitutionalism has not been able to shake off the tensions, paradoxes and limitations of domestic constitutionalism: the foundational paradox, the tension between politics and society,[154] the need to unify *and*

---

[151] Bobbitt, *Constitutional Fate*, p. 94.   [152] *Ibid.*

[153] As Anne Orford has argued in her review of Simma's *Commentary to the UN Charter*, international constitutionalism offers us 'the gift of formalism': 'a gift of faith, of careful and loving attention to an organisation and the ideals it embodies'. Orford, 'The Gift of Formalism', 193.

[154] This paradox has been discussed extensively in systems theory. Luhmann, for example, has pointed out that (domestic) constitutions claim to unify society and yet confine themselves to the political process: N. Luhmann, *Die Politik der Gesellschaft* (Frankfurt am Main: Surhkamp, 2000). Teubner has pointed at the same tension in relation to constitutionalisation at the international level: G. Teubner, 'Societal

limit politics and the limited possibilities to contain politics or to create society after a constitutional image. The limitations of constitutionalism can be regarded as, in the words of Orford, 'a reminder of that which cannot be enclosed, of that which escapes the law, of the unknown ... [of] the impossibility of ever finally securing the grounds of law'.[155]

Constitutionalism', in C. Joerges, I. Sand and G. Teubner (eds.), *Transnational Governance and Constitutionalism* (Oxford: Hart Publishing, 2004), p. 8.
[155] Orford, 'The Gift of Formalism', 195.

INDEX